Religion, Politics and Law in the European Union

EU enlargement – to countries in Central and Eastern Europe in 2004, the inclusion of Bulgaria and Romania in 2007, and increasing debates on Turkey's membership – has dramatically transformed the European Union into a multi-religious space. Religious communities are not only shaping identities but are also influential factors in political discourse. This edited book examines the activities of religious actors in the context of supranational European institutions and the ways in which they have responded to the idea of Europe at local and international levels. By bringing together scholars working in political science, history, law and sociology, this book analyses key religious factors in contemporary EU architecture, such as the transformation of religious identities, the role of political and religious leaders, EU legislation on religion, and, the activities of religious lobbies.

This book was previously published as a special issue of *Religion, State and Society*.

Lucian N. Leustean is Lecturer in Politics and International Relations, School of Languages and Social Sciences, Aston University, Birmingham.

John T. S. Madeley is Senior Lecturer in Government in the Department of Government, London School of Economics and Political Science.

Religion, Politics and Law in the European Union

Edited by Lucian N. Leustean and
John T. S. Madeley

Routledge
Taylor & Francis Group
LONDON AND NEW YORK

First published 2010 by Routledge
2 Park Square, Milton Park, Abingdon, Oxon, OX14 4RN

Simultaneously published in the USA and Canada
by Routledge
270 Madison Avenue, New York, NY 10016

Routledge is an imprint of the Taylor & Francis Group, an informa business

Typeset in Times by Value Chain, India

British Library Cataloguing in Publication Data
A catalogue record for this book is available from the British Library

ISBN10: 0-415-46627-X
ISBN13: 978-0-415-46627-1

Contents

Notes on Contributors

Benoît Challand is Marie Curie Research Fellow in the History Department at the European University Institute, Florence. He teaches in Bologna and Fribourg. He works in the field of political and historical sociology, with a particular interest in the sociology of religion and social theory. His major publications include the books *La Ligue Marxiste Révolutionnaire en Suisse Romande (1969–1980)* (Fribourg University Press, 2000) and *Palestinian Civil Society: Foreign Donors and the Power to Promote and Exclude* (Routledge, 2009). He has contributed to the *European Journal of Social Theory*, *Middle Eastern Studies* and the *International Journal of Middle East Studies*. Email: benoit.challand@eui.eu

Blandine Chelini-Pont is an assistant professor in history, law and religion in the Faculty of Law and Political Science at Paul Cézanne University, Aix-en-Provence, and regional supervisor of the Institut Européen en Sciences des Religions (IESR) (Paris). She completed her PhD on relations between the United States and the Vatican, 1939–1953, at the Institut d'Etudes Politiques de Paris. She has published many articles and book chapters, and the following books: *L'Eglise de Jean-Paul II face à l'Europe* (Paris, Nouvelle Cité, 1990); *Histoire de l'Eglise catholique* (Paris, Cerf, 1995); *Géopolitique du Christianisme* (co-editor) (Paris, Ellipses, 2003), *Dieu, en France et aux Etats-Unis: quand les mythes font la loi* (with Jeremy Gunn) (Paris, Berg International, 2005); and *Les Etats-Unis, le Saint-Siège et l'Eglise catholique américaine de l'Indépendance à la guerre froide* (Paris, Desclée de Brower, forthcoming 2009). Email: blandine.chelini-pont@univ-cezanne.fr

Norman Doe is a professor of law and director of the Centre for Law and Religion, the Law School, Cardiff University. He studied at the universities of Cardiff, Oxford and Cambridge. He specialises in canon law, and his books are *Fundamental Authority in Late Medieval English Law* (Cambridge, 1990), *The Legal Framework of the Church of England* (Oxford, 1996), *Canon Law in the Anglican Communion: a Worldwide Perspective* (Oxford, 1998), *The Law of the Church in Wales* (Cardiff, 2002), and *An Anglican Covenant: Theological and Legal Considerations for a Global Debate* (London, 2008). Email: doe@Cardiff.ac.uk

Paolo Orlando Ferrara is a PhD candidate in international studies at the University of Trento (Italy). His dissertation project analyses the main Catholic approaches to European integration in postwar Italy and France. His main areas of study include the history of European integration and the development of the nation-state and the international community in the twentieth century. He has also conducted organisational analyses in various international institutions, including the European Training Foundation (ETF), the International Training Centre of the International Labour Organization (ITC-ILO) and the Local Economic and Employment Development Centre of the Organization for Economic Cooperation and Development (OECD-LEED). Email: paolo.ferrara@sis.unitn.it

François Foret is director of political research in the Institute of European Studies and member of the Centre d'Etude de la Vie Politique (CEVIPOL) at the Université Libre de Bruxelles. His research interests are: European integration politics and policies; legitimisation of the European Union; symbolic dimensions of politics; interaction between religion and politics. His publications include : *Légitimer l'Europe: Pouvoir et symbolique à l'ère de la gouvernance* (Paris, Presses de Sciences Po, 2008); (editor) *L'espace public européen à l'épreuve du religieux* (Brussels, Editions de l'Université de Bruxelles, 2007); (with Philip Schlesinger) 'Political roof and sacred canopy? Religion and the EU constitution', *European Journal of Social Theory*, 9, 1, 2006. Email: fforet@ulb.ac.be

Max Fras is a PhD candidate in the Department of Religious Studies of the Open University and a teaching assistant at the UCL School of Slavonic and East European Studies. His research interests include secularisation, religion and civil society, and democratisation in Europe and the Middle East. Email: M.Z.Fras@open.ac.uk

David Herbert is currently a senior lecturer in sociology at the Open University. His research interests are in religion and society in Europe. His book *Religion and Civil Society* was published by Ashgate in 2003. Email: D.E.J.Herbert@open.ac.uk

Mark Hill is a practising barrister with chambers in Middle Temple, London, who has acted in several leading cases concerning religious organisations. He is honorary professor of law at Cardiff University and a fellow of its Centre for Law and Religion. He is a member of the European Consortium for Church and State Research and a member of the International Consortium for Law and Religion Studies. His recent publications include the third edition of his leading textbook *Ecclesiastical Law* (Oxford University Press, 2007) and *Religious Liberty and Human Rights* (University of Wales Press, 2000) as well as regular articles in legal periodicals. He is editor of the *Ecclesiastical Law Journal* and a member of the editorial team producing the third edition of *Jowitt's Dictionary of English Law* (forthcoming, 2010). He sits on the Legal Advisory Commission of the General Synod of the Church of England and is chancellor of the Diocese of Chichester and of the Diocese of Europe and one of Her Majesty's recorders, assigned to the Midland Circuit. His research interests relate to contemporary issues of church and state and freedom of religion in particular. Email: mh@3pumpcourt.com

Kenneth Houston is a final-year PhD candidate in the School of Policy Studies at the University of Ulster. His research interests are mainly in the area of social conflict and its analysis, with a specific interest in the role of institutionalised religion in the public space. Other interests include mechanisms of conflict resolution and European integration as conflict transformation. He is a research associate of International Conflict Research (INCORE) based at the Magee Campus, Derry, Northern Ireland. Email: achouston09@yahoo.ie

Carin Laudrup is a sociologist of religion at the University of Copenhagen. Her academic interests and publications cover multifarious aspects of civil religion. She has taught RE and English in a sixth-form college and sociology of religion and civil religion at the University of Copenhagen. For a number of years she was on the board of the European Forum for Teachers of Religious Education (EFTRE). At present she is writing a textbook for sixth-form colleges and teachers' training colleges on civil religion which will include extensive fieldwork, specifically participant observation of civil religious rituals in the USA, the UK, Northern Ireland and Denmark. Email: claudrup@gmail.com; laudrup@hum.ku.dk.

Lucian N. Leustean is a lecturer in politics and international relations at Aston University, Birmingham, UK. He holds degrees in international relations, law and theology and completed his doctorate in the Department of Government at the London School of Economics and Political Science. He is the author of *Orthodoxy and the Cold War: Religion and Political Power in Romania, 1946–65* (Palgrave, 2009) and the editor of *Eastern Christianity and the Cold War, 1945–91* (Routledge, forthcoming 2009). Email: l.leustean@aston.ac.uk

John Madeley is senior lecturer in government at the London School of Economics and Political Science. In recent years he has taught a masters course on religion and politics and his research has concentrated principally on comparing religion–state relations across the 50-odd countries of Europe. In addition to several journal articles and book chapters he has edited *Religion and Politics* (Ashgate, 2003) and co-edited (with Zsolt Enyedi) *Church and State in Contemporary Europe: the Chimera of Neutrality* (Cass, 2003). Email: J.Madeley@lse.ac.uk

Ken Medhurst is a canon theologian of Bradford Diocese and an honorary professor in the Peace Studies Department at Bradford University, where he teaches a course which will, he hopes, become the basis of a book on political theology. Recently he has written theological papers on the current economic crisis and on the whole question of communication.

Sabrina Pastorelli is a PhD student at the Ecole Pratique des Hautes Etudes – Sorbonne and member of the Groupe Sociétés, Religions, Laïcités (CNRS) in Paris. She holds a master's degree from University Paris V – Sorbonne (France) and from the University of La Sapienza (Italy). Her research interests include: sociology of religion; new religious movements; religious education; religious education in new religious movements; state–church relations in European countries; ecclesiastical law; European law and religion; human rights in Europe; regulation of religious pluralism; state public policy in religious matters. She has had articles published in these fields. She is a member of the International Society for the Sociology of Religion (ISSR), the Association for Sociology of Religion (ASR) and the Italian Sociological Association (AIS). Email: s.pastorelli@free.fr; Sabrina.Pastorelli@ephe.sorbonne.fr

Linda Risso is a lecturer in modern European history at the University of Reading. Her work focuses on the history of European integration and security and on the role of political parties and pressure groups in the formulation of national preferences. Her recent publications include *Divided we Stand: the French and Italian Political Parties and the Rearmament of Western Europe, 1949–1955* (Cambridge Scholars Publishing, 2007), 'Similar, yet so different: why the European Defence Community was not a forerunner of the ESDP', in A. Deighton and G. Bossuat (eds), *L'Union Européenne, acteur de la sécurité mondiale* (Paris, Soleb, 2007), and '"Enlightening public opinion": a study of NATO's information policies between 1949 and 1959 based on recently declassified documents', *Cold War History*, 7, 1 (February 2007). Email: l.risso@reading.ac.uk

Martin Steven lectures in the Department of Politics at the University of Glasgow, UK, on various aspects of British and American government. He completed his PhD there (as a university anniversary scholar) in December 2003. He has also spent time as a visiting scholar in the Department of Political Science at McGill University, Canada. His research interests focus on social capital, party behaviour and politics and religion, and he has published his findings in journals such as *Representation*, *Politics* and *Scottish Affairs*. Email: m.steven@lbss.gla.ac.uk

Giulio Venneri is an expert on multilateral political cooperation at the Italian Ministry of Foreign Affairs. He is a PhD candidate in International Studies at the University of Trento (Italy); his dissertation project assesses EU state-building policies for Bosnia and Herzegovina. Within his PhD framework, he was visiting scholar at the Brussels School of International Studies and Northwestern University in Chicago. He has also conducted research for the Organization for Security and Co-operation in Europe (OSCE), the Italian Ministry for Foreign Trade and the Military Centre for Strategic Studies (CeMiSS). His research interests include: the history of European integration; EU enlargement; state-building and sovereignty-related issues. Email: giulio.venneri@sis.unitn.it

Jean-Paul Willaime is research director in the Department of Religious Studies at l'Ecole Pratique des Hautes Etudes, Sorbonne, Paris. He has doctorates in religious studies and sociology from the University of Strasbourg. His fields of research are: mainline and evangelical Protestantism; the sociology of ecumenism; religions and school education; Europe and religions; and the history and theory of the sociology of religions. He has published many articles and books, including most recently *Sociologies et religion: approches classiques* (with Danièle Hervieu-Léger) (Paris, PUF, 2001), *Le religieux dans la commune: les régulations locales du pluralisme religieux en France* (co-edited with Franck Frégosi) (Geneva, Labor et Fides, 2001) and *Des maîtres et des dieux: écoles et religions en Europe* (co-edited with Séverine Mathieu) (Paris, Belin, 2005). Email: jean-paul.willaime@gsrl.cnrs.fr

Abstracts

European Integration, Laïcité and Religion
JEAN-PAUL WILLAIME

Laïcité, which must not be identified with the French system of church–state relations, is a European value. The fundamental principles of laïcité are established throughout Europe, though with variations according to the particular church–state relationship applicable in member countries. The three fundamentals principles of laïcité are the following: (1) freedom of conscience, thought and religion; (2) equal rights and duties of all citizens; (3) the respective autonomy of the state and religions. In Europe, the dominant model of church–state relations, which differs depending on the country in question, is one of recognised religions. This means that the respective autonomy of churches and the state is often associated with various forms of church–state cooperation. This kind of laïcité has been sanctioned by the Treaty of Lisbon.

Religion: a Solution or a Problem for the Legitimisation of the European Union?
FRANÇOIS FORET

Religion is not a competency of the European Union (EU), but has been more and more an issue on its agenda. The question is to know whether this plays in favour of the legitimisation of a supra- or transnational polity, or represents a further obstacle to it. The central hypothesis discussed here is that religion in itself is less a specific problem than a revelator of the EU difficulty in dealing with any normative reference. Several examples may be taken to illustrate this position, as a synthesis of different empirical researches. The 'Christian heritage' debate in the constitutional process has offered no key to solve the longstanding quest for a European memory. Through the institutionalisation of religions as privileged partners of European governance, the EU has tried to socialise religious actors and to make them comply with the rules of participative democracy (pluralism, mutual recognition . . .). Beyond the interactions of the policy game in Brussels, these rules do not always appear as generalised social norms. This is highlighted by the growing interventions of churches to defend their particularisms in the media or by the use of religious references – intimately linked with nationalist ones – to question European integration in old and new member states. However, these controversies on the new place of the sacred in public life tend to follow well-established patterns of political struggles, which is a reason to believe that, to a large extent, God is a 'business as usual' for the EU.

A European Battlefield: Does the EU Have a Soul?
Is Religion In or Out of Place in the European Union?
CARIN LAUDRUP

After its foundation and expansions from six to 27 member states the European Union (EU) seems to be in more disarray than ever before, whereas the Council of Europe with almost twice as many member states seems to be moving on quite successfully on a supranational level focusing on values and human rights. Both organisations were born out of the ashes of the European civil wars of the twentieth century. This article will analyse possible reasons why it is so difficult for European leaders to convince their citizens that the EU is the alternative of the twenty-first century. Why is the nation-state such a popular social construct that millions are willing to die for it? The lens through which this analysis is carried out is the concept of civil religion as part of the answer but also as part of the problem. At the core is education, specifically religious education, instilling norms and morals. The problem is seen in that civil religious myths and rituals mould and kindle not only nationalism, but also patriotism. The solution could be added awareness that (national) religious education can promote an inclusive understanding of other nations, cultures and religions.

From Hammer and Sickle to Star and Crescent: the Question of Religion for European Identity and a Political Europe
BENOÎT CHALLAND

The paper suggests that European political identity, as a fragile project, is always in need of external significant 'others' in order to buttress a sense of common fate within the sui generis political entity of the European Economic Community/European Union (EU). Adopting a historical and diachronic perspective, the paper argues that for decades the threat of Eastern European communism represented one such external other as a gathering element for Western Europe, but that with the end of the Cold War this 'other' was gradually replaced by the threat of Islam and Islamism (and by extension Turkey's possible entry into the EU). Europe's threat was first the communist sickle; it is now Islam's crescent. Such a portrayal is obviously problematic because of its populist and simplistic appeal that has served political purposes. This needs to be questioned. The return of religion through what is currently described as desecularisation is a rather recent issue for Europe and the question of multireligious Europe ought to be taken seriously. The paper argues, in the line of Delanty, that one should adopt a civilisational approach to Europe, thus giving real space to differences within Europe, and reflect on certain biases of secularity and laïcité towards the dominant religion in various countries.

European Enlargement, Secularisation and Religious Re-publicisation in Central and Eastern Europe
DAVID HERBERT & MAX FRAS

This article investigates the relationship between closer integration into the European Union and the vitality and public presence of religion in three relatively recent accession states: Poland, Hungary and Romania. Using Moyser's (T. Moyser, Politics and Religion in the Modern World, London, Routledge, 1991) model of five levels of political secularisation, we find that there is evidence of growth of religious influence in public life in each of these societies between 1989 and 2007, while using World Values Survey data we find that different patterns of religious vitality are exhibited: growth in Romania, decline from a high level in Poland, and decline from a modest level in Hungary. We argue that to explain this religious 're-publicisation' (growth in the public presence of religion) and different patterns of religious vitality, it is necessary to move beyond secularisation theory to a model which views the social processes identified as underlying secularisation not as the direct cause of decline in religious vitality, but rather as second-order factors creating conditions which can tend, depending on intermediate variables, as much towards growth in public presence of religion as to decline.

Cracks in a Façade of Unity: the French and Italian Christian Democrats and the Launch of the European Integration Process, 1945–1957
LINDA RISSO

Despite the fact that Christian Democracy is generally considered the main engine behind the launch of European integration, closer inspection reveals that behind a façade of unity the Christian Democratic parties supported the integration process for very different reasons and to very different degrees. Historical research has often overlooked the parties' internal disagreements and the heterogeneous reasons behind their political action. To demonstrate this point, this article focuses on the European policies of the French and Italian Christian Democratic parties between the end of the Second World War and the launch of the Common Market in 1957. By taking into account the party's internal divisions and continuous debates, this article challenges the view that Christian Democracy was united behind the integration project.

Alcide De Gasperi and Antonio Messineo: a Spiritual Idea of Politics and a Pragmatic Idea of Religion?
GIULIO VENNERI & PAOLO O. FERRARA

Examining and interconnecting two parallel lives, this article presents the abstract thoughts of a religious scholar vis-à-vis international political issues and the evolution of the attitude and sensibility of a political leader who found inspiration in his intimate religious convictions. The subjects of this study are Antonio Messineo, an international expert in politics and law and editor of the journal La Civiltà Cattolica, and Alcide De Gasperi, statesman and leader of the Italian Christian Democrat Party. The key features of their thought and actions are intimately interconnected and linked to the cultural and political context of their time. Specific attention is paid to the different approaches to European integration that Messineo and De Gasperi developed in the Christian cultural environment of post-Second World War Italy. The time-frame considered spans the period from the first years of the Italian economic, democratic and social reconstruction to the initiatives undertaken in the early 1950s for the institutional reorganisation of Western Europe. Though dealing in biographies, this paper is not a comparative biographical study, but aims to highlight the interdependence between culture and politics, theory and pragmatism.

Papal Thought on Europe and the European Union in the Twentieth Century
BLANDINE CHELINI-PONT

'Europe' has been treated in a number of different ways in papal thought in the twentieth century. At first, under Benedict XV and Pius XI, European unity was presented as the only means to avoid wars and to tame aggressive nationalisms. With Pius XII, Europe became a vision, founded on a sacred past where 'Faith' and 'Truth' had been given by Christ (and the Catholic Church) to the peoples of Europe. The pope's role was unceasingly to defend federalism, and to condemn communism and Cold War politics. The popes of the 1960s and 1970s recast Catholic doctrine on Europe as a new utopia, imbuing Europe with a new concern for the situation of Eastern Europe. They aimed to revive the opportunity for all European peoples to live in a secure, democratic and developed continent thanks to the protective cultivation of Christian values. John Paul II took the view that a common Christian identity pre-existed de facto and was outside any institutional union. Europe had always lived as a 'spiritual miracle'. The Christian heritage of Europe had to be heard, transmitted and respected both by individual European states and by the Union; otherwise the risk was that the unity project would fail and Europe would disappear, falling into decadence and permissiveness.

Towards a 'Common Law' on Religion in the European Union
NORMAN DOE

The development of the European Union (EU), in both composition and competence, has led to an expansion in the volume of its laws and other regulatory instruments dealing with religion. So much so that scholars are increasingly today talking about 'EU law on religion' as a distinct legal category. This study proposes that a juridical approach provides a concrete insight into the posture of the EU towards religion. The study examines a wide range of legal sources, including treaties (among which the Lisbon Treaty is significant), directives, decisions and case-law as they touch directly or indirectly on religion. From all these sources it is evident that key religious phenomena are now formally known to EU law – religious associations, beliefs, rules, teaching, rites and authorities. It is suggested that underlying its legal instruments seem to be eight key principles at work in the approach of the EU to religion: the value of religion; cooperation with religion; religious freedom; religious autonomy; religious equality; special protection for religion; and the concept of religious privilege. In turn, however, the study asks whether these accurately represent the general principles of law on religion common to member states of the EU.

Voices in the Wilderness: the Established Church of England and the European Union
MARK HILL

The interrelation between church and state in the UK is informed to a considerable degree by the anomalous status of the Church of England as the established church for a major part (though not by any means all) of its territory. This paper examines the historical inheritance of establishment and evaluates the manner in which this informs the dynamic between the secular and spiritual authorities. It considers the place of religion within the European Union (EU) as viewed by its institutions and by individual faith communities. While there is discernible evidence of respect being afforded to the sacred within the organs of EU governance in terms of the recognition of Christian roots of Western Europe and dialogue with religious representatives, this is neither systematic nor universal. The Church of England in particular is yet to find its voice in the corridors of influence in Brussels, and it is ventured that the anachronism of establishment may be part of the reason for this.

Religious Lobbies in the European Union: from Dominant Church to Faith-Based Organisation?
MARTIN STEVEN

The political behaviour of national, state or dominant churches in Western Europe is being affected by European Union (EU) integration in two ways. First, supranational legislation – especially the harmonisation of fundamental citizen rights in policy areas such as education and employment – has led to the political privileges that these churches have traditionally enjoyed being challenged. While the Amsterdam Treaty protects the right of the individual citizen to freedom of religious expression, the EU is an inherently secular body with no mention of Christianity in any of its treaties or directives. Second, the transfer of power to Brussels has meant that the territorial political influence of national churches is no longer clear, in any case. These two factors combined give evidence to suggest that this changing policy environment is leading churches increasingly to adopt interest-group behaviour. Does 'ever closer union' inevitably mean a less certain – if not necessarily less influential – political role for Christian churches throughout Europe?

The European Union and the New Religious Movements
SABRINA PASTORELLI

The paper looks at how European institutions, namely the European Union (EU) and the Council of Europe, deal with new religious movements (NRMs). Drawing upon the jurisprudence of the European Court of Human Rights and the European Court of Justice, the paper addresses the question of the place of new religions in the 'transparent dialogue' with the European Commission. In order to answer this question, fieldwork has been conducted to find out which NRMs are present in Brussels and are dialogue partners of the Bureau of European Policy Advisers (BEPA). The article points out what is at stake for a new religious movement in participating in the EU debates over the role of religion and its contribution to the construction of Europe. The preliminary findings allow us to claim that some movements frequently considered as 'cults' or 'sects' in the parliamentary reports of several member states (as well as in reports of specialised state agencies of 'cult' control) have been recognised as possible partners in discussions with the EU Commission. Even though the dialogue is supposed to be open and transparent, this paper raises the question of the qualities needed in a religious movement to be represented at the EU level. The paper shows how European institutions have participated in the debate on NRMs and raises questions over the possible influence of EU institutions, direct or indirect, on the policy of member states on religious matters. It also shows how governance in the relations between EU, civil society and religions could constitute a possible model for member states in dealing with the growing pluralistic landscape of the EU.

The Logic of Structured Dialogue between Religious Associations and the Institutions of the European Union
KENNETH HOUSTON

Aside from the controversy surrounding the proposed inclusion of an Invocatio Dei in the preamble to the European Union's (EU's) defunct Draft Constitution, a more muted controversy centred on the inclusion of a provision for structured dialogue between the institutions of the EU and communities of faith and conviction. This provision for dialogue, previously Article I.52.3 of the Draft Constitution, was retained in the Lisbon Treaty of 2007 as Article 17.3. The following article evaluates the logic for the inclusion of such a dialogue provision, focusing on the rationale of the European Commission body tasked with its coordination, as well as its potential role in intercultural understanding, the crystallisation of a European identity and core values, and the promotion of religious freedom and social justice. The putative imperatives examined are found to be insufficient to justify a differentiated dialogue provision.

Religion, Politics and Law in the European Union: an Introduction[1]

LUCIAN N. LEUSTEAN & JOHN T. S. MADELEY

On 11 June 2008, the eve of the Irish referendum on the Lisbon Treaty, Pope Benedict XVI publicly declared his support for a united Europe in front of a large crowd in Saint Peter's Square. He invoked the name of Saint Columbanus, an Irish saint of the sixth century who is held to have been important for converting wide swathes of the British Isles and Western Europe. The pope's comments did little to avert the constitutional crisis which followed Ireland's narrow rejection of the treaty however – which came despite the fact that the country's 1937 Constitution was declared 'In the name of the Most Holy Trinity, from Whom is all authority and to Whom, as our final end, all actions both of men and of States must be referred'.[2] This unusually direct, if unsuccessful, papal intervention serves as a reminder of how closely religion has on occasion been associated with the politics of European integration – as well as more widely in European politics – since the Second World War. It highlighted the concerns of some religious actors about the political evolution of the European Union (EU) and showed that religious and political leaders often have common agendas if sometimes divergent stances on those agendas. As will be seen below, a number of the most controversial issues associated with the ongoing project of European integration have indeed involved deep disagreement about the role of religion in politics and public life. In some ways this might seem surprising, since on most conventional measures Europe, especially in its western and central parts, can be seen as the most secular region of the world, one furthermore where secularisation continues to advance while elsewhere the contrary tendency, desecularisation – or the resurgence of religion – seems to be prevalent (Norris and Inglehart, 2004; Davie, 1994, 2000, 2002; Davie and Hervieu-Léger, 1996; Casanova, 1994, 2006, Berger, 1999; Berger *et al.*, 2008).

The contributions to this volume do not concentrate on the normative issues which still counterpose religious and secular political trends and forces, however. While taking note of the debates about the appropriate role of religion in the public sphere in which, for example, Rawls, Rorty, Habermas and others (including the current pope) have vigorously engaged themselves, they address more empirical questions (Ratzinger, 1989, 2007) The principal focus is on examining the role of religion within the political evolution of the EU and its institutions and to identify the ways in which religious communities have related to the challenges of an expanded united Europe. What role have religious communities had in the construction of the EU? Is there a common European identity rooted in religion as claimed by some? In which ways have religious communities entered into dialogue with the European institutions? To what extent and by what means can religious communities be seen to influence decision-making processes in the EU? In the political field, religion sometimes seems to transcend national barriers and have a direct impact on loyalties, legitimacy and networks of power. It is occasionally directly linked to social transformations and the establishment of new political entities. By analysing the ways in which religious actors respond to political affairs and political actors relate to their religious interlocutors at both national and supra-national levels, the volume addresses these issues in an interdisciplinary manner by bringing together perspectives from scholars working in the fields of political science, history, sociology and law.

Religion and European Institutions

In the aftermath of the Second World War which had wreaked such devastation on the European continent religious institutions and bodies were both directly and indirectly closely involved in the efforts of political, economic and cultural reconstruction. In the western part of the continent Christian Democratic parties became dominant players in the domestic politics of many countries and from the late 1940s formed a transnational network which was critical to the launch of the project of European integration (Irving, 1979; Buchanan and Conway, 1996; Gehler and Kaiser, 2004; Greschat and Loth, 1994; Hanley, 1994; Lücker and Hahn, 1987; Meyer, 1980; Durand, 1995; Malcolm, 1996; Papini, 1997; Lamberts, 1997; Pulzer, 2004; Van Hecke and Gerard, 2004; Kselman and Buttigieg, 2003; Kaiser 2007). The onset of the Cold War from 1948 cemented the growing division of the continent, in the eastern part of which Soviet domination led to the marginalisation of religious institutions, the suppression of some groups and the persecution of individual religious activists. In this context the partisan commitment of Christian Democrats to the building of institutions for cooperation and coordination in Western Europe is easily understood. For Casanova the strength of the linkage was such as to justify his claim that 'the initial project of a European Union was fundamentally a Christian Democratic project, sanctioned by the Vatican, at a time of a general religious revival in post-World War Two Europe, in the geopolitical context of the Cold War when "the free world" and "Christian civilization" had become synonymous' (Casanova, 2006, p. 66). This claim, he argues, is however little recognised by Europe's contemporary liberal elites – it remains a sort of hidden history as though it were something rather shameful – while for George Weigel and J. H. H. Weiler, the failure to acknowledge the historic debt can be traced directly to a 'Christophobic' mind-set which is all of a piece with the progressive marginalisation of religious influences in Europe's public life (Weigel, 2005). Wolfram Kaiser's study of the role of the Christian Democratic cross-national networks in launching the integration project has however done something to redress the balance (Kaiser, 2007).

The birth of the first European institutions took place in the midst of the ideological conflict between the two blocs. The Council of Europe, which began operation in August 1949, was intended to promote European unity by providing a common forum for debate and through the work of a series of commissions and the European Court of Human Rights. In 1950, however, a far more ambitious plan for promoting unity was launched with the promulgation of the Schuman Plan, which eventually led to the Treaties of Paris (1951) and Rome (1957), the foundation documents of the European Coal and Steel Community and the European Common Market respectively. Despite the Christian Democratic dominance of the political scene in the western part of the continent and the strong Catholic identity of most of the 'founding fathers', neither treaty made any reference to religion. A European policy towards religion was completely absent from the life of the Community (Maritain, 1951; Haas, 1958; Chenaux, 1990, 1991; Vincent and Willaime, 1993; Willaime, 2004; Basdevant-Gaudemet and Messner, 1999; Madelin, 2007; Weninger, 2007; Zeilstra, 1995; Barnett, 2005).

Religion was a sensitive issue in Cold War Europe (Kirby, 2003; Leustean 2009a, 2009b; Barrett *et al.*, 2001). It highlighted the ideological differences between East and West, being perceived as a marker of historical conflict and geographical separation. In the communist-controlled territories, leaders of many mainstream religious communities were encouraged or required to engage in peace propaganda, something which made relations between the two sides of the continent difficult. Religion remained connected with the political logic of the Cold War rather than that of European integration. Although political leaders aimed to engage a wide range of social actors in the evolution of the European Community, religious communities were largely kept outside the decisional process. Religious issues were present on the agendas of international institutions dealing with human rights and security, such as the Council of Europe, rather than on those of the European institutions.

Despite the almost entirely secular concerns of the project of European integration, the Catholic Church was the first religious community to monitor the activity of the European institutions through a Catholic office in Strasbourg (*Office Catholique d'Information pour l'Europe*) in 1957 (Willaime, 2002, p. 183; De Charentenay, 2003; Durand, 2008). The Vatican had promoted the idea of a united Europe immediately after the Second World War, with Pope Pius XII (1938–59) directly supporting the idea of a federal Europe, a vision that would become even clearer with the next pontificates. Pope John XXIII issued his 1961 encyclical *Mater et Magistra*, reinforcing the principle of subsidiarity which was adopted as Community policy (De Montclos, 1994, pp. 85–104; Haguenau-Moizard, 2000). An apostolic nuncio for Belgium and Luxembourg, who also monitored the European institutions, was appointed in 1970, although the establishment of official relations between the Vatican and European institutions took place only in 1980 with the establishment of the Commission of the Bishops' Conferences of the European Community (COMECE).[3] Finally, a nuncio for the EU was appointed in 1999.

If the Vatican displayed an active interest in political and religious reunification in Europe, after the Second World War Protestant and Orthodox churches were more concerned with interreligious dialogue. Ecumenical relations had been established in the interwar period, and in the new international context, Christian communities re-established contacts with each other. The World Council of Churches (WCC) was the most significant organisation which brought together religious communities on the European continent. However, the theme of European unity was not of major interest for its member churches, drawn as they were from the whole world. An independent branch of the WCC, the Conference of European Churches (CEC), was founded in 1959 with the aim of fostering dialogue between east and west. Meetings between the two sides were not always easy; CEC's congress to adopt its Constitution in 1964 was held on a boat on the Baltic Sea in order to avoid visa difficulties.

An Ecumenical Centre was established in Brussels in 1965 by representatives of the Protestant churches in the first EEC member states. The Centre brought together clergy and bureaucrats but had little influence on the official position of churches towards European integration. More direct interest in the activities of European institutions grew after the powers of the European Parliament increased in the 1970s. A rising number of religious communities were interested in the work and policies of the European Community, some of which opened offices in Brussels. Thus, the

Quaker Council for European Affairs opened an office in Brussels in 1979; the European Ecumenical Commission for Church and Society, which represented the position of the Church of England and other Protestant churches, opened offices in Brussels in 1979 and Strasbourg in 1986;[4] and the EKD (*Evangelische Kirche in Deutschland*) opened an office in Brussels in 1990. Protestant churches developed a more intensive network of dialogue with the European institutions after the fall of communism, when interconfessional bodies (the Leuenberg Fellowship (1974) and the Porvoo churches in the 1990s) publicly debated European issues. Orthodox churches, Humanists and Jewish and Muslim communities took up a similar position and opened offices in Brussels after 1990.

The recent interest of the European institutions in religious issues is also connected to the relatively late official contact with religious communities. In September 1983, President Gaston Thorn appointed Umberto Stefani, director at the secretariat general, as special counsellor in charge of conducting a census of religious communities and of representing the Commission in contact with European churches (Massignon, 2007). This informal liaison was later strengthened under President Jacques Delors who transferred these roles to the Forward Studies Unit in June 1992 under the coordination of Marc Luyckx, a Catholic theologian. The relaunch of political and economic integration after the Maastricht Treaty led Delors to suggest the re-analysis of the spiritual dimensions of Europe. In a speech to representatives of religious communities, he stated that

> We are now entering a fascinating time . . . a time when the debate on the meaning of European construction becomes a major political force . . . . If in the next ten years we haven't managed to give a soul to Europe, to give it spirituality and meaning, the game will be up. This is why I want to revive the intellectual and spiritual debate on Europe. I invite the churches to participate actively in it. The debate must be free and open. We don't want to control it; it is a democratic process, not to be monopolised by technocrats. I would like to create a meeting place, a space for free discussion open to men and women of spirituality, to believers and non-believers, scientists and artists. (Newsletter, 1992)

In October 1996, Luyycks was replaced by Thomas Jansen, former secretary general of the European People's Party, and under President Romano Prodi, Michael Weninger, former Austrian ambassador in Belgrade, took on the position (Jansen, 2000). Weninger remained in charge of the dialogue with religious communities until October 2007, when Jorge César das Neves took his role within the Bureau of European Policy Advisers which replaced the former Unit. The most significant decision on religious issues was the establishment of a European programme promoting religious dialogue entitled 'A Soul for Europe: Ethics and Spirituality', by the European Parliament (1999–2005). However, the programme did not have any legal implications and the dialogue between faiths resulted only in a few conferences and meetings of religious leaders discussing the spiritual consequences of European enlargement and integration.

Until the Convention on the Future of Europe (2001) which drafted a Treaty establishing a Constitution for Europe, religion was largely kept outside the main documents of the EU. The term 'religion' was present only in Article 13 of the Treaty of Rome as amended by the Treaty of Amsterdam in September 1997, and mention of 'religious rites, cultural traditions and regional heritage' was made in Protocol 33 annexed to the Treaty of Rome, which refers to the protection and welfare of animals, enforcing transnational implementation. The document which specified the position of the EU towards religious communities was Declaration 11 on the Status of Churches and Non-Confessional Organisations attached to the Treaty of Amsterdam (Declaration, 1997).

The debates on religious terms in the Preamble of the European Constitution showed the growing presence of religious communities and their transnational influence (Leustean, 2007). For the first time, Article I-52 of the European Constitution recognised the role of churches and non-confessional organisations in the EU, officially considering them as partners in dialogue. The article was virtually identical to Declaration 11; however, this time it did not take the form of an attached protocol but rather was placed within the most important document of the Union. After the Constitution was rejected by the French and Dutch referenda, Article I-52 was replaced by Article 17 of the Lisbon Treaty, which stated that

> 1. The Union respects and does not prejudice the status under national law of churches and religious associations or communities in the Member States;
> 2. The Union equally respects the status of philosophical and non-confessional organisations;
> 3. Recognising their identity and their specific constitution, the Union shall maintain an open, transparent and regular dialogue with these churches and organisations.

Religion and European Identity

Controversy about the role of religion or of religious institutions, groups, movements and individuals in public – and especially political – life has become more prominent in recent decades in Europe. While 60 years ago the strong Roman Catholic identity of most of those who launched the project of European integration provided a bond which did not prevent the eventual formation of a wider consensus embracing those of other traditions and party families, questions of confessional identity have recently been associated more with conflict than consensus. There have of course from the first been differentials in the levels of support and enthusiasm which the European integration project inspired in different populations characterised by the dominance of one confessional form of Christianity or another (Nelsen *et al.*, 2001; Nelson and Guth, 2003a, b; Nelson, 2004, 2005; Nexon, 2006; Philpott and Shah, 2006). The idea that Protestantism fosters Euroscepticism or is, as such, at least significantly ambivalent about European integration is supported by evidence from the countries which have historically been either overwhelmingly or mainly Protestant since the sixteenth century: the countries which constitute Scandinavia, the Netherlands and the United Kingdom (Freston, 2004; Vollard, 2006; Madeley, 2009b). Both Denmark and the UK, the first of these countries to join the EU in 1974, have often played the role of reluctant – and even obstructive or 'awkward' – partners within the EU (Miljan, 1977; George, 1990; Malcolm, 1996; Gstoehl, 2002; Hagevi, 2002; Jenssen *et al.*, 1998; Mathieu, 1999; Sundback, 2003; Sørensen and Stråth, 1997; Ludlow, 1997; Coupland, 2006).

If the contrast between the Europhile attitudes found in the leadership of the mainstream denominations and the extreme sectarian versions of Euroscepticism undermines the hypothesis that Protestantism as such generates anti-EU sentiments, the observation that similarly hostile sentiments are to be found also among sections of Catholic, Orthodox and Islamic opinion further weakens it (Taggart, 1998). To illustrate this claim it is necessary only to consult the contents of the Byrnes and Katzenstein edited volume *Religion in an Expanding Europe* (2006). There Casanova identifies a category of 'Catholic europhobes' in Poland 'who are against European integration because today's Europe has lost its Christian identity and therefore its secularist, materialist, hedonist values represent a threat to Poland's Catholic identity and values' (Casanova, 2006, p. 69). Ramet writes of 'Orthodoxy's war with the EU' which has been directed against the enshrining of liberalism within the EU's projected Constitution – with liberalism understood as 'an amalgam of select features associated with the liberal project (tolerance of homosexuality, neutrality of the state in matters of religion), pathological symptoms of social decay (pornography, drug abuse), and an assortment of groups of whom [Orthodoxy] disapproves (Jehovah's Witnesses, prostitutes, and advocates of globalization)' (Ramet, 2006, p. 166). In the same volume Tibi argues that the Islamists among Europe's burgeoning Muslim diaspora population support a version of Islamisation, which regards Europe's states gathered together within the EU as irredeemably corrupt, and aims at their eventual incorporation into *Dar-al-Islam* (the House of Islam), an ambition which, he argues, 'runs totally counter to Europeanization' (Tibi, 2006, p. 208). On the basis of these observations alone it is clear that Eurosceptic sentiments of the most vigorous sort are to be found across all the principal confessional families represented in Europe: Protestant, Catholic, Orthodox and Islamic.

Controversy about the role of religion in the European integration project turns no longer mainly around differences between Catholics and Protestants, Eastern Orthodox and Muslims, mainstream liberals and fundamentalists, however (although issues along these lines of cleavage continue to occur); it is also now a matter of those who insist that religious viewpoints be heard in debates about public policy against those who maintain that they have no place. Especially since the terrorist outrages of 9/11 – and in Europe itself, 11 March 2004 in Madrid and 7 July 2005 in London – there has been something of a moral panic not just about jihadist Islam but more generally about the role of religion in public life. This agitated public debate was prefigured in normative political philosophy by the secular liberal theses of such as Rawls, Rorty and Habermas to the effect that under liberal democratic arrangements debates about public policy should be conducted in terms equally accessible to all so that those which relied on premises (for example, religious premises) which were not universally shared should either be translated into secular terms or excluded from consideration (Audi and Wolterstorff, 1997; Gauchet, 1998; Greeley, 2003). From 1973, when the Copenhagen Declaration on European Identity was promulgated, the fundamental elements which were identified as corresponding to the 'deepest aspirations' of Europe's peoples were presented in political, legal and philosophical terms without prejudice to cultural specificities: 'the principles of representative democracy, of the rule of law, of social justice – which is the ultimate goal of economic progress – and of respect for human rights'. As already noted, it is remarkable that, despite the religious connections via Christian Democracy, the principal legal instruments of European integration are almost entirely silent about religion. The most notable mention prior to the controversies around the preamble to a possible Constitution for Europe was Declaration 11 on the status of churches and nonconfessional organisations attached to the 1997 Treaty of Amsterdam. This declaration, far from promoting any linkage between religious bodies and the EU, established a *caesura* between the two, to the effect that the EU 'would not prejudice the status under national law of churches and religious associations or communities in Member States'. It should also be noted that the Declaration concluded: 'The

European Union equally respects the status of philosophical and non-confessional organisations'.

Over the last decades locally significant issues such as the French *affaire du foulard* raised questions about the appropriate boundaries for religious expression in the public sphere. In France itself the outcome of this particular debate was that not only the *foulard* or hijab, but the wearing of all ostentatious religious symbols – including crosses worn by Christians, turbans by Sikhs and kippahs by Jews – were declared banned from state schools. Meantime, as mention above of the debate about a possible *invocatio dei* in the preamble to the stillborn Constitution of Europe indicates, controversy about the role of religion in public life has nonetheless resonated at the European level. Although Europe, and especially its western part, is seen as almost uniquely secularised relative to the rest of the world, including the USA, it is evident that it is not immune to the resurgence of religion-related issues in its politics, and this tendency has only been reinforced by the enlargement of the EU to embrace states in Eastern Europe where after the collapse of communism there has been a notable desecularising trend (Thual, 1993; Casanova, 1994; Stepan, 2000; Davie, 2002; Anderson, 2003; Norris and Inglehart, 2004; Michalski, 2006; Byrnes and Katzenstein, 2006).

In the most general terms disagreements can be seen to have revolved around whether or to what degree the business of the state or of state-like structures like those of the EU should be seen as essentially secular or, to use the French word which Jean-Paul Willaime in the opening essay focuses on, *laïque*. Debates around secularisation which have relied in part on particular understandings of the term 'secular' have unsurprisingly become more intense in recent years. For Casanova writing in 1994 the secularisation thesis in its orthodox version was a compound of three disparate elements, the first of which – secularisation as differentiation – he argued to be sound, the second – secularisation as decline – he concluded to be false, and the third – secularisation as marginalisation – he held to be deeply problematic. Secularisation as differentiation entailed *inter alia* a necessary and proper separation between the secular state and religion without accepting as a consequence of this that religious bodies, institutions, voices etc. should be excluded from public policy debates as many secular liberals insisted. In this light the development of European-level regulatory institutions can be seen as a continuation of differentiating tendencies already well-established (since indeed the rise of the modern state) at the member-state level. Others meantime have questioned whether the term 'the secular state' should be taken as properly descriptive of the modern state itself in many parts of the world, including Europe – the continent which in many other respects can be seen to be more secular than any other. Thus Jonathan Fox's survey of state–religion linkages across the world finds that no state other than the USA meets up to the strict-separationist criteria which have been policed in that country by its Supreme Court (Fox, 2008). In Europe for example even states such as France offend against such strict criteria, while most maintain arrangements which involve the direct or indirect sponsorship by state authorities of particular religious organisations and traditions (Monsma and Soper, 1997; Monsma, 2002; Madeley, 2003, 2009a; Madeley and Sitter, 2003; Madeley and Enyedi, 2003; Potz, 2003). Elsewhere across the continent there is an almost bewildering variety of patterns of relationship between states and religious bodies (Rusama, 1994; Robbers, 1996; Messner, 1999; Davie, 2000).

It is Silvio Ferrari's bold claim that behind the bewildering variety of patterns of church–state relations across the fifty-odd territories of wider Europe – with local varieties and subvarieties of establishment, one form or another of separation, or accommodation or more or less direct cooperation – the outline of a common European model can nonetheless be descried. The distinctive feature of this model, which otherwise shares a commitment to religious freedom, is the privileging of religion in public space:

> A religious sub-sector is singled out within the public sector. This may be understood as a 'playing field' or 'protected area'. Inside it the various collective religious subjects (churches, denominations, and religious communities) are free to act in conditions of substantial advantage compared to those collective subjects that are not religious. The state's only role is to see that the players respect the rules of the game and the boundaries of the playing field. (Ferrari, 1999, p. 2)

Despite this seeming religious favouritism of the state, directed at least towards those bodies whose religious *bona fides* are recognised but in such a manner as to suggest a positive valuation of, even prejudice for, religion, Ferrari emphasises the secular nature of the modern state, in French, its *laïcité*; 'the fundamental principles of the common European model of relationships between the state and the religious communities… are quite rigid.… [They] have been summed up in the formula "the secular state"' (Ferrari, 1999, p. 11). In the light of the religious partiality of the state which Ferrari himself identifies as a key feature of the common European model, it might however be argued that what is distinctive about the European model is not so much state *laïcité* as state religiosity, particularly when contrasted with the US separationist model (Madeley, 2009c). If the *laïcité* of the national state is to be seen as a principle of the European model, then, it is surely one as much honoured in the breach as in the observance (Poulat, 1987; Bauberot, 1994; Barbier, 1995; Remond, 1999).

Ferrari would seem to have a stronger case for emphasising the *laïcité* of the EU institutions on the other hand. Despite the Christian Democrats' role in their creation the secularity of these institutions has often been seen as a striking feature, something which is not surprising if, following Kalyvas, the continental Christian Democrats themselves should be seen as distinctly secular while also having strong religious roots (Kalyvas, 1994; Van Kersbergen, 1995). For some religious conservative commentators this secularity is typically seen as repugnant, just as some more neutral analysts also see it as at the very least problematic. Thus, while George Weigel claims to identify a long-standing 'crisis of civilizational morale' in Europe which the EU and the liberal elites which he sees as dominating it are unwilling and anyhow ill-equipped to address, Katzenstein refers to the 'the emptiness of the core of secular Europe' and the failure of cultural initiatives at EU level to furnish this empty space (Byrnes and Katzenstein, 2006, p. 4). However it is the overall thesis of the Byrnes and Katzenstein volume, *Religion in an Expanding Europe*, that the process of 'European enlargement will feed rather than undermine the importance of religion in the EU' as 'transnational religious communities in the European periphery are reintroducing religion into the center of Europe' (Byrnes and Katzenstein, 2006, p. 2). If they are right, issues which involve the mobilisation of religious difference are quite likely to become more rather than less significant in years to come. Berger on the other hand sees the eastward expansion of the EU as more likely to have a secularising impact on Europe's east than a desecularising impact on its west (Berger, 1999).

One of the issues which have most animated debate about the role of religion in the context of European integration has arisen in connection with the EU accession negotiations with Turkey, which finally got under way in October 2005. Alongside some prominent Christian Democrats who have objected that Turkey's strong Islamic heritage prevents it from sharing core Christian values which they insist underlie the whole EU construction, other voices – not least on the extreme right – have also tried to make an issue of Europe's Christian identity. It is even notable that while the EU has acceded to the claims of the Christian denominations, for example, in allowing member states not to recognise civil partnerships between same sex couples in the 2004 Citizenship Directive, it has objected to Turkey's attempted recriminalisation of adultery. The enlargement commissioner, Günter Verheugen, noted that it was important that 'Turkey should not give the impression . . . that it is introducing Islamic elements into its legal system while engaged in a great project such as the EU' (quoted in McCrae, 2007, p. 11). The broader issue connected to Turkey's application is the position of Islam within Europe more generally, an issue which was being lent a particular urgency by speculations about a coming clash of civilisations before 9/11 and other terrorist attacks gave a specious colour to the speculations (Huntington, 1996). For Olivier Roy the spread of Islam around the globe and its significant presence among recent immigrants in Europe has blurred the connection between religion, a specific society, and a territory and given rise to a schism between mainstream Islamist movements in the Muslim world and the uprooted militants whose 'neofundamentalism' provides a universal religious identity that transcends the notion of culture (Roy, 2002; Ferrari, 2002). The focus on the threat posed by the small minority of jihadist militants has given them greater prominence than their numbers would suggest, but some commentators such as Tibi claim that much larger sections of the immigrant Muslim communities now present in Europe share a disdain for what they regard as corrupt European cultures and are resistant to the idea of a European Islam which might share the values of tolerance, equality and human rights (Ramadan, 2004; Tibi, 2006).

Summary of Key Themes

This volume is divided into four key themes, namely religious identity, religious and political leaders, religion and law, and religious lobbies.

The theme of religious identity in the EU has proved to be controversial, particularly in the context of EU enlargement to countries in Central and Eastern Europe in 2004, the inclusion of Bulgaria and Romania in 2007, and possibly the inclusion of Turkey at a later stage. Jean-Paul Willaime argues that the EU adopts a *laïcité* approach to religion. Despite the association of the term '*laïcité*' with French church–state relations only and the difficulty of properly translating it into other languages, this model suggests equal treatment of religious communities and the widespread generalisation of religious rights and freedoms. *Laïcité* has an impact on the ways in which religious identities are shaped by European integration. In his opinion, *laïcité* is at the basis of EU relations with religious communities, shaping the transposition of religious issues into national laws.

Willaime's interpretation is taken further by François Foret's analysis of the ways in which religion plays a role in the legitimacy of the EU. In his opinion, religion is part of 'the usual rules of the game'; what matters is the institutional structure of religious dialogue with the EU. Religion is a simple technical issue in the drafting of the myriad issues within the *acquis communautaire*. Foret suggests that the most potent identity mark posed by religion is visible in the mass media, for example, from the nationalist discourses of *Radio Maryja* in Poland and the public controversy around Dan Brown's *Da Vinci Code* to the growing interest in cyber-religions.

The construction of a European identity is shaped by mass education, and in this context, Carin Laudrup examines its impact on religious curricula. She points out that the concept of civil religion promoted by Jean-Jacques Rousseau and Emile Durkheim had strong resonance in postwar Europe. The link between civil religion and the project of European integration emphasises a national rather than transnational European identity.

Benoit Challand brings religious identity closer to the European institutions. By examining the European Economic Community archival material relating to Turkey, he observes that in the 1950s and 1960s there were no references to religious issues. Instead Turkey was perceived by western political leaders as a defender of European values. By analysing the occurrence of religious terms in academic articles and EU treaties, Challand argues that religious issues mattered in the process of European integration only after the 1990s. He suggests that European identity revolves around external enemies, and from this perspective, the current Islamic 'threat' replaced the communist ideology of the Cold War period.

David Herbert and Max Fras travel eastwards with their analysis of religious identity, investigating the issues of secularisation and religious re-publicisation. By focusing on Poland, Hungary and Romania, they reveal the position of the predominant religious communities in these countries towards EU accession. The EU has been an 'agent of secularisation' which predominated over religious and political differences in the Cold War era. By placing discussion into wider analysis of religion, as reflected by the European Convention on Human Rights and the World Values Survey, they argue that, after the fall of communism, religious communities extended their societal and political influence. The particular place of religion in these countries is in contrast to the predominantly secular character of the EU.

The second theme of the volume examines the role of religious and political leaders in the construction of the EU. The project of the European Community is considered to be the product of Christian Democratic parties which dominated political life after the Second World War. Linda Risso investigates the role of the French and Italian Christian Democrats from 1945 until 1957. She points out that these parties had different agendas from each other, but that both were characterised by pragmatism rather than an integrationist ideal. Significant roles in the process of European integration were played by transnational political networks of the 'founding fathers'. Giulio Venneri and Paolo Ferrara draw a parallel between the ways in which Europe was seen by Alcide de Gaspari, the Italian prime minister who led the country's negotiations with the European Community, and Antonio Messineo, a Jesuit theologian who wrote on European issues in the same period. Veneri and Ferrara suggest that despite different personal trajectories, both Italians shared similar visions of a united Europe.

A closer analysis of the Vatican's position towards a united Europe is provided by Blandine Chelini-Pont. This position is traced to the interwar period when the continent was divided between extreme forms of nationalism. The rise of totalitarianism and the Second World War were directly linked to nationalism and religious difference. From this perspective, the new European political entity refrained from being associated with religion. The Vatican engaged in dialogue with the European institutions and encouraged a federalist vision of Europe, becoming extremely active during the pontificate of John Paul II.

Religion and law in the EU is the third theme of the volume. As Norman Doe suggests, 'law is a place where religion and politics meet', and religious issues are closely connected to communitarian and national legislation. Doe argues that similarities on religious issues in EU member states lead towards a 'common law' on religion. The 'common law' takes into account the fundamental principles which are at the basis of the supranational legislation on religion. Doe's view is reinforced by Mark Hill's analysis of the Church of England's place within the EU. Hill suggests that both European institutions and religious communities are interested in developing and maintaining institutional contacts. The deepening of European integration led the Church of England to open channels influencing the decision-making process in Brussels. Hill points out that the current EU and national legislation on religion are nevertheless linked to the process of secularisation.

The fourth theme investigates the increasing religious lobbying of the European institutions. Martin Steven argues that religious communities promote similar patterns of lobbying to that of other interest groups. Religious lobbies aim to influence both national and EU legislation. Comparable examples can be drawn from the USA where lobbying is better organised and regulated. Steven focuses on the political roles of the Church of Scotland, the Church of England and the Catholic Church in France and suggests a re-analysis of church–state relations in Europe which takes into account the role of religious lobbies.

Among the most active lobbies in Brussels are the New Religious Movements (NRMs). As Sabrina Pastorelli indicates, the NRMs have an impact at both national and European levels and the European institutions and national governments are interested in monitoring their activities. Pastorelli examines the position of the main European bodies on religious issues, namely the European Parliament, the European Court of Justice, the Bureau of European Policy Advisers, the Council of Europe and the European Court of Human Rights. She focuses on Soka Gakkai's contact with the European Commission and argues that both this religious community and the European institutions benefit from the dialogue. On the one hand, Soka Gakkai gained religious recognition in the EU, while, on the other, the Commission increased legitimacy in dealing with religious issues.

The most significant result of religious lobbying of the European institutions has been the incorporation of religious communities as partners of dialogue in the EU legislation. Kenneth Houston analyses the position of the Bureau of European Policy Advisers towards religion and the ways in which the European Constitution legalised the presence of religion. Houston suggests that religion remains a controversial issue as a result of the diversity of religious and political interests in the EU. However, he points out that the drafting of the European Constitution represented positive relations between religious communities and the European institutions as their officials met and addressed issues of concern for both parties.

Acknowledgment

We are grateful to Dr Philip Walters, the editor of *Religion, State & Society*, for welcoming the publication of this volume, for his suggestions and for his thorough editing.

Notes

1 Earlier versions of the articles in this volume were presented at the international conference 'Religion and Politics in the Construction of the European Union' organised by Lucian N. Leustean and John T. S. Madeley at the Department of Government and European Institute, London School of Economics and Political Science, on 16 June 2007. Four other papers

presented at the conference are published as a special issue on 'Challenges to Church–State Relations in Contemporary Europe' in the *Journal of Religion in Europe*, 2008, 1, 3.

2 At the time of writing, widespread doubt continues about the ratification of the Lisbon Treaty since it requires unanimity by all 27 EU member states. On 12 June 2008 Ireland rejected the Lisbon Treaty in a referendum with 53.4 per cent voting against.

3 The Commission's main objective was 'to monitor and analyse the political process of the European Union' and to inform the Catholic faithful of the 'the development of EU policy and legislation' (see the website of the COMECE).

4 This Commission would later be absorbed within CEC in order to have a larger religious representation.

References and Bibliography

Anderson, J. (2003) *Religious Liberty in Transitional Societies: the Politics of Religion* (Cambridge, Cambridge University Press).

Audi, R. and Wolterstorff, N. (1997) *Religion in the Public Square* (London, Rowman & Littlefield).

Barbier, M. (1995) *La Laïcité* (Paris, Editions l'Harmatan).

Barnett, J. (ed.) (2005) *A Theology for Europe: the Churches and the European Institutions* (Oxford/Bern/Berlin, Peter Lang).

Barrett, D., Kurian, G. and Johnson, T. (2001) *World Christian Encyclopedia: a Comparative Survey of Churches and Religions AD 30–AD 2200* (New York, Oxford University Press).

Basdevant-Gaudemet, B. and Messner, F. (eds) (1999) *Les origines historiques du statut des confessions religieuses dans les pays de l'Union européenne* (Paris, PUF).

Bauberot, J. (1994) *Religions et laïcité dans l'Europe des Douze* (Paris, Syros).

Berger, P. (ed.) (1999) *The Desecularization of the World: Resurgent Religion and World Politics* (Grand Rapids, MI, Eerdmans/Ethics and Public Policy Center).

Berger, P., Grace, D. and Fokas, E. (2008) *Religious America, Secular Europe? A Theme and Variations* (Aldershot, Ashgate).

Buchanan, T. and Conway, M. (eds) (1996) *Political Catholicism in Europe 1919–1965* (Oxford, Clarendon Press).

Byrnes, T. A. and Katzenstein, P. (eds) (2006) *Religion in an Expanding Europe* (Cambridge, Cambridge University Press).

Casanova, J. (1994) *Public Religions in the Modern World* (Chicago, University of Chicago Press).

Casanova, J. (2006) 'Religion, European secular identities, and European integration', in T. A. Byrnes and P. Katzenstein (eds), *Religion in an Expanding Europe* (Cambridge, Cambridge University Press).

Chenaux, P. (1990) *Une Europe Vaticane? Entre le Plan Marshall et les Traités de Rome* (Brussels, Editions Ciaco).

Chenaux, P. (1991) 'Les democrates-chrétiens et la construction de l'Europe (1947–1957)', *Revue politique,* 1, pp. 87–101.

Coupland, P. (2006) *Britannia, Europa and Christendom: British Christians and European Integration* (Basingstoke, Palgrave Macmillan).

Davie, G. (1994) 'The religious factor in the emergence of Europe as a global region', *Social Compass,* 41, pp. 95–112.

Davie, G. (2000) *Religion in Modern Europe: a Memory Mutates* (Oxford, Oxford University Press).

Davie, G. (2002) *Europe: the Exceptional Case: Parameters of Faith in the Modern World* (London, Darton, Longman and Todd).

Davie, G. and Hervieu-Léger, D. (1996) *Identités religieuses en Europe* (Paris, La Découverte).

De Charentenay, P. (2003) 'Les relations entre l'Union européenne et les religions', *Revue du Marché commun et de l'Union européenne*, 465, pp. 90–100.

Declaration (1997) Declaration 11 on the Status of Churches and Non-Confessional Organisations, *Official Journal C 340*, 10 November.

De Montclos, C. (1994) 'Le Saint-Siège et la construction de l'Europe', in J.-B. d'Onorio (ed.), *Le Vatican et la politique européenne* (Paris, Mame).

Durand, J. D. (1995) *L'Europe de la Démocratie chrétienne* (Brussels, Complexe).

Durand, J. D. (ed.) (2008) *Cultures religieuses, églises et Europe* (Paris, Parole et Silence).

Ferrari, S. (1999) 'The new wine and the old cask: tolerance, religion, and the law in contemporary Europe', in A. Sajo and S. Avineri (eds), *The Law of Religious Identity: Models for Post-Communism* (The Hague, Kluwer Law International).

Ferrari, S. (2002) 'Islam and the western European model of church and state relations', in W. A. R. Shadid and P. S. van Konigsveld (eds), *Religious Freedom and the Neutrality of the State: the position of Islam in the European Union* (Leuven, Peeters).

Fox, J. (2008) *A World Survey of Religion and the State* (Cambridge, Cambridge University Press).

Freston, P. (2004) *Protestant Political Parties: a Global Survey* (Aldershot, Ashgate).

Gauchet, M. (1998) *La religion dans la démocratie: parcours de la laïcité* (Paris, Gallimard).

Gehler, M. and Kaiser, W. (eds) (2004) *Christian Democracy in Europe since 1945* (vol. 2) (London, Routledge).

George, S. (1990) *An Awkward Partner: Britain in the European Community* (Oxford, Oxford University Press).

Greeley, A. (2003) *Religion in Europe at the End of the Second Millennium* (New Brunswick, Transaction Publishers).

Greschat, M. and Loth, W. (eds) (1994) *Die Christen und die Enstehung der Europäischen Gemeinschaft* (Stuttgart, Kohlhammer).

Gstoehl, S. (2002) *Reluctant Europeans: Norway, Sweden, and Switzerland in the Process of Integration* (London, Lynne Rienner Publishers).

Haas, E. (1958) *The Uniting of Europe* (Stanford, Stanford University Press).

Hagevi, M. (2002) 'Religiosity and Swedish opinion on the European Union', *Journal for the Scientific Study of Religion,* 41, 4, pp. 759–69.

Haguenau-Moizard, C. (2000) *Etat et religions en Europe* (Grenoble, Presses Universitaires de Grenoble).

Hanley, D. (ed.) (1994) *Christian Democracy in Europe: a Comparative Perspective* (London, Pinter).

Huntington, S. P. (1996) *The Clash of Civilizations and the Remaking of World Order* (New York, Simon & Schuster).

Irving, R. E. M. (1979) *The Christian Democratic Parties of Western Europe* (London, RIIA).

Jansen, T. (2000) 'Europe and religions: the dialogue between the European Commission and churches or religious communities', *Social Compass*, 47, 1, pp. 103–12.

Jenssen, A., Todal, P. P. and Gilljam, M. (eds) (1998) *To Join or Not to Join: Three Nordic Referendums on Membership in the European Union* (Oslo, Scandinavian University Press).

Kaiser, W. (2007) *Christian Democracy and the Origins of the European Union* (Cambridge, Cambridge University Press).

Kalyvas, S. (1996) *The Rise of Christian Democracy in Europe* (Ithaca, NY, Cornell University Press).

Kirby, D. (ed.) (2003) *Religion and the Cold War* (Basingstoke, Palgrave).

Kselman, T. and Buttigieg, J. (eds) (2003) *European Christian Democracy: Historical Legacies and Comparative Perspectives* (Notre Dame, Notre Dame University Press).

Lamberts, E. (ed.) (1997) *Christian Democracy in the European Union (1945–1995)* (Leuven, Leuven University Press).

Leustean, L. N. (2007) 'The place of God: religious terms in the debate on the European Constitution', in A. Cohen and A. Vauchez (eds), *La Constitution Européenne: élites, mobilisations, votes* (Brussels, Presses de l'Université de Bruxelles), pp. 113–27.

Leustean, L. N. (2009a) *Orthodoxy and the Cold War: Religion and Political Power in Romania, 1947–65* (Basingstoke, Palgrave Macmillan).

Leustean, L. N. (ed.) (2009b) *Eastern Christianity and the Cold War* (London, Routledge) (forthcoming).

Lücker, A. and Hahn, K. (eds) (1987) *Christliche Demokraten Bauen Europa* (Bonn, Europa Union Verlag).

Ludlow, P. (1997) *Dealing with Britain: the Six and the First UK Membership Application* (Cambridge, Cambridge University Press).

Madelin, H. (2007) *Refaire l'Europe: le vieux et le neuf: préface Jacques Delors* (Monaco, Editions du Rocher).

Madeley, J. T. S. (2003) 'European liberal democracy and the principle of state religious neutrality', in J. T. S. Madeley and Z. Enyedi (eds), *Church and State in Contemporary Europe: the Chimera of Neutrality* (London, Frank Cass).

Madeley, J. T. S. (2009a) 'Unequally yoked: the antinomies of church–state separation in Europe and the USA', *European Political Science*, 8, 3 (forthcoming).

Madeley, J. T. S. (2009b) 'E unum pluribus: the role of religion in the project of European integration', in J. Haynes (ed.), *Religion and Politics in Europe, the Middle East and North Africa: Challenges to Citizenship, Secularisation and Democracy* (London, Routledge/ECPR Studies in European Political Science) (forthcoming).

Madeley, J. T. S. (2009c) 'America's secular state and the unsecular state of Europe', in R. Fatton and R. Ramazani (eds), *Thomas Jefferson's Church–State Separation in the Contemporary World* (Basingstoke, Palgrave), pp. 109–36.

Madeley, J. T. S. and Enyedi, Z. (eds) (2003) *Church and State in Contemporary Europe: the Chimera of Neutrality* (London, Frank Cass).

Madeley, J. T. S. and Sitter, N. (2003) *Differential Eurocepticism among Nordic Christian Parties: Protestantism or Protest?*, paper for Scandinavian Politics Specialist Group, Political Studies Association conference, Leicester, UK.

Malcolm, N. (1996) 'Conservative realism and Christian Democracy', in K. Minogue (ed.), *Conservative Realism: New Essays on Conservatism* (London, Harper).

Maritain, J. (1951) *Man and the State* (Chicago, University of Chicago Press).

Massignon, B. (2007) *Dieux et fonctionnaires: religions et laïcités face au défi de la construction européenne* (Rennes, Presses Universitaires de Rennes).

Mathieu, C. (1999) *The Moral Life of the Party: Moral Argumentation and the Creation of Meaning in the Europe Policy Debates of the Christian and Left-Socialist Parties in Denmark and Sweden 1990–1996* (Lund, Dissertations in Sociology).

McCrae, R. (2007) *Limitations on Religion in a Liberal Democratic Polity: Christianity and Islam in the Public Order of the European Union* (London School of Economics, *Law, Society and Economy Working Papers*, 18).

Messner, F. (1999) 'La législation culturelle des pays de l'Union européenne face aux groupes sectaires', in F. Champion and M. Cohen (eds), *Sectes et Démocratie* (Paris, Editions du Seuil).

Meyer, J. F. (1980) *Des partis catholiques à la Démocratie chrétienne: XIXe–XXe siècles* (Paris, Armand Colin).

Michalski, K. (ed.) (2006) *Religion in the New Europe* (Budapest/New York: Central European University Press).

Miljan, T. (1977) *The Reluctant Europeans: the Attitudes of the Nordic Countries Towards European Integration* (Montreal, McGill-Queen's University Press).

Monsma, S. (ed.) (2002) *Church–State Relations in Crisis: Debating Neutrality* (Oxford, Rowman & Littlefield).

Monsma, S. and Soper, C. (1997) *The Challenge of Pluralism: Church and State in Five Democracies* (Oxford, Rowman & Littlefield).

Nelsen, B. F. (2004) *The Reluctant Europeans: Protestantism, Nationalism and European Integration*, paper prepared for APSA Annual Meeting, Chicago, 2–5 September.

Nelsen, B. F. (2005) *Europe as a Christian Club: Religion and the Founding of the European Community, 1950–1975: the Ideological Dimension*, paper prepared for APSA Annual Meeting, Washington DC, 1–4 September.

Nelsen, B. F. and Guth, J. (2003a) 'Religion and youth support for the European Union', *Journal of Common Market Studies,* 41, 1, pp. 89–112.

Nelsen, B. F. and Guth, J. (2003b) *Roman Catholicism and the Founding of Europe: how Catholics Shaped the European Communities*, paper prepared for APSA Annual Meeting, Philadelphia, 28–31 August.

Nelsen, B. F., Guth, J. L. and Fraser, C. R. (2001) 'Does religion matter? Christianity and public support for the European Union', *European Union Politics*, 2, 2, pp. 191–217.

Nexon, D. (2006) 'Religion, European identity, and political contention in historical perspective', in T. A. Byrnes and P. Katzenstein (eds), *Religion in an Expanding Europe* (Cambridge, Cambridge University Press).

Newsletter (1992) *Newsletter of the Ecumenical Centre in Brussels* (Brussels, EECCS), May.

Norris, P. and Inglehart, R. (2004) *Sacred and Religious: Religion and Politics Worldwide* (Cambridge, Cambridge University Press).

Papini, R. (1997) *The Christian Democratic International* (Lanham, Rowman & Littlefield).

Philpott, D. and Shah, S. (2006) 'Faith, freedom and federation: the role of religious ideas and institutions in European political convergence', in T. A. Byrnes and P. Katzenstein (eds), *Religion in an Expanding Europe* (Cambridge, Cambridge University Press).

Potz, R. (2003) 'Der Status von Kirchen und Religionsgemeinschaften in den Mitgliedstaaten der Europäischen Union', in P.-C. Müller-Graff and H. Schneider (eds), *Kirchen und Religionsgemeinschaften der Europäischen Union* (Baden-Baden, Nomos).

Poulat, E. (1987) *Liberté, laïcité: la guerre des deux France et le principe de la modernité* (Paris, Le Cerf).

Pulzer, P. (2004) 'Nationalism and internationalism in European Christian Democracy', in M. Gehler and W. Kaiser (eds), *Christian Democracy in Europe since 1945* (London, Routledge).

Ramadan, T. (2004) *Western Muslims and the Future of Islam* (Oxford, Oxford University Press).

Ramet, S. (2006) 'The way we were – and should be again? European Orthodox churches and the "idyllic past"', in T. A. Byrnes and P. Katzenstein (eds), *Religion in an Expanding Europe* (Cambridge, Cambridge University Press).

Ratzinger, J. (1989) *Les difficultés en matière de foi dans l'Europe d'aujourd'hui* (Paris, Téqui).

Ratzinger, J. (2007) *Europe: Today and Tomorrow* (San Francisco, Ignatius Press).

Remond, R. (1999) *Religion and Society in Modern Europe* (trans. Antonia Nevill) (Malden, Blackwell).

Robbers, R. (ed.) (1996) *State and Church in the European Union* (Baden-Baden, Nomos).

Roy, O. (2002) *Globalised Islam: the Search for a New Ummah* (London, Hurst).

Rusama, J. (1994) 'Europe and the churches', *Finnish Institute Yearbook* (London, Finnish Institute).

Sørensen, Ø. and Stråth, B. (eds) (1997) *The Cultural Construction of Norden* (Oslo, Scandinavian University Press).

Stepan, A. (2000) 'Religion, democracy, and the "twin tolerations"', *Journal of Democracy*, 11, 4, pp. 37–56.

Sundback, S. (2003) 'The nordic Lutheran churches and the EU question in 1994', *Temenos: Studies in Comparative Religion*, 37–38, pp. 191–208.

Taggart, P. (1998) 'A touchstone of dissent: Euroscepticism in contemporary west European party systems', *European Journal of Political Research*, 33, pp. 363–88.

Thual, F. (1993) *Géopolitique de l'Orthodoxie* (Paris, Dunod).

Tibi, B. (2006) 'Europeanizing Islam or the Islamization of Europe: political democracy vs. cultural difference', in T. A. Byrnes and P. Katzenstein (eds), *Religion in an Expanding Europe* (Cambridge, Cambridge University Press).

Van Hecke, S. and Gerard, E. (eds) (2004) *Christian Democratic Parties in Europe since the End of the Cold War* (Leuven, Leuven University Press).
Van Kersbergen, K. (1995) *Social Capitalism: a Study of Christian Democracy and the Welfare State* (London, Routledge).
Vincent, G. and Willaime, J. P. (1993) *Religions et transformations de l'Europe* (Strasbourg, Presses Universitaires de Strasbourg).
Vollard, H. (2006) 'Protestantism and Euroscepticism in the Netherlands', *Perspectives on European Politics and Society*, 7, 3, pp. 276–97.
Weigel, G. (2005) *The Cube and the Cathedral: Europe, America and Politics without God* (New York, Basic Books).
Weninger, M. H. (2007) *Europa ohne Gott? Die Europäische Union und der Dialog mit den Religionen, Kirchen und Weltanschauungsgemeinschaften* (Baden-Baden, Nomos).
Willaime, J. P. (2002) *La précarité protestante: sociologie du protestantisme contemporain* (Geneva, Labor et Fides).
Willaime, J. P. (2004) *Europe et religions: les enjeux du XXIe siècle* (Paris, Fayard).
Zeilstra, J. A. (1995) *European Unity in Ecumenical Thinking 1937–1948* (Zoetermeer, Boekencentrum).

European Integration, *Laïcité* and Religion

JEAN-PAUL WILLAIME

Introduction

At the heart of Europe's identity as a civilisation there is a tension between politics and religion, and a resolution of this tension through law and the politics of religious conflict. Europe has a wealth of cultural, linguistic and religious diversity and could be said to be characterised by plurality. If this plurality is considered from a religious angle, three key elements that are historical constituents of Europe's identity as a civilisation need to be borne in mind. Europe has a wealth not only of religious heritages but also of philosophical traditions questioning faiths, and their claims and pretensions. Reason, critical questioning, free inquiry and doubt are just as much a part of European cultural heritage as the religious traditions that form part of its history. It can even be argued that a constant dialectic between faith and doubt, or belief and reason, lies at the heart of Europe's identity as a civilisation. Another constant feature of Europe's history is the debate about the respective boundaries and autonomy of the spiritual and temporal powers. The very existence of tensions between the two is evidence that in European culture there is a clear distinction between them. Admittedly, all sorts of combinations of the two powers, including their quasi-fusion (or confusion), have characterised a European history that has been scarred by wars of religion. Nor did the spiritual and the temporal achieve their independence from each other overnight and the process was often fiercely resisted. Nevertheless, the respective autonomy of the spiritual and the temporal is now a key feature of European civilisation. Confessional conflicts, religious wars and antisemitism have had a profound influence on Europe's history. If Europe's past is characterised by violence associated with religion, it is also, and above all, the story of the pacification of this violence and the emergence of democratic societies that respect freedom of conscience and thought.

Europe signifies the historic construction of civil peace and tolerance, enabling its countries to establish themselves as political communities that acknowledge the multiple religious and philosophical choices of its peoples. This process, the result of the separation of politics and law from religion, is at the heart of Europe's identity.

Laïcité: a European Value

Laïcité, which must not be identified with the French system of church–state relations, is a European value. This claim can be substantiated despite the fact that the reading of the constitutional texts and the examination of the relationships between church and state, and between school and religion, in different European countries can easily give rise to doubts about how extensive *laïcité* actually is in Europe. Indeed, references to God (Germany, UK) or to the Trinity (Greece, Ireland) in state constitutions[1] are not unusual in Europe.[2] Some states maintain privileged ties to one religion (Denmark, Greece, England and Scotland in the UK, Malta) and many others have established partnerships with various 'recognised' religious groups (Germany, Italy). As for state schools, in Europe they frequently include religion classes jointly managed by the academic and religious authorities (Germany, Belgium, Spain) (Willaime, 2004a; Jackson *et al.*, 2007). Finally, regarding the question of the wearing of religious symbols by pupils, only France and Turkey have enacted legislation to prohibit young Muslim girls from wearing the headscarf, most European countries allowing pupils to wear it (in the UK, what matters is that the headscarf's colour match that of the school uniform). In Europe – for example, in Germany – public debate centres less on the pupils' headscarves than on those of the teachers, which is another matter entirely. Does that mean that only France and Turkey remain vigilant when it comes to *laïcité*? If that were true, there would be cause for concern because Turkey is not a model of democracy and Turkish-style *laïcité* has many surprising aspects (imams are paid by the state and a Sunni religion class is offered in state schools). On the European level, French-style *laïcité* may therefore appear isolated, and one can understand that some observers see Europeanisation as a threat to *laïcité*. This becomes even clearer when one realises that the word *laïcité* itself, and the adjective *laïque* associated with it, are difficult to translate into other European languages, and that our European partners typically associate this terminology exclusively with the French historical approach to the matter. Moreover, the perception France's European partners have of this approach often has a negative connotation; they think of French-style *laïcité* as a somewhat negative neutrality toward religions. The opposition expressed in 2001 by some secular activists toward the reference to religious heritage in the preamble to the Charter of Fundamental Rights on the one hand, and the fact that the project on a European Constitutional Treaty drawn up by the Convention on the Future of Europe in 2002–2003 mentions the 'cultural, religious and humanist inheritance of Europe' and speaks of maintaining 'an open, transparent and regular dialogue' with churches as well as philosophical and nonconfessional organisations of the member states (Article I-52) on the other hand, underline for some the idea that the European Union (EU), when all is said and done, is not very secular.

To talk about *laïcité* on the European level implies first of all a need to get beyond the French historical approach to the relationships between church and state and between school and religion. If one quite simply associates *laïcité* with the French system of regulating religion (the law of 1905 separating church and state) and with the relationship between school and religion as it has been historically constituted in France, it is immediately easy to conclude that Europe is not secular. Adopting a European point of view in the matter requires taking into account each country's history. But European integration brings into close contact countries that have constructed themselves as political communities and as democracies with differing relationships to religion. In many European countries, the autonomy of the political system was not achieved, as it was in France, through an extremely confrontational relationship with the dominant religion. The construction of Europe cannot be accomplished via the generalised acceptance by other countries of one national model or another; this process is constantly on the lookout for subtle balances and compromises within the framework of respect for a few fundamental principles. *Laïcité* is one of these principles. Not, however, *laïcité* via the regulation of religion and the status of schooling as they have been institutionalised in France, but *laïcité* as the respective autonomy of political and religious systems, dissociation of citizenship and religious affiliation, implementation of the right to worship freely – or not to worship at all – and respect for human rights (Ferrari, 1999). Taking a European perspective means first of all discovering or rediscovering that a genuine separation of religious and political systems is not incompatible with various forms of recognising the role of religions in the public sphere. We observe that at the national level and just as much at the European level (Foret, 2007). It is necessary for France to appreciate the singularities that characterise it in European eyes in this area of relations between the state, religions and society.

These singularities are of four sorts: (1) the fact that church–state relations have been more confrontational in France than elsewhere: since the French Revolution and throughout the nineteenth and twentieth century the question of the place and the role of religion has been a central one, generating deep and lasting divisions; (2) the strongly ideological nature of the problem with the influence, more pronounced in France than in most other European countries, of philosophical conceptions and political critiques of religions (from freethinkers, rationalists, Marxists, Freemasons, etc.); (3) the more pronounced affirmation of the supremacy of the state and its authority over civil life, according to the tradition of a state that is on the one hand emancipatory and enlightened, and on the other hand centralising and homogenising; (4) the strong resistance toward expressions of religious affiliation in political discourse and the disappearance of religious activity from public life, which is more accentuated in France than elsewhere in Europe. Thus, in European countries, as Bérengère Massignon emphasises in a document on 'religious signs' (Massignon, 2004, pp. 117–23) drawn up for the Ministry of Foreign Affairs, 'the occasional affairs that receive media attention do not focus on the wearing of headscarves at school by pupils', and such difficulties as do arise are 'handled flexibly, case by case … on the level of school administrators and staff meetings, one that favours amicable agreements'. Even if one finds some of these same features in other European countries – in varying combinations and with varying levels of importance – what makes France a special case is the relevance that these features have had in the country's social/historical configuration.

The French terms *laïcité* and *laïque* are difficult to translate into certain European languages, particularly English and German, and the terms are often associated specifically with the French historical experience of church–state relations. In fact, it can be argued that other European countries also speak of *laïcité*/secularity

('secularity' is in my view a better translation than 'secularism') and that the concept is acknowledged by the European Court of Human Rights, which refers to it in a number of judgments. Above all, the phenomenon is more important than the word. Micheline Milot, a Canadian academic who has studied *laïcité* in Quebec, rightly stresses the need to separate the concept and its ideological application from the historic French context in which it emerged, to think of it instead as a political concept (Milot, 2002, p. 23). According to Milot, *laïcité* signifies the political, and also the legal, arrangements governing the place of religion in civil society and public institutions (Milot, 2002, p. 34). If *laïcité* concerns the political adjustment and then the legal expression of the place of religion in societies respecting the mutual autonomy of political and religious systems and dissociating citizenship from religious affiliation – if *laïcité* is a principle implementing the right to worship freely or not to worship at all in democratic societies concerned about non-discrimination and respect of human rights – then it becomes possible to talk of European *laïcité*. Indeed, it appears in this case that a real separation of religious and political systems is not incompatible with the recognition, under various forms, of the role of religions in the public sphere. This recognition is found in the countries in Europe where the autonomy of the political system and of democracy has not been achieved, as it has in France, at the cost of conflict with the dominant religion. Some countries have even had the opposite experience of a positive role of religions in the progress toward democracy. The integration into the EU of the former Soviet-bloc countries that had suffered from religious persecutions under the regime of state-sponsored atheism is in this respect very significant. As for Germany, the 'two dictatorships' of its recent history, nazism and communism, were both hostile to religions, and the churches were ready and waiting to serve when these two dictatorships fell. In other words, the defence of liberties and the protection against the dangers of dictatorship and of nationalism went hand in hand, in Germany, with the consolidation of the institutional position of churches and of their moral sway. In the Scandinavian countries, state, religion and society evolved at the same rhythm, without major conflicts. In the year 2000, a 'secular velvet revolution' took place in Sweden with a separation of church and state that maintained some privileges for the Lutheran Church.

In a number of other publications (Willaime, 2004b, c, 2006a, 2007), I have developed the notion that, far from being something distinctively French, *laïcité* is based on a number of key principles that can be applied to a variety of forms of church–state relations. There are three such principles: (1) freedom of conscience, thought and religion, which includes the freedom to have or not to have a religion, to change one's religion and to practise it, subject only to respect for the law, democracy and human rights; (2) equal rights and duties of all citizens, irrespective of their religious or philosophical beliefs, which means that government and the state must not discriminate against persons because of their religious or philosophical positions; (3) the respective autonomy of the state and religions, which signifies that they each enjoy freedom and independence with regard to the other, subject to respect for the law and democracy.

The fundamental principles of *laïcité* are established throughout Europe, though with variations according to the particular church–state relationship applicable in member countries. In varying forms and to varying degrees this European *laïcité* applies in every country of the continent, though some apply it more strictly than others. However, the existence of an operational form of European *laïcité* does not mean that everything is perfect in the best of all worlds. The different ways in which countries have related to religion have affected their nation-building process and their progress to democracy. In several countries, political autonomy has been achieved without any excessive conflict with the dominant religion. Moreover, in the countries of the former communist bloc, the return to democracy and various forms of religious recognition were achieved simultaneously. The multiple and complex reality of church–state relations in Europe should not be equated with any particular national situation. Instead, we need to identify common principles that are unrelated to any one nation's distinctive features and historical experience.

European *Laïcité* and the Recognition of Religions

It can be said that *laïcité* in Europe is basically associated with religious recognition; in other words, that while respecting the respective independence of state and confessions and safeguarding the corresponding fundamental principles of freedom and non-discrimination, it acknowledges religions' social, educational and civic roles and as such incorporates them into the public sphere. In Europe, *laïcité* does not necessarily signify an absence of cooperation between public bodies and religions. Most countries have established systems for recognising confessions and involving them in a number of public activities. The general extent of and the particular arrangements for the recognition of religious communities vary from country to country and it is not possible here to go into details (see De Puig, 2007; Dierkens and Schreiber, 2006; Robbers, 2005). We should simply note that this *laïcité* based on religious recognition is particularly influenced by whichever religion is in the majority, so that paradoxically we can speak of Catholic, Lutheran, Muslim or even Orthodox *laïcité*, and these forms of *laïcité* will be coloured, and to varying extents limited, by the size and influence of the religious majority. Another factor influencing the situation is the growing number of people who claim to have no religion and/or dispute the role accorded to faiths.

Thus, in Europe, the dominant model of church–state relations, which differs depending on the country in question, is one of *recognised religions*, where on the basis of a separation between political and religious systems, the state recognises some religions by entering into agreements with them while guaranteeing freedom of conscience, of thought and of religion for all. In most European countries, the respective autonomy of churches and the state is often associated with various forms of church–state cooperation, notably via agreements established between the state and religious authorities. These agreements show that the state acknowledges the participation of religious groups in the education of citizens and the practical exercise of citizenship in public life. In other words, in Europe, separation of religious and political systems does not prohibit the formation of partnerships and cooperative arrangements between public agencies and religious organisations. We will look at the examples of Spain, Italy, Belgium and Germany.

In Spain, Article 16 of the 1978 Constitution, while saying that 'no religion shall have a state character', stipulates that 'the public authorities shall take into account the religious beliefs of Spanish society and shall consequently maintain cooperative relationships with the Catholic Church and other religions'. At the time it was debated, this article was even accepted by the Spanish Communist Party. As for the Organic Law of Religious Freedom of 1980, it distinguishes between religious communities that have 'well-known roots in Spain' and religious groups that have established themselves in the country more recently. The idea that some religions have 'well-known roots' may be a delicate matter to handle. Let us observe that in fact, it is not the quantitative criterion that predominates here, but the time that has elapsed since the religion's establishment and its cultural importance. Using this approach, the Spanish state has recognised the 'well-known roots' of groups very much in the minority such as Protestants, Jews and Muslims (on 14 December 1984 for the first two and on 14 July 1989 for the third). This led to the signing of cooperative agreements by the Spanish state not only with the Catholic Church (in 1979) but also, in 1992, with the Protestant, Jewish and Muslim religious minorities.

In Italy, the text of the Concordat of 1984 states that 'the principles of Catholicism are part of the historical heritage of the Italian people'; the Italian Republic and the Holy See work together 'for the promotion of man and the good of the country' (Article 1). By repealing the status of 'state religion', these agreements make provisions for a regime of self-financing for religions and the freedom 'to exercise the right to benefit, or not, from religious instruction at school' (Margiotta Broglio, 1990, p. 88; 1999, p. 158). By concluding numerous agreements with different religions and with Catholicism,[3] the Italian state has adapted itself in the matter of religious freedom and has acted accordingly in its relationships with different religious groups. Decision No. 203 of 1989 of the Italian Constitutional Court declared that the principle of *laïcité* is one of the 'supreme principles' of the Italian legal system, having a higher value than other norms or constitutional laws. In Italy, the principle of *laïcité* implies, first of all, non-indifference by the state toward religions and the guarantee of freedom of religion in a system of denominational and cultural pluralism. This leads to the teaching of the Catholic religion on the basis of the evolution and the formative value of religious culture, and the integral part the principles of Catholicism play in the historical heritage of the Italian people. Second, the principle of *laïcité* implies respect by the state for the objective right to take or not to take the religion class for which the law provides.

In Belgium, *laïcité* is very apparent, but in a form intrinsically different from the one known in France. The Kingdom of Belgium is a pluralistic state, but not a secularist one. There, *laïcité* in the shape of Humanist groups is considered as the 'seventh recognised religion' next to the six others (Catholicism, Protestantism, Anglicanism, Orthodox Christianity, Judaism and Islam) (Javeau, 2005). In prison or in the army, alongside the Catholic, Protestant, Jewish or Muslim chaplains, you may also request the services of a 'Humanist' (i.e. secular) chaplain. At school, pupils may take a denominational religion class or a class in 'nondenominational ethics'. The Catholic University of Leuven is a fully fledged public university, as is the Free University of Brussels, influenced by free thought and Freemasonry.[4] In other words, in Belgium *laïcité* is not the all-inclusive framework for the whole society; it is thought of as a nonreligious conception of man and the world, that is to say a specific philosophical option treated as the equivalent of a 'religion'.

For Germany, it is immediately interesting to observe that if it was a political revolution, the French Revolution, that is a crucial moment in French history, it is a religious revolution, the Reformation, that constitutes a fundamental point of reference for German history. While the Revolution of 1789 triggered recurrent debate in France on the place and role of religion in society, a debate that has engendered the much-discussed 'war of the two Frances', the main problem in Germany has been less that of the place of religion in society than that posed by the coexistence of two religious denominations: Catholicism and Protestantism. At the time when religion and politics were interfering with each other constantly, the essential question was how to organise the exercise of political sovereignty in the presence of two denominations where neither one had managed to defeat the other. Hence, the institutionalisation of biconfessionalism and the establishment of various forms of cooperation with churches. The defence of liberties and the protection against the dangers of dictatorship and of nationalism went hand in hand in Germany, with the consolidation of the institutional position of churches and of their moral sway. As a result, one can better understand why the German state, while declaring that 'there is no state church' (Article 137.1 of the Weimar Constitution, preserved in Article 140 of the current Basic Law), 'accords . . . a part of the public sphere to religious institutions that have their origins in historical religious institutions' (Zylberberg, 1995, p. 39). When all is said and done, these institutions are recognised as political institutions contributing towards the common good. Far from reducing public action to that of the state and the autonomous regions, in Germany the churches' mission is also recognised as serving the public interest. The fact that the churches were actively involved in the founding of the Republic, and appeared as fundamental guarantors of democracy at crucial moments in German history, only underscores this recognition. Churches are recognised as 'public corporations'. This status is characteristic of the partnership with the churches that the German state wishes to maintain, one that is based on taking into account the churches' recognised *Öffentlichkeitsauftrag* (public mission). Currently, discussions are under way so that Islam will benefit from this status, but German officials are encountering the same difficulty experienced by French officials: the problem of designating a representative authority for Muslims in the Federal Republic. If no inherent obstacle exists for this status to be extended to Islam, this does not mean that it is *ipso facto* extended to any and all groups who ask for it, whether they be a religious community or whether they represent a nonreligious conception of the universe (*Weltanschauungsgemeinschaften* – 'worldview communities' or, to use the term which is now more commonly used in Europe, 'communities of conviction'). The churches' access to the media is in keeping with the 'recognition of the public nature of their mission and their place in society': they not only have access to the media, but they also participate in the management of the public radio and television services; they are part of the 'significant social groups' that are represented in the collegial bodies of the television networks. As for state schools, religion classes are given on a denominational basis, but they are not necessarily very denominational in their content and tend to be taught more along historical and/or ecumenical lines.

Why is Europe Secular?

Legally speaking, Europe is *laïque* (secular) by virtue of the European Convention for the Protection of Human Rights and Fundamental Freedoms. This Convention was formulated inside the Council of Europe, was signed in 1950, and came into force in 1953. France ratified it in 1973, and 46 other European states have done likewise. This European Convention on Human Rights guarantees, within the limits of respect for liberal democratic principles, freedom of thought, of conscience and of religion (which includes the freedom to change religions or to have none) and prohibits any discrimination, in particular that based on sex, race or religion. It upholds the dissociation in the European arena of the socio-political order and religion. In Article 9 of the Convention – included in the Charter of Fundamental Rights – it lays down the fundamental principles of a European *laïcité* guaranteeing individual and collective freedom of religion or non-religion, specifying that the only restrictions that can be placed on it come from measures that 'are necessary in a democratic society':

> 1. Everyone has the right to freedom of thought, conscience and religion. This right includes freedom to change religion or belief and freedom, either alone or

> in community with others and in public or in private, to manifest religion or belief, in worship, teaching, practice and observance.
> 2. Freedom to manifest one's religion or beliefs shall be subject only to such limitations as are prescribed by law and are necessary in a democratic society in the interests of public safety, for the protection of public order, health or morals, or for the protection of the rights and freedoms of others.

This Article guarantees the freedoms of thought, of conscience and of religion against all influences – be they religious or otherwise – while preserving the exercise of religious freedom both in its private and its public dimensions, and in its individual as well as its collective dimensions. The sense of this Article has been explained by the European Court of Human Rights in its Kokkinakis decision (1993), where the judges declared that 'as protected by article 9, the freedom of thought, of conscience and of religion represents one of the cornerstones of a democratic society'. This precedent was confirmed in 2004 in the Sahin case where the Court reaffirmed that 'secular universities may [introduce] restrictions based on place and manner, in order to ensure the diversity of students with various beliefs and thus protect public order and the beliefs of others'. As the jurist Alain Garay points out, *laïcité* has become a 'principle raised to the status of a value by the European Convention on Human Rights' (Garay, 2006, p. 98).

In addition, Article 2 of the first additional protocol (1952) to that Convention states: 'In the exercise of any functions which it assumes in relation to education and to teaching, the State shall respect the right of parents to ensure such education and teaching in conformity with their own religious and philosophical convictions.' With this text, the countries that are signatories to the Convention recognise, on the one hand, that state schools must be pluralistic, and that they must refrain from any form of indoctrination and respect the religious and philosophical convictions of pupils and their families. On the other hand, this text rules out any state monopoly over education, recognising the right of parents to choose a private school, which does not mean – even if it is often the case in Europe – that the state is required to subsidise these schools.

The European Convention on Human Rights is not only a legally binding text. It is also a document that vouches for a shared ethos – in particular a common conception of and a common respect for human rights. The European states upholding this ethos are 'driven by the same spirit and possess a common heritage of political ideals and traditions, of respect for liberties and of the pre-eminence of law' (Preamble to the Convention) – a shared ethos that manifests itself on the intellectual level by an attitude promoting critical thinking (including about oneself), freedom of judgment (*libre examen*) and the duty of knowledge. European *laïcité*, therefore, does not mean the end of religious systems but the end of religion as a system of power and the repositioning of its role in a pluralistic society freed from domination by the clergy. It is in this framework that the relationship between religion and politics is reorganising itself in various ways that can also be seen in the religious and political disputes involving the very concept of *laïcité*. *Laïcité* is anything but a dormant topic: it not only remains an important issue in many different religious circles, but it also takes on a geopolitical dimension that does not go unnoticed by those concerned about the future of democracies in an age where many have become disenchanted with politics.

Europe is also *laïque* (secular) in terms of mentalities, as shown by the surveys conducted throughout the continent (the European Values Survey and the International Social Survey Programme) (Lambert, 2003). These surveys indicate an increase in the number of young adults in different European countries who say that they are 'without religion'. They also show that those who identify with one religion, including the most faithful of believers, give proof of autonomy in their thinking, the majority of them being in favour of a separation between the political and religious systems. It is even more interesting to observe that believers are increasingly taking into account the multiplicity of faiths in their ways of being religious. In modern-day Europe, only a small minority of people think that 'truth can only be found in one religion'. There is a secularisation of religious awareness itself that contributes to *laïcité*, strengthening it on the legal level; in other words, the secularisation of mentalities strengthens *laïcité*. The media focus on the sectarian tendencies of some groups or on various radical religious movements, notably Islamic ones, must not result in this fundamental tendency, which has become solidly entrenched in Europe, being forgotten or overlooked.

Laïcité as Sanctioned by the Treaty of Lisbon

During the Brussels summit of 17–18 June 2004, Europe demonstrated its *laïque*/secular nature in adopting a text for a treaty – the first version of which had been worked out in 2002–2003 by the Convention on the Future of Europe – including a preamble that mentions the 'cultural, religious and humanist inheritance of Europe' (this treaty was not ratified by France and the Netherlands in 2005; it had, however, been ratified by 18 of the EU member states as of 2007). Today, this version is replaced by the Treaty of Lisbon adopted on 13 December 2007. While some countries (Italy, Lithuania, Malta, Poland, Portugal, the Czech Republic, Slovakia) demanded that special mention be made of Christianity, and other voices called for a reference to God in the wording of this preamble, a *secular compromise* finally prevailed. This recognition of an 'inheritance', by not naming a particular religion, allows first of all for non-Christian religions to be taken into account, Judaism and Islam in particular, as part of the religious inheritance of Europe. Second, underscoring the role played by the cultural and humanist aspects of that inheritance alongside the religious provides a way of taking into account not only the important contributions of nonreligious philosophies, but also the fact that Europe has been a region where religion and critiques of religion are in permanent confrontation with each other. This is why one can say that a secular recognition of the diversity of Europe's constitutive inheritance prevailed.

In addition, by proposing in Article 52–3 (now Article 16C in the Treaty of Lisbon) to maintain 'an open, transparent and regular dialogue' with the churches as well as the philosophical and the nondenominational organisations of the member states, the text of the European Treaty places itself in a perspective that has become common to most of the Union member states, one of a *laïcité of recognition*: 'Recognising their identity and their specific contribution, the Union shall maintain an open, transparent and regular dialogue with these churches and organisations' (Treaty of Lisbon, Art. 16C, 3). It aims to construct a *laïcité* that recognises, on an official basis, the public role of churches and philosophical organisations in the democratic life of societies, while still respecting its own fundamental principles. If the EU constitutes a field of experimentation on the socio-political level, this is also true for *laïcité*. A *laïcité* is being invented there that guarantees the autonomy of political systems and the freedom of people when confronted by religious authorities, and recognises the contribution of religions to the education of individuals and to community life, while at the same time respecting the prerogatives of member states when it comes to church–state relations. In relationships between religious institutions, the EU forms, as Bérengère Massignon (2003, p. 41) has astutely observed, a veritable 'laboratory for managing religious and philosophical diversity … where new forms of relationships between communities of conviction and political/administrative authorities are being invented' in a framework where the role of state functions and of democracy are being redefined (Massignon, 2007). This European *laïcité* under development is well in keeping with the general religious evolution of European societies toward a model of 'pluralistic secularisation' (Lambert, 2000, p. 33), in other words 'a model in which religion must not exert a hold on public life, but may fully play its part as a spiritual, ethical, cultural or even political resource in the widest sense, by respecting individual autonomy and democratic pluralism' (Lambert, 2000, p. 33).

Essentially, European integration has two consequences for *laïcité*. First of all, it reinforces its incorporation into the legal system and its inscription into the register of human rights and of fundamental principles of liberal and pluralistic democracies, whatever the particular religious nature of each country and its way of regulating religion may be. This is indicative of the success of *laïcité*; it also shows that the concept has become commonplace. The role of the European Convention on Human Rights is significant in this respect. On the European level, there is a generalised recognition of the fundamental principles of *laïcité*, one however that remains respectful of the different types of church–state relations that prevail in the member states. In addition, in the way in which religions and philosophical convictions are represented to the European institutions in Brussels, *laïcité* finds itself taken into account above all as a specific philosophical conception (with its connections to free thought and atheist humanisms) *alongside* religious conceptions of man and the world, not as a superior, all-inclusive ideology in relation to religions (thus following the Belgian/Dutch logic of 'pillarisation' where the worldview of *laïcité* is instituted as a specific segment of society alongside the worldviews of religion) (Willaime, 2008). This is the perspective of the European Humanist Federation, which groups together nonreligious, philosophical currents of opinion. By separating these two sides of *laïcité* from each other, Europeanisation might be able to contribute to a certain marginalisation of the French model of *laïcité*; assuming that the latter model remained immutable, something which is not likely to be the case. Indeed, even if one regularly observes the reactivation of a French-style *laïcité* that is especially distrustful regarding religious systems, notably when confronted with the problems of sectarian groups and of fanatical expressions of Islam, the French practice of *laïcité* has evolved to a large extent toward one recognising the social role of religions that has put it in step with the rest of Europe (Willaime, 2005). Only an anticlerical form of *laïcité*, wishing to reactivate the philosophical authority of the state and aiming to limit religious freedom, can feel threatened by Europeanisation.

Conclusion

One way of expressing the current circumstance is to say that we are currently in a time of ultramodernity, where

> ultramodernity is seen as a process that secularizes modernity and demythologises the secular ideals in the very name of which modernity previously helped to secularize religion. The transfer of sacralisation from the religious to other spheres of activity, such as economy, the polity and morality, corresponded closely to the phase of secularizing modernity. By

> contrast with this, ultramodernity takes on the appearance of a secularized modernity in which secularization gets to work on the forces of secularization themselves: it is the disenchantment of the disenchanters. (Willaime, 2006b, p. 79)

Modernity was borne along by a strong belief – as much on the left as on the right – in the capacity of politics to provide for people's happiness once heavenly salvation had been transformed into earthly salvation. Now, the current situation in western democracies is distinctive just as much for the rise of unbelief in politics as for the rise of unbelief in religion. Marcel Gauchet's (2002) book with the pointed title *Democracy Against Itself* presents an excellent summary of the problem by locating it in the emergence of a 'society of individuals' that makes it more and more difficult to exercise collective governance. The argument is that this situation affects politics directly and that talk of 'the eclipse of politics' becomes possible. This growing lack of belief in the capacity of politics to make decisive improvements in things is all the more paradoxical in the light of the tendency to expect ever more of it. In this kind of conjuncture it is not surprising that a genuine secularisation of politics is taking place and that politics is being disentangled from the grand visions of man and society. Marcel Gauchet's way of expressing the relationship between the evolution of religious belief and political belief is very apt:

> Religious belief is ceasing to be political. It is abandoning its time-honoured involvement in the form taken by human communities. This process of detachment from its original core is opening up a different future for it. Political belief is ceasing to be religious. It is shrugging off the constraint that the sacral model was secretly continuing to exercise over all possible representations of society. This emancipation from the initial framework that contained the agreement about our world ushers us into a new age of politics and, more broadly, historical action. (Gauchet, 2002, p. 18)

This new age of politics is a new stage in the secularisation of politics. It is not only the emancipation of politics from religious tutelage (that is to say, an internal secularisation of politics); but it is also a secularisation of politics itself. The relativisation of the nation-state faced with globalisation of the economy and the media as well as with the rise of the political power of the regions, together with the very effects of European integration, help to reinforce the secularisation of politics at the national level. Despite the reference to *laïcité* as a national value and the attitudes of some militants, secularisation does not spare *laïcité* in France. At the European level France is relativised both by its support for human rights and the fundamental principles of liberal, pluralist democracies and by its confrontations with other systems of church–state relations which have their own way of being *laïque*. The notion of the 'laïcisation of *laïcité*' (Willaime, 2004b, pp. 279–345) is intended to underline the fact that *laïcité* is no longer thought of as an alternative to religions but as a principle for managing the pluralism of religious and nonreligious convictions in civil society.

Notes

1 Or in the texts that are used in place of a constitution, as in the UK, which has no written constitution.

2 France is no exception to this rule, with a reference to 'the Supreme Being': the Declaration of the Rights of Man of 1789 which claims to have been adopted 'in the presence and under the auspices of the Supreme Being' is in fact part of the texts defining the set of constitutional norms (*bloc de constitutionnalité*) of the Republic.
3 With the Waldensian and Methodist Churches (1984), with the Italian Union of Adventist Churches (1986), with the Assemblies of God in Italy (a Pentecostal denomination) (1986), with the Union of Italian Jewish Communities (1987), with the Christian Evangelical Baptist Union (1993), with the Lutheran Church (1993), as well as a more recent accord with the Italian Buddhist Union and the Congregation of Jehovah's Witnesses.
4 France recognises diplomas from Belgian universities; it therefore recognises diplomas from a Catholic university like that of Leuven/Louvain, even though within France, as the state has the monopoly on conferment of grades, it does not recognise diplomas from French Catholic universities (which does not prevent it from recognising them indirectly).

References

De Puig, L. M. (2007) *State, Religion, Secularity and Human Rights*, draft report of its Committee on Culture, Science and Education to the Parliamentary Assembly of the Council of Europe, 12 April 2007, Strasbourg, Council of Europe.

Dierkens, A. and Schreiber, J.-Ph. (eds) (2006) *Laïcité et sécularisation dans l'Union européenne* (Brussels, Editions de l'Université de Bruxelles).

Ferrari, S. (1999) 'The new wine and the old cask: tolerance, religion, and the law in contemporary Europe', in A. Sajo and S. Avineri (eds), *The Law of Religious Identity: Models for Post-Communism* (The Hague, Kluwer Law International), pp. 1–15.

Foret, F. (ed.) (2007) *L'espace public européen à l'épreuve du religieux* (Brussels, Institut d'Etudes Européennes, Editions de l'Université de Bruxelles).

Garay, A. (2006) 'La laïcité, principe érigé en valeur de la Convention européenne des droits de l'homme', *Conscience et liberté*, 67, pp. 98–116.

Gauchet, M. (2002) *La démocratie contre elle-même* (Paris, Gallimard).

Jackson, R., Miedema, S., Weisse, W. and Willaime, J.-P. (2007) *Religion and Education in Europe: Developments, Contexts and Debates* (Münster, Waxmann).

Javeau, C. (2005) 'La laïcité ecclésialisée en Belgique', in J.-P. Willaime (ed.), *Des maîtres et des dieux: écoles et religions en Europe* (Paris, Belin), pp. 157–64.

Lambert, Y. (2000) 'Le rôle dévolu à la religion par les européens', *Sociétés contemporaines*, 2000, 37, pp. 11–33.

Lambert, Y. (2003) 'Religion: l'Europe à un tournant', *Futuribles* (special issue: 'Les valeurs des européens'), 277 (July–August), pp. 129–59.

Margiotta Broglio, F. (1990) 'Vers une 'séparation contractuelle': le nouveau régime des cultes en Italie', *Le Supplément*, 175, pp. 79–95.

Margiotta Broglio, F. (1999) 'Le régime administratif des cultes en Italie', *Annuaire européen d'administration publique*, 22, pp. 154–64.

Massignon, B. (2003) 'Les relations entre les institutions religieuses et l'union européenne: un laboratoire de gestion de la pluralité religieuse et philosophique?', in J.-R. Armogathe and J.-P. Willaime (eds), *Les mutations contemporaines du religieux* (Turnhout, Brepols), pp. 25–43.

Massignon, B. (2004) 'Port des signes religieux: essai de comparaison internationale', *Cités*, (special issue: 'L'Islam en France' (ed. Y. C. Zarka)) (Paris, Presses Universitaires de France), pp. 117–23.

Massignon, B. (2007) *Des dieux et des fonctionnaires: religions et laïcités face au défi de la construction européenne* (Rennes, Presses Universitaires de Rennes).

Milot, M. (2002) *Laïcité dans le nouveau monde: le cas du Québec* (Turnhout, Brepols).

Robbers, G. (ed.) (2005) *State and Church in the European Union* (2nd edn) (Baden-Baden, Nomos Verlag).

Willaime, J.-P. (ed.) assisted by Séverine Mathieu (2004a) *Des maîtres et des dieux: écoles et religions en Europe* (Paris, Belin).

Willaime, J.-P. (2004b) *Europe et religions: les enjeux du XXIe siècle* (Paris, Fayard).

Willaime, J.-P. (2004c) 'Peut-on parler de laïcité européenne?' in J. Baubérot (ed.), *La laïcité à l'épreuve: religions et libertés dans le monde* (Paris, Universalis), pp. 53–63.

Willaime, J.-P. (2005) '1905 et la pratique d'une laïcité de reconnaissance sociale des religions', *Archives de sciences sociales des religions*, 129 (January–March), pp. 67–82.

Willaime, J.-P. (2006a) 'Cultures, religions, laïcités: divergences et convergences des modèles nationaux', in A. Bergounioux, P. Cauchy, J.-F. Sirinelli and L. Wirth (eds), *Faire des européens? L'Europe dans l'enseignement de l'histoire, de la géographie et de l'éducation civique* (Paris, Delagrave), pp. 69–82.

Willaime, J.-P. (2006b) 'Religion in ultramodernity', in J. A. Beckford and J. Walliss J. (eds), *Theorising Religion: Classical and Contemporary Debates* (Aldershot, Ashgate).

Willaime, J.-P. (2007) 'Religion et politique en France dans le contexte de la construction européenne', *French Politics, Culture & Society*, 25, 3 (Winter), pp. 37–61.

Willaime, J.-P. (2008) 'The paradoxes of *Laïcité* in France', in E. Barker (ed.), *The Centrality of Religion in Social Life, Essays in Honour of James A. Beckford* (Aldershot, Ashgate), pp. 41–54.

Zylberberg, J. (1995) 'Laïcité, connais pas: Allemagne, Canada, Etats-Unis, Royaume-Uni', *Pouvoirs*, 75, 4, (special issue: 'La laïcité'), pp. 37–52.

Religion: a Solution or a Problem for the Legitimisation of the European Union?

FRANÇOIS FORET

Introduction

Relationships between the European Union (EU) and religions have been peppered with heated controversies around the influence of the sacred on the constitutional nature, the competencies and the limits of a European polity. The hypothesis of a mutual incompatibility between religious and European-integration logics has some substance, but societal changes appear to have had a more decisive bearing on the matter than the European political project itself. Dealing (indirectly) with spiritual affairs, the EU follows the same patterns and practices as in other fields and encounters the same obstacle: a structural difficulty in combining its functionalist requirements with traditional normative allegiances. This leads to the idea that the problems posed by the regulation of 'the divine' are, to a large extent, comparable to more ordinary issues. The so-called 'religious revival' has not given rise to major changes at the European level, but the whole question of the relationship of religion to the legitimisation of the EU as a viable and accountable political order remains unresolved.

Political and religious institutions are searching for the basis of a new relationship as both are facing the decrease of their social bases at all territorial (local, national, European) and functional levels. On the one hand, religion has to take account of the pluralist and relativist character of contemporary politics, especially strong in Brussels; on the other hand, religion may still have political effects, not as an authority discourse rooted in the sacred but as a cultural raw material capable of being mobilised to sustain strategies to gain power or – more likely – recognition. Actually, religion is neither a problem nor a solution for the legitimisation of Europe because its impact does not change the usual rules of the game. It appears instead as a potent symptom or marker of the underlying resistances of identity and the normative dimensions of politics summoned up by the functionalist steamroller of European integration.

This analysis can be illustrated by some examples of the interface between European integration and the world of religion. Religions appear in the guise of actors solicited by European institutions to be partners in new patterns of governance rooted in participatory democracy (see the first subsection of this article): they provide discursive resources in Europeanisation processes which affect national identities, making them fit better with the new structures or fuelling oppositions (second subsection); they set parameters of political involvement for individuals and groups in the debates related to Europe (third subsection); and they represent stakes and forces in the structuration of the communicative universe, mainly through media which remain resolutely national (fourth subsection).

Religions as Specific Actors of European Participative Democracy

The 2000s have been a period of political decay for the EU. The momentum launched by the projects of the single market and the euro has run out. Meanwhile, the fall of the Santer Commission, the difficult business of enlargement and of the euro, the electoral backlash of the 2004 European elections and the 2005 constitutional referenda shook the EU to its roots. That is the reason why the EU has tried – once more – to tackle the legitimisation issue. The main axis of the reform is the advancing of a participatory democracy, a trend also visible in many member states. According to the official discourse, the purpose is to put the citizen at the heart of European politics and policies by involving him in decision-making in a range of settings (interest representation, deliberation, political communication) and by clearly placing EU policy outputs at his service (Foret, 2008). Beyond structural and practical transformations, the main thrust of the changes has been the reinforcement of the European public sphere in combination with national public spheres. This is indicated by the diagnosis and prescriptions that can be found in major European political documents (Commission, 2001, 2006). More than institutional re-engineering, what is at stake is the renewal of communication channels between Europe and its citizens.

Dialogue with civil society is presented as an absolute priority. In the context of civil society, religious actors constitute interlocutors who are dealt with in a distinctive way (Foret and Schlesinger, 2007). Churches have long claimed a special status in respect of their historical anchorage in European societies, their representativity as intermediate bodies and their ethical message.[1] Article 52 of the draft Treaty establishing a Constitution for Europe had satisfied their demands by establishing an 'open, transparent and regular dialogue' between them and the European institutions, separately from the dialogue with the rest of civil society. The Lisbon Treaty signed in December 2007 has kept the same wording. This text, provided it should one day come into force, would offer a legal basis which has hitherto been lacking. The European Commission has already begun to institutionalise a system of concertation with the churches. This practice was first formally initiated by Delors and more or less continued by his successors. As an advance in transparency, the list of religious organisations which can be consulted has been published on the web. The dialogue is 'open', which means that, in respect of the fact that the EU has no competence about the status of religions, all organisations which are recognised as churches or as communities of faith or conviction in member states are eligible partners. Thus the Church of Scientology is included, even though it is not considered a religion in some countries.

The direct effects of this dialogue between religious and political authorities at the European level have been weak. The EU has no oversight of the regulation of religion, a field where state sovereignty continues to prevail. Since the beginning of European integration its most important competencies have traditionally been perceived to relate to economic matters and so as not directly relevant to the key interests of religious actors. The development of EU competencies in more political directions since the end of the 1980s has changed this view, but Brussels has not yet become the priority locus of power for denominational forces. The European Commission proposes a strictly consultative role for churches, among the multiple actors associated with the EU decision-making system. Religious bodies have increased their presence in the supranational arena through interest representation and political mobilisation in the European Parliament. Nevertheless, their lobbying tends to be defensive, aimed at ensuring that established positions at the national level will not be threatened. Lobbying activity also provides the opportunity to collect information and to build coalitions between themselves and others, so facilitating action at home or in supranational/international politics arenas.

The institutional and functional setting of relations between the EU and religions has, then, real but indirect and limited effects. During the process of drafting the Constitutional Treaty, the issue attracted a modest amount of attention from the wider public and the media. However, criticisms were expressed, not on the move to consult churches, but on doing so in a privileged manner relative to the rest of civil society. Humanists and some associations of believers contested the representativity of religious hierarchies and denounced what some saw as an attempt by the EU authorities to conjure up or re-impose a sense of social order 'from above' through a partnership with institutions carrying a transcendent message. This supposed collusion between temporal and spiritual powers has been held up as a betrayal of the ideals of participatory democracy which postulates the autonomisation of civil society, representing instead a wish to limit deliberative processes by submitting them to a normative religious reference or censorship (FHE, 2002a, pp. 4–5, 2002b). So far, it has been difficult to find evidence of a major impact from churches on European policies and politics. This means that the debate has been conducted above all at the symbolic level.

Religions as Discursive Resources in Europeanisation Processes

The way in which religion is addressed may determine the hierarchies of actors enabled to take part in decision-making; it may also influence the hierarchies of normative references considered as legitimate keys to interpret public issues. Despite the different forms, the stakes are similar – at least as perceived by the defenders of '*laïcité*' – in the debates on the place of churches in the deliberative process and on the

Christian heritage of Europe. To recognise the primacy of religion as a civilisational root of Europe has been thought to run the risk of giving religious institutions a right to demand a privileged place in the formation of policy. The churches' discourse has been ambivalent on this point: while trying to present mention of Christian heritage in the Constitutional Treaty as the acknowledgment of an indisputable historical fact, they have constantly brought into play the claim for influence underlying this request.

The religious factor has also been considered in respect of its potential contribution to the reinforcing or weakening of the cohesion of political communities, either at the national or at the European level. Concerns were expressed that a reference to the Christian heritage of Europe in the Constitutional Treaty would imply the exclusion of non-Christian minorities present on the continent. The same was said about candidate countries, with Turkey in the front line. By contrast Christian protagonists claimed that religion could provide cultural raw material for a European 'big narrative' able to work as a legitimisation discourse for the EU. The recurrent question about the religious meaning of the European flag (blue as the colour of the Virgin Mary and the symbolism of the twelve stars evoking the memory of the twelve apostles) should be interpreted in this light, even if such a reading has no precise historical basis in the record of the official creation of the symbol (Hersant, 2003, pp. 102–4) and is just one of the possible contested meanings. The sacralisation of the European banner has anyway remained far more modest than the celebration of the American 'Stars and Stripes' (Goldstein, 1996; Ellis, 2005), indicating that the allegiances associated with the two symbols are very different in intensity and nature. Globally speaking, religion-based theories of European identity and memory have had no greater success (actually rather less, if that is possible) than secular ones (Schlesinger and Foret, 2006). Religion could even be seen as an obstacle to the elaboration of a consensual founding narrative for Europe. In 1988 the French president François Mitterrand wanted to place Schuman alongside Monnet in the Panthéon, the sanctuary where the Republic celebrates its 'grands hommes'. Schuman's family refused this homage, considering that, as a true Catholic in expectation of beatification, the place of the late political leader was not in such a secular place inherited from the Revolution (Foret, 2003).

In numerous cases, however, religion has been instrumentalised with a certain efficacy in providing Europeanised versions of national identities. Many scenarios are possible along a continuum whose two extremes are the French case, where the nation is historically defined against religion in the name of a universal mission to lead humanity (mainly its European part at the time of the Enlightenment) towards emancipation and progress, and the Austrian imperial model as an embodiment of a Christian Europe to be defended against alien threats, whether Islam, 'the East' or a soulless modernity (Af Malmborg and Stråth, 2002). With or against religion, the path has always been to consecrate a given political community as a 'chosen people' (Smith, 2003). This charismatic type of legitimisation is not easy to reconcile with the relativism and the functionalism of European politics and policies which work through bargaining and compromise, but the spiritual dimension may offer some gratification of collective pride for some countries which compensates for concessions made in the political field. The Catholic Church in Poland has developed the 'exchange of gifts' theory to reformulate in a more acceptable way the relation between the home country and the EU in the accession process. Following this logic, Europe brings modernity and technical progress to Poland, at the price of costly sacrifices and constraints. In return, Poland is able to rejuvenate a materialist and disenchanted Europe thanks to its intact spirituality and its moral virtue attested by its fight against totalitarianism

(Urban-Hillman, 2008). Religion has played a similar role in Hungary, in the redefinition of national identity between pressures of adjustment to adhesion criteria and the promotion of the national self. This was exemplified by debates on public holidays and national symbols, or by the revival of narratives dramatising Hungary as the historical 'European fortress' against threats from the East.

Less frequently, religion has been used to nourish opposition to Europe as a whole or, more often, resistance to certain forms of integration or particular European policies. The implementation of the non-discrimination principle is particularly discussed. Conservative and extreme right forces defend national moral sovereignty against European legislation which does not take into account historically rooted traditions on the one hand and the collective meanings attached to some legal dispositions on the other. Thus the Austrian ÖVP (*Österreichische Volkspartei*) has denounced any attempt to criticise the fact that the age of consent for homosexual intercourse is higher than for heterosexual intercourse in Austria as an ill-founded supranational interference in domestic affairs. The Italian *Alleanza Nazionale*, the Lithuanian Homeland Party or the Slovak Christian Democrat Movement fear the effects of moral corruption involved in the promotion of alternative family patterns (that is, other than heterosexual marriage) by the Charter of Fundamental Rights, which is thought to endanger social cohesion. In the same way, European asylum and migration policies which lead to the building of multicultural societies are very divisive for government formations of the political right (British Conservatives or German Christian Democrats) and widely rejected by populist parties – like those in the coalition led by Berlusconi in Italy – as a threat to authentic national and European identities (Leconte, 2007, pp. 54–62).

Mobilisations using religion as a resource in favour of, or against, what comes from Brussels can of course coexist in the same country. An illustration of this can be seen in Romania, where there has been a bitter controversy about the reform of the legal status of homosexuality (Castorcea, 2007). Here the requirements of political and spiritual belonging confront each other. Being homosexual is claimed to be in contradiction with the basic sexual morality required from an Orthodox believer; the Orthodox faith remains a keystone of national collective identity, so, consequently, a homosexual is open to the charge of being a very bad Romanian. However, EU integration plays a major role in the difficult business of redefining contemporary national identity and this implies a thoroughgoing revision of moral and legal codes to comply with human rights norms. The Orthodox Church and the political forces with religious connections have to take this evolutionary process into account, often with deep distaste and not without second thoughts, if they wish to avoid losing established positions – alternatively they must choose an opposition strategy which looks perilous and might be fruitless in the long term. The Orthodox side is split between distancing itself from a soulless and alienating supranational entity and making a positive affirmation of Romania's full belonging to the Christian modern West.

In short, religion is far more effective as a tool for redesigning national identities with a view to making them fit better with the European superstructure than building an autonomous legitimacy basis for the EU. The religious factor in European integration is to be understood neither as a set of interlocutors determined to recreate an up-to-date version of the alliance between the imperial throne of an emergent European order and the altar, nor as a 'given' identity offering to European participatory democracy the foundational elements[2] it is lacking. The potential influence of religion will be indirect and diffuse. There is indeed no European common sacred to organise shared beliefs and rituals and structure a unifying memory, but the spiritual field makes it possible to assess the range and intensity of the constitutive dynamics of a European communicative community. What is at stake is not only, or primarily, the frequency of transnational exchanges with a religious purpose. Rather, it is the way the object of religion is addressed and what it reveals about the grammar of social relations in the European polity. The way religion acts in communication spaces which remain overwhelmingly national, how its normative pretentions are regulated and the degree of its influence on political behaviour are parameters for evaluating the existence of 'European cultural codes' beyond differences of values, identities and traditions.

Religions and Political Involvement

Three classical models of the relations of religions with the world are usually distinguished (Duriez, 2000). The 'autocentred model' defines a religious group which defines its own purpose, a community which takes charge of all the needs of its members, without taking part in public life beyond the defence of its specific demands. In the 'testifying model', the religious group supports in principle the political powers-that-be provided that the public authority does not harm religious requirements. Believers are encouraged to contribute to the social order, including through charitable action. The 'protester model' defines religious movements which aim to contest or reform social relations and structures, in a general way or more often on particular issues (such as immigration, disarmament, abortion). However, in contemporary Europe the distinct logics of these three models are mixed up. Unconditional support or rejection of the political order by religious groups are rare. The rule is rather a mutual arrangement with some criticisms here and there between the temporal and the spiritual. Autocentred communities may be on the rise, and this leads to a fear of communitarianism, but this does not mean a closure of these groups. On the contrary, this retreat strategy is often coupled with other strategies tending to gain maximal visibility for their own particularism in the public space. The purpose is less to make a demonstration of strength than to make oneself available for dialogue with the state and with other groups, to take advantage of the resources of a participatory democracy promoting civil society.

Moreover, the development of parareligious phenomena is spectacular. Mysticisms, esoterisms, spiritualities claiming to promote the physical and moral well-being of the individual or certain trends in political ecology taking the preservation of the planet for future generations as a new sacred duty are flourishing alternatives to the traditional quest for salvation in established patterns of belief. The growth of these movements leads to a dilution of the religious in the public space, to be understood in two ways: on the one hand, the religious constituency loses cohesion and consistency as pluralism and relativism increase; and on the other, it finds new places in different fields. Thus, the often-claimed comeback of the religious is not a restoration of past positions, but a change of content and a modification of the borders of the public space itself, which has enlarged to cover things which it did not include before.

This renewal of visibility does not mean that religion is able to act as an organised force and a direct influence on political behaviour. International values surveys show that the religious factor is mentioned by a minority of respondents when explaining their political, relational or professional choices. Nevertheless, quantitative studies confirm that there are latent correlations between individual behaviour and religious data. A deep integration in a system of beliefs is associated with a more conservative predisposition, more traditionalist, more on the right part of the political spectrum

(Bréchon, 2005). The deregulation of spiritual life has not so much suppressed its effects as made it difficult to anticipate and oversee. It was exemplified in a manner related to European integration in the French and Dutch constitutional referenda in 2005. In France, the unanimous support of the religious authorities for the 'yes' was not sufficient to deliver a positive result, even though opinion polls showed that 66 per cent of practising Catholics voted in favour of the Constitutional Treaty (Les cathos, 2005). Practising Catholics are, of course, no longer in the majority in France. Besides, they happen to be, more than the rest of their fellow-citizens, sympathisers of the majority right parties which defended the 'yes'. Their civic behaviour in this case depended more on their political orientation than on their religious belonging in itself. A psychological explanation must also be taken into account. The 'no' was linked to high levels of social anxiety and a strong demand for a protective welfare state; integration in a religious system is supposed to be a factor of reassurance which diminishes the feeling of social insecurity, and by the same token diminishes the reason to vote 'no'; the influence of religion may then be reassessed as an indirect one, but always in close interaction with socio-demographic variables (Sauger *et al*., 2007, p. 92). Defence of '*laïcité*' was a rhetorical resource during the French campaign mainly for extreme right forces, being deployed in a xenophobic manner against Muslims rather than as the expression of a spiritual commitment (Reynié, 2005, pp. 91, 220). In the Netherlands, the 'Bible Belt' coastal area from the south-west to the north-west of the country voted 'no' (Habben Jansen, 2005), but the religious dimension appears to have been a second-order motivation behind such issues as the euro, enlargement and protest against the elites (Aarts and Van den Kolk, 2006, pp. 243–50; De Beus and Mak, 2007). Earlier, in the 2004 European elections all over the continent, the controversy about recognising Europe's Christian heritage and the accession of Turkey as a Muslim country had been secondary campaign issues before coming back onto the public agenda after the vote in a debate disconnected from the devolution of power and structured more by media and intellectual lobbying.

Religion is no longer a constitutive force in Europe. The Christian tradition had been an important factor in the support of European integration, above all for Catholics. This influence is still visible at the individual level (Diez Medrano, 2003, pp. 247–48) but has been decreasing both as a force building public opinion on Europe (Nelsen *et al*., 2001) and as a common feature among the leaders (Chenaux, 1990, 2007). Today, the myth of a religious vote is not borne out in the ballot boxes and social factors are more decisive than spiritual belonging (Brouard and Tiberj, 2005, p. 64). On some societal issues, citizens' choices can be correlated with religious beliefs. Those who believe that decisions on science and technology should be based primarily on moral and ethical grounds are more inclined to confirm that they believe in God compared to those giving more importance to a risk–benefit analysis (Commission, 2005, p. 11), but it is difficult – if not impossible – for any organisation, either religious or political, to bank on such a diffuse sensitivity to build durable and efficient positions. The more a religion is established and associated with power, the more it is in danger of decline (Martin, 1996, p. 33). Religious hierarchies have taken this reality into account and often look for ecumenical coalitions to maximise the social acceptability and the likely audience of their discourses by turning it into a general rhetoric of values capable of being understood by the wider public. An example was given in spring 2006 by the criticisms of the 'Sarkozy law' on immigration made by the *Conseil des Eglises chrétiennes de France* which brings together Catholics, Protestants and the Orthodox (Coroller, 2006a). This suggests that, contrary to what some argue, what happens in Brussels is indeed a good reflection of deep changes in European societies.

Religions in the Media: the New Battlefield?

Today, most radical religious views which achieve a hearing in the media sphere come from non-institutional sources. The authoritarian pattern of discourse by the priest (the pastor, the rabbi, the imam) who questions political leaders from his pulpit is obsolete. Instead interventions in the media in the name of democratic values (pluralism, freedom of speech) are far more legitimate.

Confronted with radical rhetoric, religious hierarchies oscillate between reproach, obliging silence and embarrassment. The case of *Radio Maryja*, which contributed to the rise to power of the Law and Justice Party in Poland, is interesting, because it is a rare configuration where a private religious actor can be considered to have played a major role in crystallising the nature of the political game. Despite the nationalist and antisemitic discourse of *Radio Maryja*, the Catholic Church in Poland remained too divided to express explicit disapproval of this powerful and awkward ally (Ramet, 2006, pp. 133–34) before the visit of the Pope Benedict XVI in May 2006. Elections in 2007 showed political support for most extremist Catholic fringes. In the same year, similarly aggressive interventions by the Spanish clergy against the prime minister, Zapatero, ended in failure.

The role of the mass media has been central, both as producers of an image of otherness attributed to some religious groups (often the Muslims) (Lorcerie, 2005) and as arenas where different versions of freedom confront each other around religious issues. The Danish cartoons crisis provides a paradigm case of the alternation of cooperation or conflict in relations between religion and media. At first sight, everything seems to make for opposition between the media as symbols of modernity, structured by the imperatives of creating the event and the quest for novelty, and religion, defined by tradition and relying on repetition and continuity. However, these are two vectors of community-building whose interactions reveal the changes in the nature of social bonds (Bréchon and Willaime, 2000). From its mission and its nature, every church has to engage in communication in order to maintain or to spread its faith. It broadcasts its words across society through its discourse, its rituals and symbols, thereby eliciting the involvement of its believers. Religion is both the means and the end of its message: the medium truly is the message. By comparison, the activities of the mass media have been defined as rituals of secular modern religions in the nation-building processes (Anderson, 1983), as the reading of newspapers and, later, the watching of the same TV programmes (Dayan and Katz, 1992) act as ceremonials where the community of doing can have the capacity to create (or not) a community of being.

Despite this kinship between the churches and the media, or maybe because of it, the coexistence has for long been conflictual. The majority faith in Europe is a good example. The position of the Catholic Church (Tuffery, 2000) evolved from a position of condemning freedom of opinion in religious matters in order to protect its spiritual monopoly to one of defending freedom of expression at the end of the nineteenth century, claiming that the state had to guarantee religious liberties when religion began to be threatened by societal change. The convergence between the media and religion went on, and in the 1960s the basis of a ‘new alliance’ was formulated. In John XXIII’s words, the potential evil powers that the media might become could become instead instruments of salvation if used in a proper way aimed at developing a true and authentic sense of community. The height of this alliance was reached during the pontificate of John Paul II, the late pope revealing himself to be a master in the use of the mass media, as in the 2000 Jubilee, and above all an inexhaustible source of rich 'human interest' stories ('a young Pole in the Vatican', 'the victor over communism', 'the pop star', 'God's athlete' and so on).

However, according to some authors (Antoine, 2003), the character of John Paul II is not sufficient to hide the structural divorce between the Catholic Church and contemporary culture, especially in Europe. The Catholic authorities have brilliantly caught up at all levels with ongoing technical change, hired professionals and developed up-to-date media skills; but this has not been enough to solve the problem of their dated image. Priests are visible on the screens, but as signs inherited from the past, wearing cassocks which they scarcely ever wear in real life but which are necessary for the purpose of 'making sense' in the context of the media. Fictions about historical secrets hidden in the Vatican are blockbusters in bookshops and movies, emphasising by contrast the effective contemporary withdrawal of the Catholic Church. Catholics maintain a presence in the general media by necessity, but focus on specialised networks to speak to believers and to manage their relationship to the religious message. To a certain extent, this expresses the acceptance on the part of the Catholic Church of its having lost touch with today's culture and a kind of self-entrenchment. Some religious actors are still active and successful in the fields of marketing, TV performances, live shows in stadiums or charismatic groups: these are the American Protestant preachers or the Asiatic gurus, which do not claim to be providing the reinforcement of any European identity with a spiritual basis. Other authors note that the Christian religion is on occasion also in intense interaction with popular culture (Possamai, 2007). Movies may take inspiration from religious figures and myths, but also offer channels and communication resources to religious groups through super-heroes, religion-based role playing games, PC games and music. This is probably more accentuated in the other main world regions than in secular Europe, which is now seen as a mission territory for religious entrepreneurs in the rest of the world.

Cyber-religion is expanding daily. The internet may be a source of information, a new way to obtain sacred texts conveniently and quickly, but can be far more than that. Websites offer the possibility of making a spiritual break in a busy agenda and thus are in full harmony with the new individualised and *ad hoc* demand which prevails in the religious marketplace. In 2000 the French portal 'Notre Dame du Web' proposed a retreat on line, with advice how to pray by mail and to explore one's faith by readings. Some religions like the Universal Life Church in California ordain priests electronically. But other confessions remain more hostile to the web, precisely because of the destructured approach to faith it allows and encourages. Some, like ultra-orthodox Jews, go as far as to forbid use of the new technologies to its members or submit them to the control of Koshernet, a device allowing only the consultation of kosher websites (Une Eglise, n.d.). Religious spam inviting users of the internet to pray are more and more numerous, even if it represents less than one per cent of the total of unsolicited messages (Majendie, 2005). Sociological analyses of the internet, then, confirm that virtual communication can efficiently underlie existing social patterns, but not replace them, nor create social cohesion from scratch nor develop a Habermasian public space (Oates *et al.*, 2006; Dahlgreen, 2000). New technologies cannot affect decisively the societal decline of religion.

Regulation systems of religion in the media are different in each European country, depending on the historical matrix of the articulation between church and state (Madeley and Enyedi, 2003), but converge on some principles which both facilitate and limit religious freedom. These principles are: freedom of expression; respect for religion and equality between faiths; promotion of autoregulation for the secular media with the participation of religious groups; the possibility of having religious media provided that the law is respected; the consideration of all religions in programming; no religious advertising and no commercial advertisements during religious broadcasts (Doe, 2004, pp. 314–15). In recent years several polemical exchanges occurred in Europe over the display of Christian symbols (taken here as examples related to the majority faith in Europe, controversies about Islam referring partly to other logics). The fierce debate and physical confrontations stirred up by the film *The Last Temptation of Christ* by Martin Scorsese in 1988 remains as a potent reminder of the structural oppositions which exist between proponents and opponents of the intrusion of media in the field of religious faith. One of the most notorious related cases was the sentencing to prison (later reversed on appeal after an outcry all over Europe) in Greece in January 2005 of the Austrian cartoonist Gerhard Haderer and the banning of his book *The Life of Jesus*, where Jesus was depicted naked on a surfboard and receiving divine inspiration from the inhalation of frankincense. The publication had sparked protests in some other countries but only the Greek Orthodox Church tried – unsuccessfully in the end – actually to prohibit its publication (Papanayotou, 2005). France has been the site of some battles, through the action of the association *Croyances et libertés* founded by the episcopate for the purpose of raising court proceedings when necessary, with varying results (Cottin and Walbaum, 1999; Saint-Martin, 2006; Baffoy and Burnet, 2006; Freyssinet-Dominjon, 2000; Cossette, 1996). In 1998 an action against Volkswagen arising from the use of *The Last Supper* by Da Vinci picturing Jesus celebrating the birth of a new Golf, was finally settled with a financial settlement from the firm. The judges did not find any prejudicial material in posters for the films *Larry Flint* (a man crucified on a woman's body) or *Amen* (a mixture between the swatiska and the Christian cross). *The Last Supper* was again at the centre of public attention in France in 2005 because of the advertisement poster for Marithé and François Girbaud clothes showing top female models replacing the apostles in an allusion to *The Da Vinci Code*. The court banned the picture as 'an insult to Christians out of proportion with mercantile purpose' (Ternisien, 2005).

The major conflict came around the book and the film *The Da Vinci Code*. What is interesting is that the event may reveal a reorientation in the global strategy of the Catholic Church, both in the Vatican and at national levels. From the Catholic standpoint, the commercial success of Dan Brown's story has been so huge that to oppose its publication would have been fruitless. On the contrary, it was seen arguably to have brought back the discussion of Christian issues to the heart of public life and so provided an opportunity to reaffirm the Christian message. That is the reason why, if *The Da Vinci Code* has been widely criticised by Christian actors and some prelates have called for its boycott, the Catholic Church as an institution and Opus Dei, one of the main targets of the fiction, did not initiate a lawsuit.[3] The two organisations tried at first to negotiate with the firm Sony, the producer of the film, asking for cuts in the most offending parts. They did not obtain satisfaction, so they resigned themselves, predicting that the polemical furore would be 'a boomerang for the enemies of the Church' as an Opus Dei representative expressed it (Coroller, 2006b).

Churches have faced an alternative when dealing with the media: either to accept the opportunity structures offered by a pluralist society, with the obligation to make religious meanings and symbols available for anybody within the limits fixed by law; or to demand the accurate interpretation and a respectful treatment of sacred traditions and beliefs. The first choice (the 'let it be' option) has the advantage of maximising the chance of reaching a large audience, thereby taking advantage of the ancestral and diffuse presence of religion in all parts of social life, at the risk of trivialising and distorting the religious message. The second choice (the 'watch your mouth' option) is likely to ensure the preservation of the dogmatic harmony and cohesion of a core group of believers (notwithstanding possible conflicts with more liberal ones contesting the right of institutions to control the sacred). The danger is that of limiting the social scope of the discourse to those who are already convinced and of accelerating the withdrawal of religion from the common culture of a given society. Considering sociological practices, political settings and recent failures of authoritarian restoration, a pluralist strategy seems both more legitimate and more profitable for European churches. The hesitations of some religious actors between the 'let it be' and the 'watch your mouth' options in the media sphere illustrate the fact that the codes of participatory democracy promoted by the EU have been widely, but not totally, taken on board. This marks both the breadth and the limits of the Europeanisation of religious civil society, Europeanisation being here understood as the diffusion of common norms and as a functionalist and relativist process which threatens to undermine inherited patterns of normative belonging.

Conclusion

From a global standpoint, comparing its relations with religions to its relations with other sectors of its political environment, the EU implements the same practices, encounters the same difficulties and fails to find any new solution to its legitimatisation problem. Dealing with the religious issue, European institutions follow the path of existing Brussels policies and politics. The dialogue with the churches does not escape from the general pattern of European participatory democracy, with questions on the selection and the representativity of interlocutors embodying civil society, on their precise influence upon decision-making and on their accountability. The mobilisation of spiritual references to nourish a big narrative for Europe is hindered by the resistance of national actors and the impossibility of defining an acceptable common ground for all member states, and thus meets the usual limit of any attempt to root the EU discourse in culture and history. The main role of religion in symbolic politics is as one parameter among others in the reformulation of national identities in order to incorporate a supranational dimension.

Structural changes in the field of religion have had an impact on the EU level as on all other levels of public life. Religious groups withdraw from the political arena as organised forces facing established powers and come back as lobbies with more diffuse strategies and purposes. The public sphere is the crucial locus where collective schemes of identification and differentiation using religious factors as distinction marks are elaborated, still within national boundaries.

In the mass media, religion frequently appears either in a stereotypical and old-fashioned way reflecting the perceptions of a general audience less and less familiar with religious tradition, or as a particularism rendered banal like others. New structures of opportunity can be found in specialised channels and new technologies; in both cases, religion can successfully maintain existing faith communities or facilitate contemporary individualised and free spiritual practice, but not counter-balance the societal decline of religion. The media have also been the site of conflicts around religious issues, between competing interpretations of freedom of speech and respect for religious sensitivities. National configurations differ from each other, but a common set of regulatory principles exists and it may be possible to discern a dominant trend toward the acceptance of relativism and the rule of law by religious and political actors. European integration comes with and reinforces this trend, without being at its origin or totally restructuring it.

Notes

1 Relations between churches and states have been framed by different national histories and remain invested with a strong symbolic meaning. However, dialogue between political and spiritual authorities is a widely-acknowledged reality today in Europe. Even '*laïque*' France has established exchange channels at the highest levels. On the new functions accorded to religions in contemporary societies, see Jolly (2005).
2 Habermas (2004, pp. 6–18) uses the term '*présupposés*'.
3 The choice to surf on the *Da Vinci Code* wave rather than to resist it is particularly obvious as far as Opus Dei is concerned, with its important efforts in counter-communication (a film *Jesus Decoded* as a factual rectification, leaflets, a website) (see http://fr.be.opusdei.org/ssec.php?a=2937 (last accessed 22 May 2007)). Outside Europe there were boycotts and bans (in China, Iran, India): see Yannou (2006).

References

Aarts, K. and Van den Kolk, H. (2006) 'Understanding the Dutch 'no': the euro, the east and the elite', *Political Science and Politics,* 39, pp. 243–50.
Af Malmborg, M. and Stråth, B. (eds) (2002) The *Meaning of Europe: Variety and Contention Within and Among Nations* (Oxford, Berg).
Anderson, B. (1983) *Imagined Communities: Reflections on the Origins and Spread of Nationalism* (London, Verso Editions and NLB).
Antoine, F. (2003) *Le grand malentendu: l'Eglise a-t-elle perdu la culture et les médias?* (Paris, Desclée de Brouwer).
Baffoy, T. and Burnet, R. (2006) 'Dieux et usages de dieux: OPA publicitaire sur le sacré', *Esprit,* August–September, pp. 16–29.
Bréchon, P. (2005) 'Religion (poids de la variable religieuse dans le comportement électoral européen)', in Y. Deloye (ed.), *Dictionnaire des élections européennes* (Paris, Economica). pp. 581–86.
Bréchon, P. and Willaime, J.-P. (eds) (2000) *Médias et religions en miroir* (Paris, PUF).
Brouard, S. and Tiberj, V. (2005) *Français comme les autres? Enquêtes sur les citoyens d'origine maghrébine, africaine et turque* (Paris, Presses de Sciences Po).
Castorcea, S. (2007) 'Orthodoxie, morale et politique: le cas de l'Eglise Orthodoxe Roumaine face à la dépénalisation de l'homosexualité', in F. Foret (ed.), *L'espace public européen à l'épreuve du religieux* (Brussels, Editions de l'Université de Bruxelles).
Chenaux, P. (1990) *Une Europe Vaticane? Entre le plan Marshall et les Traités de Rome* (Brussels, Ciaco).
Chenaux, P. (2007) *De la Chrétienté à l'Europe: les catholiques et l'idée européenne au XXe siècle* (Paris, CLD Editions).
Commission (2001) Commission européenne, Gouvernance européenne: un Livre blanc, COM (2001) 428 final, Bruxelles, 25 July, http://europa.eu (last accessed November 2008).
Commission (2005) European Commission, Social Values, Science and Technology, Special Eurobarometer 225 (fieldwork January–February 2005), http://ec.europa.eu/public_opinion/index_fr.htm (last accessed November 2008).
Commission (2006) Commission européenne, Livre blanc sur une politique de communication européenne, COM (2006) 35 final, 1 February, http://europa.eu (last accessed November 2008).
Coroller, C. (2006a) 'Les plus faibles vont être acculés à la désespérance', *Libération*, 25 April 2006.

Coroller, C. (2006b) 'Croisade modérée en France contre le Da Vinci Code', *Libération*, 17 May 2006.

Cossette, C. (1996) 'L'allusion religieuse comme axe persuasif en publicité', *Communication & Organisation*, 1er semestre, http://www.ulaval.ca/ikon/finaux/1-texque/AllRel.html (last accessed 15 September 2008).

Cottin, J. and Walbaum, R. (1997) *Dieu et la pub!* (Paris-Genève, Cerf-BPU).

Dahlgreen, P. (2000) 'L'espace public et l'internet: structure, espace et communication', *Réseaux*, 100.

Dayan, D. and Katz, E. (1992) *Media Events: the Live Broadcasting of History* (Cambridge, MA, Harvard University Press).

De Beus, J. and Mak, J. (2007) *European Legitimacy and Identity Through Unlocking the Public Spheres of Nation-States: Questioning the Public Empowerment Thesis of European Integration in the Dutch Case of Euroscepsis*, paper presented at the conference 'GARNET–JERP 5.2.1 Final Conference, The Europeans: The European Union in Search of Political Identity and Legitimacy', Florence, 25–26 May, unpublished.

Diez Medrano, J. (2003) *Framing Europe: Attitudes to European Integration in Germany, Spain and the United Kingdom* (Princeton, NJ, Princeton University Press).

Doe, N. (2004) 'Religion and media law in Europe: a comparative study', in N. Doe (ed.), *Le portrait de la religion en Europe: les médias et les arts* (Leuven, Peeters).

Duriez, B. (2000) 'Introduction', in P. Bréchon, B. Duriez and J. Ion (eds), *Religion et action dans l'espace public* (Paris, L'Harmattan), pp. 11–26.

Ellis, R. J. (2005) *To the Flag: the Unlikely History of the Pledge of Allegiance* (Lawrence, University Press of Kansas).

FHE (2002a) Fédération Humaniste Européenne, *Contribution au livre blanc sur la gouvernance européenne: valeurs, état de droit – société civile – science et société – rôle du secteur public*, March, www.humanism.be/in/doc/pdfs/whitepaper-fr.pdf (last accessed 12 September 2008).

FHE (2002b) Fédération Humaniste Européenne, *Convention sur 'l'avenir de l'Union': les communautés de foi et de convictions*, 5 June, http://www.humanism.be/fr/doc/pdfs/conv07-fr-comm%20convict.pdf (last accessed 12 September 2008).

Foret, F. (2003) 'Le leadership en représentations: Jean Monnet entre mémoire nationale et mémoire communautaire', in A. Smith and C. Sorbets (eds), *Le leadership politique et le territoire* (Rennes, Presses Universitaires de Rennes), pp. 165–81.

Foret, F. (2008) *Légitimer l'Europe: pouvoir et symbolique à l'ère de la gouvernance* (Paris, Presses de Sciences Po).

Foret, F. and Schlesinger, P. (2007) 'Religion and the European public sphere', in P. Schlesinger and J. E. Fossum (eds), *The European Union and the Public Sphere: a Communicative Space in the Making?* (London, Routledge).

Freyssinet-Dominjon, J. (2000) 'L'image du religieux dans la publicité', in P. Bréchon and J.-P. Willaime (eds), *Médias et religions en miroir* (Paris, PUF), pp. 41–63.

Goldstein, R. J. (1996) *Burning the Flag: the Great 1989–1990 American Flag Desecration Controversy* (Kent, OH, The Kent State University Press).

Habben Jansen, E. M. (2005) 'Hétéroclite non néerlandais' *Libération*, 9 June.

Habermas, J. (2004) 'Pluralisme et morale' *Esprit*, 306, July.

Hersant, Y. (2003) 'Douze étoiles d'or', in L. Passerini (ed.), *Figures d'Europe/Images and Myths of Europe* (Brussels, PIE, Peter Lang).

Jolly, C. (2005) 'Religions et intégration sociale', in *Les cahiers du Plan*, 8 (Paris, Commissariat général du Plan).

Leconte, C. (2007) 'La contestation des "nouvelles politiques" de l'Union: un indicateur de clivages axiologiques dans les positionnements partisans sur l'UE', in R. Coman and J. Lacroix (eds), *Les résistances à l'Europe: figures des oppositions au modèle européen* (Brussels, Editions de l'Université de Bruxelles).

Les cathos (2005) 'Les cathos emballés par la constitution', *Libération*, 2 June.

Lorcerie, F. (ed.) (2005) *La politisation du voile: l'affaire en France, en Europe et dans le monde arabe* (Paris, L'Harmattan).

Madeley, J. and Enyedi, Z. (eds) (2003) *Church and State in Contemporary Europe: the Chimera of Neutrality* (London, Frank Cass).

Majendie, P. (2005) 'Bientôt dans votre boîte mail, le "spam religieux"', *Reuters*, 6 January, http://www.cypress.fr/developpement/index.php?cat=0202&article=22 (last accessed November 2008).

Martin, D. (1996) 'Remise en question de la théorie de la sécularisation', in G. Davie and D. Hervieu-Léger (eds), *Identités religieuses en Europe* (Paris, La Découverte).

Nelsen, B., Fraser, C. and Guth, J. (2001) 'Does religion matter? Christianity and public support for the European Union', *European Union Politics*, 2, 2, pp. 191–217.

Oates, S., Owen, D. and Gibson R. K. (eds) (2006) *The Internet and Politics: Citizens, Voters and Activists* (London, Routledge).

Papanayotou, V. (2005) 'Jesus comic enrages Greeks', *Deutsche Welle*, 8 February, www.dw-world.de/dw/article/0,1564,1480744,00.html (last accessed 15 September 2008).

Possamai, A. (2007) *Religion and Popular Culture: a Hyper-Real Testament* (2nd edn) (Bern, Peter Lang).

Ramet, S. P. (2006) 'Thy will be done: the Catholic Church and politics in Poland since 1989', in T. A. Byrnes and P. J. Katzenstein (eds), *Religion in an Expanding Europe* (Cambridge, Cambridge University Press).

Reynié, D. (2005) *Le vertige social-nationaliste: la gauche du non* (Paris, La Table Ronde).

Saint-Martin, I. (2006) 'Christ, *Pietà*, Cène, à l'affiche: écart et transgression dans la publicité et le cinéma', *Ethnologie française*, 36, 1, pp. 65–81.

Sauger, N., Brouard, S. and Grossman, E. (2007) *Les Français contre l'Europe? Les sens du référendum du 29 mai 2005* (Paris, Presses de Sciences Po).

Schlesinger, P. and Foret, F. (2006) 'Political roof and sacred canopy? Religion and the EU constitution', *European Journal of Social Theory*, 9, 1, pp. 59–81.

Smith, A. D. (2003) *Chosen Peoples: the Sacred Sources of National Identities* (Oxford, Oxford University Press).

Ternisien, X. (2005) 'La Cène détournée de Marithé et François Girbaud est interdite d'affichage', *Le Monde*, 11 March.

Tuffery, J.-M. (2000) 'Histoire des rapports de l'Eglise catholique aux médias et son illustration française', in *Religions, droit et sociétés dans l'Europe communautaire: actes du XIIIème colloque de l'Institut de Droit et d'Histoire Religieuse d'Aix-en-Provence* (Aix-en-Provence, Presses Universitaires d'Aix-Marseille), pp.165–212.

Une Eglise (n.d.) 'Une Eglise moderne? Les sites religieux sur le web', *Radio Canada*, http://archives.radio-Canada.ca/400i.asp?IDCat=10&IDDos=1468&IDCli=9770&IDLan=0&NoCli=7&type=clip (last accessed 21 May 2007).

Urban-Hillman, I. (2008) 'Religion et identité nationale en Pologne', in A. Capelle-Pogacean, P. Michel and E. Pace (eds), *Religion et identité en Europe: l'épreuve du pluriel* (Paris, Presses de Sciences Po).

Yannou, H. (2006) 'Da Vinci Code: la riposte du Vatican', *Le Figaro*, 15 May.

A European Battlefield: Does the EU Have a Soul? Is Religion In or Out of Place in the European Union?

CARIN LAUDRUP

Introduction

The development of a formalised cooperation between European nation-states in the European Union (EU) has been through a long and extremely difficult process, which met a new obstacle when the draft Constitutional Treaty was jettisoned in referenda in France and the Netherlands in 2005. This threw the project into something of a crisis. Political scientists will invariably come up with, on the one hand, explanations in reflexive hindsight as to whether this could have been predicted and, on the other hand, with proposals for how the EU train will or can be brought back on track while still respecting the voice of the people, and thus maintaining the overall aim of a single democratic institution 'united in diversity'. What follows is predicated on the idea that research in the field of civil religion may throw some light on some of these problems. The primary focus will be on two key aspects of civil religion: Jean Jacques Rousseau's concept of the good citizen and Emile Durkheim's concept of religion as a unifying factor in society. I shall investigate theories on the role of education as a means of preparing for citizenship alongside a study of religious education (RE) curricula from a number of primarily Western European countries. These will serve as a means of highlighting the educational landscape where roughly speaking the existence of two contradictory tendencies can be identified. Whether it is a question of national, government-approved, state school curricula or church-sponsored private education I find that some tend towards the construction of a 'wall' EU (a compartmentalised EU), and others towards a 'web' EU (a transnational EU), both of them being seen as reactions or responses to globalisation.

Postwar Foresight

In 1946 in Zürich Winston Churchill gave a speech which may still be said to lie behind the ideas and goals of, first, the Council of Europe (CE) and, later, the EU.

> If Europe were once united in the sharing of its common inheritance, there would be no limit to the happiness, to the prosperity and the glory which its three or four hundred million people would enjoy. Yet it is from Europe that have sprung that series of frightful nationalistic quarrels, originated by the Teutonic nations in their rise to power, which we have seen in this twentieth century and even in our own lifetime, wreck the peace and mar the prospects of all mankind. (Churchill, 1946)

Sixty years on in Europe there are two sets of institutions sharing similar goals and yet they are widely different. Theoretically they can be described in the following way. The CE includes all the countries which geographically can be said to be part of Europe. There are 47 member states (2007) and politically the CE is constituted as an interstate organisation. The main issues which come under its remit can be described as those of values such as human rights, minority rights and education. The other organisation is the EU which is based on cooperation through commerce and trade and constituted on a supranational basis. The focus in this article is on the likelihood of a spillover from the idealism of the CE to the realism of the EU.

As early as the 1950s one of the 'founding fathers' of the EU, Robert Schuman, said that the European Coal and Steel Community 'needs a soul' (Mudrov, 2007). After the fall of the Berlin Wall and in connection with talks about expanding the EU towards the East in 1990 this idea was taken up by the then president of the EC Jacques Delors when he talked about the necessity of giving Europe a soul, a spirituality, a meaning.[1] The phrase 'a soul for Europe' caught on and has to some extent taken on a life of its own. So much so that it is fair to say that it has the character of a signifier, albeit without an unequivocal signified. In this paper I interpret what Delors called 'soul' as being of the nature of what Durkheim called a collective consciousness which he saw as integral to the creation of societal cohesion.

Civil Religion as a European Integrationist Project

Article IV-I, which was included in the draft for the Constitutional Treaty in 2003, refers to symbols of the Union comprising the following elements: flag, anthem, motto 'United in Diversity', and Europe Day.[2] These symbols of the Union draw implicitly – if not explicitly – on ideas first launched by the Swiss/French Enlightenment philosopher Jean-Jacques Rousseau. In his influential work from 1762 *The Social Contract* he proposed the introduction of what he called a civil religion as a means of creating a coherent society, a society whose citizens were more concerned with civil society than with their individual private salvation. He argued that as long as Christian citizens were more focused on life after death than on the here and now, they could not become engaged, involved, active citizens. In the chapter on civil religion his argument became more pointed when he stated that not dogmas of religion but sentiments of sociability were what was needed (Rousseau, 1998, pp. 137–38).

Civil religion as a concept has been adopted and contested by sociologists of religion since the American sociologist of religion Robert N. Bellah reintroduced it in his seminal article 'Civil religion in America' published in 1967. He defined civil religion as '... this public religious dimension ... expressed in a set of beliefs, symbols, and rituals' (Bellah, 1967, p. 3), which roughly corresponds to symbolic elements of the sort whose adoption was inserted into the 2003 draft for the Constitutional Treaty.

The intention behind the inclusion of Article IV-I is quite obvious, but the proposal was frustrated by the negative votes in the 2005 French and Dutch referenda. Despite this the flag and the anthem are slowly becoming familiar EU-integrating symbols. Rituals, however, are traditionally related to an event in such a way that there is a correspondence between belief and practice, thought and action, myth and ritual. In a civil religious context it will often be specific historic events which have been ritualised in order to celebrate national unity and/or survival of the nation. Obvious examples are the French Bastille Day on 14 July, the Danish 4 May commemorating the liberation from German occupation in 1945, and the British Remembrance Sunday on 'the eleventh hour' on the Sunday closest to 11 November 'lest we forget'. Ideally, by commemorating the past and 'the glorious dead' in the present a united nation projects hopes for a prosperous future. These civil religious rituals can be seen to remind citizens of their duty to their country which is what Rousseau stated was required of a citizen 'sacrificing, at need, his life to his duty' (Rousseau, 1998, p. 137). In the case of the EU, however, hardly anyone associates any historic event with the date 9 May 1950, the day the French foreign minister Robert Schuman presented his proposal which was to become the European Union. This, despite the great implicit claims Schuman made in his opening statement: 'World peace cannot be safeguarded without the making of creative efforts proportionate to the dangers which threaten it. The contribution which an organized and living Europe can bring to civilization is indispensable to the maintenance of peaceful relations' (Declaration, 1950). For all the fine words the date has not been internalised in the consciousness of EU citizens and it cannot in any way be said to be constitutive as a creation myth. Accordingly, and most significantly, the event has not been successfully ritualised.

The national examples mentioned above are ritualisations of days of historic events which are perceived as having been influential in forming or preserving the present nation; the ritualisations engage the population in commemorating those events. The marching season in Northern Ireland would be another case in point in that the Protestant marches through Catholic areas in Belfast are instrumental in keeping alive the memory of a victory over the Catholics more than 350 years earlier. In order for rituals to work they must be based on a certain degree of consensus. Europeans feel no more or less European on 9 May than on other days of the year and as yet there is no Europe-wide agreement to remind them that this day, on which the Union was formally 'born', might be a date worth remembering. Symbolically the day is remembered in Denmark by the European flag being used on buses. The problem is that nobody really knows why, unlike when – five days earlier – the Danish flag is flown on the Danish national holiday when most people, and particularly the elderly, know why.

The European anthem, the fifth movement of Beethoven's Ninth Symphony using Schiller's text 'Ode to Joy', was adopted by the Council of Europe in 1972 and has been used by the EU since 1986, but it does not seem to bring out the same emotions as those called up when national anthems are being played, for instance at football matches. These national anthems may be said to promote chauvinism and in that respect undermine rather than promote feelings of European identity. To illustrate the point consider this scenario: What would happen if 'Rule Britannia' were to be substituted with 'Ode to Joy' at the Last Night of the Proms concert in the Royal Albert Hall, London? Would the packed concert hall and the huge crowds of people participating in this annual ritual which is broadcast on huge screens in Hyde Park in London and cities throughout the UK (Birmingham, Liverpool, Glasgow and Belfast) react with the same Durkheimian 'effervescence' as they now do to Elgar's 'Pomp and Circumstance'? Scenes like this throughout Europe, for example at football matches, are clear evidence of the fact that it is still possible to awaken strong emotions by means of public rituals. In a conversation in May 2003 Jürgen Habermas and Jacques Derrida called 15 February another Fourth of July: it was a day when a 'genuine shared European conscience was born' as millions of Europeans poured out into the streets protesting against the war in Iraq which was about to be launched (Bauman, 2004, pp. 140–41). This event was not ritualised, but the point is quite clear. Durkheim described what he called the intense 'effervescence' unleashed by collective rituals,[3] and drawing heavily on Durkheim, Bellah introduced the functionalist idea of civil religion as an integrating factor in American society (Bellah, 1967, p. 10). According to Bellah (and Durkheim) this can explain the important functions of the rituals mentioned above in maintaining a national sense of unity. Bellah reached this conclusion based on an interpretation of the American case, and for a couple of decades sociologists of religion tended to see this notion as relating specifically to the USA because of its special history of being a 'nation of immigrants'. A similar sense of identity does not exist in a Europe consisting of nation-states. On the contrary, identity is in this specific context by and large limited to a national identity, be it Danish, British, French, Austrian or whatever, rather than a European one.

Over the past 20 years most European nation-states have witnessed an increased focus on national identity to the exclusion of all other identities. More often than not, and to varying degrees, immigration is seen as a threat in many European countries. Nationalist rituals like the ones just referred to seem to function all too well, in the sense that they may be seen to work in a way which is counterproductive if the goal is European integration. Take the example of Denmark. The focus on Denmark as a 1000-year-old Christian monarchy is extremely popular with most Danes since they learn about it in school. This national image is particularly exploited by the highly influential right-wing party *Dansk Folkeparti* (Danish People's Party), ostensibly for promoting national identity as a defence mechanism against the threat from the 'outside world'. They express the view that it is time to stand up against the threat of globalisation and European integration and to build a (symbolic) wall so as to exclude foreign (in particular, Islamic) influence, and in this context the EU is itself perceived as a part of that threat. Other Danes tend to see national feeling as a remnant of ethno-nationalism which can be usefully revived in Europe as a protest against a European project beyond nations (Baumann, 1999, p. 35). The totemic flag is useful in this respect. Danes are renowned for being fond of their flag, which according to an oft-repeated myth was sent from heaven to the Danish people in 1219, and they tend to use it on many occasions which are not associated with nationalist fervour, for example, on birthday cakes and as decorations on Christmas trees. This habitual use of the flag without the fervent passion to go with it is what Billig calls 'banal' nationalism (Billig, 2004, p. 6). In present circumstances, where the flag is being used more and more for ethno-nationalist purposes, more cosmopolitan-minded Danes are beginning to feel slightly embarrassed if they are called upon to use it.

Attention to rituals and the use of symbols confirms Durkheim's analysis of cohesion in organic modern societies. Early in his writings he saw the dangers which could arise if the notion of cohesion is taken to extremes so that the focus is on nationalistic exclusivity rather than on a more cosmopolitan-oriented inclusivity. In his later writings this led him to focus on the 'cult of man' as the only viable successor to nationalism. Although he did not himself use the term 'civil religion', his writings seem to incorporate the basic concept in many shapes and forms. One of his most important works in this context was his collection of lectures on moral education. In Durkheim's view the role of the state consists in part in calling the individual to a moral way of life and as a consequence the way in which children are taught in state schools is of the utmost importance in forming the national character.[4] Moral consensus presupposes collective values and it is the function of the state to develop and inculcate this consensus. Therefore education is an imperative means for promoting such values (Durkheim, 2002, pp. 3–14). The example of the flag serves as an obvious case in point. A piece of cloth of a certain combination of colours will not in itself inspire a nation to respect and honour it unless the people have been taught the intrinsic symbolic national value it represents. Maltreatment and burning of this particular piece of cloth may be a criminal offence, or strong emotions may be provoked if other nations do not respect it. A person is not born knowing this, but learns it as part of his or her socialisation and integration into the nation. On this point there is agreement between Rousseau and Durkheim. In sum, in the developed views of both of them on the subject civil religion accounts for, explains and promotes cohesion in individual European states by focusing on the idea of the sacred status of the nation and on the way in which this is celebrated in rituals, symbols and beliefs embedded in the nation's history. There is nothing natural in any of this – on the contrary: nationalism is inherently a social construction and must be analysed as such. This also means that other constructions of social identity are possible.

Christianity in the European Union

Before turning to the role of RE it is instructive in this context to examine the role of the churches – and of the Holy See in particular – in the construction of the EU. The ideals behind the Constitutional Treaty draft are universal ideals and the Charter of Fundamental Rights of the European Union (Charter, 2000) might even some day constitute the creedal basis for a civil religion for Europe. Some maintain that the ideals referred to are basically Christian rather than universal. Others would argue that they are the products of the Enlightenment break from Christian dogma and look back instead to Antiquity for Greek models of democracy and Roman concepts of law. The religious wars that ravaged Europe in the wake of the Reformation and the general political upheaval had helped to bring about the view that Christianity had become fragmented and could no longer function as the basis for a common morality and a universal vision. In the debates during the drafting of the Constitutional Treaty in 2003 one of the bones of contention was the question of the role of Christianity in European history. A number of church organisations saw a possibility of regaining some of the influence they had plainly lost on the institutional as well as the individual level, with declining membership, belief and observance. On the basis of an analysis of the speeches of Pope John Paul II during a tour of European institutions, Jean-Paul Willaime has argued that these visits could be seen as part of a project for developing a civil religion for Europe with the Catholic Church as the guardian of the European soul (Hervieu-Léger, 2003, pp. 8–9), but this is perhaps to misinterpret Rousseau's concept of civil religion. To Rousseau traditional institutionalised religion could not be civil religion – on the contrary. Updating Rousseau, my contention is that if civil religion is proposed as a means of Catholicising the integration process, the term is being abused. Civil religion understood in this way would not only not be able to serve to integrate EU citizens, since it would disregard their individual religious affiliations, but it would also become an instrument of exclusion rather than one of inclusion. European citizens who did not identify themselves as Christians, let alone Catholics, would automatically feel excluded. Civil religion understood in this way would in fact add a further dimension to exclusivity. 'We' Europeans, who are at present distinguished by nationality, would also be distinguished from each other by religious affiliation.

It is important to remember that Christians are not a single homogeneous group or even one large family of believers broadly united in a common set of meaning systems. Only very recently the Greek Orthodox Church was appalled when the Greek government proposed 'to make Greeks more European by removing their religious affiliation from state identity cards' (Smith, 2000). Human Rights Watch saw the existing practice as 'a labelling that has facilitated the discriminatory treatment of religious minorities. Human rights groups hailed the decision to reform the system as a step toward eliminating entrenched religious discrimination' (HRW, 2001). The controversy involved one Christian organisation using its virtual state monopoly to discriminate against other Christians. In arguing for an explicit mention of Christianity in the preamble to the draft Treaty, Christian church leaders occasionally referred to values such as human rights and democracy as being basically Christian ones, but this insistence on monopolising values could be seen to endanger the whole treaty project, giving priority to one set of meaning systems over others. Not only is there no general academic agreement as to the validity of the claim, but many secularised 'Europeans' see it as highly provocative.

This issue has been dealt with at great length by Delanty (Delanty, 2000, pp. 19–120, Delanty and Rumford, 2005, pp. 38–39). One conclusion relevant in this context is that when particular religions claim ultimate truth as part of their argument there is no place for deliberative democratic debate. In its idealised version democracy means that debate, the exchange of opinions, and a readiness to be influenced and moved by reasonable, rational arguments is fundamental to the democratic process. An important question arises here, and one that is central to the civil religion debate: to what extent is civil religion able to serve as an integrating force in society? Habermas calls it 'the uniting bond of civic solidarity' in a 'community integrated by constitutional values' which stresses the idea of consensus rather than *a priori* truths (Habermas, 2006, p. 13). In her book on civil religion Marcella Cristi argues that civil religion of the sort introduced by Rousseau and Durkheim can be analysed as two ideal types at opposite ends of a continuum. Rousseau's model indicates a top-down state-dictated version, whereas that of Durkheim can be seen as a bottom-up people-instigated version (Cristi, 2001, p. 4). Solidarity, public trust and civic engagement cannot be brought about by coercive methods. Yet it is quite simple to document, empirically, a high degree of participation in nationalistic rituals. The important question is why and how this comes to be the case. The observation that civil religion takes two contrasting forms does suggest some highly interesting approaches when it comes to translating theory into practice in the context of the very important goal of integrating 27 nation states into one unified, yet diversified, European 'nation'.

Education in the European Union

It is important to point to civil religion as a means of enhancing integration in the EU and the integral role RE can play if the project is to succeed. While culture and education have had a high priority in the CE, education and RE specifically have only in recent years become a focus of attention in the EU.[5]

Education moulds the minds of future generations, and is therefore seen to be too sensitive an area to remove from the national level to a suprastate level, which would have to be the case if the contents of the educational systems were to be harmonised within the EU. Coordination is, however, quite a different and less sensitive matter. Empirical studies support the view that there is a connection between a feeling of national identity and education. Thiel Sunier has explored how national identities (French, English, Dutch and German respectively) were created for Turkish immigrant pupils in the four countries in question (Sunier, 2000, pp. 306–10). The research was based upon the hypothesis that curricula in the following areas of study were particularly relevant when it came to identifying the successful nurturing of a civil culture: (1) the construction of a national history; (2) the role of religion; (3) lessons on National Socialism; and (4) education on immigration and multiculturalism. Later studies of curricula in European educational systems which also testify to the way in which identities are built and exercised in educational spheres can be found in Soysal, 2002, pp. 269–73 and Schiffauer *et al.*, 2004.

Religious Education in EU countries

At the opening of the twenty-first century religion is not on the decline even in Europe; one might say on the contrary, but religion plays a different role. On the one hand religion is relegated to the private sphere while at the same time it plays an increasing role in the public sphere. Add to this an added awareness that religion cannot be contained in set formulae of meaning systems or well-defined categories, but should instead be seen as 'a free-floating phenomenon' (Beckford, 2003, p. 232) or a cultural resource. Whether as an RE teacher one advocates a confessional or an non-confessional RE, European teachers of RE claim that their subject is extremely important when it comes to teaching young people how to interact and understand the society of which they are a part and into which they have to be integrated.

France is the striking example of a European country in which RE is not a standard school subject. Religion is not taught in French state schools because of the principle of *laïcité*[6] and French representatives involved in drafting the Constitution were also some of the most outspoken in arguing against the idea of including a reference to a Christian heritage of Europe. There is some justification in the statement that 'the French' are afraid of religion, and this might explain what many others feel are drastic attitudes and policies, such as banning 'ostentatious' religious symbols in schools and opposing Turkey's proposed membership of the EU in spite of the fact that in many respects Turkey is as secular in the public sphere as France, and perhaps even more so than for instance Denmark, where the annual opening of parliament is preceded by a Christian service.

RE in Europe can best be described as lying on a continuum between the two extremes where at one end confessional education is carried out by church-educated teachers or theological experts while at the other end (more or less) strictly nonconfessional teaching is carried out by teachers educated at universities or colleges of education.

My personal experience from working in a network of RE teachers representing all the views in this particular field leads to the conclusion that teachers with a confessional approach to their teaching are very concerned about what they see as a lack of interest in traditional religion in their pupils and in society in general. If children are not taught Christianity these teachers are afraid that the (religious) chain of memory will break and that society will become amnesic (Hervieu-Léger, 2000, pp. 127–30). This is why these teachers deem RE so important, but even without a confessional approach there is general consensus among European RE teachers that it is imperative for young people to know about religion. The obvious reason is that ignorance promotes prejudice, while knowledge, insight and understanding are vital elements in the processes of communication and dialogue, which are in turn fundamental to democratic societies.

The landscape of RE in Europe was surveyed in a report in 1992 which was later updated in 2000. These surveys were not limited to EU member countries. With France as a notable exception RE was found to be a subject on the school curriculum almost everywhere. There were two main approaches to the subject. One involved a distinction between confessional and nonconfessional approaches. The second could roughly be characterised as the question whether the providers were religious organisations in faith schools or formally value-neutral state schools. Members of the European Forum for Teachers of Religious Education (EFTRE, 2008) tried to expand on the 2000 report in an effort to work out ways and means of cooperating, coordinating and exchanging experiences and ideas, but this turned out to be a hopeless task. Practical problems such as different national curricula were not the major problem. The main obstacle was the differences that arose between teachers from faith schools and those from secular state-run schools. There were ideological and theological differences just as much within nations as between nations. The Netherlands can serve as an example of multiple approaches. Two thirds of all pupils, in primary as well as secondary school, attend private, church-run schools. These schools can be divided into Catholic schools and Protestant schools. They exist as small entities with curricula drawn up locally and with no kind of inspection from the authorities (Schreiner, 2000, pp. 117–22). A parallel situation in Northern Ireland has far more deleterious consequences for the whole of society. From a bird's-eye view the European RE landscape could be seen to consist of numerous small communities set behind walls – a condition which does not enhance European integration.

RE in Danish state schools at primary and secondary level (ages 8–16) provides a case in point. The school subject is called Christianity but it is possible for pupils to opt out. The reasoning behind the explicit confessional basis of RE is that a particularly close connection is deemed to hold between being Danish and being Christian, so close indeed that for many the two terms are conceived as synonymous. Danes are Christians – and this identification is supported by the fact that about 85 per cent of the population continue to be members of the state church, the Danish Lutheran Church. The majority of Danes regard christening as a rite of passage with social implications rather than an expression of faith that the child is adopted into the kingdom of Christ. When a child is baptised he or she automatically becomes a member of the state-run national church. But this is a case of belonging and not believing, to use Davie's catch phrase (Davie, 2000, pp. 93–94), as according to the European Values Study of 1999 only about 2–3 per cent of the total Danish population attend church regularly (at least once a week) (EVS, various dates).

RE is being challenged and changed on several levels and although the EU does not interfere in national sovereignty in religious, educational and cultural matters a changing picture of the educational landscape across Europe is beginning to emerge. This has happened over the last ten years or so and is reflected in the themes of the EFTRE conferences held every three years. These conferences were attended by representatives from many European countries representing different approaches to RE and with different educational backgrounds ranging from theologians to secularists. The themes of the conferences were decided on through various rounds of democratic discussion.

The Eighth Conference in 2001 was entitled 'Handling Truth Claims in the RE Classrooms of Europe'. It looked at the nature of truth and the delivery and teaching of truth claims to pupils in the classroom in the New Europe of the twenty-first century. It considered what questions of ethics arise from the teaching of the philosophy of religion and the nature of truth.

The Ninth Conference in 2004 was entitled 'RE: Educating the Whole Person'. It looked at how RE is an essential part of a wider holistic educational process of the person as a human being.

The Tenth Conference in 2007 was entitled 'The Contribution of RE to Active Citizenship'. It considered how RE could contribute to the development of active citizenship in an expanding and plural Europe.

It is interesting to observe that in 2001 truth claims were seen as a fundamental part of religion in general and RE in particular. The focus was very much on what happened in the classroom with pupils faced by different truth claims. That religion made truth claims was hardly questioned. Six years later the debates about citizenship were brought into the debate about RE from the legal and the theoretical fields. Expressed in other words the perspective of these representative RE teachers would seem to have moved from the local and inward-looking to more inclusive concern with developments in the world beyond the school systems.

The debates in organisations such as EFTRE are merely one indicator of what is going on in the field of RE in Europe. Other bodies of evidence are the textbooks used in RE. Studies carried out by Danish MA students show that school textbooks tend to see religions as stable, static and monolithic, something which gives children a very restricted view of religion and one which is little in accord with the world outside the classroom.

Citizenship and RE in the Classroom

Professor and theologian John M. Hull has proposed three principal models of approach to RE which can be found in Europe, each one identified by the formal content of RE.

The first approach is called *Learning Religion*. This is an explicitly confessional approach aiming at teaching pupils to understand philosophical and ethical issues from within a particular tradition. Typically the churches are responsible.

The second approach is called *Learning About Religion*. This is a nonconfessional approach which focuses on objectivity, the comparative method and historical awareness. This might be called secularised RE. Several religions are taught and the teachers are educators and not theologians. Each religion is regarded as one of many, and one religion is presented as, in principle, having no greater truth claim than any other. The second approach is predominant in the three Scandinavian countries and to a certain extent in the UK. In Denmark it applies only at the sixth-form college level (18–20-year-olds). The stated objective is to help young people discover who they themselves are and that no one religion and no one truth claim has priority over others.

The third approach is called *Learning From Religion*. This approach presupposes the view that by learning about religion pupils also learn from religion. It is intended therefore to promote an understanding of various religious groups and traditions and also an understanding that there are people who take religion seriously. In other words the idea is that through meeting 'the other' pupils get to know themselves (Hull, n.d.). In Denmark pupils in sixth-form colleges are exposed to this approach and introduced to fieldwork inspired by anthropological methods; RE is thus taken out of the classroom.

There are of course those who propose other approaches to the subject. Cultural anthropology may inspire the view that religions can and perhaps should be presented typically as fuzzy, with a degree of inner diversity often related to debates about the nation-state, ethnicity and culture. Professor Robert Jackson[7] calls this 'the interpretative approach'. Students of RE would here be expected to reflect on and examine their own assumptions and those of their peers and so to reflect on their own identity (Jackson, 2003, pp. 78–82). This approach involves the idealistic goal of promoting tolerance as a crucial element in RE teaching. It might nonetheless be considered a possible means of instilling attitudes which could mould 'good' citizens who would be active, respected members of society.

Globalisation and mass migration are social facts in post-traditional societies. This means that there is no general agreement on what citizenship really means and on which contents would be relevant in an educational context.

One way of thinking citizenship is as being more or less similar to national identity. This understanding of citizenship would or could lead to a disregard of the rights of ethnic minorities which are to be found in all modern societies, as they are subjected to pressure to assimilate to the norms of the majority, as can be seen in Denmark where citizenship has been included in the new RE curriculum at colleges of education alongside Christianity and (Christian) ethics.

Another view looks at modern societies as existing in a post-national era. This view could lead to thoughts about creating a kind of European citizenship perhaps based on some kind of agreement about what it means to be European and coming closer to defining 'a European soul' for instance as embodying 'tolerance' – as recently proposed by the German chancellor Angela Merkel (Speech, 2007).

Citizenship interpreted as a basic human right leads to another interpretation which might be introduced into the classroom: human rights as a new secular religion based on universal values such as tolerance, respect for the individual, freedom of speech and liberty. But these need to be interpreted in a post-national context since in themselves they are not well defined. An example of what can happen can be seen in the use the Danish People's Party made of these very same 'ideals' in its election campaign in 2007, promoting them as traditional Danish – and therefore Christian – values. Søren Krarup, one of the most influential politicians from the Danish People's Party who is also a minister in the Danish national church, warns against man-made laws, such as human rights, taking precedence over god-given laws.[8]

The American sociologist of religion James Spickard sees human rights in a rather different perspective. He argues that in a global perspective it may seem that fundamentalism, fanaticism and tendencies to react against the spread of human rights are gaining ground. The Bush administration in the USA was highly sceptical about the UN and the United Nations Declaration of Human Rights (1948) and hardly thought twice before putting force behind what it thought was right.

'Human rights' as a concept is just as ambiguous as 'soul' or 'citizenship' – as are so many of the other concepts dealt with in the social sciences. Through the lens of religion they may be said to constitute a system of sacred symbols representing the existing moral order. Human rights claims are, however, not just symbolic; they are also moral in themselves. From the first generation UN charter in 1948 focusing on individual rights to the second generation which concerns purported group rights there are parallels to the ideas of citizenship (Spickard, 2002, pp. 3–6).

In order to be protected by (for example) human rights conventions you have to belong to a group which can be identified within the constructions of national culture, ethnic culture and religion which guarantee your civil, ethnic and religious rights. This leaves behind many minority groups, 'those who are not same enough to be equal', which therefore do not fit into recognised categories and which therefore are not protected by these rights (Baumann, 1999, pp. 13–15). Enemy combatants who are not protected by the Geneva Convention could also be mentioned as a case in point, just as there are cultures and nations which do not qualify for membership of the United Nations because they are not acknowledged and recognised as 'nations'.

Conclusion

Will Europe consist of numerous walls built up by socially constructed meaning systems behind which future European citizens group and hide in religious, national enclaves, in which RE teaches them to hold on to 'historical truths' rather than man-made social constructions? Or will RE incorporate ideas and methods which prepare pupils for a post-national world in which they will have learnt from the tragedies which are the backdrop of the foundation of the EU and the CE? Adopting the latter option could be one means of countering the danger that ideological, cultural and ethnic wars will be fought on the European battlefield with religion as the ammunition. There are many complex aspects of the relationship between the EU as a future political entity and the education of its citizens which could have bearing on the likely development of an EU consensus. The argument here has been that religion, in its broadest signification, may at one and the same time be as much in place as out of place. In place, because religion, as moral education in the Durkheimian perspective, can contribute to a focus on the 'cult of man', on education for mutual understanding and human rights, thereby helping to create webs of cosmopolitans instead of walls built on ethnocentrism and chauvinism. Out of place, because RE can just as easily be used to entrench nations or religious groups in their separate identities and thus raise a barrier against integration. Web and wall models of European society are under development at one and the same time and in this contested process RE can be argued to play a role – if not a leading role, then certainly a significant one.

Notes

1 'We won't succeed with Europe solely on the basis of legal expertise or economic know-how. If in the next ten years we haven't managed to give a soul to Europe, to give it spirituality and meaning, the game will be up' (Delors, 1993).

2 These elements have been removed from the Lisbon Treaty which EU leaders signed on 13 December 2007. This fact does not interfere with the core argument presented in this paper. Not only are they still to be found on the official website, but the fact that they have been on the agenda for several years now means that Europeans are aware of their existence.

3 'The very act of congregating is an exceptionally powerful stimulant. Once the individuals are gathered together, a sort of electricity is generated from their closeness and quickly launches them to an extraordinary height of exultation. The effervescence often becomes so intense

that it leads to outlandish behaviour; the passions unleashed are so torrential that nothing can hold them. People are so far outside the ordinary conditions of life, and so conscious of the fact that they feel a certain need to set themselves above and beyond ordinary morality' (Durkheim, 1995, pp. 217–18).

4 'It is in our public schools that the majority of our children are being formed. These schools must be the guardians par excellence of our national character. They are the heart of our general education system. We must, therefore, focus our attention on them, and consequently on moral education as it is understood and practised in them and as it should be understood and practised' (Durkheim, 2002, pp. 3–4).

5 For a very useful introduction to developments in this field see Jackson (2007).

6 This concept refers to the separation of church and state which dates back to the time after the Revolution and which was formalised in 1905, as well as to a positive sense of a Republican secular ethos that prizes rationality more highly than ethnic or religious values.

7 Professor Jackson is involved in REDCo (Religion in Education: a Contribution to Dialogue or a Factor of Conflict in Transforming Societies of European Countries), http://www.redco.uni-hamburg.de/cosmea/core/corebase/mediabase/awr/redco/flyer/Redco_flyer_final_kor_mar07.pdf (last accessed 3 November 2008) and in WRERU (Warwick Religions and Education Research Unit), http://www2.warwick.ac.uk/fac/soc/wie/research/wreru (last accessed 3 November 2008).

8 'On the basis of Christian thoughts on what it means to be a *human being*, which in Denmark means being Danish, I denounce the whole present political correctness as one huge falsification of life and human existence – or with a Christian expression: as idolatry or a false religion' (Krarup, 2001 – my translation).

References

Baumann, G. (1999) *The Multicultural Riddle: Rethinking National, Ethnic, and Religious Identities* (New York, Routledge).

Bauman, Z. (2004) *Europe: an Unfinished Adventure* (Cambridge, Polity Press).

Beckford, J. (2003) 'Social movements as free-floating phenomena', in R. K. Fenn (ed.), *The Blackwell Companion to Sociology of Religion* (Oxford, Blackwell).

Bellah, R. N. (1967) 'Civil religion in America', *Daedalus,* 96, pp. 1–21.

Billig, M. (2004) *Banal Nationalism* (London, Sage).

Charter (2000) Charter of Fundamental Rights of the European Union, http://www.europarl.europa.eu/charter/default_en.htm (last accessed 29 October 2008).

Churchill, W. (1946) *Winston Churchill's Speech to the Academic Youth*, http://www.europa-web.de/europa/02wswww/202histo/churchil.htm (last accessed 11 October 2008).

Cristi, M. (2001) *From Civil to Political Religion: the Intersection of Culture, Religion and Politics* (Waterloo (Canada), Wilfred Laurier University Press).

Davie, G. (2000) *Religion in Modern Europe: a Memory Mutates* (Oxford, Oxford University Press).

Declaration (1950) Declaration of 9 May 1950, http://europa.eu/abc/symbols/9-may/decl_en.htm (last accessed 11 October 2008).

Delanty, G. (2000) *Citizenship in a Global Age: Society, Culture and Politics* (Buckingham, Open University Press).

Delanty, G. and Rumford, C. (2005) *Rethinking Europe: Social Theory and the Implications of Europeanization* (London, Routledge).

Delors, J. (1993) Quotation from his speech to European church leaders, February, http://www.liebreich.com/LDC/HTML/Europe/04-Religion.html (last accessed 11 October 2008).

Durkheim, E. (1995) *The Elementary Forms of Religious Life* (New York, The Free Press).

Durkheim, E. (2002) *Moral Education* (New York, Dover).

EFTRE (2008) European Forum for Teachers of Religious Education, http://www.eftre.net/ (last accessed 11 October 2008).

EVS (various dates) European Values Study, http://www.europeanvalues.nl/ (last accessed 4 November 2008).

Habermas, J. (2006) 'Religion in the public sphere', *European Journal of Philosophy*, 14, 1, pp. 1–25.

Hervieu-Léger, D. (2000) *Religion as a Chain of Memory* (New Brunswick, Rutgers University Press).

Hervieu-Léger, D. (2003) *The Role of Religion in Establishing Social Cohesion*, http://ec.europa.eu/research/social-sciences/pdf/michalski_210503_contribution01_en.pdf (last accessed 11 October 2008).

HRW (2001) 'Greece: human rights developments', *World Report 2001*, http://www.hrw.org/wr2k1/europe/greece.html (last accessed 11 October 2008).

Hull, J. M. (n.d.) *The Contribution of Religious Education to Religious Freedom: a Global Perspective*, http://www.iarf.net/REBooklet/Hull.htm (last accessed 29 October 2008).

Jackson, R. (ed.) (2003) *International Perspectives on Citizenship, Education and Religious Diversity* (London, Routledge).

Jackson, R. (2007) 'European institutions and the contribution of studies of religious diversity to education for democratic citizenship', in R. Jackson, S. Miedema, W. Weisse and J. P. Willaime (eds), *Religion and Education in Europe: Developments, Contexts and Debates* (Münster, Waxmann Verlag).

Krarup, S. (2001) *Hvad er det at være dansk*? (*What Does Being a Dane Mean?*), http://www.nomos-dk.dk/skraep/krarup3.htm (last accessed 4 November 2008).

Mudrov, S. (2007) *Religious Dimension of the European Union: Attitudes of Christian Churches towards European Integration*, MA thesis, University of Maastricht, http://www.intreview.com/EMTA/mt/retrieve/sergeimudrov.pdf (last accessed 14 April 2008).

Rousseau, J.-J. (1998) *The Social Contract* (Ware, Wordsworth Classics).

Schiffauer, W., Baumann, G., Kastoryany, R. and Vertovec, S. (eds) (2004) *Civil Enculturation: Nation State, School and Ethnic Difference in The Netherlands, Britain, Germany and France* (New York, Berghahn Books).

Schreiner, P. (ed.) (2000) *Religious Education in Europe: a Collection of Basic Information about RE in European Countries* (Münster, ICCS).

Smith, H. (2000) 'Greek church at war over plans to change ID cards', *The Guardian*, 22 May, http://www.guardian.co.uk/international/story/0,3604,223516,00.html (last accessed 11 October 2008).

Soysal, Y. N. (2002) 'Locating Europe', *European Societies*, 4, 3, pp. 265–84.

Speech (2007) *Speech by Angela Merkel, Chancellor of the Federal Republic of Germany, to the European Parliament in Strasbourg on Wednesday, 17 January 2007*, http://www.eu2007.de/en/News/Speeches_Interviews/January/Rede_Bundeskanzlerin2.html (last accessed 11 October 2008).

Spickard, J. V. (2002) 'Human rights through a religious lens: a programmatic argument', *Social Compass*, 49, 2, pp. 227–38, http://scp.sagepub.com/cgi/content/abstract/49/2/227 (last accessed 29 October 2008).

Sunier, T. (2000) 'Civil enculturation: nation-state, school and ethnic differences in four European countries', *Journal of International Migration and Integration*, 1, pp. 305–30.

From Hammer and Sickle to Star and Crescent: the Question of Religion for European Identity and a Political Europe

BENOÎT CHALLAND

Introduction

In *Inventing Europe: Idea, Identity, Reality*, Delanty (1995, p. vii) complained that while there were many works dealing with the 'Orient' as an invention of Europe, (almost) nothing existed on the idea that 'Europe' (the common political roof embodied by the European Communities and Union) was a construction and that it should be critically re-thought. More than ten years have passed since his seminal book was published and many authors have taken up the challenge of understanding what was the meaning of 'Europe' and how it was historically and thematically constructed to reinforce a sense of cohesion beyond national allegiances (Shore, 2000; Passerini, 2003; Stråth, 2000a,b; Joas and Wiegandt, 2005; Persson and Stråth, 2007).

Focusing on an aspect that has been, in my view, until now neglected, I want to assess critically the meaning and importance of religion for Europe. I shall adopt here a deconstructivist approach towards Europe, understood as the political project to create a common European community in the aftermath of the Second World War that was first designed around economic projects in the early 1950s and merged into a single Union in 1992. The creation of such a supranational entity has involved the establishment of an increasing array of domains where Europeans are invited to feel part of a community of fate (*Schicksalsgemeinschaft*) with the creation of a political union in the 1990s and to share basic norms through the attempt to adopt a truly European Constitution. From Europe, a geographical zone, one moved to a political project gathering independent states willing to surrender part of their sovereignty to a supranational entity. As a result, some argue, in these complex processes a European identity that is distinct from (and at times also surely conflicting with) national identities has emerged and has added a new layer of identification for Europeans. Those defending the idea of a European identity suggest different bases of common identification, ranging from a common legacy of enlightened rationality to a common set of historical experiences (going beyond wars), or from a concert of European nations to a common religious identification (Joas and Wiegandt, 2005).

The focus of identification for a political Europe through religious means is the particular concern of this paper. The last years' debate about the reference to the common legacy of Christianity in the draft European Constitution reflects this quest for a positive common European identity, but is it so that religion and in particular Christianity can provide the common point of reference for all Europeans? When and why did we start thinking of Europe in terms of religion? What does this type of reasoning tell us about Europe and its project?

This article radically questions such an identification of Europe in religious terms. Despite the high number of conferences and papers published on Europe and religion in the last few years, I suggest that the collocation of Europe and religion is only a very recent construction. Moreover I will argue that to understand this 'hyperactivism' of religion on the European scene one has to read it against the backdrop of another recent construction, namely of an external 'other' (in our case the 'problem of Islam', as it is very often referred to in the British media) that makes the overlap between European identity and religion possible. By external other, I refer to the process of stark differentiation between a Self and an Other that is branded as not being part of a given group, the end product of which is to produce polarised identities and to create (symbolic) borders between different imagined groups. To create a sense of common self, one uses an 'other', reinforcing thereby the sense of division. Religion, as an identity marker, is only one of many possible ways to create a differentiation between various social groups.

The dichotomy produced by such 'othering' processes is highly problematic since it entails profound biases, for it does not leave space to move within and between these two blocks. One should depart from simplistic and one-sided dichotomisation towards a more complex and pluriform quest for identity. Such an approach would translate, on the European level, into a research agenda for a cosmopolitan Europe, as argued for by Delanty (2006). Such a critical approach allows us to escape the absolutist tendency of creating what are artificial divides between a European 'we' and a non-European 'other' expressed in terms of religious belongingness.

Nonetheless it is heuristically interesting to study the use of external others and their polarising effects in historical terms to understand what is (or has been) at stake in our societies and what a political Europe is about. The external others we shall focus on in this paper are that of Eastern European communism for European identity in the 1950s and 1960s and that of Islam and Turkey for our contemporary societies (although we shall concentrate mostly on the latter one, for obvious reason of space). Creating a European political identity is indeed a fragile project: there are national identities, but 'European identity' is only a recent construct promoted by European elites, as illustrated by Shore (2000) or Stråth (2007). One of the claims of this paper is that Europe, because of the lack of a clear internal legitimacy, is always in need of external significant 'others' in order to buttress a sense of common fate within the *sui generis* political entity of the EEC/EU. In a historical and diachronic perspective, the paper argues that such an external other was for decades the threat of Eastern European communism as an element providing cohesion for Western Europe, but with the end of the Cold War, this 'other' was gradually replaced by the threat of Islam and Islamism (the one often misleadingly conflated with the other) and by extension Turkey's possible entry into the EU. To put it into a nutshell, Europe's threat was first that of the communist hammer and sickle and it is now that of Islam's star and crescent. This, I shall argue, is the main source of the current reduction of European identity to religious characteristics, rather than some alleged cultural roots to a 'European essence' premised on religion.[1]

I shall examine two bodies of evidence in an attempt to demonstrate the thesis that the identification with religion is only a recent phenomenon for Europe. To illustrate the shift from hammer and sickle to star and crescent, I shall first explore what Turkey has represented for Europe in the last 50 years by looking through the archives of the nascent European Communities around 1959 and 1963 (the period in which Turkey negotiated an Association Agreement with the European Economic Community (EEC)) for evidence of what European bureaucrats and legislators had to say about Turkey then. I shall contrast this with a brief overview of the current debates about Turkey as an EU candidate member. A second source of data about the religion-Europe nexus will suggest that these two terms have only recently been pressed together. A discourse analysis of the key European treaties will demonstrate the very late appearance of religion in official European texts.

Are 'Europe' and 'Religion' Historically Linked to One Another?

Let us first of all assess the claim that religion is only a very recent topic of interest for Europe. In order to do so I conducted three brief quantitative research surveys on the topics of 'Religion' and 'Europe'. These surveys looked at (1) the number of scholarly articles that include both keywords in the same article since 1950; (2) the number of newspaper articles dealing with religion and Europe in the last three decades, and (3) the content of key European treaties of the last 50 years. An analysis of these surveys, I suggest, will provide an indication of the place of religion for Europe. The purpose is to shed a diachronic light on the evolution of the relation between Europe and religion, thus exposing the contemporary illusion that it has always been present. All three types of material reinforce the claim that religion is only a recent 'European' topic and that it had not been a priority in previous decades.

(1) Scholarly Articles (1950–2001) in JSTOR

The first investigation was done through JSTOR, a search-engine for scholarly journals.[2] This electronic databank of academic articles offers access to articles only five or seven years after their original printed publication (and this is why Figure 1 stops in 2001).

The keywords introduced for this search were 'Religion AND Europe'. This means that one could find articles that are not *specifically* dedicated to religion in Europe (but articles that mention both concepts in the same paper, not automatically related). Because the purpose of this first partial research was to find *trends*, we are at least sure

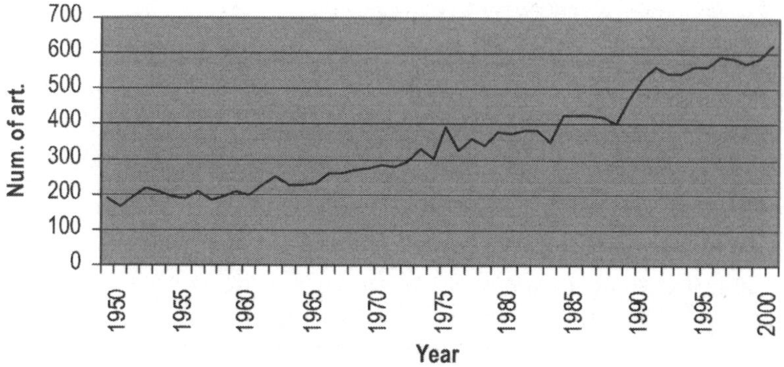

Figure 1. Number of occurrences of 'religion and Europe' in academic articles

to capture the papers dealing specifically with the question of religion in Europe (so what matters is not the actual number but the tendency for the number of papers to increase or decrease with time). It should be noted that a keyword search of this sort is not biased, in the sense that the proportion of articles actually dealing with the nexus religion – Europe should be statistically the same throughout the period chosen, namely all articles including these two words between the years 1950 (the time where the first talks about European construction started) and 2001.

The search produced nearly 19,000 hits. These articles (book reviews and opinion articles were not included in this list) come from journals publishing in the fields of history (71 journals), philosophy (26 journals), political science (43 journals), sociology (46 journals) and religion (26 journals). The result, presented in Figure 1, illustrates the increase of articles over the whole period.

One immediately notices the gradual increase of articles over the period studied. There were about 200 articles per year mentioning both Europe and religion between 1950 and 1960; the proportion then gradually increases to reach 400 articles a year after 1985, and reaches nearly 600 in the late 1990s.

(2) News Articles from Lexis-Nexis

A second quantitative search dealt with newspaper articles. This search was made possible through a corporate web-platform (Lexis-Nexis), gathering news wires and articles from a large number of international news agencies and daily newspapers. Since there are many languages included in the Lexis-Nexis database, the key words were Europe and religion (in English, German, French, Spanish and Italian), producing searches such as 'Europe AND religion(e)', 'Europa AND religione', 'Religion AND EEC', 'Religion AND EU', and 'Religion AND UE'. 506 hits were produced in total (see Figure 2).[3]

Here as well one can see a very significant increase in the number of articles dealing with religion and Europe since 2000. The attacks of 9/11, the crisis of the Mohammed cartoons in 2005–2006 and other 'clash of civilisations'-type articles have reinforced the link between religion and Europe in the last 5 or 6 years. It seems as if we are living in an epoch where the only lenses through which most of the people can make sense of political developments are those which see things in terms of the paradigm of a clash of civilisations.[4]

Certainly, the findings from these first two surveys ought to be received with caution (the first included many articles that do not directly link religion to Europe, while the

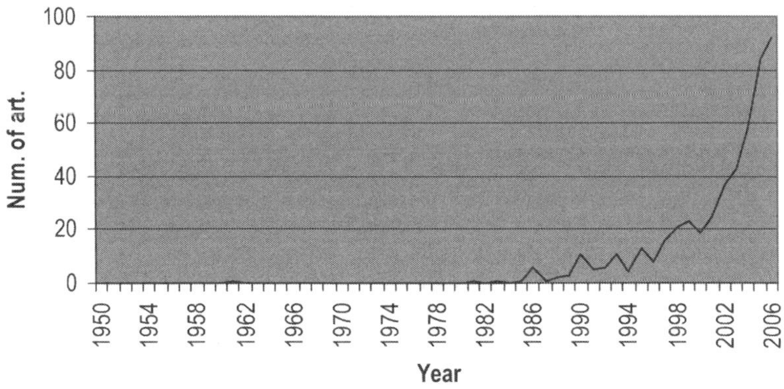

Figure 2. Number of occurrences of 'religion and Europe' in news articles

second is a selective database of news articles by no means representative of all newspapers). Nonetheless, there is little doubt that there is a quantitative increase in the occurrence of articles dealing with religion and Europe as a focus.

The third survey is a more qualitative study of the presence of 'religion' inside official treaties of the European Communities and European Union.

(3) A Discourse Analysis of Official European Treaties

This last set of indicators about the relative unimportance of religion for a political Europe comes from a discourse-analysis of European treaties. Using the software Atlas.ti,[5] I analysed nine fundamental treaties of the European Communities/Union, and my findings here demonstrate that the question of religion is *not* a central topic at all in legal terms for Europe itself. I analysed the following treaties:

- European Coal and Steel Community (1951)
- Rome Treaty and the creation of the European Economic Community (1957)
- Rome Treaty and the creation of EURATOM (1957)
- Single Act (1965)
- Single European Act (1986)
- Maastricht Treaty (1992)
- Amsterdam Treaty (1997)
- Nice Treaty (2001)
- European Constitution (2004)

These treaties total 755 pages;[6] the theme of religion comes up only 15 times. It appears first and once in the Treaty of Amsterdam of 1997 (in the context of banning discrimination of any type) and 14 times in the projected text of a European Constitution of 2004. In that last treaty (which includes the European Charter of Fundamental Rights and therefore incorporates basic human rights protection into the European Constitution), religion is also mentioned three times in the context of preventing discrimination on religious grounds, four times in the context of guaranteeing religious freedom, and once in the context of declaring that the Union respects 'the status under national law of churches and religious associations or communities in the Member States' (Article I-52). Only once does the issue of 'religion' have to do directly with the theme of European identity, in the Preamble of the Constitution ('Drawing inspiration from the cultural, religious and humanist inheritance of Europe . . . .').[7]

Even if one were to add other important texts of the EEC/EU dealing explicitly with the need to bolster a common European identity (such as the 1973 Copenhagen Declaration[8] or the 1983 Stuttgart Declaration[9]) the result of this discourse analysis would not be altered. In these two documents, religion is not mentioned at all. Should we interpret this absence as another sign that religion had not *yet* become an item on the agenda of a common European identity? If so, what was then the leitmotiv of European integration and what was central to European identity before the sudden eruption of the theme of religion for Europe in the last decade?

The Case of Turkey and the External Priorities of the European Union

Turkey and Europe after 2002

I now turn my attention more specifically to the meaning of Turkey for Europe. Turkey is now the most conspicuous candidate to join the EU, but the road to its 'integration' is still paved with many stumbling blocks, including human rights violations, the lack of democratic accountability of key institutions (including military leadership and the National Security Council), the only partially solved problems with Cyprus and Greece, and of course the religious profile of the country. Despite the staunchly secular pedigree imposed on the Turkish Republic by its founding father Atatürk and defended on many occasions by the military establishment (with coups in 1960, 1970 and 1981 and even a silent coup in the 1990s) (Yapp, 1996, pp. 309–29), it seems as if in the last years, and in particular since the EU Copenhagen Summit in 2002 discussing the opening of formal negotiations with Turkey, the main problem of Turkey's accession has been the fact that it is a Muslim country. The statement by Valérie Giscard D'Estaing[10] that Europe would lose its soul were it to accept a Muslim-majority country as part of the European club (2002) is only one example of how the Turkish–European debate has taken a very emotional turn and become polarised on religious grounds. Why this sudden turn away from the core issue of the political problems that Turkey has to deal with before being able to be part of Europe?

A look at recent academic literature in this field suggests that the Turkish religious problem (understood here as the fact that the main hurdle for Turkey's inclusion in the EU arises out of its Muslim background) has two roots. One is very straightforward, and consists in the fact that the EU's enlargement towards the East, to include twelve new members, has shifted the new frontier of Europe further east and south-east, thereby giving rise to new questions that had no priority before that. As anthropologists have shown, one's identity is not defined at the centre but at the borders of a given group (Barth, 1969). The border for Europe in the 1990s was that of Central and Eastern Europe and any expansion required the commitment of possible new members to the rule of law and the free market. Now the new frontier is Turkey, the remnants of ex-Yugoslavia and the former Soviet republics. Commitments to the rule of law, human rights and the free market certainly remain at the top of European priorities. The question of religious differences between western Catholic/Protestant and eastern Orthodox traditions was never an issue in recent years for the inclusion of the Orthodox populations of Romania and Bulgaria. Yet Muslim identification has become a burning issue for Europe. Why?

Sociologists of religion have tried to explain this shift and the use of what might seem a sort of double standard towards those of different religious backgrounds. Casanova notes that despite the fact that Turkey is very much westernised and is totally committed to a secular system the idea of including Turkey in the EU arouses fear among many Europeans. As he puts it, 'indeed, the closer Turkey gets to meet the political conditions, the more the unstated cultural conditions of already belonging to a European civilisation tend to gain prominence in the debate' (Casanova, 2006, p. 236). It seems that irrational and simplistic arguments about the existence of fundamental, even essential, differences between civilisations and about an alleged Islamic threat take the upper hand and that rational arguments about the fact that Turkey fulfils most of the criteria to enter the EU are washed away.

Casanova observes that the religious argument against Turkey actually overlaps with different dimensions of the Turkish 'otherness' and that the Muslim identity of Turkey refers back to the presence of Muslim migrants in the heart of Europe (Casanova, 2006, p. 242). Göle, in the same vein, underlines the fact that 'the two countries that voted against the European Constitution were those where Islam was most debated publicly', namely The Netherlands and France (Göle, 2006, p. 251). So the question of Turkey (or, formulated differently, the fact that Turkey's otherness is expressed in religious terms) is deeply inter-related with the quest of Europe for its own identity. One has to acknowledge that the 'otherness' of Europe is not and cannot be uniquely expressed in religious terms (be this in terms of Christianity versus Islam or in terms of a secular self-understanding of Europe versus a region where Islam is described as determining almost the entire public life), without creating serious problems by doing so.

The shift of the EU's border towards Turkey is very important for its identity. Kocka argues that borders are a 'must' for any entity and, indeed for any identity to be created. In his view, if Europe is not able to choose and commit to some borders, it will fail in its political project. In the light of what he describes as historical arguments based on common values, the discussion of a European culture and the democratic capacity of Europe, Kocka concludes that for the time being Turkey should remain outside Europe (Kocka, 2007, p. 47), not so much because there exists a clearly European set of values or a common culture (he highlights the historical entanglements of European cultures and norms with Asian ones, for example), but because of the impossibility of determining whether Turkey will commit finally and completely to democratic principles.

Such an exercise in 'border drawing' shows the very fluctuating nature of the exercise itself and the plasticity of the criteria used to decide whether to include Turkey in the EU or not, or to subsume Turkey's identity in the European identity. The question of identity becomes more difficult to answer when one speaks of large societal groups such as national groups (as Wagner (2005, pp. 495f.) puts it, 'can we assume that all Germans share the same identity?'), and of course almost impossible to answer when one wants to speak of a 'European identity', an agglomeration of so many different identities. One should therefore at least acknowledge that any discourse about identity (national or European) is highly political and that it depends on what one wants to create. The invention of tradition, or a selective use of what has historically 'existed', does not guarantee automatically that an identity project will succeed and that its discourse is 'valid'.

Turkey and Europe, 1959–1963

I now turn my attention to the *political* dimension of identity formation in addressing a diachronic questioning of the 'otherness' of Turkey for European identity. What did

Turkey represent at different times? To answer this question, I shall turn to the first connections between 'Europe' and Turkey a few years after the creation of the first European communities (the European Coal and Steel Community of 1952 and the European Economic Community (EEC) of 1957). The time frame of reference of 1959–1963 is that of the first attempts by Turkey to knock on Europe's door, by requesting to sign an agreement of association, a form of agreement dealing mostly with economic and trade issues, but whose long term perspective could be (and was originally) that of adhesion to the EEC. The documents used here are deposited at the Historical Archives of the European Union, hosted in Florence. The sample consists mostly of internal documents of the EEC (in particular documents from the *Direction Générale I* of the European Commission (in charge of external relations), notes of national ambassadors to the EEC (of the Six as well as from Turkey itself), notes from the Council of Ministers, documents from the COREPER (*Comité des Représentants Permanents*) and documents of the president of the Commission (at that time Walter Hallstein)), as well as public debates from the European Parliament and from two of its commissions (the political affairs commission and the external trade commission). 1959 represents the beginning of the Turkish request and 1963 the moment where Turkey and the EEC signed the Association Agreement.

In none of all these is there *a single word* addressing the different cultural (let alone religious or confessional) backgrounds of the Europe of the Six and of Turkey. The words 'Muslim', 'Islam' or 'religion' never appear in any documents of the time, be they public (such as parliamentary debates) or confidential secret memoranda.

Turkey started enquiring about a possible association with the EEC in early 1959, a few months after Britain asked for a redefinition of a tariff agreement with the EEC. Turkey felt it would be advantageous to ask for an association with the EEC, of the sort that the Greek government was making at the same time, rather than to negotiate single import/export quota or *ad hoc* agreements. The first internal EEC document dealing with Turkey's request dates from March 1959. It is an internal technical memorandum of the Commission on the economic difficulties of Turkey, in particular in the field of international credit lending from other countries, agricultural production and state debts (Doc. 1).[11] The economy was the first and main field of 'enquiry' for European bureaucrats. Other matters came up later at the time of the debate within the European Parliament, but in the first year Turkey also insisted very much on stressing its economic capacity to become an associate member of the EEC. Turkey also stressed its European dimension, in economic, military and geographic terms (see for example Doc. 4).[12] But overall, the first question about Turkish association was simply an economic one.

A second issue then appeared that has to do with the Turkish population. In the first in-depth analysis of 20 pages about the candidate country that one can find in the European archives the German delegation to the EEC concentrated its attention on a particular feature of the Turkish population, namely the fact that beyond the 26 million Turks living in Turkey another 23 million of Turkish origin lived in territories then controlled by the USSR. The report argued that since the standard of living inside the Soviet Union was higher than in Turkey it was important for the West to help Turkey as soon as possible (Doc. 6). In no place in this detailed report (dealing with general features of Turkey, its domestic and international political situation, its economy, agriculture and investment plans) was there any mention of the Muslim confession of the country. Turkey, which became part of NATO only three years after its foundation, was on the front line of the communist threat, and this very fact seemed to trump all other considerations about the country's interest in creating links with political Europe.

This eminently political aspect of Turkey's request (supporting Turkey meant defending it against communism) was acknowledged in a note of the *Conseil des Ministres* (September 1959) to the Commission stating that it was the duty of the ministers, not of the Commission, to decide upon the fate of Turkey's demand and that a strict parallel track should be kept for both the Greek and Turkish requests for association (Doc. 8). Is the fact that the Commission was aware of the necessity of keeping parallel tracks an indirect acknowledgment that the two requests risked *not* being treated equally, denoting a bias for one country over the other?

One can find an answer to this question in another confidential document of the Commission. There one can find the reason why there could be grounds for preferential and faster treatment of the Greek request: not because of a closer cultural heritage, but because of the different *scale* of the economic challenges that the two countries represented for the EEC. While both were less developed than the Six and shared much the same type of agricultural production, Turkey was much more populous and more industrialised but had much greater difficulties in setting its financial affairs in order than Greece (Doc. 11). In any case, an internal Turkish coup would slow down the pacing of its request to be associated with the EEC.[13] In May 1960 the Turkish army (the defender of Kemalist order since the inception of the modern Turkish state) staged a coup to oust the government of the Democratic Party (DP) led by Adnan Menderes, the initiator of Turkey's European request (Yapp, 1996, pp. 312–15). Because of the disturbances that followed this coup the Turkish dossier was put on hold for a few months (see for example Doc. 14). Once the discussions were resumed with the new government run by the Kemalist Republican People's Party, again the main stumbling block between the EEC and Turkey was the precarious state of the Turkish economy and tariff disagreements (Doc. 15). Eventually the path was smoothed for Turkey and an agreement of association was signed first in Brussels on 25 June 1963 and then in Ankara on 12 September 1963.

I next examine the reaction of public opinion[14] and of the European Parliament to this important news. It cannot be said that the Turkish request to become an associate member of the EEC stirred a lively debate. The only debate in the European Parliament was not about the 'European-ness' of Turkey, nor about the contrasting cultural backgrounds of Turkey and Europe; it was instead almost entirely about internal questions on the relative competence of the European institutions: members of the European Parliament (MEPs) were upset by the fact that the Parliament was consulted about such association only *after* the signing of the treaty. In the first debate about Turkey, Fernand Dehousse, a Belgian MEP, lamented that once more the Council of Ministers would take the lead with the question of association of the United Kingdom, the Scandinavian countries, Turkey and Greece, without referring formally to the European Parliament (Doc. 18, pp. 85–87). This type of worry would occupy most of the debates inside the Parliament, in particular at the time of the ratification of the treaty by the Parliament in November 1963 (Docs. 16, 17 and 25). In the course of the debates in the Parliament, no one ever underlined any cultural or religious differences (even in terms of commitments to values) between Turkey and Europe. There was only one type of opposition to Turkey's association, and that was expressed in economic terms. Italy for example saw the emergence of certain Turkish products (including oil, dried fruits and tobacco) as a dangerous source of competition for its own agricultural goods.[15] Overall, what comes out of the debates within the European Parliament is a general commitment to help a country that was considered as an important ally of the West. The speech of the Dutch MEP Paul Kapteyn (the author of the final report on Turkish association on behalf of the External Trade Commission) is worth quoting here:

> I believe that considerations about the principle of adhesion must be trumped by political necessities. Indeed, I am thinking of the role played by countries such as Greece and Turkey in the defence of western civilisation, a role that grants them, in my view, the right to become associate members.[16]

A similar statement was made by Eugène Schaus, president of the Council of Ministers in June 1963, on the day Turkey signed the association agreement:

> I am delighted to give you the notification that the association agreement with Turkey is to be signed today. Turkey has been one of the first European countries to express its trust in the Community and its leading role in the organisation of the free world underlines the importance of its participation in our common endeavour.[17]

Here as well no sign of dissidence can be found about Turkey, a fully 'European' and 'western' country, part of the same 'civilisation'. The context of the Cold War and the pivotal role played by Turkey not only for NATO but also in the West's attempts to extend its containment policies towards the Middle East (with the creation of the so-called Baghdad Pact) surely helps to explain why there was not a single word of dissidence about its association agreement with the EEC. When the president of the Commission, Walter Hallstein, announced that the treaty had been signed with Turkey, and that such an occasion 'was even more welcome since Turkey, a country geographically and politically in an imperilled situation, has always been faithfully and courageously linked to the cause of the free world', the Parliament stood up and applauded (Doc. 23, p. 68, translation mine).

Sickle and Crescent – the Now and Then of External Others

In the last documents analysed, the dividing line between 'us' and 'them' related not to Islam's Star and Crescent but surely to the communist Hammer and Sickle. The context of the Cold War and active containment by western countries helps to explain why no one ever questioned the association agreement with Turkey on grounds of cultural or religious differences. What mattered then was to maintain the public unity of western and Atlanticist countries, with or without cultural, religious or even economic differences amongst them.

In the present post-Cold War epoch, however, where the threat of the sickle has totally disappeared, a huge space has been left empty, and the symbol of the Islamic crescent has crystallised in the collective imaginations of Europeans (and certainly also of Americans, albeit for different reasons). If religion has acquired such a central place for our politics and our identities in recent years, it is partly because the international context has allowed for this topic to gain prominence again and for the possibility of otherness expressed in religious terms to become a vivid reality (especially after 9/11). Be it because of the appeal of the clash of civilisations thesis or because of a lack of knowledge of each other, the notion of a clash between the 'West' and 'Islam' is increasingly widespread among the European populace, even if the idea of the opposition of these entities is deeply problematic (Asad, 2003).

Elsewhere I have analysed at length the representation of Europe as a political project in French, German and Italian history textbooks from the 1950s to the present (Challand, 2009). These textbooks, which were written for European teenagers, represent a valuable articulation of wider academic discourses about the 'others' (not only historical, but also in the anthropological, religious and cultural fields) and their dissemination to wider national audiences through the teaching of history and contemporary politics. The study of history school textbooks is an interesting means of assessing the 'bottom line of what a society "knows"' (Jonker, 2009, p. 3) while at the same time analysing what are the techniques employed for inculcating certain forms of knowledge in the young audiences targeted by such national history textbooks: 'Textbooks are the instruments *par excellence* with which a society promotes its basic values' (Jonker, 2009, p. 3).

The more time that passes, the less the threat of Eastern European communism can be perceived in the ways in which European construction is represented in European textbooks, and especially in the case of Germany, which was cut in two in communist times. Through this emancipation from the communist threat that is best perceived from the mid 1990s, Europe becomes a topic of its own, and gains, so to speak, its own historical subjectivity (Challand, 2009). In other words, political Europe appears more and more as an autonomous project, without international implications other than the will emanating from European nations to build a peaceful order, but this is done also by recreating some direct links to a distant past, to an Enlightened Europe, to a Christian Europe, or even to a Greco-Roman Europe, in order to give Europe its own centre of gravity and to project historical continuities. So this process of projecting the image of an independent Europe (in the sense that it is no longer historically indebted to the Cold War and to the USA) is made possible only by creating a rather artificial sense of unity around European cultures, or values, and it is at this point that religion can serve as a binding element for a common European identity. The representations of religion as the 'other' and a return to a contemporary representation of Turkey are suggestively presented in a cartoon dealing with Turkey in a German textbook (Figure 3).

Dickes Ende

Figure 3. 'May I enter?' 'Sure, no problem!' (Cartoon reproduced in H.-J. Lendzian *Zeiten und Menschen 2* (1st edn, vol. 2) (Braunschweig, Verlag Ferdinand Schöningh, 2005), p. 364. Copyright: CCC-Cartoons.)

The drawing shows a welcoming Gerhard Schroeder (at the time (2004) German chancellor) who is willing to let Turkey enter the EU, seeing no problem, while Angela Merkel (the soon-to-be chancellor) notices the dual nature of Turkey, half-human (with flowers), half-animal (with 'Economy, Islamism and Kurds' as its main stigmata). Here the 1960s sense of unity between Turkey in Europe has totally disappeared and cultural, social and religious features (not to mention the stronger dehumanising symbols left by the animal Turkey on the ground) serve to demarcate one from another. This caricature (that thousands of students can find in their textbooks) illustrates how the 'othering' process draws on different repertoires to create simplistic accounts of the other: religion (expressed through the 'repellent side' of Islamism) serves as one of the possible *negative* markers of this Turkish otherness.

Conclusion

From all the material reviewed in these pages one can perceive the rather biased and selective use that can be made of religion as a *positive* marker of an alleged European community by stressing a *negative* view of an 'other'. The evidence shows that attempts to identify Europe in religious terms are only a recent narrative. At other times, European identities totally ignored the issue of religion, since Turkey was not seen as a significant 'other' for Europe. At that time Turkey was seen as part of the same occidental civilisation. The situation has evolved over the last ten years with the shift of political Europe's borders towards the south-east: the result is that Turkey is now taken to symbolise another civilisation (and religion).

Two things should be emphasised. First, this does not mean that religious arguments serve uniquely to advance a biased and possibly dangerous othering process. After all, religions have always been and remain one way to answer common metaphysical questions that human beings ask about their fate and lives. Religion can therefore serve as a bridge between social groups and should not automatically be read in a negative manner. Second, the evidence simply highlights the fact that Europe-and-religion is only a very recent 'civil marriage', which furthermore can serve more *political* functions than religious ones. There is therefore no reason why religions should not play a role in people's identification. Rather, as Zucca (2009) suggests, one should avoid a blithe secular confidence that dismisses all too simply anything that has to do with religion. Religion has something to say about Europe's peoples and their neighbours, but religions should not have a privileged access to politics *per se* and should not be used to create stark boundaries between in-groups and out-groups.

The question of a multireligious Europe ought to be taken seriously; it is a question rendered more important with the enlargement of Europe towards an Orthodox East and a Muslim South-East. Thus a thorough reflection on secularism should be undertaken away from simplistic portrayals of threats in terms of religious otherness (which eventually create simplistic and homogeneous blocks opposed to one another). This is true not only for those who describe Islam/Turkey as a problem for a European identity, but also for those who assume that 'secularism' is implicitly part of the European self-understanding. As Shore notes in his work on the creation of a European identity,

> Creating the 'European identity', as depicted in EU discourse, entails a degree of exclusion of the Other. ... European identity tends to become meaningful only when contrasted to that which is not Europe. As Europe consolidates and converges, and as the barriers between European

nation-states are eliminated, so the boundaries separating Europe from its Third World 'Others' have intensified. ... The problem with this approach to identity is its absolutism: its failure to recognise cultures as composite and hybrid entities. (Shore, 2000, p. 63)

The challenge is therefore to look at processes of hybridisation, thereby avoiding monocausal types of explanation. In the 2006 volume edited by Delanty the plea is made to adopt a view of Europe that goes beyond mere geographical boundaries (which are themselves arbitrary) and beyond the East–West dichotomy (Delanty, 2006). Instead, the suggestion is that a cosmopolitan approach to Europe should be adopted, one that acknowledges the rich diversity which characterises its past, present and future – a view which, furthermore, would allow us to see the goods and evils that religions have represented for this continent not least in its deep entanglement with its neighbours.

Acknowledgment

The author would like to thank Bo Stråth and Piers Ludlow as well as participants at the LSE conference for their comments, and the European Commission for the generous Marie Curie grant allowing this research at the European University Institute.

Notes

1 My argument thus differs from that of Katzenstein (2006) who deals with how religion contributes or not to Europeanisation *from within*. We nonetheless share the view that religion risks being more a stumbling block than a stepping stone for Europeanisation.

2 JSTOR, a search-engine for scholarly journals, www.jstor.org (last accessed 12 October 2007).

3 The search was operated by highlighting the option 'All news in All languages'. Available at www.lexisnexis.com (last accessed 12 October 2007). The historical depth of the articles available is obviously very short since apart from a few articles from 1962 and 1963 the series of articles available comes from the 1980s

4 The clash thesis has become one of the most powerful political myths of our time, so as to become a self-fulfilling prophecy (Bottici and Challand, 2006).

5 For a presentation of the software and its function see www.atlasti.com (last accessed 12 October 2007).

6 The treaties were downloaded from the European Navigator, www.ena.lu (last accessed 10 May 2007).

7 This recital has been kept in the Lisbon Treaty agreed upon during the Intergovernmental Conference that took place in Lisbon on 18 October 2007. See http://europa.eu/reform_treaty/index_en.htm (last accessed 14 November 2007).

8 Document on 'The European Identity' published by the Nine Foreign Ministers on 14 December 1973, in Copenhagen, available at www.ena.lu (last accessed 10 May 2007).

9 Solemn Declaration on European Union (Stuttgart, 19 June 1983), available at www.ena.lu (last accessed 10 May 2007). For an explanation of how these declarations have been instrumental in the need to create a common identity, see Shore (2000, in particular pp. 15–65) and Stråth (2000b, in particular pp. 401ff). http://news.bbc.co.uk/2/hi/europe/2420697.stm (last accessed 28 May 2007).

10 All quoted archival documents will be referred in the core of the text with a number ('Doc. 1'). A full description of the documents can be found in section (b) of the References.

11 'La Turquie qui fait géographiquement partie de l'Europe, constitue également un élément inséparable de celle-ci tant au point de vue économique que politique et militaire'. (Doc. 4).
12 Turkey had formally complained about what it perceived as the preferential treatment of Greece by the EEC.
13 I did a quick search in *Le Monde*, the leading French daily newspaper, around the dates of the signing of the Agreement in order to see whether this stirred debate. No opinion pieces were published, and even the news itself received only a small mention on the last page of the 11 September 1963 edition.
14 Speech by Edoardo Battaglia (MEP), 19 September 1961, in Doc. 19, pp. 46–48.
15 Our translation. The original reads: 'Je crois que dans ce cas [i.e. demande de la Grèce et de la Turquie] le principe d'adhésion doit céder le pas à un impératif politique. Je songe en effet au rôle que jouent des pays tels que la Grèce et la Turquie dans la défense de la civilisation occidentale, rôle qui, à mon avis, leur donne en tout cas le droit d'entrer en ligne de compte pour ce genre d'association' (Doc. 21, p. 90).
16 Our translation. The original reads: 'Je suis heureux de pouvoir vous annoncer que l'accord d'association avec la Turquie doit être paraphé aujourd'hui. La Turquie a été l'un des premiers pays européens à exprimer sa confiance dans la communauté et son rôle dans l'organisation du monde libre souligne l'importance de sa participation à notre œuvre commune' (Doc. 23, p. 42).

References

(a) Books, Articles and Papers

Asad, T. (2003) 'Europe against Islam: Islam in Europe', in B. S. Turner (ed.), *Islam: Critical Concepts in Sociology*, vol. IV: *Islam and Social Movements* (London, Routledge), pp. 345–56.

Barth, F. (1969) 'Introduction', in F. Barth (ed.), *Ethnic Groups and Boundaries: the Social Organization of Culture Difference* (London, Allan and Unwin), pp. 9–38.

Bottici, C. and Challand, B. (2006) 'Rethinking political myth: the clash of civilizations as a self-fulfilling prophecy', *European Journal of Social Theory*, 9, 3, pp. 315–36.

Casanova, J. (2006) 'The long, difficult and tortuous journey of Turkey into Europe and the dilemmas of European civilization, *Constellations*, 13, 2, pp. 234–47.

Challand, C. (2009) 'The sequences of Europe: European identity and its external others in history textbooks (1950–2005)', *Contexts, the Journal of Education Media, Memory and Society*, 2, 1 (forthcoming).

Delanty, G. (1995) *Inventing Europe: Idea, Identity, Reality* (London, Macmillan).

Delanty, G. (ed.) (2006) *Europe and Asia Beyond East and West* (London, Routledge).

Göle, N. (2006) 'Europe's encounter with Islam: what future?, *Constellations*, 13, 2, pp. 248–62.

Joas, H. and Wiegandt, K. (eds) (2005) *Die kulturelle Werte Europas* (Frankfurt a.M., Fischer Verlag).

Jonker G. (2009) 'Imagining Islam: European encounters with the Muslim world through the lens of German textbooks', in H. Yilmaz and C. Aycak (eds), *Perceptions of Islam in Europe: Culture, Identity and the Muslim Other* (London, I.B. Tauris) (forthcoming).

Katzenstein, P. (2006) 'Multiple modernities as limits to secular Europeanization?', in T. Byrnes and P. Katzenstein (eds), *Religion in an Expanding Europe* (Cambridge, Cambridge University Press), pp. 1–33.

Kocka, J. (2007) 'The mapping of Europe's borders: past, present, and future', in H.-A. Persson and B. Stråth (eds), *Reflections on Europe: Defining a Political Order in Time and Space* (Brussels, P.I.E. Peter Lang), pp. 37–48.

Passerini, L. (ed.) (2003) *Figures d'Europe: Images and Myths of Europe* (Brussels, P.I.E. Peter Lang).

Persson, H.-A. and Stråth, B. (eds) (2007) *Reflections on Europe: Defining a Political Order in Time and Space* (Brussels, P.I.E. Peter Lang).

Shore, C. (2000) *Building Europe: the Cultural Politics of European Integration* (London, Routledge).
Stråth, B. (ed.) (2000a) *Europe and the Other and Europe as the Other* (Brussels, P.I.E. Peter Lang).
Stråth, B. (2000b) 'Multiple Europes: integration, identity and demarcation to the other', in B. Stråth (ed.), *Europe and the Other and Europe as the Other* (Brussels, P.I.E. Peter Lang), pp. 385–420.
Stråth, B. (2007) 'The political, the social and the economic in a European political order', in H.-A. Persson and B. Stråth (eds), *Reflections on Europe: Defining a Political Order in Time and Space* (Brussels, P.I.E. Peter Lang), pp. 137–58.
Wagner, P. (2005) 'Hat Europa eine kulturelle Identität?', in H. Joas and K. Wiegandt (eds), *Die kulturelle Werte Europas* (Frankfurt a.M., Fischer Verlag), pp. 494–511.
Yapp, M. (1996) *The Near East Since the First World War: a History to 1995* (2nd edn) (London, Longman).
Zucca, L. (2009) 'The crisis of the secular state: a reply to Prof. Sajo', *International Journal of Constitutional Law* (forthcoming).

(b) Archival Material

All this material is located in the Historical Archives of the European Union, Villa Poggiolo, Piazza Edison 11, I–50133 Firenze, Italy. The description of each archival item includes: the nature of the document; who wrote it and to whom it is addressed; and a date (when available). The page numbers indicated give the location of the document within the relevant box in the archive. In the text the documents are referred to as 'Doc. 1' and so on.

(i) *Non-Printed Material*

1. Note interne au Dr Seeliger, Direction Générale I, 10 mars 1959, BAC 003/1978–285, pp. 3–9.
2. Aide-mémoire pour Conseil de la CEE, du Gouvernement Turc, 11 Mars 1959, BAC 003/1978–285, pp. 10–13.
3. Note pour Membres de la Commission, de F. Braun, Chef Division du Conseil des Ministres, 11 août 1959, BAC 003/1978–285-SECRET, p. 14.
4. Lettre à Hallstein, Président de la Commission, de Hikem Bensan, ambassadeur Turc, 31 juillet 1959, BAC 003/1978–285, pp. 15–17.
5. Lettre à Dr Gunther Seeliger DG relations extérieures CEE, de la *Vertretung BRD bei den EG*, 21 August 1959, BAC 003/1978–285, p. 18.
6. Vor-Entwurf: Assoziierung der Turkei bei der EWG, IG1/Rs, 27 August 1959, BAC 003/1978–285, pp. 19–38.
7. Note Direction Générale pour le Président Walter Hallstein, DG I de la part de Jean Rey (Commissaire pour les Relations Extérieures), 8 sept. 1959, BAC 003/1978–285, pp. 48–49.
8. Note du Conseil [des Ministres] R/644/59, 9 sept. 1959, BAC 003/1978–285, pp. 50–51.
9. Note complémentaire à R/644/59, 10 sept. 1959, BAC 003/1978–285, pp. 67–68.
10. Lettre au Représentant Permanent Belge Joseph van der Meulen, DG Rel. Ext., 16 sept. 1959, BAC 003/1978–285, pp. 74–75.
11. Note sur l'ouverture de négociations avec la Turquie pour accord d'association, CEE – DG RELEX, 4 mars 1960, BAC 003/1978–286 CONFIDENTIEL, pp. 33–41.
12. Note du service de presse CEE, pour W. Hallstein, et membres de la Commission, 17 mars 1960, BAC 003/1978–286, p. 42.
13. Aide-mémoire pour le Conseil, Groupe d'experts, 25 avril 1960, BAC 003/1978–286 CONFIDENTIEL, pp. 49–53.
14. Note au COREPER (Ambassadeur Berschette), de la part de Seeliger – DG 1, 20 juin 1960, BAC 003/1978–286, p. 17.

15. Résumé des discussions 14–21 oct., Commission, 27 oct. 1960, BAC 003/1978–286 CONFIDENTIEL, pp. 133–38.
16. Projet de Rapport concernant la consultation du Parlement Européen par le Conseil de la Communauté Economique Européenne sur l'Accord créant une association entre la CEE et la Turquie, Commission Politique du Parlement Européen (rapporteur Fernand Dehousse), 11 novembre 1963, PEO 426,1.
17. Projet d'Avis pour la commission politique sur l'Accord créant une association entre la CEE et la Turquie, Commission du Commerce Extérieur du Parlement Européen (rapporteur Paul J. Kapteyn) (n.d., probably October or November 1963), PEO 426,1.

(ii) *Printed Material* (*Minutes of Parliamentary Debates*)

18. APE (Assemblée Parlementaire Européenne), *Débats. Compte rendu* in extenso *des séances. Session 1961–1962. Séances du 7 au 10 mars 1961*, VII/61, N. 38. Edition de langue française, Communauté Européenne du Charbon et de l'Acier (CECA), Communauté Economique Européenne (CEE), Communauté Européenne de l'Energie Atomique (CEEA).
19. APE (Assemblée Parlementaire Européenne), *Débats. Compte rendu* in extenso *des séances. Session 1961–1962. Séances 18–19 septembre 1961*, XI/61, N. 44. Edition de langue française, CECA, CEE et CEEA.
20. APE (Assemblée Parlementaire Européenne), *Débats. Compte rendu* in extenso *des séances. Session 1961–1962. Séances 20–24 novembre 1961*, IV/62, N. 48. Edition de langue française CECA, CEE et CEEA.
21. APE (Assemblée Parlementaire Européenne), *Débats. Compte rendu* in extenso *des séances. Session 1961–1962. Séances du 22–25 janvier 1962*, IV/62, N/ 52. Edition de langue française CECA, CEE et CEEA.
22. APE (Assemblée Parlementaire Européenne), *Débats. Compte rendu* in extenso *des séances. Session 1962–1963. Séances du 27 au 30 mars 1962*, VIII/62, N. 56. Edition de langue française, CECA, CEE et CEEA.
23. APE (Assemblée Parlementaire Européenne), *Débats. Compte rendu* in extenso *des séances. Session 1962–1963. Séances du 24–28 juin 1963*, X/63, N. 64. Edition de langue française, CECA, CEE et CEEA.
24. Parlement Européen, 1963 'Document 91. Accord créant une association entre la CEE et la Turquie et documents annexes (14 nov. 1963)', in APE (Assemblée Parlementaire Européenne), *Documents de Séance 1963–1964 (nov.–déc.). Bulletin No. 32 du 31 octobre 1963*, Edition de langue française, CECA, CEE et CEEA.
25. Parlement Européen, 1963 'Document 94. Rapport fait au nom de la Commission Politique sur l'accord (doc. 91) créant une association entre la CEE et la Turquie, Rapporteur Fernand Dehousse (23 nov. 1963)', in APE (Assemblée Parlementaire Européenne), *Documents de Séance 1963–1964 (nov.–déc.). Bulletin No. 32 du 31 octobre 1963*, Edition de langue française, CECA, CEE et CEEA.

European Enlargement, Secularisation and Religious Re-publicisation in Central and Eastern Europe

DAVID HERBERT & MAX FRAS

> In Hungary, religion has become truly de-privatised during the last decade. Following Casanova's terminology, public religions are not only present in civil society, but also have a presence in political society and the state. (Enyedi, 2003, p. 173)

> In terms of trust placed on religion and religious institutions, the [Romanian Orthodox] church ranks at the top of the Romanians' list, with 86% compared to other institutions, followed by the army with 69%. At the bottom of the list are the political parties, the judiciary, the parliament, and markers of the free market. (2006 survey, in Rogobete, 2006, p. 37)

> Today, Poland is a model country where lay law is constructed according to the Catholic Church's will, in all spheres in which the clergy is interested . . . . How is it possible that in a democratic society small groups of fanatics can terrorise society, under the rule of both right-wing and left-wing parties? (Brach-Czaina, 2003, in Burdziej, 2005, p. 169)

> Religion is one of the most vital elements that go to make up the identity of believers and their conception of life, but it is also a precious asset for atheists, agnostics, sceptics and the unconcerned. (*Kokkinakis v Greece*, 1993, para. 31, in Wallace, 2005, p. 599)

Introduction

From scholarly observation to opinion poll data to secularist frustration, the first three quotations here testify to the strength of religion in the public spheres of Eastern European societies since the fall of state socialist regimes. Yet this trend apparently stands in some tension with another, perhaps better known process – incorporation into the European Union (EU), a body with a markedly secular institutional history which presides over arguably the most secularised populations and societies on the planet (Bruce, 1999, p. 117; Halman and Draulans, 2006). However, the secularising impact of the EU institutions may be less pronounced than their predominantly secular rationalist discourse – which emphasises religion as personal choice rather than as constitutive of core human identity – might at first sight suggest. For as the final quotation above indicates, key institutions such as the European Court of Human Rights (ECHR) have been cautious in challenging perceived cultural norms, and have in fact tended to adopt a tacit model of religion as constitutive of collective culture rather than an individual choice at crucial junctures, as in the verdict of the *Kokkinakis* case quoted, which upheld Greek antiproselytisation laws against an appeal by a Jehovah's Witness.

This paper examines the impact of EU enlargement on the relationship between religion, politics and society in three recent accession states – Poland, Hungary and Romania – and the attitudes and role of key religious institutions in the integration process. While each society is unique, we have chosen these three as offering three distinct types of religious composition among postsocialist societies: one Catholic, one Orthodox, each with a high degree of religious homogeneity (Poland and Romania respectively), and Hungary with its more mixed composition (52 per cent Roman Catholic, 16 per cent Reformed, 3 per cent Lutheran and 3 per cent Greek Catholic according to the 2001 census (Schanda, 2003, p. 344)). All three share a common postsocialist heritage, but the role of religion in each of their histories is quite distinct, ranging from substantial Catholic opposition and resistance to the communist state in Poland to partial absorption in state structures for the Orthodox Church in Romania during the same period (Gautier, 1997, 1998).

Our paper will first locate these country studies in the context of two broader debates. The first concerns the contested concept of secularisation and a counter trend of 're-publicisation', a term we propose using to refer to processes whereby religions become more visible and active in the public spheres of contemporary societies. The second concerns the implications of the interpretation of the European Convention on Human Rights by the ECHR in areas related to the public manifestation of religions. We shall then introduce the individual country studies by way of a consideration of World Values Survey data pertaining to each, which provide some opportunities for comparison and identification of trends over time.

Secularisation and Re-publicisation

Secularisation is a contested term, and its use involves particular complexities in postsocialist societies. In sociological terms, secularisation refers to the decline of religious influence in social systems. This may be enforced, as with the Henrician dissolution of the monasteries in Tudor England, in which the verb 'to secularise' was first used in English, or with the confiscation of church property as part of the attack on civil society in the late 1940s and early 1950s across Eastern Europe, as Stalinist regimes consolidated their grip on power. The predominant understanding of secularisation in sociological discourse is not as a deliberate policy act, but rather as a function of modernisation itself, and specifically of the development and extension of modern functional systems into every aspect of social life in a process variously referred to as social or structural differentiation (Bruce and Wallis, 1992, p. 8; Scott and Marshall, 2005). This process has been identified as 'absolutely central to all secularisation theories, without exception' (Tschannen, 1991, p. 404). In this process, public religions, like hunter-gatherers in the face of combine harvesters, are driven to the margins of the social world. However, the idea of secularisation as 'a natural, inevitable, and abstract by-product of modernisation' has recently come under attack from scholars who see it rather as 'the outcome of a struggle between contending groups with conflicting interests' (Smith, 2003, p. vii). If this can be contested in western societies (Smith's comment relates to the USA), how much more is this agonistic dimension of secularisation relevant in Eastern Europe; for while the narrative of social progress in which concepts of secularisation are embedded has been shaken in the West, it has arguably been more profoundly twisted, broken and uprooted in the postsocialist world. As Froese comments on the conclusions of a study of belief among young people in Hungary in 1990, 'Scientific atheism didn't so much transform the youth into atheists, as disillusion them into nihilistic hedonism' (Froese, 2001, p. 262).

Thus it may be that the politicisation of the very social processes identified by secularisation theory as the neutral drivers of secularisation, and the failure of modernisation as a political project, have long-term consequences for the course of secularisation in Eastern Europe. Another difficulty with transposing secularisation theory developed in western societies to Eastern Europe is the different construction and meaning of public/private distinctions in western and socialist societies. A core aspect of secularisation in western societies is the privatisation of religion, which included the sedate retreat of religion not only into the domestic sphere but also into civil society. In socialist societies the state did not recognise the autonomy of the private sphere (although in practice this could not be entirely eliminated – privacy instead was warped into secrecy), while civil society was either crudely coopted or suppressed. Again, the legacy of these processes in postsocialist societies needs to be taken into consideration. This is partly why in describing the re-emergence of religion in the public sphere of postsocialist societies we have used the term 're-publicisation' (in the sense of 'becoming public again' rather than 'becoming a republic') in place of 'deprivatization' (Casanova, 1994), to avoid the problematic assumption that religion was ever privatised in Eastern Europe in the sense of becoming a matter of personal choice, because it in fact remained the focus of state policies and (sometimes) communal loyalties. (Similarly, in many postcolonial contexts religion was never privatised in a western, Enlightenment sense, although it often did play a less prominent role in political society in the immediate postcolonial period than previously or at present, as indigenous elites adopted western political ideologies (Herbert, 2007).) Following Smith's (2003, p. vii) Habermasian understanding of the public life, we define re-publicisation as those processes through which religion re-enters fields of shared social life in which it was previously inactive or from which it had been excluded, social fields in which culturally diverse groups coexist through shared normative and institutional arrangements. These include legal, educational, mass media and public welfare fields.

In spite of its emphasis on the role of religion in social processes, sociological measurement of secularisation has tended to take levels of individual belief and practice as indicative of levels of secularisation. However, while such indicators may provide a measure of the reservoir of private religiosity from which religions may draw for public activities, they give no direct sense of the significance of religion in public social systems. Political science discourse on secularisation, however, has gone further in delineating gradations of the withdrawal of religion from public life. Thus Moyser (1991) distinguishes five levels of secularisation: constitutional, policy, institutional, agenda and ideological. 'Discursive' is perhaps better than 'ideological', we shall use it instead here; Moyser's sense seems to be that under conditions of ideological secularisation religious terms no longer form part of the repertoire in which public debate is framed, and we believe that 'discursive' is a less loaded term for this. We shall use these categories to assess the extent of the secularisation/re-publicisation of religion in Hungary, Romania and Poland since 1989, adding the categories of religious beliefs, membership and identification to assess religious vitality, as an indicator of the reservoir of religious sentiment and commitment from which public mobilisations of religion may draw.

One complexity in comparing the evidence for secularisation and re-publicisation is that secularisation theory allows for temporary reversals of secularisation if modernisation processes trigger ethno-religious or nationalist reactions (Bruce, 1998, pp. 24–25). However, while secularisation theory envisages structural causes of secularisation and agent-based resistance to these, it envisages no structural causes of re-publicisation, of religion's re-entry into public life. Reversals in secularisation then, may be attributed to a positive re-publicisation process where they can be linked to some kind of structural change, and not simply to agents' resistance on the grounds of not liking the effects of modernisation. Indeed, some observers are beginning to point towards structural features underlying re-publicisation in other regions of the world. For example, new configurations of relationships between religion, politics and increasingly diverse and deregulated media in postcolonial contexts (including Ghana, India, Egypt and Brazil) have created a public sphere in which religious and secular symbols and discourses jostle and compete, loosely but sometimes powerfully articulating with a range of commercial and political interests, and leading Meyer and Moors to argue that '[T]he marked articulation of religion in the public realm destabilises the narrative of modernity as defined by the decline of the public role of religion, and this urges us to critically rethink the nexus of religion and media in regard to (trans)national politics and the modern nation state' (Meyer and Moors, 2006, p. 6).

In Eastern Europe many of the same structural conditions can be observed, resulting in some parallel phenomena in Poland, Romania and Hungary. The growth of the *Radio Maryja* broadcasting empire in Poland with its close links to two political parties (*Prawo i Sprawiedliwość* (Law and Justice) and *Liga Polskich Rodzin* (The League of Polish Families)) stirred significant waves of political controversy over the issues of abortion, homosexuality and European integration (Ramet, 2006, pp. 133–35; Fras, 2007). In Romania competition in broadcasting between new religious arrivals and the Orthodox Church and in Hungary close links between new political parties and religious groups may also be seen as re-publicisation phenomena (Enyedi, 2003). Yet in contrast to most postcolonial contexts, in Eastern Europe the EU and related institutions provide a powerful transnational influence reinforcing state authority, market regulation of social interests and strong traditions of secular republicanism. The region thus provides an interesting test-case for debates over changing global trends in the public influence of religion.

The European Union as Agent of Secularisation? Intentions, Accidents and Ethno-National Reactions

How might the EU impact on accession states as a secularising influence? We have described secularisation as possibly the consequence of the deliberate actions of states and other collective actors, and as a by-product of structural change. Thus the EU's possible secularising effects can be analysed both in terms of the impact of the secular character of the EU and related institutions such as the Council of Europe and the ECHR, and as an accidental consequence of the incorporation of new members into wider functional systems of communication, market exchange, migration, production and social regulation as a result of closer integration into EU structures.

Taking accidental effects first, it should be noted that a range of factors may be expected to produce a secularising effect regardless of the variety of secularisation or neosecularisation theory chosen. Thus in one variant Norris and Inglehart (2004) see the improved sense of security produced by an effective welfare state as a key factor in the decline of conventional religiosity; so the EU may be seen as an agent of such change through its social rights provisions. For neosecularisation theorists it is the declining scope of religious authority that it is the hallmark of secularisation (Chaves, 1994). Here EU institutions may be seen as contributing to this process by creating a transnational network of secular institutions circumscribing the power of national institutions at which level religion may have been powerful. The core process of all secularisation theories, social differentiation, may be predicted to have a marginalising effect on the social roles of religion by incorporating Eastern European nations into wider regionally and globally based functional social systems operating according to their own internal logic, so that any local 'residual' functions performed by religion are gradually eroded.

However, the 'orthodox' model of secularisation (Bruce and Wallis, 1992) also allows that EU incorporation may trigger ethno-nationalist reactions which may mobilise around religion ('cultural defence' (Bruce, 1998, p. 25)), and that religious organisations may, as in the American case, function to support the transition of new migrants while they are settling into European societies (Bruce, 1998, p. 24), in which case religious mobilisation would be expected to increase. A key question here is whether such reversals of secularisation – re-publicisation – can successfully be incorporated within a secularisation narrative, or whether there is evidence of sustained reversal and new public religious phenomena which require a different explanatory framework, and in particular whether structural causes may be identified which underpin re-publicisation phenomena.

Turning to the EU's secular character, one recent example of its articulation is found in the recent failed EU Constitution, which, while now redrafted in more modest form as a result of rejection in national referenda (for reasons unrelated to the current discussion), is nonetheless arguably indicative of the outlook of dominant elements of Europe's elites. Thus Ahonen (2007, p. 11) describes the document as possessing a 'rationalist liberal democratic tone', one which was identified and resisted by many of the delegates at the Constitutional Convention, including the Polish delegation (see Muszyński, 2002). More broadly, Ahonen identifies the EU's universalising and rationalist elements as at odds with strong ethno-nationalist currents in Eastern Europe. This is perhaps most clearly seen in the human rights aspect of EU membership, flagged strongly in the 1993 Copenhagen criteria which laid the ground rules for EU accession for postsocialist states, including 'stability of institutions guaranteeing democracy, the rule of law, human rights and respect for and protection of minorities' (Ahonen, 2007, p. 9).

In particular, EU accession requires prior membership of the Council of Europe, and, as part of that, incorporation and (in theory) implementation of the European Convention on Human Rights. The concern with the rights of religious minorities in this document in particular stands in tension with the claims to national representative status claimed by some churches in Eastern Europe, notably the Romanian Orthodox Church (Rogobete, 2006). However, it may be argued that the Convention has been less of a secularising influence than its rhetoric might suggest, for in spite of its having the strongest enforcement regime of any international convention in history, the extent of enforcement remains limited, especially in the case of religion. This is because of a perception – articulated by an ECHR judge in a crucial ruling – that Europe is characterised by an 'absence of a uniform conception of the significance of religion in society' (*Kokkinakis v Greece*). In such circumstances the ECHR is likely to be influenced in its decisions by representations of national cultures produced by member-state governments. We shall now consider some relevant provisions and their implementation, in order to assess the likely secularising impact of the European Convention on Human Rights on Romania, Hungary and Poland.

The European Convention on Human Rights and Secularisation

It might be thought that the Convention's measures to protect religious freedom and minorities could impact on the opportunities of powerful national churches to exert influence at the level of constitution and policy, so here we consider the potential for the Convention to do so in the context of the precedents established so far, and discussed below. Several articles have been invoked in cases relevant to religious minorities, but probably the most important are Article 9 (freedom of thought, conscience and religion (see Janis *et al.*, 1995, pp. 468, 471)) and Protocol 1 Article 2 (education – see Janis *et al.*, 1995, p. 483), and these will be central to the discussion here.

Religious Education and Freedom from Indoctrination

Protocol 1, Article 2 enshrines a universal right to education within the scope of existing state provision, and requires the state to respect parental religious and philosophical conviction in such provision. While the former has been interpreted as a guarantee that the state must provide at least primary education, the latter has been interpreted narrowly, such that after a review of the relevant case law one commentator observes that 'parents can now only object to education in the tenets of religions or philosophies other than their own if the purpose of such education can be equated with indoctrination' (Evans, 1997, p. 356). However, 'there is yet to be a case in which the Commission has found that the practice of a school amounted to indoctrination contrary to Article 2' (Evans, 1997, p. 357). Parents may provide their own alternative educational provision, but the state is not obliged to fund them to do so, even where state provision exists for other religions or denominations. Thus Evans concludes: 'taking Article 14 in conjunction with Article 2 of the First Protocol is unlikely to improve significantly the position of those seeking access to funds in order to set up or maintain educational establishments that accord with their religious or philosophical convictions' (Evans, 1997, p. 362). Thus in the cases we shall consider below, where the Roman Catholic Church in Poland and the Romanian Orthodox Church have sought to ensure their dominance in the field of provision of religious education in state schools, it is unlikely that the ECHR will act as a significant brake on their influence.

Restrictions on Public Culture: Freedom of Speech

Perhaps of even greater significance for religious minorities in Central and Eastern Europe are the decisions relating to Article 9 in the *Kokkinakis* and *Otto-Preminger-Institut* cases, because these suggest discrimination in favour of majority religious traditions. Of particular concern here is the circumscription of minority rights to express dissent from the majority religious view, whether through attempts at evangelism in the former case or satire in the latter.

As Evans comments, 'the *Kokkinakis* case permits a state to prevent a believer from manifesting a belief if improper means are used' (Evans, 1997, p. 335). The state is obliged to demonstrate that improper means have been used, but is given broad discretion to define impropriety. Thus the Greek antiproselytisation law was deemed legal by the ECHR. This prohibits

> any direct or indirect attempt to intrude on the religion or beliefs of others of a different persuasion, with the aim of undermining those beliefs, either by any kind of inducement or promise of inducement or moral support or material assistance, or by fraudulent means or by taking advantage of his inexperience, trust, need, low intellect or naïvety. (Section 4 of Law no. 1363/1938, quoted in Evans, 1997, p. 333)

This would seem to restrict severely the legal scope of missionary activity, and to read into Article 9 an obligation to respect majority religious views not immediately evident from its wording. This process was extended further in the *Otto-Preminger-Institut* case when the court ruled that

> the respect for religious feelings of believers as guaranteed by Article 9 can legitimately be thought to have been violated by provocative portrayals of objects of religious veneration; and such portrayals can be regarded as malicious violation of the spirit of tolerance, which must be a feature of democratic society. (Quoted in Evans, 1997, p. 336)

Again, the state is given broad discretion to determine the content of this 'respect', the reason given for this being the 'absence of a uniform conception of the significance of religion in society' (*Otto-Preminger-Institut v Austria*) across Europe. It is notable that this case originated in the predominantly Catholic Austrian Tirol, while the *Kokkinakis* case originated in predominantly Orthodox Greece; in other words, these are restrictions on the liberty of minorities in favour of a conservative interpretation of majority sensibilities. This means that dissenting minorities are given least protection where they are likely to need it most. Furthermore, the case suggests that the ECHR will risk challenging states only where it perceives that there is already a Europe-wide consensus. It follows from this that rapid expansion of the Council of Europe (and subsequently the EU) is likely to be followed by a diminution of challenges by the ECHR to states in controversial areas such as religion. As with the state's obligation to respect parental and philosophical conviction, it seems that in the area of the rights of religious minorities to manifest their beliefs the ECHR is likely to present little challenge where religious majority institutions hold a privileged position in the public cultures of accession states.

The European Union, Property Restitution and the Regulated Market

Other evidence also suggests that the secularising effects of EU institutions on new members may be limited. Dempsey (2006) reports that the Greek Catholic minority in Romania, whose property was confiscated by the communist authorities after the Second World War and given to the Orthodox Church to administer, has been disappointed that EU pressure for restoration prior to Romanian membership in January 2007 did not produce any government action, and that the EU delegates responsible did not see the issue as a priority. One observer even goes so far as to argue that 'Freedom of religion for members of minority faiths could end up being limited in the new societies of eastern Europe and the former Soviet Union *because* of the growing ties with European institutions, not in spite of these developing connections' (Richardson, quoted in Enyedi, 2003, p. 173). Richardson argues that this is because, as with economic matters, the EU operates a regulated rather than a free 'market', which allows larger and older religious organisations to establish and maintain dominant 'market' positions (Richardson, 1999). Thus it would appear that, in general, constitutional secularisation in EU institutions has thus far had only a limited effect at national level. In this context we turn to consider our three country studies, beginning with an analysis of data from the World Values Survey, which provides points of comparison across the three societies.

Secularisation or Re-publicisation in Eastern Europe? Religion and Society in Poland, Hungary and Romania in the World Values Survey

The World Values Survey (WVS) provides valuable longitudinal opinion poll data on a range of issues connected with moral, social and political opinions and across an increasing range of societies since the 1980s. The Survey presents some evidence on the level of increased religious vitality (or 'spiritual capital' (Wuthnow, 2000)), which we conceptualise as a resource on which religions may draw for public mobilisation, but which is not necessarily of direct social or political significance. Thus between 1990 (1993 for Romania) and 1999 the proportion of those saying that they 'get comfort and strength from religion' increased slightly in Hungary (from 45.1 to 47.1 per cent), Poland (from 71.7 to 74.9 per cent) and Romania (from 73 to 79.8 per cent) (Survey, 2007). However, over the same period church attendance rose only in Romania (from 30.6 per cent claiming at least monthly attendance in 1993 to 46 per cent in 1999), with falls recorded between 1990 and 1999 in Poland (from 83.6 to 77.8 per cent) and Hungary (from 23 to 17.4 per cent) (Survey, 2007). Trust in religious institutions and confidence in their ability to provide answers to problems in family life and on moral, social and political questions all follow the same trends as church attendance rather than personal sustenance: thus confidence and trust increased in Romania but decreased in Poland and Hungary during this period (Survey, 2007). Thus public perceptions in Poland and Hungary suggest some privatisation of religion (increase in personal sustenance value, but decrease in confidence in religious institutions), in contrast to the Romanian case.

A series of new questions concerning the relationship between religion and politics were added in 1999. On a core issue concerning the separation of religion and politics in democratic systems, majorities in all three societies agreed that religious leaders should not influence how people vote (71.6 per cent in Hungary, 84.5 in Poland and 71.2 in Romania), with only small minorities disagreeing (6.9, 6.2 and 7 per cent). However, on the question of whether it would be better if more people with strong religious beliefs were in public office there is again a striking bifurcation between Romania, where 58.7 per cent agreed, and Poland and Hungary where 28 and 23.3 per cent agreed respectively. Intriguingly, in the Polish case, this is exactly the same proportion as those who voted for the Law and Justice party in the 2005 elections, with its overtly Catholic nationalist leadership – with the result that that party led the ruling coalition from 2005 to 2007 (Kohn, 2005).

Taken together, the WVS data present some evidence of the increased importance of religion for people in their personal lives in these three societies in 1990s, but only in Romania is there evidence for an increase in support for religion playing a more active role in public life through the decade, with contrary downward trends evident in Poland and Hungary. However, as the evidence cited above from postcolonial contexts suggests, re-publicisation may not translate directly into changes in public opinion, but rather, by making religious symbols and discourse more widely available, provide a resource for future political mobilisations (Rajagopal, 2001, p. 283). Is there any evidence of such re-publicisation phenomena in Eastern Europe? In this context we turn to our national case studies.

Poland

Symbolically, discursively and organisationally, the Catholic Church was crucial to the mobilisation of the Solidarity movement (Kubik, 1994; Żaryn, 2003). The opposition wave created in the 1970s and 1980s, although decisively a trade union movement, had deep roots in the Catholic Church and its teachings, as well as in earlier actions of anticommunist resistance undertaken by the Polish Roman Catholic Church (PRCC) (Osa, 1997). The alliance between opposition and the PRCC became particularly visible in the 1980s, in the decade of Solidarity and other opposition movements in Poland. The episcopate not only symbolically supported Solidarity following the strikes in Gdańsk and other cities on the Baltic coast in 1980, but also provided logistical support for opposition groups (Żaryn, 2003, pp. 419–75). This was possible only because the PRCC was the biggest non-state structure in the People's Republic of Poland that was relatively independent from the communist authorities and largely opposed to their main policies – especially those related to separation of church and state and suppression of religion in the public realm.

In this context by the 1960s the PRCC was already presenting an openly pro-European stance – expressed for example in the historic letter to the German bishops (in 1965, when the Polish episcopate wrote 'we forgive and we ask for forgiveness'). During his first papal visit to Poland in 1979 John Paul II said that preserving good relations with neighbours was just as important as preserving the Polish national heritage. In 1981 Solidarity issued a declaration of solidarity with the nations of Central-Eastern Europe – another expression of the pro-European views of the Polish opposition (Jackowska, 2003, pp. 25–35), and in a speech given at the European Parliament in 1988 John Paul II referred to East and West Christendom in Europe as the 'two lungs' of the continent, that can allow it to breathe properly only if working together. After the fall of the communist government the PRCC instantly sought influence on the integration process and tried to present it as much more than an economic development. In 1997 the Polish episcopate went on a collective tour of

Brussels, after which the bishops unanimously supported the integration process (Integracja, 2002). Polish Catholic intellectuals, particularly the liberals, were very supportive of EU integration (Mazowiecki, 2002; Knotz, 2003). The official PRCC portal, *Opoka*, lists the numerous advantages of EU integration, even citing official government publications to support its stance. The advantages include that: the EU respects national models of church–state relations and does not interfere in them; guarantees religious freedom and the right of religious education (France is listed as the only example where this has to take place outside the school setting); allows for state financial support for the church; supports charitable activities of the churches; and respects the church's right to authorise marriages (Kościoły, n.d.).

In 2001 the Polish primate Glemp met Günter Verheugen, the then European commissioner for enlargement, and expressed the opinion that EU enlargement was a historical necessity, reassuring him that there was no rift within the episcopate as far as supporting EU integration was concerned (Prymas, 2001). However, the very need for reassurance suggests the presence of some division, and recent statements suggest more ambivalence on the issue. Thus in 2002 the episcopate issued a special communique, *Biskupi polscy wobec integracji europejskiej* (*Polish Bishops toward European Integration*), moderately in favour of european integration, but also calling for preservation of Polish national culture, religious identity and values (Biskupi, 2002). A strong pro-European stance was forcefully reiterated just three weeks before the EU accession referendum in 2003, when John Paul II addressed the participants in the National Pilgrimage to Rome, using the title 'Europe needs Poland. The Church in Europe needs the Poles' Testimony of faith. Poland needs Europe' (Pope, 2003). Yet despite the pope's largely Euro-enthusiastic speech, the episcopate issued a more ambivalent document entitled *Słowo biskupów polskich w sprawie wejścia Polski do Unii Europejskiej* (*The Polish Bishops' Word on Poland's EU Accession*) just a week before the EU referendum (1 June 2003). While cautiously optimistic about the prospect of European integration, the document declares that support for EU integration cannot be drawn from Catholic teaching as such, and that every voter should make up his or her own mind according to his or her own convictions and moral conscience (Słowo, 2003). Two possible readings of this document may be suggested. First, it could be argued that its authors share something like Casanova's (1994) reading of the implications of the Second Vatican Council and are trying to maintain the Catholic Church's role as a voice with a contribution to make to public debate in civil society, but which should not intervene at the level of political society or the state unless there are vital issues of principle clearly at stake. Alternatively, a more *Realpolitik* reading is that the noncommittal stance could reflect either divisions in the hierarchy or a sense of division in the electorate, or among important constituents of it, and a wish to avoid alienation from them.

The latter reading is the more consistent with earlier actions. For example, in the immediate postcommunist period (in 1989 and 1993 respectively), and concerning religious instruction in schools and the restriction of Poland's previously relatively liberal abortion laws, the PRCC did not seek merely to present its case in public debate and leave the outcome up to the democratic process, but rather to influence government policy by negotiating directly with ministers. In the case of religious education the process bypassed the *Sejm* (parliament) altogether. Subsequently, on a series of issues from homosexual marriage to further developments in religious education to the Polish and European Constitutions, the PRCC has continued to attempt to influence public policy through direct government contacts rather than by opening up debate by addressing the wider civil society. As contributors to a debate on the influence of the PRCC in the pages of the daily newspaper *Rzeczpospolita* wrote in 2003, 'If we are to be a civil society, various agreements made over the heads of society, for example the decision of the government not to hold a referendum over abortion or the "back door introduction" of religious education into schools should again be made public' (Dunin and Sierakowski, 2003, in Burdziej, 2005, p. 169).

Thus the relationship between the PRCC, the media and the government in Poland raises doubts about the extent to which the PRCC fully 'accept[s] the principle of self-organization of an autonomous civil society' (Casanova, 1994, p. 109), and provides evidence of re-publicisation parallel to that observed in postcolonial contexts, namely produced through a combination of changing structural conditions (including media diversification and greater global and transnational connectivity) and the actions of key institutions and actors. On the question of the articulation between religion and democracy, while on the one hand there is no evidence that the PRCC seeks to stifle free speech or to seek formal recognition from the state as a national church (in contrast to the Romanian Orthodox Church, as we shall see below), on the other hand its actions seem more consistent with 'promot[ing] the principle of a homogeneous Polish Catholic community' than actively encouraging the expression of diverse opinions, particularly where that expression of diversity might lead to a conclusion contrary to the teaching of the church (Casanova, 1994, p. 109).

Such evidence, alongside the PRCC's fierce support for a God clause in the EU Constitution preamble, supports the view that a desire to maximise political influence at any level rather than a principled abstention from interference in politics lay behind the episcopate's guidance to voters in the accession referendum. If one considers a range of actions, it seems that the PRCC aims at maximising its political influence across civil and political society and the state, and that its moderately pro-EU stance in this case was an attempt to maintain support both of the audience of *Radio Maryja* and of EU supporters in liberal circles.

If we take this situation together with incidents such as the church's dispute with the ombudsman for citizens' rights (Herbert, 2003, pp. 219–22), it would seem that the PRCC's influence at constitutional, policy, institutional, agenda and ideological levels is increasing rather than declining. However, as comparison with the WVS data suggests, the PRCC is increasingly politically assertive at a time when elements of its grassroots support appear to be in decline, trends which have continued since 1999. For example, church attendance has continued to fall – though only from extra-ordinary to merely very high levels (Norris and Inglehart, 2006, p. 122), and decline is more marked in areas closer to the social and political role of the church, such as trust and support for the influence of the church on politics (Większość, 2007). At the same time the circulation of religious discourse in the media, building on the basis of an already prolific Catholic press under communism, has grown considerably, especially at the right-wing populist end of the market, exemplified by *Radio Maryja*. Thus the trend towards religious re-publicisation appears to be in the opposite direction to the extent of public support for the church, especially in terms of political engagement. This bifurcation between decline in religious vitality and increasing influence in politics underlines the importance of considering different dimensions of secularisation/re-publicisation separately.

Romania

Gautier (1997, 1998) sees Romania alongside the Soviet Union as typifying the 'church within socialism' model of church–state relations. This means that the

Romanian Orthodox Church (ROC) collaborated with the state apparatus and became part of the establishment (Radu, 2005, p. 9). The ROC's identification with the ethnogenesis of the Romanian people and the process of nation formation (Lordache, 2003, p. 239), combined with the model of church–state relations inherited from Byzantine history (Stan and Turcescu, 2000; Guran, 2006), meant that the communist regime was able to coopt the church in building its nationalistic model of state socialism.

Romania continues to exhibit very high levels of religious identification according to a range of polling evidence gathered since 1999 (the last publicly available WVS data). For example in the 2002 national census 99.96 per cent of the population claimed to belong to an officially recognised denomination, with 86.8 per cent identifying with the ROC (Rogobete, 2006, p. 37). In a poll conducted on behalf of the *Wall Street Journal* in 2004 Romania topped the world league table in terms of the percentage of the population identifying as religious, some 97 per cent (Rogobete, 2006, p. 36). Church attendance is also reported as high, with 43 per cent claiming to attend services once a week or more, and a further 37 per cent at Christmas and Easter and on other holy days (Rogobete, 2006, p. 38). What seems remarkable, compared with the effect that evidence of collaboration with socialist authorities has had on churches in other postsocialist societies – for example East Germany (Gautier, 1997, 1998) – is the continued high level of public trust in the ROC. In a recent poll 58 per cent of respondents said they had 'very much' trust in the ROC, and a further 32 per cent had 'much' trust, way ahead of the second-highest institution, the army, with 20 and 19 per cent respectively (Rogobete, 2006, p. 37).

The ROC opposes religious pluralism and has sought to entrench its position as the national church in Romania (Gillet, 2001, in Rogobete, 2005, p. 288). This can seen both in the position it has taken on the drafting of new laws to replace the communist legislation on issues such as the regulation of religious groups and property confiscated from the Greek Catholic Church, and in the writings of theologians and church leaders (Radu, 2005). Furthermore it 'has managed to maintain a strong political voice that cannot be ignored by the country's political elite' (Stan and Turcescu, 2000, p. 1485), as can be seen in its influence in legislation concerning religious education (on which it maintains a monopoly), gay rights and the media (Alexandru, 2006, p. 64; Romocea, 2007).

Such stances place it strongly at odds with the EU elite's secularist discourse, and indeed elements within the ROC have openly opposed closer EU integration. Radu (2005) quotes from a monthly magazine published by an Orthodox theological college and apparently written with the blessing of Patriarch Teoctist, which opposes EU membership on just about every substantive point, and thus it rejects (i) the adoption of European international legislation; (ii) the renunciation of territorial ambitions required as a condition of EU membership; (iii) the granting of full citizen's right to immigrants (referred to as 'the social garbage of Asia, Africa and America'); (iv) the granting of rights (called 'privileges') to Romania's internal minorities; (v) proposed legislation allowing foreigners to buy land, and other forms of inward investment (called 'subordination to foreign capital'); (vi) the influence of American and French culture ('the pressure of the Empire'); (vii) 'atheistic liberalism, the chaos of rights ... to speak, ... opinion, ... information, etc.'; and (viii) Romania becoming a 'field of propaganda for ... schismatic cults' (Andreescu, 1998, quoted in Radu, 2005; exact quotations indicated). However, while such views represent an aspect of Orthodox opinion, they should not be taken as representative of the Orthodox Church as a whole.

In spite of such opposition Romania joined the EU in January 2007, which suggests that such views are of limited influence on either the political elite or the voting population. Nonetheless, when the evidence of political secularisation is reviewed it is clear that the ROC exercises substantial influence at the policy (religious education), institutional (control of property), agenda (the media) and ideological (gay rights) levels. When one combines this influence with high levels of religious identification and public trust and relatively high levels of church attendance, all on an upward trajectory since 1993, it is apparent that Romania, like Poland, evidences a pattern of religious re-publicisation, in which the dominant church has asserted itself powerfully in public life. The difference in the Romanian case is that religious vitality indicators continue on an upward trend. All this suggests that the possibility of increased political mobilisation remains high.

Hungary

Active religious participation is lower in Hungary than Romania or Poland, and with a monthly church attendance figure of 23 per cent in 1990, dropping to 17.4 per cent by 1999, closer to Western European norms (Froese, 2001, p. 265; Survey, 2007). In its 1990 Constitution Hungary opted for a clear church–state separation. Thus it is perhaps surprising to find, since as the first quotation given at the start of the paper asserts, religious organisations in Hungary have succeeded in becoming embedded in civil, political and state society. How has this been possible? Enyedi argues that the Constitution provided a loophole that the churches, aided by the interpretation of the Constitutional Court, have been able to use to ensure a material basis for their activities:

> By accepting the principles of equality and neutrality, the makers of the constitution have severely limited the scope for state discrimination or even differentiation between churches, but they did not foreclose on it completely. In defining relevant roles, the Constitutional Court had a particularly prominent role. According to the Court's decision ... the state should be neutral, but the differential treatment of churches, taking into account social and historical reality, need not be a breach of neutrality. (Enyedi, 2003, p. 161)

This fact has allowed the four historical churches privileged access to state resources, and the concept of active neutrality, whereby the state has a 'duty to provide the churches with the means ... necessary for their operation' (Enyedi, 2003, p. 161) has meant that state funding for churches was permitted from 1990 to 1997, and replaced in 1998 with a voluntary church tax system whereby taxpayers can contribute up to one per cent of their income tax contribution to the registered religious organisation of their choice, with registration contingent on length of period in existence, period of registration in Hungary and taxpayer demand criteria (Schanda, 2003, p. 345; Enyedi, 2003, p. 170).

Furthermore, in spite of self-imposed restrictions on political participation by clergy (Catholic clergy are entirely forbidden to hold political office, and Lutherans must suspend their clerical duties for the period of political office), churches have become involved in political campaigning by issuing guidance for voters to consider when weighing up how to vote (Enyedi, 2003, p. 165), and close links have developed between some Calvinist clergy and right-wing political parties (Enyedi, 2003, p. 164). The churches have also been active in some political campaigns on issues of public morality, for example concerning reciprocal rights for ethnic Hungarians in neighbouring Romania and vice-versa in 2001 (Enyedi, 2003, p. 165). There has also, as in Poland, been an agenda shift to the right within the mainstream political parties in which appealing to a perceived religious nationalist constituency has been a significant factor (Enyedi, 2003, p. 168; Fras, 2007). Interestingly too, Hungary had (as of 1991) a rather high proportion of the population agreeing with the statement 'It would be better for the country if more people holding religious beliefs held public office', at 27 per cent (compared with 18 per cent in Britain and 39 per cent in the USA (Froese, 2001, p. 264); though by 1999 this had dropped to 23.3 per cent (Survey, 2007). However, Hungary also had a rather high proportion of people in the early 1990s believing that the churches should speak out on various aspects of public life (Froese, 2001, p. 264).

If we consider Hungary in terms of levels of political secularisation, then, it seems that the main areas of religious influence are at the level of agenda and discourse, and that this has been exercised via public opinion and 'normal' (in western democratic terms) channels of lobbying, rather than through a direct relationship between church and state, as in Poland or Romania. The key variable here would seem to be religious plurality: Hungary simply lacks a dominant church which is able to intervene in politics in the manner of the PRCC or the ROC, and hence the opportunities for direct policy influence are limited, in spite of growing links between churches and some political parties. The Hungarian Constitution exemplifies the European model of a state-regulated market in religion, with special privileges accorded to the large historical institutions. While these 'big players' are recognised by the state and funded through a state-administered mechanism, their roles are also circumscribed, and the levels of trust in the churches (more than 50 per cent of the sample in 1999 had 'not much' or 'no' trust in the churches (Survey, 2007)) suggest there is little chance of increased political mobilisation at national level. On the other hand the high levels of support for the church to have a voice in public affairs found in the early 1990s suggest that the churches may have an opportunity to play an influential role as public voices in civil society, along the lines envisaged by Casanova (1994).

Conclusion

What may be concluded from the evidence presented here? One striking finding from the country studies is that in each society and on each of the levels of political secularisation delineated by Moyser (1991) religious influence increased between 1989 and 2007. This is in spite of accelerating modernisation, brought about in part by EU enlargement, and integration into EU institutions, many of which have a markedly secular character. Of course some increase in the public presence of religion might be expected after decades of religiously repressive socialist rule; but it is also striking how effectively religious institutions in these societies have adapted to changing social and political conditions in order to maximise their interests, in spite of some decline in religious vitality and public support (in Poland and Hungary). These latter cases demonstrate that it is possible to increase public religious activity (re-publicisation) even when religious observance is in decline, which suggests that religious mobilisation at a public level and religious vitality at a private level operate with considerable autonomy. This in turn suggests that any model of religious change and its articulation with the politics of contemporary societies needs to be subtle enough to detect and account for these apparently contradictory trends.

In this context it is notable that there is some evidence in Eastern Europe of new configurations of relationships between religion, politics and increasingly deregulated media, enabling an increased circulation of religious symbols and discourse in the public sphere, parallel to that found by Meyer and Moors (2006) in postcolonial contexts. Such evidence suggests that, while data on religious vitality and public support for religious mobilisation show contradictory trends rather than any overall movement towards secularisation or re-publicisation across Eastern Europe, secularisation theory's account of why these changes are occurring is inadequate, because structural factors are involved in producing re-publicisation, which cannot be reduced to the management of cultural transition or cultural defence. Rather, what is needed is a theory which sees structural change as a second-order factor creating possibilities in a cultural field theorised as much more autonomous than in secularisation theory, rather than seeing social differentiation as the immediate cause of changes in the religious sphere. As the Eastern European cases show, such possibilities can be realised in the direction of re-publicisation as much as of secularisation, even in the presence of a stabilising and regulating transnational influence like the EU, depending on the interaction between structural conditions and the 'struggle between contending groups with conflicting interests seeking to control social knowledge and institutions' (Smith, 2003, p. vii).

References

(a) Books, Articles and Papers

Ahonen, P. (2007) 'Ethnonationalism in the European east–west borderlands: *Weltanschauugen* in the European Union and Central and Eastern Europe', *Religion, State & Society*, 35, 1, pp. 5–41.

Alexandru, F. (2006) 'Church–state relations in post-communist Romania', *The Romanian Journal of Political Sciences*, 2, pp. 57–69.

Andreescu, G. (1998) 'International relations and Orthodoxy in Eastern and South-Eastern Europe', *International Studies* (Galaţi), 4, pp. 1–32.

Biskupi (2002) 'Biskupi polscy wobec integracji europejskiej' ('Polish bishops towards European integration'), *Tygodnik Powszechny Online*, 21 March, http://www.tygodnik.com.pl/numer/279606/biskupi1.html (last accessed 10 October 2008).

Brach-Czaina, J. (2003) 'Polska w cieniu kościoła' ('Poland in the shadow of the church'), *Rzeczpospolita*, 105, 7 May.

Bruce, S. (1998) *Conservative Protestant Politics* (Oxford, Oxford University Press).

Bruce, S. (1999) *Choice and Religion: a Critique of Rational Choice Theory* (Oxford, Oxford University Press).

Bruce, S. and Wallis, R. (1992) 'Secularization: the Orthodox model', in S. Bruce and R. Wallis (eds), *Religion and Modernization: Sociologists and Historians Debate the Secularization Thesis* (Oxford, Clarendon Press), pp. 8–30.

Burdziej, S. (2005) 'Religion and politics: religious values in the Polish public square since 1989', *Religion, State & Society*, 33, 2, pp. 165–74.

Casanova, J. (1994) *Public Religions in the Modern World* (Chicago, Chicago University Press).

Chaves, M. (1994) 'Secularization as declining religious authority', *Social Forces*, 72, 3, pp. 749–74.

Dempsey, J. (2006) 'Romania at EU's door, seeks church restitution', *International Herald Tribune*, 7 April.

Dunin, K. and Sierakowski, S. (2003) 'Jaki kościół, jaka lewica, dialog' ('What church, what left, what dialogue?'), *Rzeczpospolita*, 155 (5–6 July), p. A7.

Enyedi, Z. (2003) 'The contested politics of positive neutrality in Hungary', *West European Politics*, 26, 1 (January), pp. 157–76.

Evans, M. (1997) *Religious Liberty and International Law* (Cambridge, Cambridge University Press).

Fras, M. (2007) *Fourth Republic or Fourth Rome? Religion and Politics in Poland after the 2005 General Elections*, paper presented at the conference 'Life in Motion: Shifting Spaces, Transcending Times, Crossing Borders', Masaryk University, Brno, Czech Republic, 28 June, unpublished.

Froese, P. (2001) 'Hungary for religion: a supply-side interpretation of the Hungarian religious revival', *Journal for the Scientific Study of Religion*, 40, 2 (June), pp. 251–68.

Gautier, M. (1997) 'Church attendance and religious belief in postcommunist societies', *Journal for the Scientific Study of Religion*, 36, 2 (June), pp. 289–96.

Gautier, M. (1998) 'Church elites and the restoration of civil society in the communist societies of Central Europe', *Journal of Church and State*, 40, 2 (spring), pp. 289–318.

Gillet, O. (2001) *Religie şi nationalism: ideologia Bisericii Ortodoxe Române sub regimul comunist* (*Religion and Nationalism: the Ideology of the Romanian Orthodox Church under the Communist Regime*) (Bucharest, Compania).

Guran, P. (2006) 'Byzantine ecclesiology in a new member state of the European Union: the Romanian case', *The Romanian Journal of Political Sciences*, 6, 2, pp. 149–54.

Halman, L. and Draulans, V. (2006) 'How secular is Europe?', *British Journal of Sociology*, 57, 2, pp. 263–88.

Herbert, D. (2003) *Religion and Civil Society* (Aldershot, Ashgate).

Herbert, D. (2007) *Why Has Religion Gone Public Again? Towards a Theory of Religious Re-Publicisation*, paper presented at the symposium 'Religion and Spirituality in a Post-colonial Context', University of Kwazulu Natal, Pietermaritzberg, SA, 9 January, unpublished.

Integracja (2002) 'Integracja europejska wyzwaniem dla Kościoła w Polsce' ('European integration is a challenge for the Polish church'), *Katolicka agencja informacyjna*, http://ekai.pl/europa/?MID=3790 (last accessed 21 November 2008).

Jackowska, N. (2003) *Kościół katolicki w Polsce wobec integracji europejskiej* (*The Catholic Church in Poland and European Integration*) (Poznań/Gniezno, Instytut Zachodni/Prymasowskie Wydawnictwo Gaudentinum).

Janis, M., Kay, R. and Bradley, A. (eds) (1995) *European Human Rights Law Text and Materials* (Oxford, Oxford University Press).

Knotz, O. (2003) 'Concerns and hopes: Roman Catholics and the European Union', *The Polish Foreign Affairs Digest*, 3, 1, pp. 111–20.

Kohn, M. (2005) 'Poland's beacon for Europe', *Open Democracy*, http://www.opendemocracy.net/globalization-institutions_government/election_poland_2597.jsp (last accessed 17 February 2009).

Kościoły (n.d.) *Kościoły w Unii Europejskiej* (*Churches in the European Union*), http://www.opoka.org.pl/biblioteka/X/XU/kosciolwobecue.html (last accessed 21 November 2008).

Kubik, K. (1994) *The Power of Symbols Against the Symbols of Power: the Rise of Solidarity and the Fall of State Socialism in Poland* (Philadelphia, Pennsylvania University Press).

Lordache, R. (2003) 'Church and state in Romania', in S. Ferrari and W. Durham (eds), *Law and Religion in Post-Communist Europe* (Leuven, Peeters).

Mazowiecki, T. (2002) 'The Europe we want', *The Polish Foreign Affairs Digest*, 2, 4, pp. 13–29.

Meyer, B. and Moors, A. (eds) (2006) *Religion, the Media and the Public Sphere* (Bloomington, Indiana University Press).

Moyser, T. (1991) *Politics and Religion in the Modern World* (London, Routledge).

Muszyński, Abp. H. (2002) 'Abp Muszyński: nie "klerykalizujemy" konwentu lecz szukamy wspólnych wartości' ('Abp Muszyński: we are not "clericalising" the convent but looking for common values') (interview), 8 May, *Katolicka agencja informacyjna*, http://ekai.pl/europa/?MID=3944 (last accessed 21 November 2008).

Norris, P. and Inglehart, R. (eds) (2004) *Sacred and Secular: Religion and Politics Worldwide* (Cambridge, Cambridge University Press).

Osa, M. (1997) 'Creating solidarity: the religious foundations of the Polish social movement', *East European Politics and Societies*, 11, 2, pp. 339–65.

Pope (2003) 'Pope speaks of his own coming judgment day', *USAToday.com*, 19 May, http://www.usatoday.com/news/religion/2003-05-19-pope-judgement_x.htm (last accessed 10 October 2008).

Prymas (2001) 'Prymas: wstąpienie do Unii to konieczność' ('Primate: entering EU is a necessity'), *Katolicka Agencja Informacyjna*, 19 November, http://ekai.pl/serwis/?MID=1125 (last accessed 10 October 2008).

Radu, B. (2005) 'The Romanian Orthodox Church and European integration: a conflict of values?', *Studia Universitaris Babes-Bolyai*, June.

Rajagopal, A. (2001) *Politics after Television: Hindu Nationalism and the Reshaping of the Public in India* (Cambridge, Cambridge University Press).

Ramet, S. (2006) 'Thy will be done: the Catholic Church and politics in Poland since 1989', in T. Byrnes and P. Katzenstein (eds), *Religion in an Expanding Europe* (Cambridge, Cambridge University Press), pp. 117–47.

Richardson, J. (1999) 'New religions and religious freedom in Eastern and Central Europe, with a special focus on Hungary', in A. Sajo and S. Avineri (eds), *The Law of Religious Identity: Models for Post-Communism* (Alphen aan den Rijn, Kluver International Law).

Rogobete, S. (2005) 'Morality and tradition in postcommunist Orthodox lands: on the universality of human rights, with special reference to Romania', *Religion, State & Society*, 32, 3, pp. 275–97.

Rogobete, S. (2006) 'Some reflections on religion and multiculturalism in Romania: towards a reappraisal of the grammar of traditions', *Romanian Journal of Political Science*, 6, 2, pp. 35–55.

Romocea, C. (2007) *Religious Media in Romania: Pluralism or Monopoly?*, paper presented to the British Sociological Association Study Group, Oxford, April, unpublished.

Schanda, B. (2003) 'Religion and state in the candidate countries to the European Union – issues concerning religion and state in Hungary', *Sociology of Religion*, 64, 3 (fall), pp. 333–48.

Scott, J. and Marshall, G. (2005) 'Structural differentiation', in *A Dictionary of Sociology* (Oxford, Oxford University Press).

Słowo (2003) *Słowo biskupów polskich w sprawie wejścia Polski do Unii Europejskiej* (*The Polish Bishops' Word on Poland's EU Accession*) 2 May, http://www.opoka.org.pl/biblioteka/W/WE/kep/slowo_ue_02052003.html (last accessed 10 October 2008).

Smith, C. (ed.) (2003) *Power, Interests and Conflict in the Secularization of American Public Life* (Berkeley, University of California Press).

Stan, L. and Turcescu, L. (2000) 'The Romanian Orthodox Church and post-communist democratization', *Europe-Asia Studies*, 52, 8 (December), pp. 1467–88.

Survey (2007) *World Values Survey*, www.jdsurvey.net/bdasepjds/QuestionMarginals.jsp (last accessed 2 December 2007); data up to 2004 are available at www.worldvaluessurvey.org (last accessed 12 December 2007).

Tschannen, O. (1991) 'The secularization paradigm: a systematization', *Journal for the Scientific Study of Religion*, 30, 4, pp. 395–415.

Wallace, J. (2005) 'Challenges and opportunities facing religious freedom in the public square', *Brigham Young University Law Review*, 3, pp. 597–610.

Większość (2007) 'Większość Polaków: kościół ma zbyt duże wpływy' ('Majority of Poles: church has too much influence over politics', *Gazeta Wyborcza*, 20 February, www.gazetawyborcza.pl (last accessed 22 November 2007).

Wuthnow, R. (2000) 'How religious groups promote forgiving', *Journal for the Scientific Study of Religion*, 39, 2, pp. 125–39.

Żaryn, J. (2003) *Dzieje Kościoła katolickiego w Polsce 1944–1989* (*History of the Catholic Church in Poland 1944–1989*) (Warsaw, Neriton).

(b) Court Cases

Kokkinakis v Greece, Case No. 408, 25.5.1993, Serial A, No. 260-A, http://cmiskp.echr.coe.int/tkp197/portal.asp?sessionId=15545365&skin=hudoc-en&action=request (last accessed 5 November 2008).

Otto-Preminger-Institut v Austria, Case No. 474, 20.9.1994, Serial A, No. 295-A, http://cmiskp.echr.coe.int/tkp197/portal.asp?sessionId=15545417&skin=hudoc-en&action=request (last accessed 5 November 2008).

Cracks in a Façade of Unity: the French and Italian Christian Democrats and the Launch of the European Integration Process, 1945–1957

LINDA RISSO

Introduction

Christian Democracy is considered the initiator of the European integration process. The so-called 'Fathers of Europe' – Robert Schuman, Alcide De Gasperi and Konrad Adenauer – were indeed Catholics, and the Vatican was supportive of the project. Closer inspection reveals however remarkable differences in the reasons why, and the degree to which, each group supported or opposed the integration process. More often than not the official position of a political party was the result of an ongoing compromise between different opinions existing side by side within the same political group. Particularly in the case of Christian Democracy, historians have oversimplified the degree of unity within each party. Identified as the promoters of the integration process itself, their internal disagreements and the heterogeneous reasons behind their political action have not yet been examined in sufficient detail and their idealism has often been overestimated.[1] The French and Italian Christian Democratic parties provide a good case study with which to challenge the prevalent view that they stood solidly united behind the federalist project. By looking at the period between 1945 and the launch of the Common Market in 1957, this article examines their pragmatism and the fierce debate about the integration process, thus challenging the view that Christian Democracy was united behind the integration project.

Christian Democracy and European Integration

A well-researched examination of Western European Christian Democracy is particularly important because of the party family's political weight in the postwar years. By 1950, approximately two-fifths of the MPs of the six founding members of the European Economic Community were Christian Democrats and Christian Democratic was the largest single group in the Assembly of the Coal and Steel Community. Thanks to such a massive presence, Christian Democracy exerted significant political pressure and significantly influenced the direction that the integration process would take.[2]

European Christian Democratic parties supported the integration of Western Europe as a means of rebuilding the economies of their countries in the aftermath of the war, ensuring more stable political systems and overcoming nationalism. The Christian Democratic parties based their political programme on the radical view that western civilisation was embedded in Christian values and that it needed to be protected both from the seduction of modern lifestyles and from the even greater dangers of communism. With the beginning of the Cold War, communism became the European Christian Democrats' main enemy and as such it needed to be fought both at home and at the international level. It was argued that in order to stem the communist tide, the western governments should rebuild their economies, rearm and coordinate their defensive policies to respond to an imminent Soviet attack, and strengthen their relations with the USA. The Christian Democratic leaders believed that because of its economic and military strength the USA was the only country able to counterbalance the increasing power of the USSR and that it was therefore essential to the survival of Western Europe that the USA remained committed to the Old Continent.

The Christian Democratic parties rapidly developed an Atlanticist orthodoxy and became the staunchest supporters of the need to protect western civilisation through the creation of a strong military framework built around the economic and military capability of the USA. The American presence on the Continent was seen as essential for protecting national and international democracy, and for this reason, the US primacy in the Alliance was not only accepted but considered to be vital (Lundestad, 2003).

In France, the postwar federalist approach to European problems had its roots in the Catholic movement in favour of European unity pushed forward by Marc Sangnier between 1919 and 1932. Sangnier promoted collaboration with other Western European Christian-inspired political groups, such as Luigi Sturzo's Popular Party, as a means of resolving the problem of Franco-German rivalry. The so-called *Jeunes Equipes* (also called *groupes briandistes*) promoted federalism and transnational cooperation as a way of overcoming German isolationism and fascism (Delbreil, 1993a).[3] After the Second World War, such groups continued their cooperation in favour of a united Europe in the form of the *Nouvelles Equipes Internationales* (NEI), founded in March 1947. The NEI gathered together political parties of Christian inspiration, thus including for example the Protestant wing of the CDU-CSU (*Christlich Demokratische Union – Christlich-Soziale Union in Bayern*). The French Christian Democrats of the MRP (*Mouvement Républicain Populaire*) did not join as a group but on an individual basis in order not to compromise the party's non-confessional image in French politics. Although Sturzo had played a pivotal role in the interwar contacts among Catholic politicians, the new DC (*Democrazia Cristiana*) did not join immediately but followed the NEI's works from the outside.

During the first decade after the Second World War the NEI put forward a vision of a new, integrated Western Europe as elaborated during their interwar transnational cooperation. The NEI campaigned for the creation of a federal Europe, closely associated with the USA. There was a general consensus that transnational cooperation was the only way to control German recovery while at the same time protecting Western Europe from Soviet aggression and a communist takeover in general. Thus, the NEI supported the foundation of the Council of Europe and campaigned actively in favour of the European Coal and Steel Community and the European Defence Community in the early 1950s. Afterwards, they worked on the re-launch of Europe at Messina (Bacharan-Gressel, 1993). Although it is difficult to evaluate the actual significance of such contacts in shaping the postwar integration process, they played a prominent part in creating a network, in preparing the ground for a Franco-German rapprochement soon after the conflict and in sustaining the launch of the integration process.

The structure and performance of the Christian Democratic parties varied considerably from one country to another, but it can safely be said that Christian Democracy was essentially a post-Second World War phenomenon and partially filled the political void left by the fall of the Nazi and Fascist regimes. French Christian Democracy had its roots in the ideas of Lamennais and Lacordaire. After the limited success in the interwar period of the *Parti Démocratique Populaire* (PDP) and of Marc Sangnier's *Jeune République*, French political Catholicism opened a more successful phase with the foundation of the *Mouvement Républicain Populaire* (MRP) in 1944.[4] The MRP can be seen as the symbol of the Fourth Republic, just as the Radicals were of the Third. Between 1946 and 1958, the MRP never had fewer than 85 deputies in the National Assembly and at the first elections approximately one elector in four voted for them. The MRP took part in 23 out of the 27 governments of the Fourth Republic and supported all of them except the government led by Pierre Mendès-France.

The Italian *Democrazia Cristiana* (DC) was founded in September 1942, and only six years later it was confirmed to be the major government party, gaining 48.5 per cent of the votes and leading a coalition that would rule Italy for 50 years. The DC was strengthened by the support of numerous Catholic associations, such as Catholic Action, the *Coldiretti* and the CISL (*Confederazione Italiana Sindacati Lavoratori*), the Catholic trade union (Allum, 1990; Gambino, 1988; Scoppola, 1988; Orfei, 1976; Galli, 1993). Under the leadership of Alcide De Gasperi, the DC brought Italy into NATO and enthusiastically supported European integration.

Both the MRP and the DC were interclass parties and their heterogeneous composition allowed them to represent different social groups, from capitalist elites to Catholic peasants and workers. Their presence in all layers of society, coupled with support in every corner of both their countries, gave them a powerful political presence. Both parties were Christian-inspired political groups but, while the MRP refused to be a confessional party, the DC capitalised on its close ties with the Vatican. The DC exploited its collaboration with the clergy to maintain its presence in the south and strengthen it in the north-east. The overwhelming predominance of Catholicism in Italian society made the DC's definition of a 'confessional' party very narrow – thus excluding non-Catholics and nonbelievers. Conversely, the MRP rejected the definition of 'confessional' party and its founding manifesto called upon 'men and women from all social classes ... to create with us a truly new political party driven by the revolutionary spirit of the French people and to exclusively serve national grandeur', with no actual reference to their religious belief (as quoted in Béthouart, 2004, p. 86).

After the first postwar elections the DC emerged as the leading party within the governing coalition. The extreme right was of negligible political weight and this meant that the DC and their allies saw themselves as the only opponents of the Italian Communist Party. In France the MRP was equally anticommunist but carried only slightly more political weight than the Radicals, the Socialists and later the Gaullists. As shall be discussed, anticommunism was not the sole reason behind the MRP's European policies: while for the DC European integration was a means to bind the USA to Europe and to fight against communism, for the MRP it was primarily a tool to solve the Franco-German problem. Yet Europe was a source of division among French Catholics – particularly at the level of intellectuals and leaders – to an extent unknown in Italy, where the party leadership was overwhelmingly in favour of Atlanticism and Europeanism. The Gallic tradition meant that for some of those in the top echelons of French Catholicism, nationalism was an obstacle in the federalist project (Tranvouez, 1993). In both cases, the idealism behind the Europeanist effort of both parties should not be overestimated. The European question was omnipresent but it was also always instrumental: as a means to solve problems in home affairs, as an anticommunism weapon, or as a means to solve economic problems. The support of the DC and the MRP for Europe was pragmatically based on the knowledge that their electoral support was rooted in the middle classes and rural areas and that the main concerns of their electorate were anticommunism, economic reconstruction and the need to anchor the USA to Europe in an anti-Soviet alliance, as has been well demonstrated by the historical survey carried out by Jean-Claude Delbreil (1993b).

In the immediate postwar years the MRP was torn between nationalism and reconciliation. As a resistance party, it first capitalised on nationalism and supported the idea that France should be a world power and not a victim of the two blocs' competition. For the same reason, it supported the efforts to keep control over the colonial empire. However, the beginning of the Cold War and France's economic problems led the MRP to abandon nationalism and to move towards reconciliation with Germany. The same could also be said for the DC: as long as Alcide De Gasperi was prime minister, the DC was consistently supportive of Europe.[5] De Gasperi and his foreign minister, Carlo Sforza, endorsed the European integration process as a way to keep the USA committed to Europe and to rehabilitate the country politically on the international stage. As well as being aware that European integration could secure peace, De Gasperi also recognised the economic advantages it could bring to Italy. At that time the Italian economy was characterised by cheap labour costs, a weak currency and a lack of raw materials and technologies. A more integrated European economy could provide the Italian economy with huge benefits: contracts for raw materials, easier movement of the Italian unemployed throughout Europe, and a huge market for cheap Italian products. Thus national-oriented goals were certainly factors in Italy's enthusiastic support for the integration of Europe's economy. Unemployment, in particular, was one of De Gasperi's main concerns and, given the size of the problem, he saw emigration as the only solution.[6]

For these reasons Robert Schuman's proposal for a coal and steel pool was welcomed by both the MRP and the DC. In France, the European Coal and Steel Community (ECSC) was seen not only as a way to resolve the historical competition for the resources of the Saar and the Ruhr but also as a way to bind West Germany more tightly to Western Europe. Not surprisingly, therefore, the Schuman declaration was approved unanimously and greeted with a standing ovation at the MRP Congress in Nantes in 1950. In Italy, the government saw the ECSC as a way to allow the emigration of Italian unemployed to northern Europe, thus relieving pressure at home. The Christian Democratic parties' unanimous support for the ECSC was easily obtained. The second step towards further integration, however, was about to be much more problematic. In October 1950, the project for the formation of the European Defence Community (EDC) put the federalist credentials of the Christian Democratic parties to the test and highlighted the contradiction between nationally oriented goals and genuine federalist commitment.

The Christian Democrats and the European Army

The EDC debate influenced French politics in a way that had no equivalent in any other Western European country. Governments rose and fell because of the EDC issue, and the EDC Treaty was repeatedly amended by successive French governments (Risso, 2007). Pinay was officially defeated on a budget issue in December 1952 but in practice his fall was due to the fact that the MRP had grown tired of his delay with regard to the EDC project. In January 1953 René Mayer had to replace Schuman with Bidault at the Quai d'Orsay in order to get Gaullist support for his government, and when he openly supported the Paris Treaty he was overthrown by the Right after a debate on fiscal policy. In the governmental crisis that developed between May and June 1953, Mendès-France failed to be appointed prime minister because a minority of 37 MRP members refused to vote for him, on the grounds that he had not committed himself to the ratification of the EDC. Paradoxically, a few weeks later Laniel was appointed prime minister thanks to his vagueness with regard to the EDC (Rioux, 1987; Grosser, 1984).

The MRP has usually been depicted as the keenest advocate of the European army, and for this reason many historians have overlooked its fierce internal disagreements regarding the project.[7] In fact, behind its apparently unanimous support for the European army project a lively debate took place within the party. While Pierre-Henri Teitgen led the EDC partisans, Schuman's attitude towards the Treaty of Paris was rather negative, while Bidault reluctantly supported it as a military necessity, but still loathed the European Political Community because he regarded it as being too far-reaching. Finally, a minority led by André Monteil and Léon Hamon actively opposed the whole project.[8]

Pierre-Henry Teitgen, the party's president, led the fiercest supporters of the European army and the European Political Community. This group consisted mainly of anticommunists, who believed that the only way to fight communism was through political union. In October 1950 Teitgen explained that 'what we are proposing to Germany is not revived militarism, but Europe' (JO-AN, 25 November 1950, pp. 7203–08). A less enthusiastic, but still supportive, group was led by Robert Schuman and Alfred Coste-Floret, who were in favour of European integration but demanded that political and economic union take place before military integration (Schuman, 2000, p. 35). In his report to the MRP Congress of Lille in 1954, Etienne Borne explained that 'We regard the EDC as the most reasonable solution to the problem of European defence; nevertheless we favour it not as a primary objective, but as a means to the construction of a united Europe' (Irving, 1973, p. 180). The support of this group – which gathered together a large number of MRP deputies – for the EDC is an essential part of any explanation of their subsequent opposition to the Western European Union.

Despite his support for the EDC, Robert Schuman – who at the time was foreign minister – did not submit the treaty to the National Assembly for ratification immediately after it was signed. In fact, eight whole months elapsed between the signing of the treaty in May 1952 and its submission to the National Assembly on 30 January 1953 by his successor, Georges Bidault (Poidevin, 1986). Schuman's decision to postpone the ratification debate must be correctly contextualised. In May 1952 serious criticism of the European army project pervaded the French public and political parties, criticism that was reinforced by the signing of the Contractual Agreements, which replaced the Occupation Statute and granted West Germany national sovereignty, albeit within limits. Although only the Communists openly opposed the treaty, the first signs of dissent were visible among the Radicals and the Gaullists. Historians have suggested that a decisive governmental initiative supporting ratification would have overcome the still weak opposition, and that Schuman should have acted more promptly before the situation within the National Assembly degenerated to the point of rendering ratification impossible (Fauvet, 1956, pp. 28–29).[9] In the following months the criticism within the Socialist and Radical parties grew stronger and the Gaullists joined the Communists in their anti-EDC campaign. Compared to this, the opposition of May 1952 may seem trifling indeed, but in addition to the fact that Schuman could not predict such degeneration, he also knew that, since the EDC Treaty implied substantial constitutional amendments, it required the favourable vote of a strong majority. Indeed, it is probable that Schuman hoped to postpone the ratification debate until the disagreement within the Socialist Party was resolved and the highest degree of approval for the EDC was likely.

Other MRP members were not enthusiastic about the new direction undertaken by the integration process. Georges Bidault agreed with the general idea of a European army, but opposed its supranational implications and the Political Community in particular.[10] He feared that such ambitious projects would lead to the demise of the French Union and would reduce French influence in the Atlantic Alliance by removing the power that its overseas territories provided. Bidault also argued that the Saar question had to be settled before the Contractual Agreements and the EDC were ratified, because if German sovereignty was restored before the international status of the Saar was decided, Bonn would claim jurisdiction over the region (Soutou, 1993; Elgey, 1993, pp. 329–30; Bidault, 1954).

When appointed foreign minister in January 1953, Bidault stated that he would favour the ratification of the EDC only if certain conditions were met, such as attenuation of the supranational features of EDC, more clearly defined British involvement, and the possibility of France keeping control over a part of its national army, which would be used in the overseas territories. Bidault proposed the Additional Protocols (1953), through which he hoped to resolve the Assembly's main concerns (Protocoles, 1953).[11] The reasoning behind the Additional Protocols was the assumption that the ratification of the EDC Treaty required the support of a significant part of either the Socialists or the Gaullists; and, since supranationality failed to appeal to more than half of the Socialists, the only hope of ratifying the EDC was to appease the conservatives. In order to do so, it was imperative to persuade the Gaullists that the treaty did not excessively infringe national sovereignty. However, the foreign ministers of the Six opposed the French document, which they saw as an attempt to tailor the EDC to French needs, and refused to discuss them.[12]

Finally, there was a small group of outright opponents of the European army led by André Monteil in the National Assembly and by Léo Hamon in the Council of the Republic. Even though they supported a united Europe and fully endorsed the Political Community, they denounced German rearmament as premature, since it could jeopardise the development of the new West German democracy. They also accused the EDC of exacerbating the internal divisions of Europe while provoking the USSR (Irving, 1973, p. 175). Their main argument was that military union should be the last and not the first step towards European integration; to them, premature ratification of the EDC Treaty meant putting 'the cart before the horse' (L'Armée, 1952). The group was in favour of reopening negotiations with Moscow and believed that only if that failed should the Six proceed with the ratification of the EDC (André Monteil in JO-AN, 11 December 1952, p. 586).[13]

The Italian government wanted to be very sure that any step towards further integration did not alienate US sympathies. In February 1951 *Il Popolo*, the DC's newspaper, published a long interview with Paolo Emilio Taviani, a DC member who led the Italian delegation at the EDC conference. Taviani clarified the party's position: 'We admit European union only if it respects Atlantic solidarity. Europe is for us the second pillar of the Atlantic Union: the more solid it is, the more stable the transatlantic union will grow' (Inaugurata, 1951; see also Resoconto, 1951).[14]

When after the summer of 1951 Washington became supportive of the European army and pressed for a fast and successful end to the talks, the DC changed its attitude. Under the leadership of the newly appointed Ivan Matteo Lombardo, the Italian delegation became much more cooperative and De Gasperi's proposal of the Political Community marked the peak of Italian endeavour. The reasoning behind the Political Community proposal lay in De Gasperi's belief that since the integrated army was going to be created, it was vital not only to provide it with sufficient democratic control in order to ensure the correct deployment of European forces, but also to spell out the rights and duties of the new supranational authority and the member states. Quite apart from these considerations, however, De Gasperi clearly had in mind the benefits that the creation of the EPC could bring to Italy. In addition to the economic benefits linked to the ECSC, the integrated procurement policy envisaged in the EDC Treaty would allow Italian heavy industry to participate in the rearmament of Europe. Moreover, according to De Gasperi's proposal for a Political Community, the new supranational institution would encourage tighter economic integration, opening the market to cheap Italian products and workers.

Some of the Italian Christian Democrats, however, remained doubtful not only about allowing German rearmament but also about engaging in a major battle both inside and outside parliament with the Communist Party. Giovanni Gronchi and Giuseppe Dossetti, in particular, were critical of the government's domestic and foreign policies and opposed them both in parliament and at the party's congresses, to the great embarrassment of the party leadership, which was striving to convey the impression that the Christian Democrats stood solidly behind their professed Atlanticism and Europeanism. Gronchi and Dossetti headed two left-wing factions within the DC, and although their approaches to foreign policy differed slightly, they both agreed on the need to continue the dialogue with the Communists and Socialists, in order to promote a solid economic and social programme, and to open new diplomatic relations with the East.[15] Dossetti in particular criticised De Gasperi for the economic reforms his governments had passed, which he said undermined the working class, whose civil rights were gradually being eroded by legislation designed to protect the interests of the employers. As to foreign policy, Dossetti accused the government and the main leaders of the DC of exposing the country to dependence on the USA and possible conflict with the East.[16]

The Collapse of the European Dream

Between 1950 and 1954 the Christian Democrats shifted from confident support for European integration to a more cautious attitude. The changing nature of East–West relations after the death of Stalin in 1953 and the increasing fear that excessive supranationality might jeopardise the nation-state forced the Christian Democrats to slow their pace. In addition, the increasingly bleak electoral prospects led them to move the European issue to the back burner and to focus on problems at home. The rejection of the EDC by the National Assembly in August 1954 gave way to a hectic diplomatic exchange which led to the amendment of the Brussels Treaty of 1948, whereby Italy and West Germany entered the Brussels Treaty Organisation (renamed Western European Union, WEU), and consequently to West Germany obtaining full sovereignty and NATO membership (Risso, 2007).

After the rejection of the European army, the EDC supporters within the National Assembly formed a united front with the critics of German rearmament to oppose the WEU. The MRP lamented the limited political independence of the WEU and many Socialists and Radicals thought that Germany should not be rearmed under the EDC or under the WEU. The Communists provided the third pillar of the opposition front: insisting on the need to reply to the Soviet diplomatic notes, they pushed for the postponement of the ratification debate until after the Four Powers had met to discuss Moscow's proposals for a peaceful settlement of the German problem. After a lengthy and problematic ratification debate, the Paris Agreements were approved by the National Assembly at the end of December 1954 (JO-AN, 29 December 1954, pp. 6960–61). Everybody was relieved by the solution of a problem that had haunted European foreign and defence policies for five years, but the result was a compromise that did not fully satisfy anybody: not the anti-Germans; not the Europeanists, who saw the WEU as an imperfect copy of the EDC; not the Communists, who wanted a completely neutral Europe; and not the Gaullists, who criticised the excessive submission to NATO and the USA.

Despite Adenauer's appeals to his fellow Christian Democrats to vote for the treaty, 53 MRP members followed Georges Bidault, Maurice Schumann and Pierre-Henri Teitgen in voting against it. A dozen others abstained, and only a few voted for the treaty (JO-AN, 29 December 1954, pp. 6959–60). This division clearly stemmed from the trauma of the rejection of the European Defence Community. The failure of the EDC had been a severe blow for the MRP, which had committed its best men and great efforts to it. The MRP had ascribed the rejection of the EDC to Mendès-France, whom it accused of having sold the EDC for the Indochina settlement at Geneva (Gladwyn, 1972, p. 272; Mendès-France, 1954). It believed that in August 1954 the handful of votes necessary for the ratification of the EDC could have been brought in if Mendès-France had thrown the authority of the government against the motion, instead of disclaiming all responsibility for the project's failure. Evidence of the MRP's resentment is provided by the fact that in October 1954 almost the whole party refused to give a vote of confidence to the Mendès-France government and on 30 November they abstained from a vote on constitutional reform sponsored by Mendès-France. Quite apart from this resentment, there were more factual reasons behind the MRP's opposition to the new WEU. Although the party recognised the importance of British commitment, it warned the Assembly that 'behind the appearance of a European organisation, the new agreements will set up a German army, British control and an American command' without supranational guarantees (Teitgen in JO-AN, 22 December 1954, p. 6749). The lack of supranational control over armament production was the party's main concern: it believed that the lack of any 'spirit of community' meant that Germany would be rearmed without the necessary safeguards. The party also criticised the fact that the WEU was under the SACEUR (Supreme Allied Commander Europe) command, which transformed the Brussels organisation into a merely operational extension of NATO (De Menthon, 1954; Schuman, 1954;

Simmonnet, 1954). Finally, the MRP had supported the EDC because it considered it a step towards a closer union, but it saw the WEU as a step backwards (Massigli, 1978, p. 481). For the MRP the defeat of the European army implied the triumph of nationalism over supranationalism, and the party's hope of becoming the leader of European Christian Democracy and of European integration was shattered.

In Italy, the signing of the Paris Agreements had been welcomed by the majority of the political forces, and a wide coalition of parties expressed its support for the WEU. Besides the governing coalition, which included the DC and the Republicans, Liberals and Social Democrats, the Right expressed its intention of voting in favour of the WEU as well. Appeased by the solution to the problem of Trieste, the Right was open to a closer relationship with the Western Allies and, although a deep dislike for British leadership of the WEU had initially hampered their support, both the Monarchists (PNM) and the Neo-Fascists (MSI) eventually supported the new military organisation. The Communists and the Socialists were thus left to fight alone against the WEU. The DC was solidly in favour of the Paris Agreements, although for some of its members the parliamentary debate was an occasion to regret the defeat of the EDC and criticise the lack of supranationality under the WEU. Since the death of Alcide De Gasperi, however, the party had been undergoing a fierce internal conflict which left room for more independent voices, some of which spoke in parliament against the WEU. Ugo Bartesaghi and Mario Melloni, in particular, expressed their disagreement with the government's foreign policy. Bartesaghi expressed – in a private capacity – his doubts about the wisdom of ratifying a military alliance before the international position of Germany and relations with Moscow were settled (AP-CD, 15 December 1954, pp. 15235–42). On similar lines, Mario Melloni proposed a motion delaying the debate for six months, a suggestion too close to the Italian Communists' position to please the DC leadership, which a few days later suspended and eventually expelled – the two deputies, a measure very rarely taken by the Christian Democrats (Bartesaghi, 1954).[17] On 23 December the Paris Agreements were ratified by the Italian parliament by 335 votes to 215, the largest majority the Scelba government ever received on a foreign policy vote. Only the Socialists and Communists voted against ratification, along with five other MPs, who were probably Christian Democratic supporters of Melloni and Bartesaghi, taking advantage of the secret ballot to rebel against official party policy.[18] Overall, however, the DC approved the WEU, and criticism was contained.

Overall, it is nevertheless clear that European Christian Democracy burned its fingers on the European Defence Community and decided to abandon such ambitious projects in the future and to opt for a more cautious approach. Functionalism gradually pushed aside the creation of an all-embracing community and gave way to a more pragmatic strategy. As Gehler and Kaiser (2001) have demonstrated, European Christian Democracy thought of the creation of an integrated economic space before the end of the EDC but it was only after the vote of August 1954 that they pressed ahead with the project. The Christian Democrats pressed for further specialised communities in sectors such as agriculture and transport. On 23 April 1955, *Forces Nouvelles* warned that 'The first task is to re-establish a European atmosphere in order to revive confidence which has been shaken by the defeat of the EDC. Concrete and precise initiatives, which are immediately realizable, must restore coherence and authority to the construction of Europe' (quoted in Irving, 1973, p. 189).

Only after the Suez crisis did the MRP express moderate enthusiasm for the possibility of launching a common market as envisaged at Messina. At the Montrouge Congress of 1956 the MRP affirmed its support for the relaunch of the European idea in the form of economic integration. Robert Schuman explained in the National Assembly that without continuous pressure towards integration West Germany would relapse into neutralism and turn to the East. Teitgen presented the Common Market as a way to help Europe compete with the USA and the USSR (JO-AN, 3 July 1957, pp. 3176–79 and 3183–85). Both in January 1957, when the Common Market was discussed in the National Assembly, and during the ratification debate in July 1957, all the MRP MPs voted in favour of economic integration, although the most federalist members did not miss the opportunity to complain about the lack of democratic control and the weak political structure of the new institution (JO-AN, 22 January 1957, p. 239; JO-AN, 9 July 1957, p. 3495). In their view, the Council of Ministers was too powerful and the extent of the use of the veto too great, and furthermore the lack of direct elections made the whole structure undemocratic. The Common Market was 'like a heavy lorry with a two-horse engine' (JO-AN, 15 January 1957, p. 11).

In Italy, the fall of the EDC coincided with the death of Alcide De Gasperi in August 1954. Although his successor, Giuseppe Pella, reconfirmed that the Atlantic Pact and European integration remained the cornerstones of Italian foreign policy, he also affirmed 'Italian sovereign rights over Trieste' and, if he did not revise the DC's pro-European programme, he did speak of a more 'moderate Europeanism' (La conferenza, 1953; Concorde, 1953; Canavero, 1990). Pella's improvident attempt to get control over Trieste by sending the army over the border caused the premature fall of his government. Amintore Fanfani was appointed prime minister but stayed in power for only 12 days before Mario Scelba replaced him.[19] From the death of De Gasperi onwards, the DC evolved into a party divided into increasingly organised factions. Each of these factions revolved around one or more leaders, was soundly based in one region and demanded its share of power (Galli, 1993; Pasquino, 1980). The foundation of established factions led to the disintegration of the party's monolithic structure and to the creation of a plurality of cultural and political groups, a tendency which would be further exacerbated by the Second Vatican Council.[20]

French and Italian Christian Democracy: Similarities and Differences

The comparative examination of how French and Italian Christian Democratic support for integration evolved between 1950 and 1957 highlights some interesting similarities between the two parties as well as some significant differences. Pragmatism was paramount for both parties; their European policies were instrumental in achieving a strong economy and in fighting against communism. In the case of France, there was also the need to normalise Franco-German relations and in Italy there was the desire to achieve political rehabilitation and to solve the country's economic problems. Both parties needed to respond to the interests and anxieties of their core middle class and rural electorate and there was little room for idealism.

By anchoring the USA to Western Europe in an anticommunist and anti-Soviet alliance and by relaunching the economy, the integration process seemed to offer the right answer to some of the most urgent problems. By taking the lead, the French government – and the MRP with them – could also claim that France was still a great power, thus downplaying the effects that the problems in the colonies could have on France's role on the international stage. The DC was eager to find a solution to the endemic unemployment that was crippling the Italian economy, and the ECSC as well as the European Economic Community (EEC) offered the ideal solution. Both parties, however, witnessed an intense internal debate with members expressing doubts about how a new integrated Europe could make the division of Europe permanent and how the creation of supranational institutions might jeopardise the nation-state. The opponents of the project expressed their concerns at the parties' congresses and very rarely did they challenge the parties' leaderships in parliament. Even when they dared to do so, they eventually voted in support of their party's policy. In the very few cases in which they did refuse to do so, they were isolated within the party and eventually forced to leave, as in the case of Dossetti.

Between 1950 and 1957 both countries had highly unstable political systems which, because of the delicate balance of their governmental coalitions, were highly sensitive to external influence as well as to the equilibrium of power within their parliaments.[21] Yet while in France governmental crises had a direct impact on the composition of the governmental majority and its political programme, in Italy this was not so much the case. In Paris the fall of all governments was followed by complicated discussions and attempts to find a compromise between the almost equal weights of the major parties; in Italy the centrality of the Christian Democrats reduced the effect of political crises to a redistribution of ministries among the party members. The instability in the case of the French was compounded by the fact that the governing parties had little in common besides wanting to be part of the government, and disagreement on both foreign and domestic policies was rife. Each prime minister considered his appointment as a chance to correct the current state of affairs and adapt the government's policy to his party's – if not his personal – programme, and this was true for the MRP members too as the Schuman – Bidault competition demonstrates. However, rapid government turnover often prevented them from implementing significant changes to France's European policy, and the result was a confused 'wait-and-see' attitude. The rejection of the EDC crushed the MRP's dream of leading the construction of a united Europe and it was only after the Suez crisis that it turned back to Europe.

In Italy, the governmental composition was stable and there was little talk of including new parties, or at least such talk did not go beyond an indirect flirtation on the part of some Christian Democrats with the Right in order to obtain their external support.[22] During the first legislature (1948–1953) – and to a certain degree during the second (1953–1958) as well – the large consensus of the Christian Democrats dwarfed their allies. Had these allies decided to leave the governing coalition, they would have been crushed between the Christian Democrats and the Communists, with little hope of influencing the government at all. Because of the exclusion of the Communists from the government and the absence of an alternative to the DC, the Italian government remained firmly based on the centrality of the DC and this meant that even within the party there was little debate about issues of foreign policy. Between 1948 and 1953 the central role of Alcide De Gasperi provided a further element of stability. Thanks to his prewar experience and his personal charisma, De Gasperi managed to control the growing factionalism of his party and his leadership role in European affairs was undisputed. With his electoral defeat, internal divisions broke out and a fierce battle for the leadership took place, disrupting Italian support for European integration. Although De Gasperi's successors were more cautious, they continued to support further integration with little change. Except for very few cases, notably those of Ugo Bartesaghi and Mario Melloni, the party continued in its consistent support of the integration of Western Europe.

Conclusion

In the postwar years, Christian Democratic Europeanism was more than the simple sum of nationally oriented goals and anticommunism; it was rooted in the interwar idealism and in the belief that Western Europe shared common Christian values and that such values needed to be protected and supported. The interwar cooperation, developed through networks like the NEI, produced a new transnational debate about the future of Europe and brought together political leaders of different countries who shared similar values and ideas. Such contacts developed into mutual trust and friendship and created fertile ground for a new form of Europeanism and close collaboration. In the aftermath of the Second World War such ties grew stronger and contributed to the transnational Christian Democratic support for the integration process.

After the war, in both France and Italy, anticommunism became a crucial element in holding the governing coalitions together, but anticommunism alone does not fully account for the Christian Democratic Europeanism. The electoral support for the DC and the MRP was rooted in the middle classes and rural areas, whose main concerns included economic reconstruction and modernisation. For the party leadership of the MRP and the DC, European integration was also a means to tighten Europe's ties with the USA, which was seen as a crucial element for the economic relaunch and political stabilisation of Western Europe and for the organisation of an effective defence system across the Atlantic. In addition, the DC looked at an economically integrated Europe as a way to solve Italy's economic problems and for the MRP it was primarily a tool to stabilise Franco-German relations. Because of the heterogeneous nature of Christian Democratic Europeanism, a different degree of support was present within each party and party factions often disagreed on what Europeanism should entail and what direction the parties' support for economic and political integration should take. Political parties witnessed fierce debates, disciplinary measures and expulsions that tore the parties apart behind a façade of unity.

Acknowledgment

I would like to thank Dr Martin Conway (Balliol College, Oxford) for his help in revising this article.

Notes

1 While the work by Wolfram Kaiser (2007) offers an excellent analysis of the delicate balance between Christian Democratic idealism and pragmatism, the parties' internal disagreements and debates are not studied in depth.
2 For an introduction to Christian Democracy and the EEC/European Union, see Kselman and Buttigieg (2003), Gehler *et al.* (2001), Lamberts (1997), Buchanan and Conway (1996), Hanley (1994), Fogarty (1957) and Kaiser (2007).
3 On the contacts among European Catholic politicians in the interwar period, see Gehler *et al.* (2001), Kaiser (2000) and Papini (1995).
4 For the origins of French Christian Democracy, see the old but still valuable book by Irving (1973); for the MRP foreign policy and particularly its European commitment, see Berstein *et al.* (1993), Zéraffa-Dray (1993) and Letamendia (1996).
5 De Gasperi was prime minister from December 1945 to July 1953 and also acted as foreign minister between 1951 and 1953.
6 A further example is provided by the meeting of Santa Margherita Ligure of February 1951, which saw Pleven and Schuman, De Gasperi and Sforza discussing the project of a Franco-Italian customs union. The meeting lasted three days, after which De Gasperi successfully obtained French authorisation to allow Italian immigration (Résolutions, 1950).

7 See Irving (1973) and Rioux (1987). Letamendia even speaks of a 'great unity and strong will' of the party (see Letamendia, 1993, p. 103). The alleged unity of the MRP behind the EDC has been reconfirmed by Bruno Béthouart (2004).
8 There were four debates regarding the European army: in October 1950, when René Pleven introduced his project to the National Assembly, two MRP members voted against it and one abstained (JO-AN, 25 October 1950, pp. 7234–44); in February 1952 the number of dissenting members grew to seven with six votes against and one abstention (JO-AN, 19 February 1952, pp. 787–804); in November 1953 it held steady at five, with three votes against and two abstentions (JO-AN, 27 November 1953, pp. 5639–40); and finally, in August 1954, when the Paris Treaty was rejected, three Christian Democrats voted against the EDC and three abstained (JO-AN, 30 August 1954, pp. 4473–74).
9 Irving (1973, pp. 178–79) argues that the delay was due to Schuman's lack of political conviction regarding the feasibility of the EDC.
10 Georges-Henri Soutou (1993) maintains that Bidault's support for European integration was stronger than is usually believed.
11 Soutou retraces the origins of the Additional Protocols back to the negotiations Bidault initiated to gain the Gaullist support in the summer of 1952, when he demanded British commitment and limited supranationality (Soutou, 1993, pp. 218–19).
12 The French Protocols were discussed at the Anglo-French ministerial meeting of February 1953 (French, 1953).
13 The fear that the creation of the EDC might provoke a Russian attack was discussed at the MRP Congress in Paris of October 1953 (see Herriot, 1952).
14 The archives of the Istituto Luigi Sturzo in Rome keep the minutes of the DC congresses as well as the diaries of Francesco Bartolotta, who was De Gasperi's personal secretary in the period 1950–53. For the party's internal debate on foreign policy between September 1949 and August 1950, see Resoconto (1950).
15 In 1949 both Gronchi and Dossetti had criticised the ratification of NATO, and although they eventually voted for it, they often condemned Italy's subordination to Washington and the anticommunist hatred within the DC.
16 Both Dossetti and Gronchi expressed their criticism at the party meeting of July 1951 (see Verbali, 1951). A few months later, in October 1951, Dossetti left the DC and politics altogether and entered a monastery. When in 1955 Gronchi was appointed president of the Republic, he reiterated his idea that Italy should act as mediator between the USA and the USSR.
17 After his expulsion Melloni became a columnist of *L'Unità* under the name of Fortebraccio and eventually joined the *Partito Comunista Italiano* (PCI). In July 1955 other DC members (Chiarante, Magri and Zapulli) were expelled for supporting Melloni and Bartesaghi.
18 This phenomenon, quite common in the Italian parliament, was known as *franchi tiratori*.
19 Pella was prime minister from 17 August 1953 to 5 January 1954, Fanfani from 18 to 30 January 1954, and Scelba from 10 February 1954 to 22 June 1955.
20 Allum (1990) and Meneguzzi Rostagni (1990, 1992) offer a detailed analysis of the impact of the Second Vatican Council on the DC.
21 Between January 1950 and June 1955 Italy had six governments, four of which were led by De Gasperi. In the same period, France had nine governments.
22 The major change in the composition of the governing coalition took place in December 1963, when the Socialist Party joined the government.

References

Allum, P. (1990) 'Uniformity undone: aspects of Catholic culture in postwar Italy', in Z. Baransky and R. Lumley (eds), *Culture and Politics in Postwar Italy: Essays on Mass and Popular Culture* (Basingstoke, Macmillan), pp. 79–96.

AP-CD (various dates) *Atti Parlamentari, Camera dei Deputati: Discussioni: Seconda legislatura, 1953–1958* (Rome, Tipografia della Camera dei Deputati).

Bacharan-Gressel, N. (1993) 'Les organisations et les associations pro-européennes', in S. Berstein, J. M. Mayeur and P. Milza (eds), *Le MRP et la construction européenne* (Brussels, Editions Complexe), pp. 38–50.

Bartesaghi (1954) 'Gli on. Bartesaghi e Melloni esclusi dalla Democrazia Cristiana', *Il Corriere della Sera*, 18 December.

Berstein, S., Mayeur, J. M. and Milza P. (eds) (1993) *Le MRP et la construction européenne* (Brussels, Editions Complexe).

Béthouart, B. (2004) 'Entry of the Catholics into the Republic: The Mouvement Républicain Populaire in France', in M. Gehler, W. Kaiser and H. Wohnout (eds), *Christian Democracy in 20th Century Europe* (Vienna, Böhlau), pp. 85–100.

Bidault (1954) 'M. Bidault: Il faut s'ôter de l'esprit la notion d'ennemi héréditaire', *Le Monde*, 20 March.

Buchanan, T. and Conway, M. (eds) (1996) *Political Catholicism in Europe, 1914–1965* (Oxford, Clarendon Press).

Canavero, A. (1990) 'La politica estera di un ministro degli interni: Scelba, Piccioni e Martino e la politica estera italiana', *Storia delle Relazioni Internazionali*, 1, pp. 63–97.

Concorde (1953) 'Concorde e solenne affermazione alla Camera del diritto dell'Italia sul Territorio Libero di Trieste', *Il Corriere della Sera*, 7 October.

Delbreil, J. C. (1993a) 'Les démocrates d'inspiration chrétienne et les problèmes européennes dans l'entre-deux-guerres', in S. Berstein, J. M. Mayeur and P. Milza (eds), *Le MRP et la construction européenne* (Brussels, Editions Complexe), pp. 15–39.

Delbreil, J. C. (1993b) 'Le MRP et la construction européenne: résultats, interprétations et conclusions d'une enquête écrite et orale', in S. Berstein, J. M. Mayeur and P. Milza (eds), *Le MRP et la construction européenne* (Brussels, Editions Complexe), pp. 330–45.

De Menthon (1954) 'M. De Menthon: le MRP a toujours combattu la reconstitution de l'armée nationale allemande', *Le Monde*, 25 December.

Elgey, G. (1993) *Histoire de la IVe République: la République des illusions (1945–1951)* (2 vols) (Paris, Fayard).

Fauvet, J. (1956) 'Naissance et mort d'un traité: du plan Pleven au vote du 30 décembre 1954', in R. Aron and D. Lerner (eds), *La Querelle de la CED: essais d'analyse sociologique* (*Cahiers de la Fondation Nationale des Sciences Politiques*, 80), pp. 23–57.

Fogarty, M. (1957) *Christian Democracy in Europe, 1820–1953* (Notre Dame, University of Notre Dame Press).

French (1953) 'French fears of Germany', *The Times*, 11 February.

Galli, G. (1993) *Mezzo secolo di DC* (Milan, Rizzoli).

Gambino, A. (1988) *Storia del dopoguerra: dalla liberazione al potere DC* (Bari-Rome, Laterza).

Gehler, M., Kaiser, W. and Wohnout, H. (eds) (2001) *Christian Democracy in 20th Century Europe* (Vienna, Böhlau).

Gehler, M. and Kaiser, W. (2001) 'Trasnationalism and early European integration: the *Nouvelles Equipes Internationales* and the Geneva Circle, 1947–1957', *The Historical Journal*, 44, 3, pp. 773–98.

Gladwyn, Lord (1972) *The Memoirs of Lord Gladwyn* (London, Weidenfeld & Nicolson).

Grosser, A. (1984) *Affaires extérieures: la politique de la France, 1944–1984* (Paris, Flammarion).

Hanley, D. (ed.) (1994) *Christian Democracy in Europe: a Comparative Perspective* (New York, Pintler Publishers).

Herriot (1952) '"MM. Herriot et Daladier ont raison: la négociation avec l'Est est encore possible", affirme Denis, député du MRP', *Le Monde*, 25 October.

Inaugurata (1951) 'Inaugurata la conferenza per un esercito europeo', *Il Popolo*, 16 February.

Irving, R. E. M. (1973) *Christian Democracy in France* (London, George Allen & Unwin).

JO-AN (various dates) *Journal Officiel de la République Française, Débats parlementaires, Assemblée Nationale, 1949–1955* (Paris, Direction des Journaux Officiels).

Kaiser, W. (2000) 'Co-operation of European Catholic politicians in exile in Britain and the United States during World War II', *Journal of Contemporary History*, 35, pp. 439–65.

Kaiser, W. (2007) *Christian Democracy and the Origins of European Union* (Cambridge, Cambridge University Press).
Kselman, T. A. and Buttigieg, J. A. (2003) *European Christian Democracy: Historical Legacies and Comparative Perspectives* (Notre Dame, University of Notre Dame Press).
La conferenza (1953) 'La conferenza della "Piccola Europa" si apre stamani a Villa Aldobrandini', *Il Corriere della Sera*, 22 September.
L'Armée (1952) 'L'Armée Européenne serait-elle un risque pour la paix?', *Le Monde*, 29 January.
Lamberts, E. (ed.) (1997) *Christian Democracy in the European Union, 1945–1995: Proceedings of the Leuven Colloquium,* 15–18 November 1995 (Leuven, Leuven University Press).
Letamendia, P. (1993) 'La place des problèmes européens dans la vie interne du parti sous la IVe République', in S. Berstein, J. M. Mayeur and P. Milza (eds), *Le MRP et la construction européenne* (Brussels, Editions Complexe).
Letamendia, P. (1996) *Le Mouvement Républicain Populaire: histoire d'un grand parti français* (Paris, Beauchesne).
Lundestad, G. (2003) *The United States and Western Europe since 1945: from 'Empire' by Invitation to Transatlantic Drift* (Oxford, Oxford University Press).
Massigli, R. (1978) *Une comédie des erreurs, 1943–1956* (Paris, Plon).
Mendès-France (1954) 'M. Mendès-France et le Mouvement Républicain Populaire', *Le Monde*, 23 July.
Meneguzzi Rostagni, C. (1990) 'La Santa Sede e la politica estera italiana (1945–1949)', in E. Di Nolfo, R. H. Rainero and B. Vigezzi (eds), L'*Italia e la politica di potenza in Europa, 1945–1950* (Settimo Milanese, Marzorati), pp. 169–94.
Meneguzzi Rostagni, C. (1992) 'Il Vaticano e la costruzione europea (1948–1957)', in E. Di Nolfo, R. H. Rainero and B. Vigezzi (eds), L'*Italia e la politica di potenza in Europa, 1945–1950* (Settimo Milanese, Marzorati), pp. 143–72.
Orfei, R. (1976) L'*occupazione del potere* (Milan, Longanesi).
Pasquino, G. (1980) 'Italian Christian Democracy: a party for all seasons', in P. Lange and S. Tarrow (eds), *Italy in Transition* (London, Cass), pp. 88–109.
Papini, R. (1995) *Il coraggio della democrazia: Sturzo e l'internazionale popolare tra le due guerre* (Rome, Edizioni Studium).
Poidevin, R. (1986) *Robert Schuman: homme d'état, 1886–1963* (Paris, Imprimerie Nationale).
Protocoles (1953) *Protocoles additionnels au Traité instituant la Communauté Européenne de Défense* (Paris, Ministère des Affaires Etrangères, Centre d'Information et Presse).
Resoconto (1950) *Resoconto della seduta del Consiglio Nazionale della DC*, Archivio Storico dell'Istituto Luigi Sturzo, Via delle Coppelle 35, Rome, Fondo Bartolotta, 14 October 1950, vol. XVI, pp. 1551–54.
Resoconto (1951) *Resoconto della riunione del gruppo parlamentare della DC al Senato*, Archivio Storico dell'Istituto Luigi Sturzo, Via delle Coppelle 35, Rome, Fondo Bartolotta, 10 January 1951, vol. I, pp. 10bis–10quater.
Résolutions (1950) 'Les résolutions franco-italiennes et les entretiens de Santa Margherita', *L'Année Politique*, pp. 54–55.
Rioux, J. P. (1987) *The Fourth Republic 1944–1958* (Cambridge, Cambridge University Press).
Risso, L. (2007) *Divided We Stand: the French and Italian Political Parties and the Rearmament of West Germany, 1949–1955* (Newcastle-upon-Tyne, Cambridge Scholars Publishing).
Schuman (1954) 'M. Schuman: il faut s'orienter vers une communauté fondée sur la confiance', *Le Figaro*, 9 October.
Schuman, R. (2000) *Pour l'Europe* (Genève, Nagel).
Scoppola, P. (1988) *La proposta politica di De Gasperi* (Bologna, Il Mulino).
Simmonnet (1954) 'M. Simmonnet: lier l'Allemagne à l'Occident par des solutions politiques', *Le Figaro*, 9 October.
Soutou, G. H. (1993) 'Georges Bidault et la construction européenne 1944–1954', in S. Berstein, J. M. Mayeur and P. Milza (eds), *Le MRP et la construction européenne* (Brussels, Editions Complexe), pp. 197–228.

Tranvouez, T. (1993) 'Europe, Chrétienté et Catholiques français: débats en marge du MRP', in S. Berstein, J. M. Mayeur and P. Milza (eds), *Le MRP et la construction européenne* (Brussels, Editions Complexe), pp. 87–102.

Verbali (1951) *Verbali del Consiglio Nazionale della DC*, Archivio Storico dell'Istituto Luigi Sturzo, Via delle Coppelle 35, Rome, Fondo Democrazia Cristiana, 2–3 July 1951, box 12, f. 23–24.

Zéraffa-Dray, D. (1993) 'Le Mouvement Républicain Populaire et la construction de l'Europe', in G. Trausch (ed.), *Die Europäische Integration vom Schuman-Plan bis zu den Verträgen von Rom* (Baden-Baden, Nomos), pp. 231–40.

Alcide De Gasperi and Antonio Messineo: a Spiritual Idea of Politics and a Pragmatic Idea of Religion?

GIULIO VENNERI & PAOLO O. FERRARA

Introduction

In the aftermath of the Second World War, Italy was a complex mosaic of interconnected problems. After almost two years of nazi occupation the northern part of the country was liberated, but political activities were only slowing restarting. The post-fascist government was striving – with more failures than successes – to regain credibility. Although its immediate aim was to improve its international reputation, most of its initiatives seemed bridled by a sense of political impotence. Socio-economic stabilisation was hard to achieve, as a result of social and geographical divisions that had been exacerbated during wartime. Witnessing this unstable environment, Pope Pius XII called for direct action: all those holding political, intellectual and social positions should participate in the reconstruction of the country. Any doctrinal elaboration could not remain in a 'pure form'; concrete problems had to be considered, and theoretical discourses strengthened with issues in the real world. Simultaneously, spiritual values and doctrinal convictions had to be encompassed in the political decisions and material actions of all Catholics involved in the front-line of policy-making. The pure theoretical and the practical concrete must intersect and support each other, reaffirming complementarities between intellectuals and politicians. The former were to use their capacity for interpreting events and problems and provide rational bases for the understanding of politics. The latter were to act in the 'here and now', immersed in mundane activities, but benefiting from cultural and spiritual equipment consolidated by their faith. The spiritual and political dimensions were to become for them two sides of the same coin. Ideally, this division was embodied in the encounter between the thought of one of the most widely recognised Catholic intellectuals of post-war Italy, Antonio Messineo, and the most influential politician in the history of the Italian First Republic, Alcide De Gasperi.

The spiritual beliefs that illuminated De Gasperi's political commitment complemented the pragmatic arguments of Messineo's doctrinal exegesis. The former guided the Italian Republic for eight years (1945–53), experiencing a subtle and constant tension between pragmatism and idealism. Italy emerged from the war as a destabilised, politically divided and economically troubled country, and De Gasperi looked at Europe as an opportunity for its moral rehabilitation. He let his internationalist and Christian ideas flourish and openly strove for supranational political integration. Meanwhile Messineo, who wrote for over four decades in *La Civiltà Cattolica* (considered since its foundation in 1850 as the 'official voice' of the secretary of state of the Holy See), constantly paid attention to an idea of Europe based on three pillars: integration, grounded in the spiritual traditions of 'Latin Europe'; the prestige of its history; and the strength of its values. From inside the Vatican, Messineo escaped the plethora of problems conditioning Italian politicians like De Gasperi in their daily activities; nonetheless, 'pragmatic' considerations dictated by political contingencies can be identified in his thought, in line with the Jesuit distinction between 'thesis' and 'hypothesis'.

Theory and Practice in the Works of Messineo

Antonio Messineo emerged within the group of writers of *La Civiltà Cattolica* – to which he contributed between 1932 and 1978 – as a point of reference in the field of international politics, particularly during the pontificate of Pius XII (Campanini, 1982, pp. 371–74). Although at first glance his commentaries reveal a doctrinal integrity that cuts across the years, a close study of his works shows a serious consideration of contingencies and a 'flexibility' of argument in dealing with concrete exigencies. Theory and practice went hand in hand: the concrete applications of his arguments and doctrinal standpoints could be contextualised in the evolution of the political situation in Italy as well as in the international environment.

In line with the pope's message, the reorganisation of the international community after the Second World War aimed to spread Christian ideals of universalism, solidarity and interdependence (Riccardi, 1993, pp. 21–23). Following the Jesuit doctrines of Luigi Taparelli D'Azeglio, a discrepancy between *general ideas* and *contingent situations* was a marked feature of the works of Messineo. First, it emerged in the use of the concept of nationalism; its meaning changed and adapted itself to the specific issues of domestic and international politics. A constant element in Messineo's articles was the concern to contribute to the creation of an intellectual climate useful for the preservation of social order, in Italy and elsewhere. Second, it emerged in Messineo's different approach before and after 1947 to the analysis of international politics and the role of the superpowers. Messineo moved from a critical position on American liberalism towards a recognition of the USA as the only political and military force that could prevent the spread of Marxism throughout the world. Even the process of European integration – in principle a clear expression of the affirmation of universalism, solidarity and interdependence – was explained in relation to the political development of the international system.

Nationalism in the 1940s and 1950s

Nationalism has followed a continuous process of redefinition and reinterpretation in relation to universalism and interdependence (Messineo, 1944a). It reached its apex during the first half of the twentieth century, when it was perceived as a carrier of contrasting sentiments, accentuating ideas such as people's common destiny, barriers between states and the disintegration of the international community (Hobsbawm, 1990, pp. 131–62). The 'cult of the state' contrasted with the Catholic doctrine reflected in the *Syllabus* of Pope Pius IX issued in 1864 (Oddone, 1946, pp. 241–48). State-centred ideologies were condemned by the Catholic Church on the grounds that they undermined the survival of 'revealed religions' by replacing them with 'secular religions' (Bracher, 1985, p. 9). Messineo's articles in the 1930s were characterised by a constant ambiguity. The author tried to achieve a difficult balance between Catholic political doctrine and the dominant ideology of the Fascist regime in Italy; however, too many aspects of the regime's doctrine were not consistent with Catholicism. Hierarchical relations among races (Taradel and Raggi, 2000, pp. 98–123), the incentive to autarchy and the myth of national welfare at the expense of other peoples were all in disaccord with the Catholic position (Alix, 1962, pp. 303–9). These conflicts were made explicit in the encyclicals *Mit Brennender Sorge* and *Summi Pontificatus*; the latter, issued by Pope Pius XII, was repeatedly quoted by Messineo and the other writers of *La Civiltà Cattolica* as the main source of political and doctrinal guidance.

According to Pope Pius XII (and Messineo), two 'errors' characterised the beginning of the twentieth century. Political disregard for the human being and the hubris of all materialistic ideologies had induced public authorities to overstep their limits (Pius XII, 1995, pp. 37–43). Both liberal and leftist ideologies were accused as being sources of injustice. Italy was marked by a political dialectic between two opposing poles, those of the detractors of the Catholic Church and of its defenders (Veneruso, 1982, pp. 9–17). The country needed guidance to find the 'right path'. Highlighting the importance of nationalism as a decisive factor for the pursuit of common goals against class divisions, Messineo indicated the main values to be taught:

> The protection of nationalities has never represented a theoretical or a practical issue for the Catholic Church ... [The church] has recently condemned only political nationalism that goes against the laws of solidarity and universal charity, but it does not diminish the relevance of nationalities, definable as a natural value for the human being and as a fundamental tool for the general order of the universe which comes directly from God. (Messineo, 1946a, p. 269)[1]

Messineo's warning stemmed directly from that of the pope, who condemned the lack of universal principles implicit in the exasperations of nationalistic movements. Making reference to the pope, he did not aim to undermine 'the love for the traditions and the glories of the homeland' that nationalism generated, neither did he pose obstacles to 'the promotion of its prosperity and the pursuit of its legitimate interests' (Pius XII, 1995, p. 41). Transforming nationalism from an absolute to a relative value was his key message. He followed an analogous logic on the role of the state. States were not only helpful but necessary tools for the maintenance of social order and stability, particularly in Italy, where the attractive power of the Socialist and Communist parties risked undermining the Catholic Church (Messineo, 1944b, p. 36). However, after the electoral victory of the Christian Democrat Party (*Democrazia Cristiana*) in April 1948 the country was presented with a chance for a moderate transition, and the focus on nationalism and the authority of the state faded in Messineo's works.

The argument in Messineo's book *La Nazione* (1944b) and in his articles appears to conflict with the postwar search for a supranational reorganisation of the system. To his eyes, the ultimate objectives presented by Catholic doctrine were functional to the post-1945 environment: the affirmation of the *bene comune* ('common good') of the international society (a formula that always remained vague); and the creation of organisations that mediated between individuals and naturally aggregated societies (families and nations) and between the multitude of peoples of all countries. States had the duty of exerting authority over people, but at the same time they had to overcome the limitations encompassed in the traditional idea of sovereignty, enlarging the natural community of peoples at a supranational level (Verucci, 1988, pp. 201–3). In Messineo's works the concepts of 'nationalism' and 'state authority' underwent various changes. Between the late 1940s and the early 1950s Messineo contributed to the *Enciclopedia Cattolica* and presented the *nazione* as a collective actor decisive in the education of the human person by transmitting 'the basic elements of his culture' and by perpetuating 'the heritage of spirit, ideas, traditions, language and religion' (Messineo, 1952, pp. 1711–14). He focused on this concept and on its beneficial effects for the harmonious coexistence of the people. The principle of nationality contained undeniable 'elements of truth', and states had to respect it; in the words of Messineo, 'nationality is a social fact ... with its own, inalienable rights' (Messineo, 1944c). The mixture of the two concepts of 'nationalism' and 'state authority' should continue to preserve public order. They were complementary, although their importance was not equivalent, as the latter prevailed over the former in two respects: nations were simple forms of 'inorganic societies', nothing more than groups imperfectly integrated; the state, by contrast, was instead entitled to reign over citizens, with the rule of law as its only limitation. Finally, states were the 'true source of independence' and 'finalistic societies' (Messineo often used this expression in order to underline the material purposes that were inherent in the essence of nations) aimed at determining the general welfare of the people (Messineo, 1953, p. 1261). Messineo showed the interconnectedness between politics, law and morality, and he reaffirmed the validity of Natural Law through the ontological explanation of states and nations; this argument was also developed by another Jesuit intellectual contributing to *La Civiltà Cattolica*, Francesco Oddone (1945, pp. 230–36).

The Superpowers and the New World Order

In the first two years after the Second World War Messineo's articles were marked by strong disapproval of the new international system and, particularly, of the hegemony of the superpowers. He accused the USA and the Soviet Union of developing policies that conflicted with the noble principles that they had previously advocated. The commitment of their leaders to implement agreed principles through the creation of a multilateral system centred on the United Nations seemed to have become a memory of the past (Messineo, 1947a, pp. 97–105). Messineo saw Washington and Moscow as reliable allies until 1947; after this time, he presented the United States as the 'lesser evil' in the world reorganisation. The principle of nationality – which satisfied the needs generated by the evolution of Italian politics, such as national economic reconstruction, currency and prices stabilisation, containment of social turmoil – found a different application. In his articles Messineo argued that the behaviour of two superpowers which were seeking only their own political interests represented a new stage for the defence of nations. His response to the treatment received by Italy (the loss of all colonies, the Adriatic islands, Fiume and Istria; the transfer of the border territories of Briga and Nizza to France; the recognition of the independence of Albania and Ethiopia; the cancellation of the preferential commercial agreements with China; the renunciation of sovereignty over the city of Trieste) was suggestive: long before expressing his disappointment with the negotiations of the Paris peace treaty in 1947 he had already criticised American and Russian realism and remarked that 'everybody understands that the willingness to take action in the name of a common interest was nothing more than camouflage and veiled forms of imperialism' (Messineo, 1945a, p. 72). Moreover, the political principles of international peace and economic solidarity which had been proclaimed in August 1941 by President Roosevelt and Winston Churchill and subsequently encompassed in the Atlantic Charter at the beginning of the following year were neglected: when the war turned in the Allies' favour, the commitment to apply these principles faded (Messineo, 1948, p. 227). The denial by the two superpowers of the eight principles affirmed by the American and British leaders in wartime (renunciation of territorial enlargement, freedom of the people, autonomy of national governments, freedom of trade, promotion of economic collaboration among the nations, lasting peace, liberty of navigation, renunciation of the use of all military means), which were at the basis of the 1945 United Nations Charter and had generated the clear enthusiasm of Pius XII, and the failures of the new system stimulated Messineo's drastic judgments. To his eyes, the critical situation at the international level could not serve as a justification for the superpowers to refrain from respecting the core principles of the UN Charter. The pillars of this Charter could not be interpreted flexibly. On the contrary, however, political leaders claimed the right to consider the Charter merely as some kind of 'letter of intent' which had been completely superseded by the latest developments in international relations, as the division of the international community into two blocs created a system where 'international life is paralysed, the urgent problems of European reconstruction do not find a solution, nor can they possibly find one in the future, and the long series of international conferences do not produce any substantial results' (Messineo, 1948). Messineo advanced two arguments against this position. He supported the validity of the Charter, emphasising the multilateral approval of the document by numerous governments with the manifest intention of developing new policies for a safer international community; and he noted that the political statements by the leaders of the superpowers had been implemented through further developments of the international system, in particular through the formal incorporation of norms that generated duties into bilateral and multilateral treaties between various states, as for example the Anglo-Russian treaty of May 1942 and the American-Russian agreement of June 1944 (Messineo, 1945b, pp. 283–91). Messineo saw that in the current situation European countries found it hard to realise their right to prosper in autonomy and freedom. On the one hand, the Soviet Union was the Hobbesian Leviathan that devoured the rest of the community; on the other hand, the two liberal powers embodied the principle *homo homini lupus*.

> On the territories that are militarily occupied by Anglo-American troops, true liberty and complete autonomy are nothing but dreams, veiled by the

> pretence of monitoring operations in a soft and human way as a political necessity, but in fact with rigid and sometimes even harsh methods; this is even more the case for the populations subject to Russian control, whose destiny everyone can easily imagine. (Messineo, 1945c, p. 5)

In Messineo's opinion, the use of both political and military force transformed democracy into a chimera. As Angelo Brucculeri pointed out (1945a, pp. 269–77), if the superpowers wanted to become truly democratic, they had to respect the Christian roots of Europe. Their joint control over Europe was illegitimate as it rejected Natural Law. In the aftermath of the Second World War, Anglo-American liberalism did not constitute an optimal option for Messineo; he considered it responsible for the crisis of civilisation that derived from the invalidation of all Christian traditions and values.

The beginning of the Cold War led Messineo to rethink his view of the liberal states. This change of opinion was partly prompted by the vicissitudes of Eastern European countries. After 1947 Messineo invited 'Latin Europe' to make a choice between the two systems. Influenced by the Truman Doctrine and the Marshall Plan, he supported the idea of a common reply from the West to the threats coming from East. Whereas before he had pushed for a common policy for the European nations grounded in the principle of neutrality and equidistance from the superpowers, now he began to promote American projects aimed at halting Soviet expansion. The construction of the European castle suited this new paradigm. Messineo gave voice to the Vatican's abandonment of its equidistance since 1947, and his contraposition of the blocs and their models of civilisation became from this moment onwards stronger and stronger. At that time the pope saw the destiny of Eastern Europe as compromised, and *La Civiltà Cattolica* reflected this sense of loss, closely following the evolution of the crises.

Civil wars in Greece and Turkey and political uncertainties in Italy and France strengthened Messineo's personal struggle for the church's protection. Exchanging messages, Pius XII and Truman fortified their cultural and political alliance (Messineo, 1947b, pp. 481–85). The American exaltation of economic liberties over transcendent values became acceptable: 'within the American objectives, the recreation of a domestic and an international system of freedom comes first' (Anon., 1947).

Washington was, therefore, important for Europe. However, not only Messineo but the other writers on the journal – Angelo Brucculeri, Francesco Oddone and Andrea Barbera – were insistent that Europe must preserve its historical and cultural specificity (Brucculeri, 1945b, pp. 369–77). Europe had to learn again to draw its own trajectory and to block any attempt at imposing conditionality on its autonomy: 'It is undeniable that the criteria established by the United States for distributing economic aid for the reconstruction provoke the loss of liberty of the beneficiaries and increase the influence of the Americans, which can even turn into hegemony' (De Marco, 1948, p. 125). Messineo depicted the Organization for European Economic Cooperation (OEEC) as a precious multilateral mechanism for the preservation of European autonomy and the defence of the nations involved in the project (Messineo, 1946b, p. 5), and this idea would remain dominant in the following years after the establishment of the first European Community: 'between two large blocs and a less efficient area like the British Empire, only the creation of an area economically and politically united, that is to say Europe, can become successful and influential within the international community' (Messineo, 1957, p. 125). The idea of Europe that emerged from his pages required, at this stage, the development of a mixture of nationalism, solidarity and universalism, and the integration of Catholic doctrine with elements of liberalism. Thus the correlation of *theoresis* and *praxis* found its complete accomplishment.

De Gasperi and the Dichotomy between Pragmatism and Idealism

De Gasperi held the reins of government at one of the most critical periods in Italian history. His political activities were characterised by a subtle and constant tension between pragmatism and idealism, which emerged as a dichotomy between political laicism and mysticism (Venneri, 2008). Rocco Buttiglione argues that 'faith in Jesus Christ [was] at the centre of the life of Alcide De Gasperi' (Buttiglione, 2006, p. 146), while Pietro Scoppola suggests that De Gasperi's political sensibility stemmed from a connection between 'tough realism ... and an intense moral tension' (Scoppola, 2006, p. vii). His spiritual background was central to his political activity. Politicians assuming key governing positions often start their career implementing high-minded principles and sophisticated ideals, which they tend to marginalise as soon as their impetus is hindered under the burden of daily political activities. De Gasperi, by contrast, seems to have moved from efficient political realism to a kind of romantic 'Europeism', but was this truly a step from pragmatism to idealism? To paraphrase Giulio Andreotti – who worked with De Gasperi after 1947 – the latter was actually 'made of realism and idealism' (Andreotti, 1964).

Political Commitment, 'Faith' in the Democratic Method and 'Respect' for Providence

A few months after De Gasperi's death, Mgr Franco Costa warned that no one writing about his life should neglect his spirituality. The assistant general of *Azione Cattolica* described this spirituality as a 'unique richness' (Costa, 2004, pp. 244–50), the foundation and source of De Gasperi's social and political activism. For Roberto Morozzo della Rocca, De Gasperi's life unfolded 'on the basis of a strong connection between faith and historic commitment' (Morozzo della Rocca, 2005). Apart from few sporadic exceptions (Andreotti, 2006a; Corsini and Repgen, 1984; Goio, 2004; Morozzo della Rocca, 2005), Italian historians have largely marginalised the connections between De Gasperi's spiritual and political lives. Even the recent biography by Piero Craveri suffers in this respect: Craveri recalls that De Gasperi hoped to be remembered as 'a man of faith' rather than as an astute politician (Craveri, 2006, p. 16), but he nevertheless limits references to his spirituality.

Two questions remain unanswered. First, how did De Gasperi view his responsibility towards the *res publica* during the difficult Italian rehabilitation process? Second, what kind of Catholic was De Gasperi?

A few months after the liberation of Italy De Gasperi exhorted the members of the recently constituted Christian Democrat Party to work for the country, which needed stimuli 'to develop its national conscience and decide democratically its own destiny' (De Gasperi, 1945). Looking 'with Christian eyes' at the ancient Roman and Greek traditions, De Gasperi stressed that 'guiding a state produces an intimate connection with God, our Father, [and] creates an immediate responsibility towards the population, [which is] the mediator of the divine will that holds everything' (quoted in Bozza, 1956, p. 112). This bond with God as a paternal figure appears intense and profound. Writing to his daughter Lucia from a mountain retreat, De Gasperi once admitted: 'I do feel I should use this retreat to talk to God, but I hear the voices of men, calling to be served; actually, do not I serve them in God's name?' (quoted in Morozzo della Rocca, 2005). As a liberal Catholic politician, De Gasperi felt that existing parliamentary dynamics should have bridled the rising fascist movement. Documents recently declassified from the Vatican archives show that De Gasperi, then the leader of the Italian People's Party (*Partito Popolare Italiano*), had a meeting with Mussolini in December 1922, only a few weeks after the latter's March on Rome. The minutes of the meeting show that De Gasperi asked Mussolini for an explicit guarantee that pluralism through the proportional electoral system would be respected and left unaltered in the following years (Messina, 2006). After the electoral victory in 1948 De Gasperi, now the leader of the Christian Democrat Party, constantly viewed democracy as the most suitable system for Italy. How should the newly elected government cope with communist participation in the Italian reconstruction process? Both De Gasperi and his American counterparts saw the 'red threat' as a significant danger, but they held different views on the most appropriate anticommunist measures. The Italian democratic order was finding a balance thanks to the intellectual contribution of socialists and communists; hence, in De Gasperi's view, the defeat of communism had to come about by democratic and legal means. In Andreotti's opinion 'De Gasperi was firmly and absolutely intransigent in favour of the democratic method' (2006b). Democracy was a creed and a method 'to be accepted unconditionally' (De Gasperi, 1950): 'if there is anything, after my religious faith, to which I am really devoted, it is the sense of democracy . . . . My public life is given coherence by my loyalty to the democratic principle in every circumstance, in every state, and from every tribune' (quoted in Bozza, 1956, p. 131).

De Gasperi was in prison from 1927 to 1928. This constituted 'a decisive moment for his human and religious experience [because] he discovered the humiliation of being *servus inutilis'* (Morozzo della Rocca, 2005). Writing to his wife from prison, De Gasperi stressed that being in God's hands inevitably meant accepting his will: 'it is better to suffer from iniquities than being the one that makes others suffer' (quoted in Peláez, 1965, p. 29). De Gasperi was an avid reader of *De Imitatione Christi*. He often used this mystical book attributed to Thomas à Kempis as a breviary for his daily orations. Both Morozzo della Rocca (2005) and Piero Craveri (2006, p. 24) make reference to De Gasperi's affection for the messages contained in *De Imitatione Christi*; moreover, Pietro Scoppola describes De Gasperi's view even of the Bible as 'neither merely devotional or pietistic, or intellectualistic: he queries the Book and he daily compares his problems, his existential experience, with the religious sense that the Book suggests to him' (Scoppola, quoted in Tenaglia, 2001, p. 30). Stefano Trinchese says that De Gasperi's tendency to make 'constant reference to the holy texts as an element of salvation constituted the main feature of his actions, especially in moments of pain and uncertainty' (2006, p. 12).

This background suggests that De Gasperi's struggle between faith and political activism should not be interpreted negatively. Almost certainly he overcame the tension between the two through 'concrete spirituality' (Tenaglia, 2001, p. 34). In his view Christianity was materialised only through 'concrete struggle for the rule of law and social action' (De Gasperi, 1953). Elements of his concrete spirituality were made explicit by De Gasperi as early as 1909. Speaking at the national conference of the Catholic University Federation in Rome, he encouraged the association of wise realism with the most pure idealism: 'in this era of mechanical progress and economic change, we Catholics have the duty to keep our feet firmly planted on the ground of reality, but with our eyes fixed towards the eternal ideal' (quoted in Trinchese, 2006,

p. 85). In one of his letters to his daughter Lucia in the early 1950s he similarly confided:

> I need to be reminded that providence uses who it wants, whenever it wants, and that it does not abandon the country in which the Church has its roots. But speaking in human terms, worries obscure the sky and prior to a new serenity there will still be the need for a supreme effort. (Quoted in Catti-De Gasperi, 2005, p. 286)

De Gasperi viewed political life from a Christian perspective. Acknowledging the divine will that gives direction to everything, he recognised the importance of facing problems in human terms and striving for concrete solutions. One of his daughters, Maria Romana, suggests that her father's conception of politics was 'rigorously realistic' (Catti-De Gasperi, 2005, p. 37). She tells us that he kept two Latin quotations visible underneath the glass of his working desk. One was from Horace, '*aequam memento rebus arduis servare mentem*' ('remember to maintain a serene mind when difficult times arrive'), and one was from Ovid, '*perfer et obdura: multo graviora tulisti*' ('hold on and persist: you have endured much more difficult things') (Catti-De Gasperi, 2005, p. 159). In her eyes, one of De Gasperi's main gifts was 'to be free from a negative understanding of the present that leads one to meditate only on the absolute and to marginalise the contingent as if the latter is not *Deus rei*', in other words, that belongs to God (Catti-De Gasperi, 2007). She also quotes De Gasperi as voicing his intimate thoughts on the relationship between politics and the divine a few hours before his death:

> I have done all that was in my power, and my conscience can rest in peace. The Lord makes you work, He allows you to design projects; He gives you energy and life; but suddenly, when you start to think that you are *necessary, indispensable* to your work, then He takes everything away from you. And He proves to you that you are not indispensable; all you can be is useful: and thus He tells you: it is enough, now you can leave. (Quoted in Aga-Rossi *et al.*, 2004, p. 305, emphasis added)

European/Supranational Hope: 'a More Powerful Harmony'

Daniela Preda suggests that De Gasperi was influenced by Altiero Spinelli – promoter of the *Manifesto di Ventotene* for a federalist reorganisation of Europe – when he reached the apex of his Europeism and showed some federalist tendencies (Preda, 1989, 2004). His political activity in Vienna, prior to the First World War, inevitably projected him from the peripheral Trentine regional dimension into the lively centre of a multinational and complex conglomerate. The multinational ferment of the Austro-Hungarian Empire showed him solidarity between European peoples. He developed the conviction that politicians should acknowledge, prior to the state, 'the natural rights of the human being, the family, and human society'; the state represents a political organisation that 'does not coincide with freedom, does not stand upon freedom, but recognises it and coordinates its use' (De Gasperi, 1922). Later in his life, reflecting on Italian reconstruction, he defined the state as an agency responsible for 'imposing democratic legislation, equal for every citizen' (De Gasperi, 1948b), but the state is not necessarily the ultimate form of efficient political organisation. As the process of European integration was successfully launched De Gasperi had no hesitation: the promotion of social justice, peace and democracy should be delegated to a supranational entity (De Gasperi, 1950). Explaining his ideas on inter-state integration, he placed Europe at a crossroad between 'reason and sentiment, liberty and justice' (De Gasperi, 1948a). The perspective of the European supranational integration meant nothing but a further, physiological development of the experiments in national reunification that had exploded in Europe in the nineteenth century. He foretold that 'Europe will exist, but nothing will be lost of all that gave glory and happiness to every nation. It is indeed in a wider society, in a more powerful harmony, that the human being can affirm himself and determine the extent of his intellect' (De Gasperi, 1953). Umberto Corsini emphasises that De Gasperi's pro-Europe attitude was deeply rooted in 'Christianity and Catholicism, [which] provided the foundations for the ideals of reunification of different populations within the same faith, moral law and a rule of law that goes beyond breeds, languages, cultures and customs' (Corsini and Repgen, 1984, p. 252). European integration was functional to the achievement of two basic Christian values: universalism and solidarity. First, in the eyes of De Gasperi universalism was a value to be respected:

> Christianity, which is a divine gift for us, actually belongs to, and is addressed to, humanity as a whole. Circumscribing Christianity solely to the European experience would mean to impose limits on it, to downgrade it. At the same time, how could we conceptualise a European construction without taking into account the Christian element, how could we ignore the lessons of fraternity, unity and social value that stem from it? (De Gasperi, 1953)

Second, De Gasperi saw Christian solidarity as mediating between the possible excesses of liberalism and the threat of intrusive tendencies on the part of the state, but to what extent were Christian ideals unfolding in the European political edifice? De Gasperi reconciled his lay vision of politics and religiosity as follows:

> When I affirm that Christianity is at the origin of the European civilisation I do not intend to introduce any kind of exclusive confessional criterion into the evaluation of our history. I refer to the common European common heritage, to that unitary morality that puts emphasis on the human being and his responsibility. (Quoted in Guiso, 2004, p. 22)

Efforts for a Political Europe

Political discussions for the institutional reorganisation of Western Europe were inaugurated in January 1948, when the British foreign secretary Ernest Bevin exhorted the Benelux countries to join the Anglo-French Dunkerque Alliance. Italy was part of the 'European family', but was not encouraged to participate until Washington decided on its inclusion (Varsori, 1988). After the communists seized power in Prague in February 1948 the United States intensified support, sending the message that the communists were not to take over in Italy. Official documents from the Foreign Relations of the United States book series (FRUS) confirm that after the Czech *coup d'état* General George C. Marshall alerted the US diplomatic delegations in Paris and London that a communist success in Czechoslovakia would stimulate vigorous subversive initiatives in Western Europe, particularly in Italy (FRUS, 1974, pp. 735–36). At a meeting of the Cominform in Białystok in Poland the Soviet Union promised funds and weapons to Italian communists. The funds were to be used for a series of general strikes and the weapons for insurrectional activities (Di Nolfo, 1978, pp. 549–52).

De Gasperi was deeply concerned about the capacity of left-wing parties to control labour parades and he achieved two major successes. First, he used the Białystok episode to strengthen cohesion within the Christian Democrat Party in the crucial pre-electoral weeks (De Gasperi, 1948b). Mario Scelba had warned him that a Catholic fifth column – the *Movimento Cristiano della Pace* led by Guido Miglioli – had decided to support the communist front in the 1948 elections (Andreotti, 2005, p. 38). Second, he obtained more American support: diplomatic acknowledgment for the return of Trieste to Italian jurisdiction, weapons to be sent via Germany, and the inclusion of Italy in the enlarging Dunkerque Alliance. Following US advice, Bevin asked De Gasperi to join the European club; however, De Gasperi declined the invitation (Pastorelli, 1987, p. 138). The 'nationalist' aspects of De Gasperi's decision were a reflection of the trauma suffered by the Italian political class over the terms and conditions of the peace treaty signed in Paris on 10 February 1947 (Formigoni, 2000, p. 392). De Gasperi did not sign the 1948 Brussels Treaty mainly because Italy had different security concerns; the agreement was creating a military alliance that was inconceivable for many Italian politicians; and the alliance would have left unaltered the position of inferiority imposed by the political–military clauses of the peace treaty. Anxiety for international parity was shared among the leading figures of the Italian government. De Gasperi criticised the enlargement of the Dunkerque Alliance, defining the project as 'dangerously anti-Germany' (Andreotti, 2005, pp. 281–84). In his opinion 'Germany had to be strongly integrated in a common European construction', instead of being marginalised as an enemy (quoted in Guiso, 2004, p. 25).

This firm criticism was a prelude to the Europeist attitude that characterised De Gasperi's political activity in the early 1950s. In July 1948 he undertook his first formal 'European manoeuvre', solving a particular national problem. The conversations about the establishment of the Atlantic Alliance were about to be launched without Italy. For De Gasperi and Carlo Sforza, the minister of foreign affairs, Europe was the key to achieving the definitive securitisation of Italy under the Atlantic umbrella. By showing concrete commitment to European integration they now hoped to overcome the previous misunderstandings between Italy and the Western partners and at the same time to create consensus on the domestic front. A military alliance hinged around Washington was not an acceptable option for most members of the parliament. According to Sergio Romano the Italian 'neutrality party' was a well-matched group of Catholics, communists, liberal-nationalists and socialists (Romano, 2004, p. 13). Moreover, even a 'progressive branch' of the Christian Democrat Party proposed to remain 'far from the Atlantic' and to turn Italy – possibly with Switzerland and Sweden – into a beacon of neutrality (Di Nolfo *et al.*, 1990, p. 5). Italian diplomats considered that neutrality and equidistance were ethically admissible and also convenient. However, commenting on De Gasperi's decision to leave the foreign ministry to Pietro Nenni, the leader of the Italian Socialist Party, in the summer of 1946, the ambassador Alberto Tarchiani defined Nenni as the most committed promoter of a neutralism that was perhaps desirable but 'unfortunately' inapplicable for clear 'geographical, juridical, and economical reasons' (Tarchiani, 1955, p. 14). Brussels represented only a 'midway stop' on the way to reaching Washington as smoothly and quickly as possible.

With the aim of overcoming this complex network of adverse currents, Sforza and De Gasperi presented the Italian 'way' towards European integration: the Paris-based OEEC should be the embryo of the new Europe (Sforza, 1953). In 1949 Italy signed the North Atlantic Treaty (FRUS, 1975, pp. 233–34) and was one of the founding members of the Council of Europe. With these two steps, Italy achieved full membership in the Western block; at the same time, the USA, France and Britain abolished the military restrictions imposed by the earlier peace treaty, even without the assent of the USSR, the fourth signatory of that treaty. During discussions on the establishment of the European Coal and Steel Community (CECA) Italy had been at the margin of the European ferment; however, during the negotiations for the creation of the European Defence Community (EDC), De Gasperi promoted Italy as one of the most active supporters of integration. He strove for the inclusion in the EDC treaty of Article 38, which proposed that the EDC Assembly should work for the adoption of a draft constitution for a political Europe (Quagliariello, 2004, pp. 247–86). Later, acknowledging difficulties about the treaty's coming into effect, he strove with the French statesman Robert Schuman to assign the role of proto-Assembly to the already operative CECA Parliamentary Assembly. Unfortunately, this last strenuous attempt to promote a formal supra-national political community was to end in failure. Writing to Amintore Fanfani, secretary-general of the Christian Democrat Party, De Gasperi defined the EDC as 'a thorn in his side' (Catti-De Gasperi, 1975, pp. 334–35). Despite this debacle, De Gasperi made a substantial mark on the construction of Europe. Perhaps it is not by chance that the European Union's motto 'united in *diversity*' was present in De Gasperi's vision of integration. In 1953 he foresaw a reunification based on 'unity in *variety*, a variety of natural and historical forces'. In his own words, 'it will be possible to reach [such a unity] only by walking on the path of a new European humanism; in respect for traditions, with a momentum towards progress, in the exercise of freedom' (De Gasperi, 1953).

Conclusion

'The real world out there' and the decision-making process are often presented as distant from, or clashing with, the higher strata of ideas and abstract conceptualisations. This dualism is evident in the behaviour of many politicians and intellectuals. Particularly in contemporary politics, decision-makers seem to be immersed in a political life of constant input and instant communication which has nothing in common with the reflective attitude of intellectuals and academics. The cases of De Gasperi and Messineo, however, show that the 'reality-ideas' dichotomy does not apply in all situations and cannot be generalised to every individual. Politicians can be motivated by idealism. Idealism might not be a necessary and sufficient condition to generate desired results; however, ideals influence in a substantial way the development of political projects and proposals. European integration cannot be explained independently from economic analyses and practical opportunism. However, De Gasperi's cultural and spiritual predisposition towards a renewed context of international solidarity and universalism undoubtedly gave incentive to the process. Messineo, an intellectual belonging to the Catholic Church, followed pure theoretical elaboration in order to give his blessing to or reject developments in international relations. In particular, he supported European integration by taking into consideration the intrinsic compatibility between a phenomenon that exhibited a lexicon familiar to Christian doctrine and the official teachings of the Catholic Church. Nonetheless, his views were not simply the products of theoretical arguments. Considering the main problems of his time, Messineo kept his eyes on Italy and the political evolution of the international system. De Gasperi and Messineo are striking examples of men in whom the two domains of the ideal and the practical overlap and interplay.

Note

1 All quotations from Italian sources are the authors' translations.

References

Aga-Rossi, E., Ballini, P. and Carioti, A. (2004) 'Intervista a Maria Romana Catti-De Gasperi: mio padre, cristiano e uomo libero', *Ventunesimo Secolo*, 3, 5, pp. 287–305.

Alix, C. (1962) *Le Saint-Siège et les nationalismes en Europe* (Paris, Sirey).

Andreotti, G. (1964) 'La concezione della politica: la politica come missione', *Concretezza*, 10, 16, http://www.degasperi.net/navipage_percorsi.php?id_cat=p2&id_tm=t3 (last accessed 27 October 2008).

Andreotti, G. (2005) *1948: l'anno dello scampato pericolo* (Milan, Rizzoli).

Andreotti, G. (2006a) *De Gasperi* (Palermo, Sellerio).

Andreotti, G. (2006b) Speech at the ceremony for the 'Premio Alcide De Gasperi: Costruttori d'Europa', Trento, 19 August (untitled, unpublished).

Anon. (1947) 'Cronaca contemporanea', *La Civiltà Cattolica*, 2, pp. 94–95.

Bozza, T. (1956) *Alcide De Gasperi: discorsi politici*, vols 1–3 (Rome, Cinque Lune).

Bracher, K. D. (1985) *Il novecento secolo delle ideologie* (Rome/Bari, Laterza).

Brucculeri, A. (1945a) 'Dalla guerra alla pace', *La Civiltà Cattolica*, 3, pp. 269–77.

Brucculeri, A. (1945b) 'Democrazia e morale', *La Civiltà Cattolica*, 4, pp. 369–77.

Buttiglione, R. (2006) 'Cercare il bene comune con il metodo della libertà', in G. Frigerio (ed.), *Nel solco di De Gasperi: commenti scelti* (Milan, Edizioni Bietti).

Campanini, G. (1982) 'Antonio Messineo', in *Dizionario storico del Movimento Cattolico in Italia* (Casale Monferrato, Marietti), pp. 371–74.

Catti-De Gasperi, M. R. (1975) *De Gasperi scrive: corrispondenza con capi di stato, cardinali, uomini politici, giornalisti, diplomatici*, vol. 2 (Brescia, Morcelliana).

Catti-De Gasperi, M. R.(2005) *De Gasperi: ritratto di uno statista* (Milan, Mondadori).

Catti-De Gasperi, M. R. (2007) *Dedicato a mio padre*, speech at S. Lorenzo Basilica, Rome, 24 March, unpublished, text in possession of the authors.

Corsini, U. and Repgen, K. (1984) *Konrad Adenauer e Alcide De Gasperi: due esperienze di rifondazione della democrazia* (Bologna, Il Mulino).

Costa, F. (2004) 'La spiritualità di De Gasperi', in N. Guiso, *Dovuto a De Gasperi: testimonianze e documenti nel 50esimo anniversario della morte* (Milan, Edizioni Ares), pp. 244–50 (originally published in *Civitas*, 1954).

Craveri, P. (2006) *De Gasperi* (Bologna, Il Mulino).

De Gasperi, A. (1922) *Discorso sullo stato cattolico*, http://www.degasperi.net/show_doc.php?id_obj=1705&sq_id=0 (last accessed 27 October 2008).

De Gasperi, A. (1945) 'Perché ci chiamiano Democratici Cristiani', *Il Popolo*, 145.

De Gasperi, A. (1948a) *Le basi morali della democrazia: discorso alla Grande Conférence Catholique*, http://www.degasperi.net/show_doc.php?id_obj=3336&sq_id=0 (last accessed 27 October 2008).

De Gasperi, A. (1948b) 'Non serviamo l'America, non osteggiamo la Russia: difendiamo l'Italia: discorso pronunciato al Convegno dei Gruppi Giovanili della Democrazia Cristiana Roma 15 febbraio 1948', *Il Popolo*, 41.

De Gasperi, A. (1950) *L'idea Europea nel solidarismo cristiano: discorso pronunciato al Convegno delle Nouvelles Equipes Internationales*, http://www.degasperi.net/show_doc.php?id_obj=3302&sq_id=0 (last accessed 27 October 2008).

De Gasperi, A. (1953) *La tendenza all'unità è una delle costanti della storia*, http://www.degasperi.net/show_doc.php?id_obj=3311&sq_id=0 (last accessed 27 October 2008).

De Marco, A. (1948) 'Piano Marshall e orientamenti politici europei', *La Civiltà Cattolica*, 3, p. 125.

Di Nolfo, E. (1978) *Vaticano e Stati Uniti, 1939–52: dalle carte di Myron C. Taylor* (Milan, Franco Angeli).

Di Nolfo, E., Raniero, R. H. and Vigezzi, B. (1990) *L'Italia e la politica di potenza in Europa 1945–1950* (Milan, Marzorati).

Formigoni, G. (2000) *Storia della politica internazionale nell'età contemporanea 1815–1992* (Bologna, Il Mulino).

FRUS (1974) *Diplomatic Papers 1948 – Eastern Europe; the Soviet Union*, vol. 4 (Washington, DC, United States Government Printing Office).

FRUS (1975) *Diplomatic Papers 1949 – Western Europe*, vol. 4 (Washington, DC, United States Government Printing Office).

Goio, M. (2004) *Alcide Degasperi: la sua parola* (Trento, Reverdito Editore).

Guiso, N. (2004) *Dovuto a De Gasperi: testimonianze e documenti nel 50esimo anniversario della morte* (Milan, Edizioni Ares).

Hobsbawm, E. J. (1990) *Nations and Nationalism since 1780: Programme, Myth, Reality* (Cambridge, Cambridge University Press).

Messina, D. (2006) 'Così Mussolini mentì a De Gasperi: salverò il proporzionale', *Corriere della Sera*, 19 September.

Messineo, A. (1944a) *Il diritto internazionale nella dottrina cattolica* (Rome, La Civiltà Cattolica).

Messineo, A. (1944b) *La Nazione* (Rome, La Civiltà Cattolica).

Messineo, A. (1944c) 'La nazionalità e l'ordinamento internazionale', *La Civiltà Cattolica*, 1, p. 294.

Messineo, A. (1945a) 'Il convegno dei Cinque', *La Civiltà Cattolica*, 4, p. 72.

Messineo, A. (1945b) 'Il naufragio della Carta Atlantica', *La Civiltà Cattolica*, 1, pp. 283–91.

Messineo, A. (1945c) 'Le incognite della ricostruzione europea', *La Civiltà Cattolica*, 3, p. 5.

Messineo, A. (1946a) 'La Chiesa e le nazionalità', *La Civiltà Cattolica*, 1, pp. 249–60.

Messineo, A. (1946b) 'I paradossi della politica internazionale', *La Civiltà Cattolica*, 2, p. 5.

Messineo, A. (1947a) 'La seconda assemblea delle Nazioni Unite', *La Civiltà Cattolica*, 1, pp. 97–105.

Messineo, A. (1947b) 'Per una pace vera e duratura', *La Civiltà Cattolica*, 3, pp. 486–95.

Messineo, A. (1948) 'L'Europa alla svolta del suo destino', *La Civiltà Cattolica*, 1, p. 227.

Messineo, A. (1952) 'Nazione', in *Enciclopedia Cattolica* (Città del Vaticano, Ente per l'Enciclopedia Cattolica e per il libro cattolico), vol. 8, pp. 1711–14.

Messineo, A. (1953) 'Stato', in *Enciclopedia Cattolica*, vol. 9 (Città del Vaticano, Ente per l'Enciclopedia Cattolica e per il libro cattolico), p. 1261.

Messineo, A. (1957) 'Evoluzione politico-sociale dell'Europa contemporanea', in A. Muñoz-Alonso *et al.* (eds), *Le basi culturali dell'unità europea: atti del primo incontro internazionale dell'Istituto Internazionale Studi Superiori 'Antonio Rosmini'* (Bolzano, Athesia), p. 125.

Morozzo della Rocca, R. (2005) *La spiritualità di De Gasperi*, http://www.degasperi.net/navipage_percorsi.php?id_cat=p2&id_tm=t2 (last accessed 27 October 2008).

Oddone, A. (1945) 'L'autorità sociale e l'osservanza delle leggi', *La Civiltà Cattolica*, 1, pp. 230–36.

Oddone, A. (1946) 'La politica dei fatti compiuti', *La Civiltà Cattolica*, 1, pp. 241–48.

Pastorelli, P. (1987) *La politica estera italiana del dopoguerra* (Bologna, Il Mulino).

Peláez, M. (1965) 'Volontà di resistere', *Studi Cattolici*, 49, pp. 28–32.

Pius XII (1995) 'Summi Pontificatus', *Enchiridion delle Encicliche* (Bologna, Edizioni Dehoniane).

Preda, D. (1989) 'De Gasperi, Spinelli e l'art. 38 della Ced', *Il Politico*, 152, p. 4.

Preda, D. (2004) *Alcide De Gasperi federalista europeo* (Bologna, Il Mulino).

Quagliariello, G. (2004) 'La Ced, l'ultima spina di De Gasperi', *Ventunesimo Secolo*, 3, 5, pp. 247–86.

Riccardi, A. (1993) *Il potere del papa da Pio XII a Giovanni Paolo II* (Rome/Bari, Laterza).

Romano, S. (2004) *Guida alla politica estera italiana* (Milan, Rizzoli).

Scoppola, P. (2006) 'Prefazione', in S. Trinchese, *L'altro De Gasperi* (Rome/Bari, Laterza).

Sforza, C. (1953) *Cinque anni a Palazzo Chigi: la politica estera italiana dal 1947 al 1951* (Rome, Atlante).

Taradel, R. and Raggi, B. (2000) *La segregazione amichevole: 'La Civiltà Cattolica' e la questione ebraica (1850–1945)* (Rome, Editori Riuniti).

Tarchiani, A. (1955) *Dieci anni tra Roma e Washington* (Verona, Arnaldo Mondadori).

Tenaglia, A. (2001) *Religione e politica in Alcide Degasperi* (Reggio Emilia, Pozzi Editore).

Trinchese, S. (2006) *L'altro De Gasperi* (Rome/Bari, Laterza).

Varsori, A. (1988) *Il Patto di Bruxelles (1948): tra integrazione Europea ed Alleanza Atlantica* (Rome, Bonacci Editore).

Veneruso, D. (1982) 'Movimento cattolico, nazionalismo e fascismo', in F. Traniello and G. Campanini (eds), *Dizionario storico del movimento Cattolico in Italia* (Casale Monferrato, Marietti), pp. 9–17.

Venneri, G. (2008) 'Man of faith and political commitment: Alcide De Gasperi in the history of Europe', *Journal of Modern Italian Studies*, 13, 1, pp. 89–92.

Verucci, G. (1988) *La Chiesa nella società contemporanea: dal primo dopoguerra al Concilio Vaticano II* (Rome/Bari, Laterza).

Papal Thought on Europe and the European Union in the Twentieth Century

BLANDINE CHELINI-PONT

> I'm sending out a cry of love to you, old Europe: find yourself again, be yourself, discover your origins, revive your roots, revive those authentic values which make your history glorious and your presence beneficent on other continents. (John Paul II, 1982)

Introduction

Papal thought on the uniting of Europe is of fairly recent date, having been elaborated over less than a century. In its early form, it was closely related to the major objective of twentieth-century papal teaching and pontifical diplomacy, which was aimed at building and preserving peace. At first, it was a practical commitment to finding an 'institutional solution' which would bring to an end the quarrelsome propensities of the old continent. Considering the appalling violence and loss of life of the First World War, Pope Benedict XV (1914–22), who defined it as 'the suicide of civilised Europe', thought of establishing a unified working organisation of the states of Europe, dedicated to preventing a future war. His successor Pius XI (1922–39) was also favourable to an institutional and diplomatic solution of this sort. However, both of them lacked a positive political vision of a united Europe, being instead preoccupied with the establishment of organisations devoted to the avoidance of war. The task of developing substantive ideas on the subject of European unity fell to Pius XII (1939–58). The Second World War and the death of European fascism encouraged him to create a Catholic vision of Europe which had not existed before. During the pontificate of Pius XII ideas about Europe's Christian vocation and its 'real' significance began to develop and spread, taking the form of a predominantly federal project of unity and directed towards counteracting the advance of communism (Durand, 2007, pp. 385–91).

The advent of the European Community and the process of integration inaugurated a period of increased commitment in papal speeches, not only regarding the central question of maintaining peace on the old continent, but also European federalism and the construction of Europe itself. In the 1960s and 1970s the papacy added further priorities for maintaining peace, which ceased to be centred exclusively on Europe, although responsibility for the unity of Europe remained 'a duty', according to Paul VI (1963–78). Europe's unity was returned to the heart of Catholic teachings, however, by a new pope who came from the East, John Paul II (1978–2005). In his view, Europe comes to figure as part of Catholic doctrine, going beyond and transcending the geopolitical balance of the continent. John Paul II even spoke of Europe as a cultural and spiritual miracle, albeit surrounded by turmoil (John Paul II, 1982).[1]

With this pope, the peaceful and steadily growing European community underwent a change of perspective. Previously, the objective of unity was justified by reference to a common Christian identity and was meant to protect the continent from war and further splintering. John Paul II took the view that a common Christian identity pre-existed *de facto* and was outside any institutional union. Europe had always lived by its Christian culture and values. This culture and these values had to be respected both by individual European states and by the Union, at the risk otherwise of the unity project failing and Europe disappearing, falling into decadence and permissiveness.

The 1920s: Avoiding the Return of War in a Europe Threatened by Rival Nationalisms

The idea of building European unity through peaceful diplomacy emerged during the pontificate of Benedict XV. In the encyclicals *Ad Beatissimi* in 1914 and *Pacem Dei Munus* in 1920 the papacy promoted 'the politics of peace' from which it has not since departed. In its beginning it was closely focused on the European continent (Vaillancourt, 1990, pp. 49–64). Benedict XV, who replaced Pius X one month after the beginning of the First World War, immediately adopted a neutral position with regard to the conflict and devoted his energy to stopping the war (Renoton Beine, 2004, p. 420; Pollard, 1999, pp. 76–78). He was accused by the Allies of favouring the Germans, as he tried to prevent Italy from joining the Allies, while the Germans accused him of supporting the French. In his first world message, *Ubi Primum*, on 8 September 1914, he described the war as 'the bane of God's wrath'. He encouraged the belligerent parties to 'enter into the path of peace and reach out to one another'. In his encyclical *Ad Beatissimi* on 1 November 1914 he spoke out about the horror he felt over the dreadful war massacres and condemned what he took to be its moral causes, namely, hatred, disdain for authority, class struggle, and greed (Vaillancourt, 1990, p. 57).

At the Christmas celebrations of the same year Benedict XV proposed a 'truce of God', which was not followed. At the beginning of 1915 he composed a prayer for peace to be recited in all European churches, while on 28 July in *Allorché Fummo Chiamati* he described the war as a 'horrible carnage that dishonours Europe'. In his opinion victory would serve only to foster hatred and bitterness and prepare for new wars. He intervened by trying to prevent the USA from sending weapons to the powers of the Alliance. He spoke of the entire world becoming a hospital and an open grave, and on 4 March 1916, in *Al Tremendo Conflitto*, he compared the war to the suicide of civilised Europe, imploring the belligerents to renounce their intentions of mutual destruction.

In his famous note addressed to the heads of state on 1 August 1917 (Renoton-Beine, 2004, pp. 397–99)[2] the pope proposed a negotiated peace plan; however, it was rejected (Renoton-Beine, 2004, pp. 278–96). He spelled out three conditions required to reestablish a durable and equitable peace: a ceasefire; a simultaneous and reciprocal reduction in arms; and the establishment of an arbitration procedure with sanctions for those who opposed its results. He wanted the belligerents to recognise the moral force of law and gradually to demobilise their armed forces. A few weeks later, through his intermediary Cardinal Pietro Gasparri, the secretary of state, Benedict XV suggested the simultaneous and reciprocal abolition of compulsory military service and the creation of an arbitration tribunal; however, these suggestions failed to attract a consensus (Vaillancourt, 1990, p. 57; Renoton-Beine, 2004, pp. 367–75). At the end of the war he received President Wilson (4 January 1919) in Rome and supported his objectives for building a new international order, intended to help Europe emerge from the disastrous consequences of its long tradition of *Realpolitik*. In his encyclical *Pacem Dei Munus* on 23 May 1920 Benedict XV deplored the fact that both the Treaty of Versailles, described by him as the 'peace of the victors', and the League of Nations, the first real international organisation, failed to erase the sources of rivalry between states. He even foresaw the possibility of another war as a result of continuing hatred and the absence of a true brotherly society of nations.[3]

Benedict XV's successors were largely inspired by his pronouncements in their teachings, especially by his encyclical *Pacem Dei Munus*, which addressed some of the most significant questions at the time: How to avoid war between Europeans? How to reduce the strength of the rival nationalisms? And how to build peace in Europe?

This picture of Europe, destroyed yet constantly on the brink of conflict, was the backdrop for the development of a 'concrete' conception of peace, no longer focused on doctrines about the conditions for a just war (Bacot, 1989, p. 250). This active papal diplomacy in favour of building a European order of peace founded on the primacy of law and on moral values remains largely overlooked by historians. The actions and speeches of Benedict XV and Pius XI produced between the two world wars suggest a continuity in the internationalist and European orientation of the Catholic Church.

Pius XI began his pontificate with the encyclical *Ubi Arcano Dei* in 1922. The encyclical's main objective was to prevent the otherwise ineluctable return of the war in Europe, by supporting the creation of an organisation for maintaining peace.[4] Although the Holy See was excluded from the League of Nations at Italy's behest, the pope was represented in the process of its creation by his unofficial representative, Mgr Bonaventura Cerretti, who was known in France for his diplomatic abilities, having as nuncio negotiated the integration of Catholic dioceses into the framework of the 1905 law on the separation of church and state.

In a comparable way to his predecessor, Pius XI expressed serious reservations concerning the reparations demanded by France from Germany (Note, 1921). He unreservedly supported the English and later the American mitigation of the disastrous economic and financial consequences for Germany of the 'merciless' Treaty of

Versailles. His attitude was vigorously denounced in France, by parliament and the media, as an obvious sign of germanophile papal partisanship (Chenaux, 2007, pp. 24–25). Although the Vatican was fairly hostile to the beginning of the League of Nations as first established, the entry of Germany through the Locarno Accords (16 October 1925) changed this position. The League became a real object of hope for the Vatican. The Locarno Accords were in line with the reconciliation logic of the papacy, and Pius XI's Consistorial Allocution on 20 December 1926 condemned the *Action Française* as a nationalist-Catholic political party hostile to Franco-German reconciliation. With his dismissive caustic reference to 'this immoderate nationalism, this new heresy to be fought', Pius XI reaffirmed his commitment to the strong condemnation of any political ideals that contradicted the laws of brotherhood and of 'the universal human family' (Prévotat, 1996, pp. 359–95; Prévotat, 2001, p. 450). He issued the encyclicals of the 1930s condemning communism and nazism and opened the way for the Holy See to come out in favour of European integration after 1945.

Pius XI was enthusiastic about the signing of the Briand–Kellog Pact which renounced war (Il Patto, 1928, cited in Chenaux, 2007, p. 33). He was strongly in favour of the proposal of French minister and diplomat Aristide Briand, made before the League of Nations in September 1929, to establish a 'federal link' among Europeans (Società, 1929, cited in Chenaux, 2007, p. 33). The notion was that if they were bound together by political and economic systems, Europeans would abandon intra-European war. Briand's plan for a European Union had a particular place in the Holy See's European thought. Several copies of the plan were received by the Secretariat, and its points discussed and commented upon by Cardinal Eugenio Pacelli, the Holy See's secretary of state and future Pope Pius XII, and by nuncio Luigi Maglione in Paris. Allusion to this plan was found in the encyclical *Quadragesimo Anno* of 15 May 1931 praising the constitution of regional economic unions (Chenaux, 2007, pp. 24–28). The inspiration of Briand's plan was equally recognised in the pope's remarks to the French ambassador Charles-Roux in July of 1932:

> The present political construction of Europe, divided into a number of countries which are ruled by jealous nationalism, no longer responds to the conditions of a time when one can circle the continent in 24 hours. The future of Europe lies in a European agreement leading towards a United States of Europe. (Charles-Roux, 1932)

The 1930s and the 1940s: Combatting Inhuman Totalitarianisms: the Birth of Catholic Doctrine on Europe and Support for Federalism

In the 1930s the Vatican took the position that the solution for a politically united Europe would be an 'ideological' one. Moving on from the commitment to achieving peace by practical measures of reconciliation, it became urgent to create an ideal to substitute for the quarrelsome totalitarianisms of the continent which were leading irrevocably in the direction of war. It was an ideal which was nurtured at the same time as the Catholic Church's 'conversion' to democracy and to human rights, a conversion explicitly confirmed during the Second World War by Pius XII, but which was already well under way in the period between the two world wars (Chenaux, 2003, p. 462).

From 1922 to 1939 Pius XI's pontificate was confronted with an unprecedented challenge. The denunciation of totalitarianism was developed by means of reinterpretation of Catholic theology on the two powers, namely, the temporal (political order) and the spiritual (that of the church) which ought to collaborate for the common good. In the encyclical *Iniquis Afflictisque* of 18 November 1926 Pius XI in a 'traditional' rebuke criticised the interference of the Mexican state in the internal affairs of the Catholic Church. However, with his encyclical *Acerba Animi* of 29 September 1932, on the same subject, he insisted for the first time on going beyond the traditional defence of the 'inalienable rights' of the church and on the freedom of a civil society faced with a state which attempted to restrain it ideologically. The encyclical *Non Abbiamo Bisogno* of 29 June 1931 denounced Italian fascism, the encyclical *Mit Brennender Sorge* of 14 March 1937 denounced nazism as 'racist', and the encyclical *Divini Redemptoris* of 19 March 1937 denounced communism as inhuman and 'atheist'. In these encyclicals taken together Pius XI presented an entire body of reflection on totalitarianism and a conception of 'a good regime', representing its exact opposite. Totalitarianism was an ideological vision of the world, exclusive and incontestable, imposed in the face of all opposition. This vision required complete control over a society, the disappearance of the separation between state and civil society, the monopolisation of power by the party or the ruler, and the elimination of any opposition and independent organisation.

In Pius XI's opinion, totalitarianism represented a new variant of the historical secular movement born in the sixteenth century, which had already been denounced by Pope Leo XIII in the encyclical *Quod Apostolici Muneris* on socialism (28 December 1878). Totalitarian ideology was presented as directly opposed to the Catholic doctrine of the state founded on the role of intermediary bodies and the principle of subsidiarity (*Quadragesimo Anno*, 15 May 1931). It was in this context of incipiently democratic Vatican political thinking that the Catholic European idea took root.

The idea of European unity has developed through several stages. 'Europe', like 'democracy', did not spring from the Catholic world of ideas and doctrines. In the nineteenth century continental unification projects provoked aversion among many Catholics because of their liberal and nationalistic origins, which were in line with the fight for collective emancipation from church authority (Chenaux, 2007, pp. 24–28; see also Hugo, 1849). The idea of a 'United States of Europe' and European federalism had a strong anti-Catholic tonality and was overtly Kantian (Castillo, 2001, p. 125). For example, Robert de Traz (1884–51), founder of the *Revue de Genève*, a literary review which aimed to support and give new perspectives to the League of Nations, wrote that only the Protestant mind, respectful of the diversity of peoples and men, could respond to the problems of a fragmented Europe, while the Catholics, confusing unity and uniformity, were unable to see the reality of Europe, essentially diverse and plural, in which it was necessary to live together (Meylan, 1969, p. 360).

The idea of a European political union was elaborated inside Catholic thinking circles from already well-developed thematics. The concept derived in part from a 'political' nostalgia for Christendom which reappeared in pontifical speeches. The notion of Christendom was popular among Catholic authors in the 1930s, being linked with the idea of the 'West' (*Abendland*); it met with unprecedented success in Weimar Germany and the English Catholic Renaissance movement between the wars (Dawson, 1932, pp. 247–304). Their anti-Protestant and anti-modern reading of European history opposed the golden age of medieval Christendom to the period of its disintegration and decline marked by the birth of the nation-states. This reading remained prevalent in the Catholic culture of the 1930s and still sustained the Catholic imagination in the days following the Second World War.

Pius XII borrowed from this imagination a positive reading of European history, which presented Christian culture as foundational (Mayeur, 1981). He put forward a summary account of 'the extraordinary common heritage', on which he based his first major European encyclical of 1947, *Fulgens Radiatur*, proclaiming St Benedict as the patron saint of Europe. Pius XII's recognition of the spiritual paternity of St Benedict summed up a 'romantic' vision of Europe's origins, which later reappeared in full force with John Paul II. This perception was promoted by a particular romanticism, that of the Germany of Friedrich Novalis, Adam Müller and Friedrich Schlegel, who developed an idealist and overtly nostalgic vision of Christian Europe (Dawson, 1932, pp. 140–67). The vision of a glorious European Christian past was also presented in Pius XII's famous speech of 11 November 1948 (*Allocution* ...) at the Convention of the Union of European Federalists in Rome. He invited the 'great European nations with their long histories filled with memories of glory and power to disregard their past greatness in order to fall into line with a higher political and economical unity' (Documents, 1948–63, doc. no. 90, 1948, pp. 23–24). In this text, the Middle Ages were considered a reference point because 'Europe formed a compact whole and its soul was Christianity'. The modern era was one of a slowly progressing disintegration and growing irreligion, which had driven Europe to misfortune. According to Pius XII, a new era was to be hoped and worked for, an era in which the ties between religion and European civilisation would be reestablished and the rights of God and the divine recognised, or at least those of the natural rights of which human rights were to be considered an integral part.

The 1940s and 1950s: Repairing Continental Divisions and Federating Europe's Eastern and Western Blocs

Pius XII put forward the concept of Europe's 'Christian vocation' and adopted the European federalist programme designed during the Second World War among Catholic intellectuals. Though these ideas were far from being shared by everyone they provided the main foundation for the new Christian Democratic parties on the continent (Durand, 1995, p. 383). From 1948 until his death Pius XII continued to manifest sympathy for pro-European unity movements. The support that he lent to governments engaged on this course, under the leadership of Catholic politicians (Konrad Adenauer, Robert Schuman, Alcide De Gasperi), gave rise to controversy around the emergence of a Vatican Europe, which looked to the Americans and adhered to Cold War logic (Chenaux, 1990, p. 364).

Affirming Europe's Christian vocation as well as supporting the federalist project was certainly, from the pope's point of view, the best means of combatting communism in Europe. The project had continued to concern the Secretariat of State since the Russian–American alliance of 1941. The Soviet Union aroused fears in the Vatican well before the beginning of the Cold War. The European unity project made it possible to step out of the Cold War logic imposed by the former Allies and it was not perceived in Vatican circles as involving a voluntary allegiance to American international politics. The project took on a new aspect in the 1950s with the adoption of the 'reunification' objective accompanied by constant reminders of the existence of 'the other Europe', with its common Christian faith, as shown by the *Apostolical Letter to the People of Russia* of July 1952. The reminder of the wider dimensions of Europe's heritage created the space for the Holy See's '*Ostpolitik*', its fight for 'religious freedom'. Seeking an alternative way outside the logic of the Cold War, Pius XII also attempted to break the nuclear escalation by unreservedly condemning atomic weapons, in his encyclical *Mirabile Illud* of December 1950.

Pius XII's European commitment to unity and federation was extremely strong. From the first days after the Second World War he indicated both the necessity and the difficulty of establishing the European Union: 'There is no time to lose.... It is high time that this happened. Some are even wondering if it is not already too late .... We are expecting [from the continent's larger nations] that they disregard their past greatness and fall in line with a higher political and economic unity' (*Allocution* ...). The slow pace of progress after the war did not correspond to papal expectations, as reflected in the address of 13 September 1952 to the pilgrims of the *Pax Christi* movement. Evoking the political personalities who worked for the unification of Europe, Pius XII said 'When we follow the work of these men of state we cannot help feeling anxious .... The appropriate atmosphere still does not exist, and without it these new political institutions will not be able to sustain themselves in the long run' (Documents, 1948–63, doc. no. 447, 1952, pp. 95–96). The Christmas radio message of 1953 also provided Pius XII with the occasion to formulate a new plea. Referring to the apparition of 'a grey vision of a worried Europe', the pope urged Christian politicians into action: 'Why continue to hesitate? The end is clear; the needs of the peoples are before everyone's eyes. To those who ask for an advance guarantee of absolute success, one must answer that it is indeed a risk, but adapted to the present possibilities, it is a reasonable one' (Documents, 1948–63, doc. no. 644, 1953, pp. 28–29).

When the first European institutions were established, Pius XII gave a positive reaction. He acknowledged this success with an expression of joy before the representatives of the European Community Steel and Coal industry (ECSC) on 4 November 1957:

> Today many apprehensions have been appeased and we can foresee that the movement which has been created cannot be stopped any more, that it is necessary to go even deeper and consent to temporary sacrifices without which this would not work .... Entering into a larger community never comes without sacrifices, but we urgently need to understand their ineluctable yet finally beneficial nature .... The results obtained make us feel optimistic about the future. (Documents, 1948–63, doc. no. 633, 1957, pp. 637–39)

Pius XII felt that the European countries which had acknowledged the principle of delegating a part of their sovereignty to a supranational organisation had 'entered on a salutary path from which a new life in all areas would emerge, a wealth that was not only economical and cultural but also spiritual and religious'.

The 1960s and the 1970s: Competing Emergencies

This period of modern history corresponded to a time of a more 'universal' redeployment of the Catholic Church, a process in which the Second Vatican Council was the landmark. Pope John XXIII (1958–63), returning to the inspirations expressed by Benedict XV, declared the Holy See's support for an institutional Europe which synchronised the European project with his own battle for peace in the face of the nuclear threat. During his brief pontificate, John XXIII introduced some major changes in Vatican policy regarding the Soviet Union and the Eastern bloc countries generally, and in his pontifical teachings on peace and disarmament. He saw himself more as a peaceful mediator between East and West than a natural ally of the United States and Western Europe. His main contribution to peace was his encyclical *Pacem in Terris*, pronounced on 11 April 1963, almost two years after his progressive encyclical *Mater et Magistra*, which cleared away various inherited obstacles in the socio-economic and political teachings of the Catholic Church (Vaillancourt, 1990, p. 63).

On 24 October 1960 John XXIII launched a call for peace, which was published two days later in the Russian newspaper *Pravda*. Several authors noted a sort of reciprocal fondness between John XXIII and Nikita Khrushchev which went back to the mutual exchanges of peace messages in the 1960s. In April 1963, a few weeks after the publication of *Pacem in Terris*, the pope agreed to meet the Adzhubei couple, Khrushchev's son-in-law and daughter, at the Vatican. Furthermore, during the Cuban missile crisis in the autumn of 1962, John XXIII played an important role as mediator between Kennedy and Khrushchev, something which both political leaders recognised (Hehir, 1990, p. 30; Stehle, 1981, p. 306). The diplomatic interventions of John XXIII can be said, then, to have contributed to preventing the outbreak of a nuclear conflict between the Soviet Union and the United States.

Some argue that the Cuban missile crisis 'convinced John XXIII that *Pacem in Terris* should become the first political priority of the Church' (Hanson, 1987, p. 310). Certainly this encyclical remained one of the most important papal documents of the Catholic Church on the subject of peace. It was addressed not only to Christians but to all men of good will and insisted on the rights and fundamental duties of human beings and on the fact that there would not be any real peace without respect for a moral order based on truth, justice, solidarity and freedom. John XXIII linked the question of disarmament to the question of development and demanded an end to the arms race:

> Hence justice, right reason, and the recognition of man's dignity cry out insistently for a cessation to the arms race. The stock-piles of armaments which have been built up in various countries must be reduced all round and simultaneously by the parties concerned. Nuclear weapons must be banned. A general agreement must be reached on a suitable disarmament program, with an effective system of mutual control. (*Pacem in Terris*, para. 112)

The Second Vatican Council, which was summoned by John XXIII but which ended under the papacy of his successor Paul VI, also reconsidered the importance of peace and the banning of nuclear arms. Chapter V of the Apostolic Constitution *Gaudium et Spes* (7 December 1965) deals with the church in today's world. Peace was not conceived as an absence of war or as a balance game between opposing forces but was rather the product of justice (Vaillancourt, 1990, p. 66). John XXIII's interest in the construction of Europe was not as central as that of Pius XII. He nevertheless made a clear statement on this subject in a letter which was read by his secretary of state, Amleto Cicognani, at the 'Social Week' in Strasbourg in July 1962: 'Europe is a reality which is growing each day. The risk has been taken and this daring has been rewarded.' This document also took note of the first positive results of the European Coal and Steel Community and spoke on the issue: 'Would a European unity once built possess its own common asset, as is the case for each country?' The answer was categorical: 'Without doubt, this European common asset exists; we must affirm it and strive to promote its accomplishment' (Jean XXIII, 1962).

Pope Paul VI explored the question of European unity more regularly and his declarations on the subject were fairly numerous. Thus during his visit to the abbey at Monte Cassino on 24 October 1964 he proceeded with the solemn proclamation of St Benedict, patron of Europe (*Lettera Apostolica*). Later, speaking to the General

Assembly of the Association of European Studies Institutes, he justified the pontifical position on European unity in the following terms, after evoking the strong involvement of his predecessors:

> Why so much interest on the part of the spiritual community in temporal questions such as the political and economic organisation of a continent? The answer is already implicitly stated in the brief historical reminder which we have outlined. So many cultural, moral and religious values are involved in the idea of Europe; it represents such a spiritual heritage in the eyes of the church; the balance of an entire continent is so important for the entire society to run properly and for world peace, that the church, concerned for the welfare of mankind, cannot be disinterested. (*Discours* . . ., 1967)

However, Paul VI's greatest concern lay elsewhere. Very early in his pontificate he was known to be greatly preoccupied with the questions of disarmament and peace. In a logical follow-up to the thinking of John XXIII and the Second Vatican Council, he condemned nuclear and indiscriminate war, as well as the arms race, remaining in favour of a general and controlled effective reduction in arms. In his 1964 Christmas message he proposed the establishment of a global and state-raised development fund for third-world countries, which would be supplied by money obtained from disarmament. During a historic visit to the United Nations headquarters in New York in 1965 Paul VI made a plea against war: 'Never again . . . . Drop the weapons from your hands.' In January 1967 he took further actions and established a Pontifical Commission entitled 'Justice and Peace'. A permanent Committee for Peace was constituted within this commission which on several occasions condemned the war in Vietnam (Vaillancourt, 1990, p. 69).

Beyond disarmament, Paul VI also connected the issue of peace with that of development. The encyclical *Populorum Progressio*, published at the beginning of 1967, established a direct link between development and peace by claiming that 'development is the new word for peace' and that 'peace is radically a work of justice, love and culture'. The encyclical asserted the necessity for a universally competent political authority at an international level:

> Everyone knows, however, that revolutionary uprisings – except where there is manifest, longstanding tyranny which would do great damage to fundamental personal rights and dangerous harm to the common good of the country – engender new injustices, introduce new inequities and bring new disasters. The evil situation that exists, and it surely is evil, may not be dealt with in such a way that an even worse situation results . . . . Who can fail to see the need and importance of thus gradually coming to the establishment of a world authority capable of taking effective action on the juridical and political planes? (*Populorum Progressio*, paras 31, 78)

Europe: an Autonomous Concept under Pope John Paul II

With Pope John Paul II Europe again became a central topic in papal teaching (Chelini, 1989, p. 208). More than 300 writings and speeches were devoted by him to this topic. John Paul II took two major ideas from Pius XII and elaborated them further: Europe included the East and it was educated in the Christian faith (Chenaux,

2004, p. 280; Durand, 2006, pp. 9–69). A few days before his pontificate Karol Wojtyła wrote an article in the Catholic Italian review *Vita e Pensiero* regarding the boundaries of Europe (Wojtyla, 1978). He condemned the 'western' vision of Europe, regretting the disappearance of *Mitteleuropa* after the end of the Second World War as a spiritual bridge between the two Europes, Eastern and Western, the 'two spiritual lungs' of the continent (Chelini, 1989, pp. 27–33).[5]

The rediscovery of 'middle' Europe, removed from the map by Nazi Germany and the Soviet Union, was characteristic of the end of the 1970s, particularly in the context of the debate over the installation of Pershing missiles on European soil. As Philippe Portier suggests, the pope's insistence on directing attention 'towards the East' was aimed at remodelling the European map in favour of the Catholic Church (Portier, 2007). First, in terms of the political map, the Polish pope publicly questioned the Yalta decisions which subjected a significant portion of the European continent to irreligious state dictatorship. He expected that by reminding Christians in Eastern Europe of their common civilisation with those in Western Europe he would symbolically separate them from the communist regimes. Second, in terms of Europe's religious map, by insisting on the continent's dual identity he recognised the full legitimacy of ancient Constantinople as the other centre of power and civilisation (Portier, 2007, pp. 47–48).

This double-edge teaching reached its acme with the proclamation of Ss Cyril and Methodius as co-patron saints of Europe, legitimately 'sent' by the Roman pontiff to evangelise the Slavic peoples (encyclicals *Egregiae Virtutis*, 31 December 1980 and *Slavorum Apostoli*, 2 July 1985). By reestablishing Eastern Orthodoxy in its patriarchal primacy, John Paul II assigned himself the task of putting an end to the fractures which had appeared in the Christian community almost a thousand years before. Similarly, along with the 'recovery' of the East, John Paul II sought to reintegrate the nations as natural and unique communities, indispensable to the integrity of Europe. His thinking on Europe was marked by his Polish education and the romanticism of Polish nationalism. His youthful reading of Adam Mickiewicz (1798–1855), Juliusz Słowacki (1809–49) and Zygmunt de Corvin-Krasiński (1812–1859) had convinced him that small nations overshadowed by powerful imperialisms were capable of liberating the continent from the 'sin of power', an expression used by Słowacki in his last poem *Król Duch* (*King Spirit*), an epic about Poland's legendary past written in 1847 (Poupard, 1981). Unity protected them from subservience to one federation, itself placed under Christian solidarity. This neo-Europeanisation called for the respect of 'the sovereignty of each nation by virtue of its own culture', as the pope told UNESCO (*Discours* . . ., 1980), and also allowed it to move away from the centre of the Europe of Brussels: 'The reunited partners', he claimed in his first speech to the European Parliament in April 1979, 'will not forget that they do not constitute all of Europe themselves' (*Discours* . . ., 1979). Europe was not to be confused with or placed entirely at the service of the European community.

Europe, 'an Ethico-Judicial Battle'?[6]

An important theme present in John Paul II's vision of Europe was that the reconstruction of the continent and of the European Union was dangerously distancing itself from its true nature without any clear consciousness of its own culture. There was a close relationship between the interest of the Holy See since the 1990s and the development of the European Union, which was no longer one of warm support, but rather one of injunction and critical support (Salin, 2005, p. 228). With the process of EU enlargement, what were its main foundations? The notion of its having exclusively liberal foundations was a matter of deep concern for John Paul II.

He tried to influence the foundational principles embedded in the draft Constitution for Europe of 2004. Before the Treaty of Amsterdam was adopted in June 1997, John Paul II and the other European church leaders had, for example, succeeded in excluding legal church–state relations from future European competences. This 'protection' was inserted again in the Treaty of Lisbon, Part I, Title 2, Article 16C, dealing with the national legal status of churches or 'philosophical and non-confessional organisations'. They were to remain within the framework of national sovereignty (Schneider, 2008). This step was significant. In the debates during the elaboration of the European Constitution, the Vatican was in favour of the explicit recognition of 'Europe's Christian roots' and the mention of God in the Preamble to the Treaty (Christians, 2004; Daups, 2006). John Paul II made this cause his own. Despite open support from several EU member states, particularly Italy and Poland, and a myriad of lobby associations, the Preamble retained a different wording about 'the inspiration of the cultural, religious and humanist heritage of Europe, from which the universal values of the inviolable and inalienable rights of human beings developed, as well as freedom, democracy, equality and the rule of law'.

The reason for the relative Catholic failure was not only the secular intention of the French government, which was condemned by Cardinal Jean-Marie Lustiger, the archbishop of Paris, in Berlin on 28 November 2000. Lustiger claimed that the EU was hanging on to a radicalised vision of Enlightenment culture as the main component of European identity (Chenaux, 1990, p. 203). However, the omission of references to Christianity and God in the European Constitution was not only the result of the Enlightenment culture, but also a question of legal consistency. If such references had been included, they might have brought about a qualitative transformation in European law and the laws of EU member states (Monial, 2004). In Philippe Portier's opinion, John Paul II certainly was not nostalgic for the *Res Publica Christiana*. He was not calling for a state which imposed a Christian society. In his address before the European Parliament in October 1988 (*Discours ...*, 1988), the pope pointed out his objections to any form of confessional state, recognising the validity of democratic regimes which are founded on the sovereignty of the people and limited government. From this perspective, John Paul II can be seen as having a 'laic' perception of politics which recognised political autonomy and the rule of law. However, he cleaved to the Thomist tradition – strongly present in contemporary Catholic social doctrine – claiming that the rule of law cannot be the unilateral producer of the legal system and the values it protects.

The rule of law is an instrument at the service of societies which precede and extend its authority. It has a transcendent nature and is 'natural' to man as the authority which governs him in the interest of avoiding injustice and chaos.[7] The encyclical *Centesimus Annus* (1991) contained the Catholic definition of democratic order: 'The Church values the democratic system inasmuch as it ensures the participation of citizens in making political choices, guarantees to the governed the possibility both of electing and holding accountable those who govern them, and of replacing them through peaceful means when appropriate' (*Centesimus Annus*, para. 46). Democracy must develop respect for civil society. The primacy of civil society over the state is ontological and exists independently of it. Authority is legitimately exercised if it seeks the common good and if it employs legal moral means. Public authority is required to respect the pre-existing fundamental and inalienable rights of each human being (*Catechism*, para. 2254). If leaders enact laws or take unjust measures – contrary to the 'natural law' – these measures may not force the collective conscience (*Catechism*, para. 2242). In this case, authority degenerates into oppression.

Two main ideas summarise this conceptual approach. First, the obligations of the rule of law must ensure the conditions for 'household prosperity' (*Catechism*, para. 2211) and the right means for the accomplishment of the common good. Second, the pre-existence of a civil society and its intermediary bodies. These bodies are able to take charge of, or undertake co-responsibility for, a number of essential and diffused aspects of the same common good (the principle of subsidiarity) (*Catechism*, para. 1883). Article 3B of the Treaty of Maastricht for the European Union recognised the principle of subsidiarity, which derived from the social doctrine of the Catholic Church, in community legislation under the name of participatory democracy. The Treaty of Lisbon also endorsed the principle of subsidiarity in an additional protocol.

Although the rule of law imposes respect for a base of common values, it does not decide what they are. According to John Paul II, these values do not need any contract. They are not negotiable and cannot be the object of transactions or contractual laws in the name of popular sovereignty. For John Paul II, these values are not to be submitted to the random demands of a section of society, according to a contractual model of liberal adjustments. They should absolutely remain judicially untouchable. In this sense, reminding Europeans of just what Europe fundamentally was and is – meaning a system based on authentic values both revealed and thought out – would, he believed, help them to encapsulate the inviolability of these values in the common Constitution. If Europeans did not include this inviolability in the Constitution under the name of God or revealed Christian rights and duties, the corruption of liberal philosophy would drag them towards an 'immoral' individual and collective existence, an immorality henceforth entrenched by law in the name of freedom. John Paul II associated the present Europe and its way of functioning with a deviation into the 'morbid culture' and civilisational crisis of liberal societies. Being permissive, indifferent, materialistic, hedonistic, these societies were heading towards the dislocation of large united families, disrespect for life from its conception to its end, the absence of moral protection for young people and the rapid rise of exclusion and poverty (*Acto Europeo* …, 1982; text also available in Salin, 2005, annexe 1, pp. 205–11).

In John Paul II's opinion, Europe was still disfigured by the confusion of the democratic game with the consensual adaptation of the values in vogue at any moment. Jean Séguy (1980) claims that his European project involved 'mobilising utopia'. Even if Europe was at peace, prosperous and fairly egalitarian, these values meant nothing if Europeans lost their profound sense of human life. Europe would find its meaningful sense again only if it returned to the truths of its pre-modern culture and worked towards re-founding the basis of its democratic system. According to Philippe Portier, this call for restoration took an 'ethico-judicial' form, by 'repositioning customs and laws, economical and political systems, the vast domains of culture, civilisation and development back under the guardianship of Christian definitions which have been authenticated by the Roman moral authority' (Portier, 2007, p. 49). The conciliatory humanism of Europeans should cease to lean on an unlimited liberalism: 'An ethical system without a transcendent reference system is incapable of creating absolute moral values', according to John Paul II. 'It remains fragile in practice and precarious in time.' This postulate explains John Paul II's project of resacralising Europe, without which, according to him, Europeans would be incapable of organising a just and viable way of living together.

Conclusion

'Europe' has been treated in a number of different ways in papal thought in the twentieth century. At first, under Benedict XV and Pius XI, European unity was presented as the only means to avoid wars and to tame aggressive nationalisms. With Pius XII, Europe became a vision, founded on a sacred past where 'Faith' and 'Truth' had been given by Christ (and the Catholic Church) to the peoples of Europe. The pope's role was unceasingly to defend federalism, and to condemn communism and Cold War politics. The popes of the 1960s and 1970s recast Catholic doctrine on Europe as a new utopia, replacing Christendom or the Christian Empire. They imbued Europe with a new concern for the situation of Eastern Europe and the need to remember that East and West belonged together. They aimed to revive the opportunity for all European peoples to live in a secure, democratic and developed continent thanks to the protective cultivation of Christian values.

John Paul II's contribution to this debate remains without doubt the most personal and original. According to him, European unity represented more than a hope for a lasting peace for its people and for the rest of the world. It had become a possible vehicle of salvation for its inhabitants and humanity. At Santiago de Compostela in 1982 he suggested that Europe was born in pilgrimage and that its maternal language was Christianity. Its aim was not to become richer or more secure. Its goal was spiritual, and Europe could not reach the best form of society unless it renewed and protected the values which Christianity had encapsulated. Jean Paul II proposed that Europe build toward this ideal of a humane society, diverse, protected, peaceful and prosperous, with a clearly delineated 'political' will aimed at preserving and promoting inalienable and God-linked values. The legacy of his pontifical teachings continues (Barberini, 2006). His successor, Benedict XVI, has shown his intention of perpetuating and developing Catholic teachings on Europe in exactly the same way (Ratzinger, 2004; Benedict XVI, 2006, 2007).

Notes

1 John Paul II (*Acto Europeo* ..., 1982, para.3) says. 'I view Europe and see a continent which has most contributed to world development, not only in the field of ideas but also in the fields of work, sciences and the arts. And while I bless the Lord for letting Europe shine its evangelical light since the beginning of apostolic preaching, I cannot keep silent on the state of crisis in which it finds itself at the doorstep of the third millennium of the Christian era.'

2 The papal notes published by Nathalie Renoton-Beine are kept in the Vatican's archives, Archivio della Congregazione degli Affari Ecclesiastici Straordinari di Secretaria di Stato, period I–III (before 1922).

3 'For if in most places, peace is in some sort established and treaties signed, the germs of former enmities remain; and you well know, Venerable Brethren, that there can be no stable peace or lasting treaties, though made after long and difficult negotiations and duly signed, unless there be a return of mutual charity to appease hate and banish enmity' (*Pacem Dei Munus*).

4 'An attempt in this direction has already and is now being made; its results, however, are almost negligible and, especially so, as far as they can be said to affect those major questions which divide seriously and serve to arouse nations one against the other. No merely human institution of today can be as successful in devising a set of international laws which will be in harmony with world conditions as the Middle Ages were in the possession of that true League of Nations, Christianity' (*Ubi Arcano Dei*, para. 45).

5 This expression was first used by John Paul II on 25 January 1988 in the apostolic letter *Euntes in Mundum* for the millennium of the baptism of Kievan Rus'. The original term in Latin is 'duo pulmones', used at part V, para. 12. The future pope had, however, expressed the idea of two complementary parts of Europe in his first article on Europe (Wojtyla, 1978).
6 Expression used by Philippe Portier (2007, p. 44).
7 Leo XIII: 'Every human community needs an authority to govern it' (*Immortale Dei*; *Diuturnum*). 'The foundation of such authority lies in human nature. It is necessary for the unity of the state. Its role is to ensure as far as possible the common good of the society' (*Catechism*, Part III, Section I, Chapter II, Article 2a., para. 1898).

References

(a) Books, Articles and Papers

Bacot, G. (1989) *La doctrine de la guerre juste* (Paris, Economica).
Barberini, G. (2006) 'La politique européenne de l'Eglise Catholique, de Pie XII à aujourd'hui', *L'Année Canonique*, 48, pp. 187–217.
Benedict XVI (2006) *Christianity and the Crisis of Cultures: the Europe of Benedict* (San Francisco, Ignatius Press).
Castillo, M. (2001) *L'Europe de Kant* (Paris, Privat).
Charles-Roux, F. (1932) 'Charles-Roux à Bonnet', 19 December 1932, *Documents Diplomatiques Français, 1932–1939*, Ière Série (1932–1935), II (15 novembre 1932–17 mars 1933) (Paris, Ministère des Affaires Etrangères, 1966), pp. 282–88.
Chelini, B. (1989) L'*Eglise de Jean-Paul II face à l'Europe* (Paris, Nouvelle Cité).
Chenaux, Ph. (1990) *Une Europe vaticane? Entre le plan Marshall et les Traités de Rome* (Brussels, Ciaco).
Chenaux, Ph. (2003) *Pie XII: diplomate et pasteur* (Paris, Cerf).
Chenaux, Ph. (2004) 'De Pie XII à Jean Paul II: une certaine idée de l'Europe', in V. Aucante (ed.), L'*Europe et le fait religieux: sources* (Paris, Patrimoines, Valeurs, Parole et Silence).
Chenaux, Ph. (2007) *De la Chrétienté à l'Europe: les Catholiques et l'idée européenne au XXème siècle* (Tours, CLD).
Christians, L.-L. (2004) 'Construction européenne et politique religieuse', in B. Chelini-Pont (ed.), *Quelle politique religieuse en Europe et en Méditerranée?* (Aix-en-Provence, Presses Universitaires d'Aix-Marseille), pp. 123–40.
Daups, Th. (2006) 'Eglises et Union Européenne: l'institutionnalisation d'une représentation participative', in B. Chelini-Pont (ed.), *Annuaire Droit et Religion*, vol. II (2006–07) (Aix-en-Provence, Presses Universitaires d'Aix-Marseille).
Dawson, C. (1932) *The Making of Europe: an Introduction to the History of European Unity*, vol. III (Washington, Catholic University of America Press).
Documents (1948–63) *Documents Pontificaux de sa Sainteté Pie XII* (21 vols) (Saint-Maurice, Editions Saint-Augustin).
Durand, J.-D. (1995) L'*Europe de la démocratie chrétienne* (21 vols) (Brussels, Complexe).
Durand, J.-D. (2006) 'Giovanni Paolo II e l'Europa occidentale: al di la della secolarizzazionne', in E. Guerrieri and M. Impagliazzo (eds), *Storia della Chiesa XXVI: i cattolici e le chiese cristiane durante il pontificato di Giovanni Paolo II (1978–2005)* (Cinisello Balsamo, San Paolo).
Durand, J.-D. (2007) 'Le Saint-Siège et la construction européenne, 1945–2005', *Documentation Catholique*, 2378 (15 April).
Hehir, J. B. (1990) 'Papal foreign policy', *Foreign Policy*, 78, Spring, pp. 26–48.
Hanson, E. O. (1987) *The Catholic Church in World Politics* (Princeton, Princeton University Press).
Hugo, V. (1849) *Opening Address to the Peace Congress* (Paris, 21 August 1849), http://www.ellopos.net/politics/hugo-addresses-europe.asp; in French at http://www.lettres.net/hugo/texte03.htm (both last accessed 29 October 2008).

Il Patto (1928) 'Il patto contra la guerra firmato a Parigi: sulla via della pace', *L' Osservatore Romano*, 29 August.

Jean XXIII (1962) 'Lettre adressée au président Alain Barrère, 49ème semaine sociale de France sur "L'Europe des personnes et des peoples"', Strasbourg, 19 July, *La Documentation Catholique*, 1033, p. 155.

Mayeur, J.-M. (1981) 'Pius XII and Europe', *Relations Internationales*, 28, pp. 413–21.

Meylan, J.-P. (1969) *La Revue de Genève, miroir des lettres européennes 1920–1930* (Geneva, Droz).

Monial, P.-Y. (2004) 'Le projet de traité établissant une constitution pour l'Europe: quels fondements théoriques pour le droit constitutionnel de l'Union européenne?', *Revue Trimestrielle de Droit Européen*, 40, 3, pp. 443–76.

Pollard, J. (1999) *Benedict XV (1914–1922): the Unknown Pope and the Pursuit of Peace* (New York, Geoffrey Chapman).

Portier, Ph. (2007) 'Jean-Paul et l'Europe', *Revue Esprit* (special issue 'Les effervescences religieuses dans le monde'), March–April, pp. 43–55.

Poupard, P. (1981) 'Respecter le droit de chaque nation: la pensée internationale de Jean-Paul II', *Revue Communio*, 6, 3, pp. 17–26.

Prévotat, J. (1996) 'La condamnation de l'Action française par Pie XI', in *A. Ratti, Pape Pie XI: actes du colloque tenu les 15–18 mars 1989* (Rome, Ecole Française de Rome), pp. 359–95.

Prévotat, J. (2001) *Les Catholiques et l'Action française: histoire d'une condamnation, 1899–1939* (Paris, Fayard).

Ratzinger, J. (2004) *Europe, Today and Tomorrow* (San Francisco, Ignatius Press).

Renoton-Beine, N. (2004) *La colombe et les tranchées: Benoît XV et les tentatives de paix durant la grande guerre* (Paris, Cerf).

Salin, L. (2005) *Vers une Europe vaticane? L'influence du Saint-Siège dans l'élargissement de l'Union Européenne* (Paris, L'Harmattan).

Schneider, H. (2008) 'Die Europäische Union, Kirchen und Religionen: Rückblicke auf eine Kontroverse', *Integration*, 31, 1 (January), pp. 37–47, http://www.iep-berlin.de/index.php?id=610 (last accessed 23 September 2008).

Séguy, J. (1980) 'La socialisation utopique aux valeurs', *Archives des Sciences Sociales des Religions*, 50, 1 (July–September), pp. 7–21.

Società (1929) 'Società delle nazioni: i lavori della decima Assemblea: le sorprese della coerenza', *L'Osservatore Romano*, 7 September.

Stehle, H. (1981) *Eastern Politics of the Vatican 1917–1979* (Athens, Ohio University Press).

Vaillancourt, J.-G. (1990) 'Cinq papes modernes, le concile Vatican II et la paix mondiale', *Sociologie et Société*, XXII, 2, http://classiques.uqac.ca/contemporains/vaillancourt_jean_guy/cinq papes modernes/cinq papes_concile_paix.pdf (last accessed 23 September 2008)

Wojtyla, K. (1978) 'Una frontiera per l'Europa: dove?', *Vita e Pensiero*, 4 (June–December), pp. 160–68.

(b) Papal Encyclicals, Apostolic Letters, Papal Speeches and Other Papal and Official Catholic Documents

Except for Pius XII, *Allocution*, these are all available online at the official site of the Holy See, www.vatican.va (last accessed 23 September 2008).

Catechism of the Catholic Church

Leo XIII

Quod Apostolici Muneris, 28 December 1878.

Diuturnum, 29 June 1881.

Immortale Dei, 1 November 1885.

Benedict XV
Ubi Primum, 8 September 1914.
Ad Beatissimi Apostolorum, 1 November 1914.
Allorché Fummo Chiamati, 28 July 1915.
Al Tremendo Conflitto, 4 March 1916.
Pacem Dei Munus Pulcherrimum, 23 May 1920.

Pius XI
Ubi Arcano Dei, 23 December 1922.
Iniquis Afflictisque, 18 November 1926.
Quadragesimo Anno, 15 May 1931.
Non Abbiamo Bisogno, 29 June 1931.
Acerba Animi, 29 September 1932.
Mit Brennender Sorge, 14 March 1937.
Divini Redemptoris, 19 March 1937.

Pius XII
Fulgens Radiatur, 21 March 1947.
Allocution aux congressistes de l'Union Européenne des Fédéralistes, 11 November 1948, http://www.ena.lu
Mirabile Illud, 6 December 1950.
Apostolical Letter to the People of Russia, 7 July 1952.

John XXIII
Mater et Magistra, 15 May 1961.
Pacem in Terris, 11 April 1963.

Paul VI
Lettera Apostolica Pacis Nuntius, San Benedetto Abate Viene Proclamato Patrono Principale dell' Intera Europa, A Perpetua Memoria, 24 October 1964.
Gaudium et Spes, 7 December 1965.
Populorum Progressio, 26 March 1967.
Discours aux membres de l'Assemblée générale de l'association des Instituts d'Etudes Européennes, 29 April 1967.

John Paul II
Discours aux membres du Parlement Européen, 5 April 1979.
Discours à l'UNESCO, 2 June 1980.
Egregiae Virtutis, 31 December 1980.
Acto Europeo en Santiago de Compostela, 9 November 1982.
Slavorum Apostoli, 2 July 1985.
Euntes in Mundum, 25 January 1988.
Discours au Parlement Européen, 11 October 1988.
Centesimus Annus, 1 May 1991.

Benedict XVI
Address to the Participants in the Convention Organized by the Commission of the Bishop's Conferences of the European Community (COMECE), 24 March 2007.

(c) Archival Material

Note (1921) Note from the Secretariat of State in December 1921 addressed to the American government, Archivio della Congregazione degli Affari Ecclesiastici Straordinari di Secretaria di Stato, period I-III, Germania, 11, http://asv.vatican.va/en/fond/index/AES.htm

Towards a 'Common Law' on Religion in the European Union

NORMAN DOE

Introduction

Law is a place where religion and politics meet. There has been a profound increase in the treatment of religion by the laws and other regulatory instruments of the European Union (EU).[1] So much so that commentators today speak of the category 'European law on religion' among the several branches of law emerging alongside the development of the EU and the fuller economic, political and social integration of its member states.[2] European law on religion may be found in four basic sources: (1) its formal sources, the laws and other regulatory instruments of the Union (treaties, regulations, directives, jurisprudence, etc); and its material sources (from which inspiration is drawn), namely (2) the general principles common to and induced from the similarities between the laws on religion in the member states (under the EU law category 'general principles common to the laws of the Member States'),[3] (3) the European Convention on Human Rights (ECHR),[4] and, perhaps, (4) the laws of the religious traditions themselves.[5] There are eight fundamental principles of the European law of religion in these species of legal regime, representing what may be styled a European 'common law' on religion.

1. The Principle of the Value of Religion

Like the ill-fated draft Constitution 2004, in its much-debated preamble (see Potz *et al.*, 2004), the draft European Union Reform (or Lisbon) Treaty 2007 (EURT), amending the Treaty on European Union and the Treaty Establishing the European Community,[6] draws 'inspiration from the cultural, religious and humanist inheritance of Europe, from which have developed the universal values of the inviolable and inalienable rights of the human person, freedom, democracy, equality and the rule of law'.[7] It also recognises the 'specific contribution' of *churches* to Europe.[8] While this provision describes the normative effect of religion, the principle of the value of religion is not new in European law (and a reference to the European 'spiritual heritage' appears in the Charter of Fundamental Rights 2000).[9] It is occasionally recognised in some EU regulatory instruments which acknowledge explicitly but in a somewhat general manner the significance of the 'religious and philosophical values of society',[10] or 'spiritual welfare'.[11] Moreover, it has been suggested in judicial proceedings that religion may be a defining characteristic of nationhood within member states: a 'nation' is 'the totality of individuals linked by the fact of sharing traditions, culture, ethnicity, religion and so on'.[12] Similarly, the Seventh Framework Programme directive, in the context of European citizenship, recognises that 'religions', along with cultural heritage, institutions and legal systems, history, language and values, are a 'building element' of European multicultural identity and heritage.[13]

As the draft 2004 EU Constitution, the Lisbon Reform Treaty does not specify *which* spiritual or religious heritage is inspirational; indeed, the Charter of Fundamental Rights, Article 22, provides that the Union must respect 'religious diversity'.[14] This expresses the neutrality of the Union towards different religions,[15] and is consistent with both the foundational instruments of the community and the practice of functional regulatory instruments. They expressly recognise the category 'religious diversity',[16] the need to work with 'religious pluralism',[17] and the growth of interaction between religions in Europe and beyond.[18] Consequently, the value of *religions*, of their diversity–plurality, is known to European law. The decision on Specific Programme Cooperation accepts that 'appreciation and understanding of differences between value systems of different religions or ethnic minority groups lay foundations for positive attitudes'.[19] The Equal Opportunities Programme seeks to facilitate and celebrate diversity, and highlights 'the positive contribution that people, irrespective of religion or belief, can make to society as a whole'.[20]

Religious neutrality is in keeping with a definition of religion in an EU directive on refugees, third country nationals with well-founded fears of religious persecution in their own country:

> The concept of religion shall in particular include the holding of theistic, non-theistic and atheistic beliefs, the participation in, or abstention from, formal worship in private or public, either alone or in community with others, other religious acts or expressions of view, or forms of personal or communal conduct based on or mandated by any religious belief.[21]

Neutrality, in terms of recognition of the value of religion, is consistent with the principle of equality: under the regulation to establish a community code on rules governing the movement of persons across borders, border guards must 'fully respect' human dignity irrespective of religion or belief.[22] At the same time, however, European instruments recognise the dangers posed by 'the radicalisation of religious groups'.[23]

The value of religion principle is a fundamental of Strasbourg jurisprudence,[24] and the general principles of law on religion common to the member states of the Union. Typically, the courts assume that 'some benefit accrues to the public from the attendance at places of worship of persons who live in this world and mix with their fellow citizens'.[25] Moreover, the value of religion to European life and development is recognised, unsurprisingly, by religious groups themselves (see for example Pope John Paul II, 2003), many of which espouse similar values to those of the Union. For example, the *Charta Oecumenica* (2001), between the Conference of European Churches and the Roman Catholic Council of European Bishops' Conferences, provides that 'Christianity constitutes an empowering source of inspiration and enrichment for Europe'; the parties undertake to participate in 'the building of Europe', and to work for 'a humane, socially conscious Europe, in which human rights and the basic values of peace, justice, freedom, tolerance, participation and solidarity prevail'.[26]

2. The Principle of Subsidiarity in Matters of Religion

Based on a declaration appended to the Treaty of Amsterdam 1997,[27] like Article 52 of the draft Constitution,[28] the Lisbon Reform Treaty in Article 15b.1 provides: 'The Union respects and does not prejudice the status under national law of churches and religious associations or communities in the Member States'.[29] Interpreted literally, this does not recognise (or protect) the competence of member states to operate their own systems of law on religion generally,[30] though it is commonly understood as an expression the principle of subsidiarity in religious matters: the regulation of religion is primarily a matter for the member states and their domestic laws.

The instances are well-known. The Union respects the special status of Mount Athos under the Hellenic Constitution on grounds of 'a spiritual and religious nature'.[31] 'Religious factors' may be important in decision-making within member states (exercising their margin of appreciation) on the regulation of gambling.[32] That a person maintained washing machines in a Bhagwan community was irrelevant to the question whether he was engaged in 'economic activity'.[33] Religious and ethical issues about abortion were irrelevant to determine the legality of restrictions on the provision by student associations of information about abortion services.[34] Sunday trading questions, and restrictions of the free movement of goods, are matters for national law.[35] The attempt to make Sunday the Europe-wide day of rest failed.[36] Subsidiarity is also used in Strasbourg jurisprudence (as to recognition or establishment of state-churches provided states protect the freedom of other religions in such systems,[37] and they must ensure state neutrality in religious affairs).[38]

Nevertheless, matters within the economic competence of the Union may have a religious dimension. Under rules on the procurement of public works contracts national authorities must apply domestic procedures adapted to the relevant EU law which might include provisions on the 'structures of the church'.[39] There are provisions on the export of cultural goods, including those elements forming an integral part of 'religious monuments'.[40] Rules on objects containing precious metals cover both secular and religious items.[41] A regulation on statistics on income and living conditions applies to 'institutions' which includes 'religious institutions (convents, monasteries)'.[42] Under the decision establishing the European Year of Equal Opportunities, actions as to religion (along with race, ethnicity, disability, age and sexual orientation) must take full account of gender differences.[43]

The widening EU interest in matters of religion is particularly evident in instruments dealing with external relations. One function of the special representative of the Union for Afghanistan is to advise on 'respect for human rights of all Afghan people, regardless of gender, ethnicity or religion'.[44] Some directives refer explicitly to the religious affairs departments of non-member states.[45] The decision on principles, priorities and conditions in the Accession Partnership with Turkey includes the requirement that Turkey guarantees 'in law and practice' the full enjoyment of human rights and freedoms by all without discrimination on grounds of religion or belief.[46] The regulation which establishes a financing instrument for the promotion of democracy and human rights worldwide enables community assistance in the fight against discrimination based on religion or belief.[47]

3. The Principle of Cooperation: Dialogue with Religion

The Lisbon Reform Treaty in Article 15b.3 provides: 'Recognising their identity and their specific contribution, the Union shall maintain an open, transparent and regular dialogue with these churches and organisations'.[48] Cooperation between the EU and associations which might include religious bodies has been on the political agenda for some time: in a declaration appended to the Maastricht Treaty (charitable associations responsible for welfare programmes and services);[49] in an opinion on the role of civil society organisations in the building of Europe;[50] and in a call for a structured channel for feedback, criticism and protest in European governance.[51] Indeed, the database of CONECCS (Consultation, the European Commission and Civil Society) carries information about formal consultative bodies and civil society organisations with a number of religious organisations listed.[52] The principle of cooperation with religious organisations may be justified on the basis of their particular expertise, including that in moral and social affairs, and enhancement of legitimacy in governance (see Rivers, 2004, pp. 286–87).

This principle merely articulates existing practices under EU law.[53] The provision which establishes a high-level advisory group on social integration, to examine the participation of ethnic minorities in the labour market, mentions religion.[54] The EU Agency for Fundamental Rights must cooperate closely with nongovernmental organisations (NGOs) and institutions of civil society active in combatting racism and xenophobia at national, European and international level; the agency is to establish a 'cooperation network' (the Fundamental Freedoms Platform) to include 'religious, philosophical and non-confessional organisations'.[55] The principle is also employed in external relations. One function of the special EU representative for Central Africa is to contribute, in cooperation with the Organization for Security and Co-operation in Europe, to conflict prevention and resolution by developing close contacts with authorities and other local actors including 'religious groups and their leaders', NGOs, political parties and minorities.[56]

The principle has been extended to financial support for religion. For the purposes of expenditure, religion is included in the classification of non-profit institutions.[57] The regulation for a financing instrument for development cooperation provides that 'churches and religious associations and communities' are eligible for funding.[58] Under the instrument for nuclear safety cooperation, non-state actors eligible for financial support include 'churches and religious associations and communities' likely to contribute to the development or the external dimensions of internal Union policies.[59] Similarly, churches and religious associations and communities are eligible for funding to implement action and joint cross-border cooperation programmes under the European Neighbourhood and Partnership Instrument.[60] The regulation which establishes the Instrument for Stability Abroad also provides that churches, religious associations and communities are eligible for financial support.[61]

The proposed Lisbon Treaty obligation to cooperate with religions, and their consequential right to cooperation, goes beyond the requirements of both the European Convention on Human Rights (it does not appear in the Convention) and the laws of member states: that states have a juridical *duty* to cooperate with religions is not a principle common to their constitutional traditions. However, there is a principle that states have a *right* to establish facilities for dialogue. Covenants, concordats and other agreements have proliferated in church–state relations within national borders. For example, agreements are entered to define church–state relations, to guarantee religious freedom, and to make provision for collaboration in matters of common concern. Protestant churches, and the Roman Catholic Church, are parties to these agreements. Agreements have also been established between alliances of churches and the state (see Puza and Doe, 2006). Similarly, some state laws enable interreligious collaboration (to enter 'covenants' to share church buildings),[62] as do the regulatory instruments of religious organisations.[63] The Constitution of the Conference of European Churches does so at EU level.[64]

4. The Principle of Religious Freedom

Under Article 6 of the Lisbon Reform Treaty, the Union recognises the rights, freedoms and principles set out in the Charter of Fundamental Rights 2000, which has 'the same legal value as the Treaties'. The Charter states that 'Everyone has the right to freedom of thought, conscience and religion. The right includes freedom to change religion or belief and freedom, either alone or in community with others and in public or in private, to manifest religion or belief, in worship, teaching, practice and observance.'[65] This principle, associated with many other rights,[66] but which does not appear expressly in the Rome or Maastricht treaties, was in the early jurisprudence of the European Court of Justice understood to be a feature of community polity.[67] The principle is embedded in the EU in numerous regulatory instruments, such as the directive on the equal treatment of men and women in the supply of goods and services: 'it is important to respect other fundamental rights and freedoms, including ... the freedom of religion'.[68] Some provisions are facilitative: respect for religious freedom appears in the directive on freedom of movement of EU citizens;[69] the Council Code on cross-border movement has rules on journeys for religious events, along with political, scientific, cultural and sports events.[70] Other rules are prohibitive: for example, staff appointments to the European Defence Agency must not refer to the religious beliefs of candidates.[71]

The principle is particularly evident in the administration of justice. A decision on extradition cooperation provides that a member state has *no* duty to extradite if that state has 'substantial grounds' to believe that the request has been made to prosecute or punish a person on religious grounds, or would 'cause prejudice' to the position of that person for this reason.[72] The framework decision on the mutual recognition of financial penalties enables a member state to refuse to execute a decision or financial penalty if it objectively believes that these aim to punish a person on grounds of religion.[73] Another framework decision, on the mutual recognition of confiscation orders, provides that a member state may refuse to confiscate property if confiscation is to punish or prosecute a person on account of their religion or belief.[74] An agreement between the EU and Iceland and Norway provides that the latter may refuse to surrender a person if they believe the arrest warrant was issued to prosecute or punish that person on grounds of religion or belief.[75] Similar rules exist as to the transit of third country nationals or stateless persons when a member state refuses transit if such persons run the risk of torture, inhuman or degrading treatment or punishment, the death penalty, or persecution because of religion (but not belief).[76]

The Union commonly makes religious freedom or equality a condition in its policies on external relations with non-member states.[77] The regulation to establish a financing instrument for democracy and human rights worldwide enables community assistance in the fight against discrimination based on religion or belief.[78] The Accession Partnership with Turkey includes the requirement that Turkey guarantees 'in law and practice' the full enjoyment of human rights and freedoms by all irrespective of religion or belief. It also requires Turkey to 'adopt and implement provisions concerning the exercise of freedom of thought, conscience and religion by all individuals and religious communities' in line with the European Convention on Human Rights as well as to take into account recommendations of the Commission against Racism and Intolerance, an institution of the Council of Europe.[79] Strasbourg jurisprudence, and the myriad micro-principles which it has developed about the terms of religious freedom under Article 9 of the ECHR, will become very important in the elaboration of religious freedom in the EU.[80] The principle of religious freedom is a well-developed fundamental general principle of laws common to the member states;[81] indeed, in the UK, for example, the statute explicitly recognises its 'importance'.[82]

5. The Principle of the Autonomy of Religious Associations

Neither the Rome Treaty nor the Maastricht Treaty expressly provides for the right of religious associations to self-governance. It is possible that the principle of autonomy is implicit in Article 15b of the Lisbon Reform Treaty on the status of religious associations, and it is certainly a necessary aspect of religious freedom.[83] Nevertheless, respect for and protection of religious autonomy has been assumed in ordinary regulatory instruments over the years. For instance, the Turkey accession partnership decision requires Turkey to establish conditions for the functioning of religious communities, including legal and judicial protection (*inter alia* through legal personality of the communities, their members, and assets, teaching, appointment and training of clergy and enjoyment of property rights in line with Protocol 1, ECHR).[84] However, one condition in the EU partnership with the former Yugoslav Republic of Macedonia is that the latter is to 'ensure the full implementation of *the constitutional principle of the separation of religious communities and groups from the State*', as well as to review 'the legal framework for religious communities and groups' (my italics).[85]

The Union sometimes explicitly allows the operation of duties under religious law.[86] For example, member states could grant exemptions from the restrictive measures against Iraq (introduced for security reasons), to prevent the entry or transit through their territories of prescribed persons, where the state decides that travel is justified on the grounds of 'urgent humanitarian need, including religious obligation'.[87] The same 'religious obligation' formula was also used in relation to the religious duties of persons seeking entry while EU restrictions were operative against the Republic of Congo,[88] in relation to persons suspected of involvement in the assassination of a former Lebanese prime minister,[89] and in relation to nationals of the Côte d'Ivoire.[90]

Perhaps the most well-known juridical expression of the autonomy principle relates to the freedom of religious organisations to discriminate on grounds of religion in the employment sphere. One directive prohibits direct and indirect discrimination on grounds of religion or belief (along with disability, age or sexual orientation).[91]

However, religious discrimination may be permitted in 'the case of occupational activities within churches and other public or private organisations the ethos of which is based on religion or belief'; this applies 'where, by reason of the nature of these activities or the context in which they are carried out, a person's religion or belief constitute a genuine, legitimate and justified occupational requirement, having regard to the organisation's ethos'.[92] Nevertheless, provided that its rules are otherwise complied with,

> this Directive shall thus not prejudice the right of churches and other public or private organisations, the ethos of which is based on religion or belief, acting in conformity with national constitutions and laws, to require individuals working for them to act in good faith and with loyalty to the organisation's ethos.[93]

Similarly, the working time directive enables states to derogate from prescribed requirements, if there is proper regard for workers' safety and health, in relation to workers officiating in religious ceremonies in churches and religious communities.[94]

An important by-product of the exercise of religious autonomy is the juridical integration of decision-making by religious authorities into the European regulatory regime; religious authorities are assigned tasks of carrying out public EU functions. Several instruments on foodstuffs deal with 'legislative or administrative decisions or customs' of member states 'relating ... to religious rites'.[95] Ritual slaughter, now within the scope of EU law,[96] is exempt from the requirement to stun animals before slaughter.[97] In the member states, 'the *religious authority* on whose behalf slaughter is carried out shall be competent for the application and monitoring of the special provisions which apply to slaughter according to religious rites' (my italics).[98] Incidentally, evisceration must be carried out no later than 45 minutes after stunning or, 'in the case of ritual slaughter, half and hour after bleeding'.[99] A regulation on foodstuffs hygiene provides that food business operators of slaughterhouses must ensure the trachea and oesophagus remain intact during bleeding, except in the case of the slaughter 'according to a religious custom'.[100]

Other examples of the legal recognition of decisions taken by religious bodies in an exercise of their autonomy include the following. The decisions of church tribunals in matrimonial cases operative under concordats between the Holy See and Portugal, Spain and Italy are afforded recognition by the Union.[101] Rules on the description and presentation of wines permit recommendations to the consumer concerning the acceptability of the wine for religious purposes;[102] such recommendations may be indicated 'only if the wine ... has been produced in accordance with the special rules laid down by the religious authorities concerned, and those authorities have given their written approval as to such indication', moreover, such recommendations may be indicated only in trade with the religious authorities concerned.[103] Rules prohibit the processing of personal data revealing religious or philosophical beliefs; but there are exceptions for processing by a foundation, association or any other non-profit-making body with a religious or philosophical aim (political or trade union aims are also covered) carried out in the course of their legitimate activities provided the processing relates solely to the members of the body or persons having regular contact with it in connection with its purposes; disclosure is subject to data subject consent.[104]

The religious autonomy principle has been developed from time to time in Strasbourg jurisprudence, but its inspiration seems to have come from its well-established place in the general principles of religion law common to the member states: in some states the principle is enunciated in the constitutional[105] or other formal laws,[106] and in others it is a principle developed in case-law (see Robbers, 2001). The principle of autonomy is asserted by the internal regulatory systems of some religious traditions and organisations, particularly in relation to governance, doctrine and discipline.[107]

6. The Principle of Religious Equality (Non-Discrimination)

Article 21 of the Charter of Fundamental Rights (which under the Lisbon Treaty enjoys the same legal value as the treaties), provides that: 'Any discrimination based on any ground such as sex, race, colour, ethnic or social origin, genetic features, language, religion or belief, political or other opinion, membership of a national minority, property, birth, disability, age or sexual orientation, shall be prohibited'.[108] This is declaratory of the existing foundational laws of the Union.[109] Indeed, 'Non-discrimination is a fundamental principle of the European Union' and provides for action to combat discrimination on account of religion and belief, in accordance with Article 13(1) of the Treaty of Rome and Article 21 of the Charter of Fundamental Rights.[110] It is a 'general principle of Community law'.[111] Non-discrimination is based on the principle of equal treatment,[112] which itself is 'a basis for democracy'.[113] Another reason for non-discrimination is social cohesion: non-discrimination on grounds of religion or belief expresses a 'basic principle of social cohesion' and should be incorporated in all levels of the strategic approach to cohesion.[114]

The prohibition against religious discrimination appears in a multitude of EU regulatory instruments,[115] and is applied in many contexts. First, community officials are beneficiaries of the principle. Discrimination on grounds of religion or belief is prohibited in the recruitment of Union personnel,[116] and specifically for staff of the European Defence Agency.[117] Second, member states must implement the directive on admitting third country nationals for the purpose of scientific research without discrimination on grounds of religion or belief;[118] the same applies to third country nationals for study, pupil exchanges, unremunerated work and voluntary service.[119] Third, member states must apply the directive on the right of EU citizens and their families to move and reside freely in the territories of member states without discrimination on account of religion or belief.[120]

The principle is applied in relation to health care. One regulation promotes health care services for lower income population groups and marginalised groups including 'persons belonging to groups suffering religious discrimination'.[121] It is also applied in relation to the application of funds. The regulation on the European Regional Development Fund, the European Social Fund and the Cohesion Fund provides for member states to take appropriate steps as to access to and implementation of the funds without discrimination on grounds of religion or belief.[122] The same applies with regard to the European Agricultural Fund for Rural Development.[123] The regulation which establishes the European Globalisation Adjustment Fund, to support redundant workers affected by major structural changes in world trade, provides that the Council and member states must ensure that the fund is administered without discrimination on grounds of religion,[124] and the regulation to establish a financing instrument to promote democracy and human rights worldwide enables community assistance in the fight against discrimination based on religion or belief.[125]

Moreover, soft-law regulatory instruments provide educative mechanisms to encourage the fight against discrimination. The Culture Programme aims to contribute to the elimination of religious discrimination.[126] The decision establishing the Youth in Action Programme links the promotion of active citizenship with the fight against discrimination on grounds of religion and belief.[127] The objective of the Equal Opportunities Programme is to raise awareness of the right to equality: all people are entitled to equal treatment irrespective of religion or belief.[128] According to this programme, the Union will take into account the different ways in which men and women experience discrimination on grounds of religion.[129]

The provision which forbids religious discrimination in the European Convention on Human Rights is somewhat similar in width to that developed in EU law: it prohibits state discrimination on grounds of religion in the exercise of convention rights and 'any rights set down by law'.[130] Prohibitions against religious discrimination are a common historical feature of the constitutions of several member states.[131] However, in the employment field, the principle has been a stimulus for (rather than a result of) the development of the general principles of religion law common to the member states of the Union. This has proved no more evident than in the UK and the dramatic effect there on the introduction of a general law against religious discrimination, elements of which were simply embryonic in the pre-Union era (Sandberg and Doe, 2007b).

7. The Principle of Special Protection of Religion

The Charter of Fundamental Rights 2000 has provisions which imply special protection for particular religious activities: Article 10.2 provides that 'The right of conscientious objection is recognised, in accordance with the national laws governing the exercise of this right'.[132] Article 14.3 states that

> The freedom to found educational establishments with due respect for democratic principles and the right of parents to ensure the education and teaching of their children in conformity with their religious, philosophical and pedagogical convictions shall be respected, in accordance with national law governing the exercise of such freedom and right.[133]

As with religious autonomy, the provision of special protection would seem to be a micro-principle of religious freedom; people cannot practise their religion freely if rules of general applicability disadvantage them in particular ways by virtue of their religious needs. The concept is not new. It is based on the current EU juridical practice in various fields.

First, special protection may be afforded to religious *associations*. A member state may provide that a trade mark shall not be registered, or if registered, shall be liable to be declared invalid, where the trade mark covers 'a sign of high symbolic value, in particular a religious symbol'.[134] Advertisements must not be inserted in any broadcast of a 'religious service', and 'religious programmes' of less than thirty minutes must not be interrupted by advertisements.[135]

Second, special protection may be afforded to *individuals*. Member states must satisfy the directive on electronic commerce but may derogate if necessary for public policy to combat 'the fight against any incitement to hatred on grounds of ... religion'.[136] The personal file of temporary staff of the European Defence Agency shall not refer to their 'religious activities and views'.[137] The system to protect personal data in the passenger name record of air passengers transferred to the US Bureau of Customs and Border Protection prohibits the use of sensitive information on religious beliefs.[138] However, personal data on religious beliefs may be processed if necessary for criminal investigations.[139]

Third, special protection may apply to religious *property*. There are provisions on the export of cultural goods forming an integral part of 'religious monuments'.[140] The return of cultural objects unlawfully removed from a member state includes objects found in the inventories of ecclesiastical institutions.[141] Some provisions are explicitly designed for the 'protection of cultural and religious sites',[142] or 'the rehabilitation of damaged and destroyed properties ... including historic and religious sites'.[143] One regulation prohibits dealing in Iraqi cultural property and items of 'religious importance', and protects inventories of Iraqi 'religious institutions'.[144]

Fourth, special protection is extended to *food*. In a regulation on foodstuffs, an applicant seeking authorisation to trade in genetically modified food or feed (different from its conventional counterparts with respect to composition, nutritional value and intended use) must send with the application 'a reasoned statement that the food does not give rise to ethical or religious concerns'; moreover, labelling of such genetically modified food or feed must include information about whether the modification 'gives rise to ethical or religious concerns'.[145] By regulation, export refunds on beef and veal should be granted for third countries which, 'for cultural or religious reasons, traditionally import substantial numbers of animals for domestic slaughter'.[146]

A good example of special protection for religion in the principles of law on religion common to the states of the Union is provided by the following provisions relating to the media field. First, under freedom of expression, freedom of the press is fundamental to democracy, and the press enjoys a discretion to cover religious matters. Second, in its coverage of religion the secular press must respect religion, it must portray it accurately, not offending religious feelings, particularly when offence may cause breaches of public order: different religions should enjoy equal protection against offensive publications. Third, the secular press should have a system of self-regulation, and the membership of self-regulatory bodies should include representatives from religious groups. Press self-regulation (codes of practice and guidance) should strike a balance between responsible journalistic freedom and protection of religious feelings by means of rights of complaint, remedial action and enforcement of standards which guard against religious discrimination and incitement to religious hatred.[147] Fourth, governmental and other bodies charged with monitoring standards in broadcasting should include representatives from religious groups; the transmission of religious programmes and services is a cultural expectation in Europe; religious groups have a right to be considered for access to transmission time, in programmes and broadcasts of religious worship. Self-regulation in broadcasting should have regard to religious pluralism, and satisfy respect for religion and non-discrimination on grounds of religion (see Doe, 2004).

8. The Principle of Religious Privilege

A principle related to special protection is that of the religious privilege which enables the enjoyment of extraordinary rights based on exemptions from rules of general applicability. This has not been articulated formally in the foundational instruments of the Union.

First, European law commonly exempts religion directly from prescribed requirements. 'Mobile churches' enjoy exemptions from requirements of vehicle harmonisation.[148] Tax exemptions may be enjoyed in relation to 'supplies of staff by religious or philosophical institutions for medical, welfare, child protection and educational purposes with a view to spiritual welfare'.[149] By way of contrast, the Turkey accession partnership decision provides that Turkey may not privilege the Muslim community over non-Muslims; Turkey must

> Adopt a law comprehensively addressing the difficulties faced by non-Muslim religious minorities and communities in line with the relevant European standards. Suspend all sales or confiscation of properties which belong or belonged to non-Muslim religious community foundations by the competent authorities pending adoption of the abovementioned law.[150]

Second, enjoyment of the privilege is at the discretion of the member state. Exceptions to working time requirements may be made for those officiating at religious ceremonies.[151] The directive on equal treatment of men and women in employment does not limit the right of a member state to exclude from its field of application those occupational activities and, where appropriate, prior training, for which, by reason of their nature or the context in which they are carried out, the sex of the worker constitutes a determining factor.[152] The directive on harmonisation of aspects of copyright enables member states to have exceptions for reproductions by the press, communication to the public or making available articles on 'religious topics' and materials for 'use in religious celebrations'.[153] As to consultation with and information for employees, member states may set special provisions for religion.[154] Likewise, member states may exempt payment service providers from requirements about the provision of information on the payer accompanying transfers of funds to organisations carrying out non-profit charitable, religious and cultural purposes provided that such organisations are subject to external reporting and audit.[155]

The principle of religious privilege, known to Strasbourg jurisprudence,[156] is a settled feature of the religion laws of the member states of the Union. In the UK, for instance, the law provides a number of statutory exemptions and common law concessions to religion. For example, Sikhs enjoy exemptions from general rules requiring the wearing of crash helmets on motor cycles,[157] and a special defence in an offensive articles prosecution in relation to carrying a *kirpan*;[158] the exemption from the general rule that a person must swear a Christian oath in judicial proceedings;[159] conscientious objection to participation in prescribed abortion treatment;[160] exemptions of ecclesiastical buildings from the general laws about works on listed buildings of historical or archaeological importance;[161] and statutory exemptions from the payment of local rates in favour of places of worship and associated properties.[162]

Conclusion

The enlargement of the EU, in composition and competence (economic, political and social), has produced an expansion in the volume of EU laws and other regulatory instruments dealing with religion. A wide range of religious phenomena is now expressly recognised in EU law: religious associations, groups, authorities, leaders, rules, customs, obligations, beliefs, teaching, ceremonies, rites, worship, observance, practice and education – all are juridical categories.

An examination of its laws and other regulatory instruments reveals the posture of the EU in terms of its own church–Union relations. The details of its laws indicate that the Union shares characteristics most in common with the so-called cooperationist model of church–state relations, though the language of separation is also employed; however, the Union is not a state–church system.

Efforts are now being made by scholars to identify from these instruments a set of fundamental principles: the value of religion; subsidiarity in religious matters; cooperation with religion; religious freedom; religious autonomy; religious equality; special protection for religion; and religious privilege.[163] The provisions of the Lisbon Treaty provide a convenient presentation and summary of these principles. It expressly lists the principles of the value of religion, subsidiarity, cooperation, freedom and equality, but it does not articulate expressly the principles of religious autonomy, special protection, or religious privilege; however, the latter seems to flow from the former.

These eight proposed principles have not been articulated *de novo* by the Union in its Reform Treaty. They may be induced from, and represent the motivating force behind, the existing foundational and functional legal instruments of the Union. Moreover, in a very general manner, it is possible to agree with the claims of the EU instruments themselves that these fundamentals are inspired loosely by the general principles common to the laws on religion of the member states. There are principles of religion law common to the member states; their existence can be factually established; each state contributes through its own religion law to this store of common principles; the principles are authoritative principles of law; they are fundamental to the self-understanding of each state in its approach to religion; and they demonstrate a workable unity in the European approach to the regulation of religion.

The draft constitutional principles of the value of religion, cooperation and religious autonomy do not formally appear in the European Convention on Human Rights; however, the autonomy principle is a feature of Strasbourg jurisprudence and a key element of common constitutional traditions of member states. The religious equality principle is causative of (rather than resulting from) common constitutional practices of member states. The special protection and privilege principles are more fully developed in the general principles of religion law common to the member states than in the formal instruments of the Union. A comparison of the emergent principles with those in the ECHR and the common constitutional traditions of the member states would be instructive.

An articulation of the general principles of religion law common to the member states is useful: (1) to test the EU claim that its fundamentals about religion are derived from the common legal traditions of its member states by functioning as a yardstick by which to measure the legitimacy of future developments in EU law on religion; (2) to help administer the idea that treaty/charter rights are to be interpreted in harmony with the common constitutional traditions of member states; and (3) to provide guidance on the balance to be struck between these principles.[164]

The EU claims that its laws and regulatory instruments are based on the constitutional traditions and principles of law common to its member states (and the ECHR). This is sustainable in relation to the growing body of EU regulatory material on religion. The evidence suggests that broadly the claim is accurate: these eight proposed principles are loosely consistent with the principles of religion law common to the member states. However, the position appears to be more complex than this. Only an articulation of the 'common law' of religion in the member states could reveal the complexities involved and yield more conclusive evidence. This is no easy task.

Acknowledgment

I am grateful to my colleagues Russell Sandberg and Mark Hill, at the Centre for Law and Religion, Law School, Cardiff University, for helpful comments on a draft of this piece, and to Charlotte Dyer at Cardiff Law School for invaluable assistance with the referencing.

Notes

1 There seem to be three broad phases: 1957–*ca* 1975, a general absence of norms on religion; 1976–1992, the side-effects of economic law on religion and the emergence of interest in religion (exemplified in, for example, *Prais v Council of Ministers* (C-130/75) 61975J0130); 1992–2007, from Maastricht to Lisbon, characterised by a growing body of substantive norms (actual and proposed) on religion. The following suggests that the next period might involve a more rigorous and critical understanding and articulation of the 'general principles of community law' on religion in member states of the Union.

2 Robbers (2004, p. 312): 'the fundamental principles of European law on religion' include regionality, neutrality, equality. See also Ventura (2001) and Davie (2000).

3 Treaty of Rome, Article 215(2); also (Lisbon) draft EU Reform Treaty 2007, Art. 6.2: rights in the ECHR result from constitutional traditions common to member states as general principles of EU law.

4 Though the ECHR, a creation of the Council of Europe, is not formally part of EU law, it has strong persuasive authority, and it has been ratified unilaterally by member states of the EU.

5 Insofar as religious laws fundamentally condition the claims which religions make upon the member states and in turn the EU itself and their responses to religion.

6 TEU retains its title; TEC becomes the Treaty on the Functioning of the European Union (TFEU).

7 European Union Reform Treaty (EURT) 2007, referred to in some sources as the Lisbon Treaty, Art. 1. See also Art. 2: the EU values are: respect for human dignity, freedom, democracy, equality, rule of law, human rights and minorities' rights; these values are common to member states in a society in which pluralism, non-discrimination, justice, solidarity and sexual equality are pursued.

8 EURT, Art. 15b (amending TEC); this repeats draft Constitution 2004 Art. 52.3.

9 Preamble: 'Conscious of its spiritual and moral heritage, the Union is founded on the indivisible, universal values of human dignity, freedom, equality and solidarity'.

10 Directive 2006/123/EC, Preamble, para. 40.

11 Directive 77/388/EEC: tax exemptions may be enjoyed as to 'supplies of staff by religious or philosophical institutions for medical, welfare, child protection and educational purposes with a view to spiritual welfare'; also Regulation EC 1781/2006, Art. 18 for exemptions for organisations carrying out non-profit charitable, religious and cultural purposes.

12 *Eman v College van Burgemeester en Wethouders van den Haag* (C-300/04) [2007] 1 CMLR 4, celex reference 62004J0300, Opinion of Advocate General Tizzano, Case C-145/04, celex reference 62004C0145, para. 79.

13 Council Decision 1982/2006/EC.

14 See also draft Constitution 2004, Art. 82; but EURT, Art. 3 refers only to 'cultural and linguistic diversity'.

15 See Robbers (2004, p. 314) for argument in favour of neutrality.

16 Decision 2006/320, Art. 22, OJ 2006 L118/9 at 13.

17 Decision 1982/2006/EC, OJ 2006 L412/1 at 24; see also Common Position 2006/795/CFSP.

18 Decision 1983/2006, Preamble (European Year of Intercultural Dialogue): EU enlargement, increased mobility in a single market, old and new migratory flows, exchanges with the rest of the world through trade, education, leisure and globalisation in general, is increasing interaction between peoples, cultures, languages, ethnic groups and religions in Europe and beyond.

19 Decision 2006/971.

20 Decision 771/2006, Art. 2 (on the basis of 2000/78/EC).
21 Directive 2004/83/EC, Art. 10(b).
22 Regulation EC 562/2006, Art. 6 (Schengen Borders Code).
23 Common Position 2005/304, Art. 11: in dealing with conflict prevention, management and resolution in Africa, the EU must evaluate possible cooperation at national and international levels, 'to address the problem of the relationship between the radicalisation of religious groups and their vulnerability to terrorist recruitment, in a conflict prevention and peace building perspective'.
24 *Kokkinakis v Greece*, 260-A Eur. Ct. H.R. (ser. A) (1993): 'Freedom of thought, conscience and religion, is one of the foundations of a "democratic society" within the meaning of the Convention. It is, in its religious dimension, one of the most vital elements that go to make up the identity of believers and their conception of life, but is also a precious asset for atheists, agnostics, sceptics and the unconcerned. The pluralism, indissociable from a democratic society, which has been dearly won over the centuries, depends on it'.
25 UK: *Neville Estates v Madden* [1962] Ch. 852.
26 *Charta Oecumenica* (2001, III.7): the alliance commits itself 'to seek agreement ... on the substance and goals of our social responsibility, and to represent in concert ... the concerns and visions of the churches *vis-à-vis* the secular European institutions; to defend basic values against infringements of every kind; to resist any attempt to misuse religion and the church for ethnic or nationalist purposes'.
27 Treaty of Amsterdam 1997, Appendix: Declaration on the Status of Churches and Non-Confessional Organisations.
28 For a discussion of this see Duffar (2006).
29 EURT, Art. 15b.1; see also Art. 15b.2 (Art. 52.2 of the draft Constitution 2004): 'The Union equally respects the status under national law of philosophical and non-confessional organisations'.
30 It merely protects rights of states to determine the legal position of religious organisations.
31 Declaration on the Status of Mount Athos 1979 (on Art. 105 of the Hellenic Constitution).
32 *Commission of European Communities v Italy*, C-260-04 celex reference 62004J0260, para. 35; see also the *Placanica* case, C-338/04 celex reference 62004J0338 and *Commission of European Communities v Greece*, C-65/05 celex reference 62005J0065; and EFTA Surveillance Authority Decision 336/94 celex reference 61994J0336: decision-making in member states as to the administration of amusement machine operations may not be justified on religious grounds alone.
33 *Steymann* Case 196/87 [1988] ECR 6159 (under Art. 2 EC), celex reference 61987J0196.
34 *SPUC v Grogan* Case C-159/90 [1991] ECR 4685, celex reference 61990J0159.
35 *Torfaen BC v B&Q plc* Case 145/88 [1989] ECR 3851, celex reference 61988J0145.
36 *UK v Council of Ministers* Case C-84/94 [1996] ECR I-5755, celex reference 61994J0084.
37 *Darby v Sweden* (1990) 187 ECtHR; *Dődsbo v Sweden*, Application No. 61564/00, 17/01/06.
38 *Refah Partisi (Welfare Party) v Turkey* (2003) 37 EHRR 1, Application numbers 41340/98; 41342/98; 41343/98; 41344/98: 'The court has frequently emphasised the state's role as the neutral and impartial organiser of the exercise of various religions, faiths and beliefs, and stated that this role is conducive to public order, religious harmony, and tolerance in a democratic society. It also considers that the state's duty of neutrality and impartiality is incompatible with any power on the state's part to assess the legitimacy of religious belief and that it requires the state to ensure neutral tolerance between opposing groups.'
39 Directive 71/305/EEC, Art. 2; Directive 92/456/EEC Annex 1 (i.e. 'church councils' in Belgium); see also Directive 2004/18/EC.
40 Regulation 3911/92, Annex, Art. 1.2.
41 Common Customs Tariff 1999/L 278/1 at 508.
42 Regulation EC 1982/2003, Annex 1(f).
43 Decision 771/2006, Preamble (2).
44 Council Joint Action 2007/106/CFSP, Art. 3(e).

45 Directive 2006/97/EC: on the accession of Bulgaria and Romania.

46 Council Decision 2006/35/EC, OJ 2006 L22/34 at 37; for Turkey, see Oktem (2002).

47 Regulation 1889/2006, Art. 2.1(b)(iii).

48 See also EURT, Art. 136a for promoting the role of the social partners at EU level and dialogue between them; Art. 17b: the right to petition EU institutions (also Art. 22, Charter of Fundamental Rights); and Art. 8b: EU institutions shall give 'representative associations' the opportunity to make known and publicly exchange their views in all areas of Union action; maintain an open, transparent and regular dialogue with these; and consult them. Under Art. 256a, the Economic and Social Committee consists of representatives of civil society organisations (including cultural ones).

49 Declaration No. 23; see also Commission Communication on Fostering the Role of Associations and Foundations in Europe COM/97/0241, celex reference 51998IP0203; see also the Commission discussion paper *Building a Stronger Partnership*, COM (2000) 11. In 1999, under President Romano Prodi, one section of the European Commission's Group of Policy Advisers was assigned the task of 'dialogue with religions, churches and humanisms'.

50 Opinion of the Economic and Social Committee on the Role and Contribution of Civil Society Organisations on the Building of Europe 1999/C 329/10, CES 851/99 D/GW 1999/C 329/10.

51 European Governance: a White Paper COM (2001) 428, 2001/C 287/01.

52 These include the Church and Society Commission of the Conference of European Churches, the Catholic European Study and Information Centre, the European Humanist Federation, and the *Centre Européen Juif d'Information*: http://www.europa.eu.int/comm/civil_society/connecs/index.htm

53 Decision 1983/2006, Preamble: see above note 18.

54 Decision 2005/85/EC (implementing Art. 13 Treaty of Rome).

55 Community Regulation EC 168/2007.

56 Council Joint Action 2007/113, Art. 3(1)(d).

57 Regulation 113/2002.

58 Regulation EC 1905/2006, Art. 24; see also Regulation EC 625/2004.

59 Council Regulation (Euratom) 300/2007, Art. 7(2).

60 Regulation 1638/2006, Art. 14(1)(h)(viii).

61 Regulation EC 1717/2006, Art. 10(2).

62 England and Wales: Sharing of Church Buildings Act 1969, s.1.

63 For example, the Church and Nation Committee of the Church of Scotland consults with the Scottish Parliament.

64 It has an office in Brussels for its Church and Society Commission. The Commission has working groups on EU legislation. There are 126 churches and 43 organisations in CEC, including the Church of England, the Church of Denmark, the Church of Finland, the Netherlands Council of Churches, the Council of Protestant Churches of Portugal, the Lutheran Church of Slovakia and the EKD. CEC is 'an ecumenical fellowship of churches in Europe which confess the Lord Jesus Christ as God and Saviour according to the Scriptures and seek to fulfil together their common calling to the glory of the one God, Father, Son and Holy Spirit' (Constitution). See also (for example) the European Network of Health Care Chaplaincy.

65 Charter, Art. 10. See also draft Constitution 2004, Art. 70.1: same wording as Art. 9 ECHR.

66 Charter, Articles: 7 (privacy and family life); 8 (data protection); 9 (marriage and the family); 11 (expression); 12 (association); 13 (the arts and academic freedom); 14 (education including religion); 17 (property); 21 (discrimination); 23 (gender equality); 24 (children); 25 (the elderly and their right to participate in social and cultural life) and 26 (disability): all potentially concern religion.

67 *Prais v Council of Ministers*, C-130/75 [1976] ECR 1589, celex reference 61975J0130: while the law on community officials (1968) forbade religious discrimination, it was held that

scheduling an examination on a Friday in the case of a Jewish candidate was not in breach of freedom of religion.

68 Directive 2004/113/EC, Preamble (3).
69 Corrigendum to Directive 2004/58/EC, Preamble (32); see also Decision 2004/513.
70 Regulation EC 562/2006, Annex I(d) (in accordance with Art. 251 of the Treaty of Rome).
71 Decision 2004/676/EC, Art. 36.
72 Decision 2004/579: OJ 2004 L261/69 at 76.
73 Council Framework Decision 2005/214, Preamble (5).
74 Council Framework Decision 2006/783, 13 (in accordance with Art. 6 of the Treaty on European Union and Chapter VI of the Charter of Fundamental Rights).
75 Agreement, OJ 2007 L129/2, Art. 1(4).
76 Agreement between the European Community and the Russian Federation on Readmission, OJ 2007 L129/40; see also Directive 2005/85/EC, Art. 27(1).
77 Common Position on Nigeria, 2002/401.
78 Regulation 1889/2006, Art. 2.1(b)(iii).
79 Council Decision 2006/35/EC, OJ 2006 L22/34 at 37,38.
80 In view of the proposal for the EU to accede to the ECHR. Currently, Art. 6.2 of the EURT states that the EU 'shall respect fundamental rights, as guaranteed by the European Convention … but does not provide for accession'; the ECJ ruled out EC accession in 1994 on the grounds that the Community lacked competence to become a party to the ECHR.
81 It appears in most member state constitutions: Robbers (2005) and Sandberg and Doe (2007a).
82 Human Rights Act 1998, s.13.
83 Art. 15b repeats the draft Constitution 2004, Art. 52.
84 Council Decision 2006/35/EC, OJ L22/34 at 38.
85 Decision 2006/57/EC, OJ 2006 L35/57 at 60.
86 See for example the *Horizon College* case C-434/05, celex reference 62005J0434.
87 Council Common Position 2007/140.
88 Common Resolution 2005/440/CFSP.
89 Common Position 2005/888/CFSP.
90 Common Position 2004/852.
91 Directive 2000/78/EC, Art. 4(1).
92 Directive 2000/78/EC, Art. 4(2): also: 'This difference of treatment shall be implemented taking account of member states' constitutional provisions and principles, as well as the general principles of Community law, and should not justify discrimination on another ground'.
93 Directive 2000/78/EC, Art. 4(2). For criticism of this (as a description of a rule rather than a rule) see Rivers (2004, p. 285).
94 Directive 93/104/EC, Art. 17.
95 Directive 2001/88/EC, Preamble (1).
96 Previously, under Directive 74/577/EEC, Art. 4, national provisions relating to ritual slaughter were exempted from the European requirement to stun before slaughter.
97 Directive 93/119/EEC.
98 Directive 93/119/EEC.
99 Directive 83/90/EEC.
100 Corrigendum to Regulation EC 853/2004, Ch. IV, 7(a); see also C321 E/314 (Protocol No. 33. (1997)) on animal welfare: 'while respecting the legislative or administrative provisions and customs of the Member States relating in particular to religious rites, cultural traditions and regional heritage'.
101 Regulation 1347/2000, Art. 40.
102 Regulation 3201/90, Art. 10(1).
103 Regulation 3201/90, Art. 10(2): however, the terms Kosher wine, Passover kosher wine, Kosher wine for Passover and their translations may appear without this restriction (in Art.

10(2)) provided that the rule in Art. 10(1) on recommendation of acceptability of use for religious purposes is satisfied.

104 Directive 95/46/EC; see Robbers (1994).

105 For example Art. 44.2.5, Constitution of Ireland: 'Every religious organisation shall have the right to manage its own affairs'; Belgian Constitution, Art. 21; German Constitution, Art. 137.

106 For example Church of Scotland Act 1921.

107 For example, in the field of internal discipline, see the Roman Catholic Code of Canon Law (1983) c.1311: 'The Church has an innate and proper right to coerce offending members of the Christian faithful by means of penal sanctions'; see also Van der Vyver (2001), p. 645.

108 See also EURT (TEC), Art. 10; and draft Constitution 2004, Arts 81, 118.

109 Treaty of Rome (Nice Version), Art. 13: 'the Council, acting ... on a proposal from the Commission and after consulting the European Parliament, may take appropriate action to combat discrimination based on sex, racial or ethnic origin, religion or belief, disability, age or sexual orientation'.

110 Decision 1672/2006, Preamble (8); see Directive 2000/78.

111 *Mangold v Helm*, C-144/04, celex reference 62004J0144; see also *Commission of European Communities v Federal Republic of Germany*, C-43/05, celex reference 62005J0043: the case concerns the failure to transpose Directive 2000/78 into German law.

112 *Palacios de la Villa v Cortefeil Servicios SA*, C-411/05, celex reference 62005J0411; for discrimination and religion, see also *Chacon Navas v Eurest Colectividades SA*, C-13/05, celex reference 62005J0013; *El Youssfi v Office National de Pension* C-276/06 celex reference 62006O0276.

113 Decision 2006/971.

114 Decision 2006/EC, Preamble (15) and Introduction to Guidelines for Cohesion Policy.

115 Regulation 1974/2006, Annex II, para. 15.2.

116 Decision 2002/621/EC (Personnel Selection Office).

117 Decision 2004/676/EC, Art. 5.

118 Directive 2005/71/EC, Preamble (4); see also Recommendation 2005/251/EC.

119 Directive 2004/114/EC; see also Directive 2004/38/EC.

120 Corrigendum to Directive 2004/58/EC, Preamble (32).

121 Regulation (EC) 1905/2006, Art. 5(2).

122 Council Regulation 1083/2006, Preamble (30) and Art. 16; see also Regulation 1080/2006.

123 Council Regulation EC 1698/2005, Art. 8.

124 Regulation (EC) 1929/2006, Art. 7.

125 Regulation 1889/2006, Art. 2.1(b)(iii).

126 Decision 1855/2006, Art. 12(d).

127 Decision 1719/2006, Art. 2(3).

128 Decision 771/2006, Art. 2 (on the basis of 2000/78/EC).

129 Decision 771/2006, Art. 4.

130 ECHR, Art. 14: 'The enjoyment of [Convention] rights and freedoms ... shall be secured without discrimination on any ground such as ... religion'; and Art. 1, Protocol 12. Also: *Moscow Branch of the Salvation Army v Russia*, App. No. 72881/01, E.Ct.H.R. 5/10/06: on registration of religious bodies.

131 For example: Germany, Constitution, Art. 136; Italy, Constitution, Art. 8.

132 See also draft Constitution 2004, Art. 70.2.

133 See also draft Constitution 2004, Art. 74.3.

134 Directive 89/104/EEC, Art. 3(2)(b).

135 Directive 89/552/EEC (amended by 97/36/EC), Art. 11(5).

136 Directive 2000/31/EC, Art. 3(4)(a).

137 Decision 2004/676/EC, Art. 32.

138 Decision 2004/535. For a challenge to and judicial consideration of the directive, see *European Parliament v Council of the European Union*, C-317/04, celex reference 62004J0317.

139 Decision 2002/187, Art. 15(4).

140 Regulation 3911/92, Annex, Art. 1.2.
141 Directive 93/7/EEC.
142 Council Joint Action 2006/304, OJ 2006 L112/19 at 19 (in Kosovo).
143 Decision 2006/56: conditions for EU partnership with Serbia and Montenegro.
144 Regulation EC 1210/2003, Art. 3 and Annex II.
145 Regulation EC 1829/2003, Preamble (22), Arts 5 and 13.
146 Regulation EC 2000/2005; see also Regulation 393/2005; Regulation 1254/199, Art. 33.
147 Freedom of expression and religion includes the right of religious groups to establish and run their own press; there is a right to freedom of expression in both public and private broadcasting.
148 Directive 2001/85/EC, Annex 1, para. 1.3.2.
149 Directive 77/388/EEC.
150 Council Decision 2006/35/EC, OJ 2006 L22/34 at 37.
151 Directive 2003/88/EC, Art. 17(1)(c). See also *Dallas v Premiere Ministre*, C-14/04, celex reference 62004J0014, on Directive 93/104 (on derogations for workers officiating at religious ceremonies).
152 Directive 76/207/EEC, Art. 2(2).
153 Directive 2001/29/EC, Art. 5(3)(c) and (g).
154 Directive 2002/14/EC, Art. 3(2).
155 Regulation EC 1781/2006, Art. 18.
156 *Iglesia Bautista and Ortega Moratilla v Spain* (1992) 72 DR 256 Application Number 17522/90: preferential tax treatment to the Catholic Church over other churches (in this case Baptist) was justifiable by reference to its special responsibilities (for example, providing public access to its monuments) under a concordat.
157 Road Traffic Act 1988, s.16.
158 Criminal Justice Act 1988, s.139.
159 Oaths Act 1978, s.1.
160 Abortion Act 1967, s.4.
161 Ecclesiastical Exemption (Listed Buildings and Conservation Areas) Order 1994.
162 Local Government Finance Act 1988, s.51, Sched. 5, para. 11.
163 There is some artificiality in these, particularly the distinction between the principle of special protection and that of religious privilege: the latter is a species of the former; and both may be illustrations of the value of religion principle. There may also be inconsistencies between them: religious privilege is difficult to reconcile with the equality principle.
164 The work of the European Consortium for Church and State is invaluable in this regard.

References

(a) Books, Articles and Papers

Davie, G. (2000) *Religion in Modern Europe* (Oxford, Oxford University Press).

Doe, N. (2004) 'Religion and media law in Europe: a comparative study', in N. Doe (ed.), *The Portrayal of Religion in Europe: the Media and the Arts* (Leuven, Peeters), pp. 287–315.

Duffar, J. (2006) 'Les relations entre l'union européenne et les églises', in R. Puza and N. Doe (eds), *Religion and Law in Dialogue: Covenantal and Non-Covenantal Cooperation between State and Religion in Europe* (Leuven, Peeters), pp. 265–84.

Oktem, N. (2002) 'Religion in Turkey', in F. Messner (ed.), *The Status of Religious Confessions of the States Applying for Membership of the European Union* (Milan, Guiffre Editore), pp. 251–76.

Pope John Paul II (2003) *Ecclesia in Europa*, papal exhortation, http://www.vatican.va/holy_father/john_paul_ii/apost_exhortations/documents/hf_jp-ii_exh_20030628_eccle (last accessed 17 November 2008).

Potz, R., Berlingo, S., Von Campenhausen, A., Margiotta Broglio, F., Robbers, G. and Ferrari, S. (2004) in 'God in the European Constitution: opinions of members of the European Consortium for Church and State Research', European Consortium for Church and State Research, *Newsletter*, 4, pp. 4–110.

Puza, R. and Doe, N. (eds), (2006) *Religion and Law in Dialogue: Covenantal and Non-Covenantal Cooperation between State and Religion in Europe* (Leuven, Peeters).

Rivers, J. (2004) 'In pursuit of pluralism: the ecclesiastical policy of the European Union', *Ecclesiastical Law Journal*, 7, pp. 267–91.

Robbers, G. (ed.) (1994) *Europäisches Datenschutzrecht und die Kirchen* (Berlin, Duncker & Humblot).

Robbers, G. (ed.) (2001) *Church Autonomy: a Comparative Survey* (Frankfurt am Main, Peter Lang).

Robbers, G. (2004) 'Diversity of state–religion relations and European Union unity', *Ecclesiastical Law Journal*, 7, pp. 304–16.

Robbers, G. (ed.) (2005) *State and Church in the European Union* (2nd edn) (Baden-Baden, Nomos).

Sandberg, R. and Doe, N. (2007a) 'Church–state relations in Europe', *Religion Compass*, 1, 5, pp. 561–78.

Sandberg, R. and Doe, N. (2007b) 'Religious exemptions in discrimination law', *Cambridge Law Journal*, 66, 2, pp. 302–12.

Van der Vyver, J. D. (2001) 'Sphere sovereignty of religious institutions: a contemporary Calvinist theory of church–state relations', in G. Robbers (ed.), *Church Autonomy: a Comparative Survey* (Frankfurt am Main, Peter Lang), pp. 645–81.

Ventura, M. (2001), *La laicità dell'Unione Europea: diritti, mercato, religione* (Turin, G. Giappichelli Editore).

(b) Legislation, Treaties, Directives, Decisions, Cases, etc.

Please note that, as far as citing these documents is concerned, we are using a slightly different convention from that used elsewhere in this volume. Inserting the references in brackets within the text would break up the continuity and make the text difficult to read. We are therefore consigning all the references to endnotes. Most of the documents cited in the endnotes (other than books and articles) can be found at EUR-LEX, http://eur-lex.europa.eu, the official website and online case and legislation library of the EU. The sources are given their full neutral citations so that they can be located in alternative places than the EUR-LEX website if the reader so wishes, but they are available from EUR-LEX. Merely select your preferred language and enter the site, go to search and enter either the citation of celex specific reference or go to simple search. Once on simple search select the type of document – case-law, legislation or treaties – and then enter the citation given. All the documents are subdivided by type. Alternatively, to find Official Journal entries (those cited as OJ L and then three numbers) on the main page of the EUR-LEX website, click on the Official Journal link at the top of the menu and enter the citation in the search boxes.

Documents which are not located at EUR-LEX are listed with their sources below. European Court of Human Rights cases can be searched on the ECHR's website at www.echr.coe.int with the application numbers and references given. Other documents are given online references to full text articles or are domestic case-law which can be found in any legal library.

(i) *Legislation, Treaties, Directives, Decisions, etc.*

Charta Oecumenica (2001) can be accessed at http://www.cec-kek.org/content/charta.shtml

Opinion of the Economic and Social Committee (endnote 51) can be accessed at http://eesc.europa.eu/sco/docs/ces851-1999_ac_en.PDF

(ii) *Court Cases*

Darby v Sweden (1990) 187 ECtHR is a decision of the European Court of Human Rights and so is not on the EUR-LEX website. It can be accessed at http://cmiskp.echr.coe.int/tkp197/view.asp?action=html&documentId=695519&portal=hbkm&source=externalbydocnumber&table=F69A27FD8FB86142BF01C1166DEA398649

Dődsbo v Sweden Application No. 61564/00 is an application to the European Court of Human Rights and so is not on the EUR-LEX website. It can be accessed at http://www.manskligarattigheter.gov.se/dynamaster/file_archive/060919/fd47bdbb69eddde6ca034f35bd2cf4bd/CASE%20OF%20ELLI%20POLUHAS%20DODSBO%20v%5B1%5D.%20SWEDEN.pdf

Iglesia Bautista and Ortega Moratilla v Spain (1992) 72 DR 256 is a decision of the European Court of Human Rights and so is not on the EUR-LEX website. It can be accessed at http://cmiskp.echr.coe.int/tkp197/view.asp?action=open&documentId=829634&portal=hbkm&source=externalbydocnumber&table=F69A27FD8FB86142BF01C1166DEA398649

Kokkinakis v Greece, http://cmiskp.echr.coe.int/tkp197/view.asp?action=html&documentId=695704&portal=hbkm&source=externalbydocnumber&table=F69A27FD8FB86142BF01C1166DEA398649

Moscow Branch of the Salvation Army v Russia, App. No. 72881/01, E.Ct.H.R: the decision of the European Court of Human Rights can be accessed either on the website of the European Convention on Human Rights or at http://cmiskp.echr.coe.int/tkp197/view.asp?action=html&documentId=809052&portal=hbkm&source=externalbydocnumber&table=F69A27FD8FB86142BF01C1166DEA398649

Neville Estates v Madden [1962] Ch 852 can be found by using the citation on any legal database. Ch means 'Chancery'.

Refah Partisi (Welfare Party) v Turkey (2003) 37 EHRR 1 is a European Court of Human Rights case reported in *European Human Rights Reports*, searchable from the website by the given citation, or available directly at http://cmiskp.echr.coe.int/tkp197/view.asp?action=html&documentId=698813&portal=hbkm&source=externalbydocnumber&table=F69A27FD8FB86142BF01C1166DEA398649

Voices in the Wilderness: the Established Church of England and the European Union*

MARK HILL

Introduction

The meaning, effect and future of establishment within the UK are complex matters of history, ecclesiology, sociology and politics.[1] However, the fact that the Church of England is the established church in England informs an understanding of its legal relationship with the state and the manner of its self-regulation, which was revisited in 2003 by the Judicial Committee of the House of Lords in the light of the provisions of the Human Rights Act 1998. Despite this, anecdotal experience indicates reluctance on the part of the Church of England aggressively to confront the government on matters of proposed legislation. Initiatives from within the European Union (EU) concerning religious organisations place emphasis on the presence of religion at the heart of modern Europe and within the institutions of the EU itself. There are also religious initiatives from faith communities, individually and collectively, which seek to inform and influence the social and political agenda of the EU. Against this background, there is an apparent anomaly as to why the Church of England seems to lack visibility at the heart of EU institutions. Various considerations can be discerned,

*An earlier version of this paper was presented at the conference 'The European Union and the Religious Dimensions of Law: Issues and Challenges' held by The Centre for the Study of Law and Religion, University of Bristol, 12–13 January 2007.

including: the lack of resources; its status as an established church; the jurisprudential anomaly of the Diocese in Europe; its numerically small membership; and the fact that European legislation, in practice, is centrally declared but nationally applied. There is merit in exploring how, both unilaterally and collaboratively, the Church of England might improve its position as a lobbyist at both the Westminster Parliament and EU institutions.

The Church of England and the State

The curtailment of papal authority at the time of the Reformation and the recognition of the sovereign as supreme governor of the Church of England created a discernible unity between the church and the state, the products of which are evident today.[2] In the context of an appeal on an obscure point of law under the Chancel Repairs Act 1932, the judicial committee of the House of Lords enjoyed a rare opportunity to consider the constitutional status of the Church of England in contemporary jurisprudence (*Aston Cantlow*). As Lord Nicholls of Birkenhead observed,

> Historically the Church of England has discharged an important and influential role in the life of this country. As the established church it still has special links with central government. But the Church of England remains essentially a religious organisation. This is so even though some of the emanations of the church discharge functions which may qualify as governmental. Church schools and the conduct of marriage services are two instances. The legislative powers of the General Synod of the Church of England are another. This should not be regarded as infecting the Church of England as a whole, or its emanations in general, with the character of a governmental organisation. (*Aston Cantlow*, para. 13)

In Lord Hope of Craighead's opinion 'the Church of England as a whole has no legal status or personality' (*Aston Cantlow*, para 61).[3] Whilst acknowledging that the Church of England had regulatory functions within its own sphere of activity, he concluded that it could not be considered to be a part of government, observing that the state has not surrendered or delegated any of its functions or powers to the church: 'The relationship which the state has with the Church of England is one of recognition, not of the devolution to it of any of the powers or functions of government' (*Aston Cantlow*, para. 61).[4] Lord Rodger of Earlsferry, in a concurring speech, suggested that 'the juridical nature if the Church [of England] is, notoriously, somewhat amorphous' (*Aston Cantlow*, para. 154). He concluded that

> The mission of the Church is a *religious* mission, distinct from the secular mission of government, whether central or local. Founding on scriptural and other recognised authority, the Church seeks to serve the purposes of God, not those of the government carried on by the modern equivalents of Caesar and his proconsuls. This is true even though the Church of England has certain important links with the state. Those links, which do not include any funding of the Church by the government, give the Church a unique position but they do not make it a department of state: *Marshall v Graham* [1907] 2 KB 112, 126, per Phillimore LJ. In so far as the ties are intended to assist the Church, it is to accomplish the Church's own mission, not the aims and objectives of the Government of the United Kingdom. (*Aston Cantlow*, para 154)[5]

These assertions may seem both obvious and self-evident; however, the Court of Appeal had previously reached the opposite conclusion on the specific question of whether a parochial church council is a public authority for the purposes of the Human Rights Act 1998.[6] The Court of Appeal regarded the established nature of the Church of England as imbuing its component institutions with a governmental function sufficient to render them public authorities. The analysis of the House of Lords is much to be preferred, being more cogent and sophisticated, and the consequent reversal of the Court of Appeal's ruling accorded with widespread academic opinion.[7]

As with all aspects of the UK's unwritten constitution, the precise relationship between the Church of England and Her Majesty's government is liable to evolution. One of Gordon Brown's first acts as prime minister was to issue a Green Paper, *The Governance of Britain* (Governance, 2007), in which he put forward proposals for further constitutional change, including the making of senior church appointments. In a statement to the House of Commons he stated that 'The Church of England is, and should remain, the established church in England. Establishment does not, however, justify the Prime Minister influencing senior church appointments, including bishops' (Hansard, 2007).[8] The Green Paper outlined the role which the prime minister and the government should play in church appointments by reference to four principles:

> 1. The Government reaffirms its commitment to the position of the Church of England by law established, with the Sovereign as its Supreme Governor, and the relationship between the Church and State. The Government greatly values the role played by the Church in national life in a range of spheres;
> 2. The Queen should continue to be advised on the exercise of her powers of appointment by one of her Ministers, which usually means the Prime Minister;
> 3. In choosing how best to advise The Queen on such appointments, the Government believes in principle that the Prime Minister should not play an active role in the selection of individual candidates. Therefore, the Prime Minister should not use the royal prerogative to exercise choice in recommending appointments of senior ecclesiastical posts, including diocesan bishops, to The Queen; and
> 4. The Church should be consulted as to how best arrangements can be put in place to select candidates for individual ecclesiastical appointments in line with the preceding principles. (Governance, 2007, para. 62; see Cranmer, 2008).

The government's initiative was subsequently welcomed by the General Synod at its July 2007 Session, regarding it, among other things, as the prospect of the Church of England achieving the 'decisive voice in the appointment of bishops' for which Synod voted in 1974.[9]

The presence of Anglican bishops in the House of Lords is but one part of the broader question of wholesale reform of the upper house of Parliament which has been on the political agenda since the Labour government came into power in 1997; although when the matter was last debated in parliament in March 2007 the two houses came to precisely opposite conclusions as to the composition of a reformed second chamber.[10] The minister of justice and lord chancellor reconvened the informal cross-party group on Lords reform in the hope of achieving some kind of consensus, but whether there is to be a continuing place for bishops, or additional places for leaders of other faith communities, remains a matter for conjecture.[11]

Influencing Domestic Legislation

Anecdotal experience would seem to indicate reluctance on the part of the Church of England to confront the government overtly on legislative policy. There are a number of possible reasons for this, which may be symptomatic of an English reticence. The sophisticated lobbying industry, familiar to Americans on Washington DC's Capitol Hill, is much less developed in the UK. The Churches Main Committee (now renamed the Churches' Legislation Advisory Service) exists as a consultative body between parliament and the major religious organisations in the UK.[12] Its remit is broad but its effectiveness is through gentle influence rather than the adoption of pressure group tactics. There is certainly no culture of the Church of England publicly lobbying government.

This is evident, for example in the Gender Recognition Act 2004. The Act permits transgendered individuals to live under their acquired gender in preference to their gender of birth. The right of a religious organisation to regulate its internal affairs in accordance with its doctrine is enshrined under Article 9 of the European Convention on Human Rights and it is a matter to which a court must have particular regard under Section 13 of the Human Rights Act 1998.[13] Members of a religious organisation are entitled to ask individuals whether they have undergone or are undergoing gender reassignment, but, in the absence of the individual's consent, a person exposes himself to criminal penalty and is liable to a fine of up to £5000 if he passes on that information. The doctrine and practice of many religious organisations make it essential that such information be communicated to other members acting in an official capacity, albeit discreetly and confidentially, and limited to individuals who have a need to know. Such necessity to communicate engages Article 9.

Thus provision needed to be made under Section 22(5) prescribing that disclosure of information in such circumstances is not to constitute a criminal offence. This provision is proportionate and appropriate having regard to competing rights of the transgendered community under Article 8 and Article 12 of the European Convention on Human Rights. A statutory defence is now to be found in the Gender Recognition (Disclosure of Information) (England, Wales and Northern Ireland) Order 2005. The exemption was hard won from the Department of Constitutional Affairs (now renamed the Ministry of Justice) with a coalition of religious organisations, animated by the Church of Jesus Christ of Latter-day Saints, but including Roman Catholics, Methodists, Baptists, Muslims, Jews, Baha'i, Sikhs and Buddhists. Several of them had no doctrinal objection to gender reassignment but wished to show solidarity with other faith communities on the fundamental issue of religious liberty. Noticeable on the fringe, however, was the Church of England, which supported the general religious exemption but was somewhat anxious not to be seen openly opposing legislation which had passed through parliament, membership of whose upper house includes Anglican archbishops and bishops. The established status of the Church of England could be seen as emasculating it from effective lobbying. The absence of lords spiritual from a reformed second chamber would free the bishops to lobby for specific legislative provision as well as to seek to shape government opinion and policy.[14] However, this is to overlook the many subtle ways in which bishops help to inform parliament of spiritual concerns across a broad range of issues. The efficacy of this benign influence, by its very nature, is not widely reported and its impact and effect are not amenable to scientific assessment. Alternative means of bringing religion into dialogue with government are currently merely embryonic and seem to lack the depth of the traditional methods.[15]

European Union Initiatives

There have been a number of initiatives amongst the institutions of the EU seeking to focus upon the spiritual dimension of Europe (Rivers, 2004). At the time of the Maastricht Treaty on European Union in 1992 a speech by Jacques Delors led to the movement 'A Soul for Europe' with its declared purpose 'to involve religious communities in dialogue with European institutions' (Soul for Europe, 2000). The movement had six members: the Commission of the [Roman Catholic] Bishops' Conferences of the European Community; the Church and Society Commission of the Conference of European Churches; the Orthodox Liaison Office; the Conference of European Rabbis; the European Humanist Federation; and the Muslim Council for Co-operation in Europe.

In 1999, on the initiative of President Romano Prodi, one section of the European Commission's Group of Policy Advisers was assigned the task of 'dialogue with religions, churches and humanisms', headed by Dr Michael Weninger. Furthermore, the Charter of Fundamental Rights 2000 guaranteed: religious, cultural and linguistic diversity; freedom of religion; the right to religious education; and prohibition against discrimination on religious grounds. The Convention on the Future of the European Union aiming towards greater integration (moving from an economic to a social and political community) set up a Forum consisting of 'structured networks' or 'organisations representing civil society' which included religious organisations. In 2003 President Prodi established a Reflection Group on the Spiritual and Cultural Dimension of Europe to debate on whether there should be a reference to God in the draft EU Constitution. The underlying concept of the EU in its present form is far removed from that of the European Economic Community out of which it has grown.

The ill-fated draft Treaty Establishing a Constitution for Europe contained no explicit reference either to God or to Christianity in the main body of the text, but its Preamble referred to religion in its very first sentence: 'Drawing inspiration from the cultural, religious and humanist inheritance of Europe, from which have developed the universal values of the inviolable and inalienable rights of the human person, freedom, democracy, equality and the rule of law ...' . Article I-52 went on to treat the status of churches and of non-confessional organisations in an even-handed way, juxtaposing harmonisation with diversity:

> 1. The Union respects and does not prejudice the status under national law of churches and religious associations or communities in the Member States.
> 2. The Union equally respects the status under national law of philosophical and non-confessional organisations.
> 3. Recognising their identity and their specific contribution, the Union shall maintain an open, transparent and regular dialogue with these churches and organisations.

The chairman of the drafting Convention, Valéry Giscard d'Estaing, deliberately left the issue open when he drafted the document, inviting a petition for the inclusion of some religious reference. 'I have chosen not to insert the reference to the Christian heritage in the constitution', he was reported as saying; 'rather, I appeal to you to persuade me of its necessity' (Evans-Pritchard, 2004).

Opinions were divided:[16] Poland was strongly in favour of some specific reference to Christianity while France, with almost a century of *laïcité* behind it, was opposed. The Commission of the Bishops' Conferences of the European Community (an official

Roman Catholic body generally known by the acronym COMECE, standing for *Commissio Episcopatuum Communitatis Europensis*) suggested that 'at a prominent place, in the centre between the cultural and the humanist inheritance, the religious inheritance of Europe forms a source of inspiration for the entire Constitutional Treaty' (COMECE, 2005, p. 14). By making reference to the religious inheritance of Europe, argued COMECE, the Treaty implicitly accepted the predominant contribution made by Christianity to the Europe of today and an explicit mention of God or of Christianity would have been a strong signal supporting the identity of Europe.[17]

The Parliamentary Assembly of the Council of Europe has been concerned with the relationship between religion and society at large for some considerable time. Reports and subsequent recommendations have included *Religion and Democracy* (1999), *Illegal Activities of Sects* (1999), *Russia's Law on Religion* (2002), *Religion and Change in Central and Eastern Europe* (2002), *Education and Religion* (2005) and *Freedom of Expression and Respect for Religious Beliefs* (2006). In June 2007 the Assembly debated three reports – on *New Steps in the Field of Intercultural and Interconfessional Dialogue*, on *The Relations between State, Religion and the Individual*, on *Blasphemy, Religious Insults and Hate Speech* – and an opinion on *European Muslim Communities Confronted with Extremism*. A related report that was not debated in June was on the *Dangers of Creationism in Education*. The concerns of the Assembly have centred primarily on social cohesion and religious extremism. In June 2007 the Assembly adopted Recommendations on The State, Religion, Secularity and Human Rights (Rec. 1804) and on Blasphemy, Religious Insults and Hate Speech (Rec. 1805). The key points of Recommendation 1804 can be marshalled into three groups.

First, historically, religion has been an important feature of European society; citizens have a right to freedom of religion, and faith communities are also part of civil society with a role to play in the wider national community; the Council of Europe welcomes and respects religious plurality; the separation of church and state is one of Europe's shared values; governance and religion should not be mixed; and the European Court of Human Rights recognises the right of individual countries to organise those relations in various ways so long as they comply with the Convention.

Second, it recognises that the practice of religion has declined markedly but, at the same time, Muslim communities in virtually all the Council of Europe member states are growing stronger; that religion has become a central issue of debate; that intercultural dialogue and its religious dimension are important but interreligious dialogue is not a matter for member states or for the Council.

Third, it shows that fundamentalism, terrorisms, racism, xenophobia and ethnic conflicts often have religious aspects; that governments should take account of the special capacity of religious communities to foster peace, cooperation, tolerance, solidarity, intercultural dialogue; that education, especially school education, is crucial, and children should be taught about the origins of all religions; that freedom of religion is protected by Article 9 of the European Convention but must not run counter to other fundamental rights, nor may states allow the dissemination of religious principles which, if put into practice, would violate human rights; and that freedom of expression is one of the most important human rights and cannot be restricted out of respect for religious sensibilities.

The Assembly proceeded to recommend, *inter alia*, setting up an institute to devise syllabuses, teaching methods and educational material for the study of the religious heritage of the member states and promoting the objective, balanced teaching of religions. More controversially, it proposed that all religious leaders should be required to undertake human rights training, especially those involved in the education of young people – but it failed to explain precisely what is 'a religious leader'.

Religious Initiatives

Religious groups see Europe itself as a particular field of religious activity on a regional basis: see, for example, the Papal Exhortation *Ecclesia in Europa* in 2003 ('Jesus Christ alive in his church, [is] the source of hope for Europe') (John Paul II, 2003). Several religious alliances have been formed to effect dialogue. The Conference of European Churches (CEC) has an office in Brussels for its Church and Society Commission. The Commission has a number of working groups on EU legislation and includes seven members: the Church of England, the Church of Denmark, the Church of Finland, the Netherlands Council of Churches, the Council of Protestant Churches of Portugal, the Lutheran Church of Slovakia, and the *Evangelische Kirche in Deutschland* (EKD). CEC is 'an ecumenical fellowship of churches in Europe which confess the Lord Jesus Christ as God and Saviour according to the Scriptures and seek to fulfil together their common calling to the glory of the one God, Father, Son and Holy Spirit'. The intention is that the churches are to support one another in the exercise of the ministry of reconciliation incumbent on them all. At its fourth assembly in 1964 the Conference adopted its first Constitution. The churches seek by the grace of the Triune God to pursue the path of growing conciliar understanding. In faithfulness to the gospel, as witnessed in scripture and transmitted in and through the church by the power of the Holy Spirit, 'they seek to grow in the fellowship (*koinonia*) of faith and love' and to make a common contribution to the church, to the safeguarding of life and the wellbeing of all humankind (CEC, 1992, Preamble).

The Roman Catholic Church has in Brussels a Commission of the Bishops' Conferences of the European Community (COMECE). CEC and COMECE have meetings with the president of the European Commission, and specialist work is done by attending meetings, presenting evidence and lobbying the EU (see McClean, 2002). Certain Protestant churches consider that the Catholic Church is over-represented in the institutions of the EU. It is certainly true that newer religious movements are under represented, in many instances to vanishing point.

The *Charta Oecumenica* (2001) is a set of 'Guidelines for the Growing Cooperation among the Churches in Europe'. It was established by CEC and COMECE and has the following main objectives:

1. *The nature and purpose of the charter*: it expresses a common commitment to dialogue and cooperation and describes fundamental ecumenical responsibilities. It is designed to promote an ecumenical culture of dialogue and cooperation at all levels of church life, but it has no magisterial or dogmatic character, nor is it legally binding under church law.

2. *The form and subjects of the charter*: a preamble and three parts. Each part consists of the statement of an objective and commitments: called together to unity in faith; proclaiming the gospel together; moving towards one another; acting together; praying together; continuing in dialogue; participating in the building of Europe; reconciling peoples and cultures; safeguarding the creation; strengthening community with Judaism; cultivating relations with Islam; encountering other religions and world views. The document is commended to the churches 'to be adopted and adapted to each of their local contexts'.

3. *The proclamation of the gospel*: 'The most important task of the churches in Europe is the common proclamation of the Gospel, in both word and deed, for the salvation of all'. 'The widespread lack of corporate and individual orientation and falling away from Christian values challenge Christians to testify to their faith, particularly in response to the quest for meaning which is being pursued in so many forms'.

4. *Inter-church conflict*: 'In the event of conflicts between churches, efforts towards mediation and peace should be initiated and/or supported as needed'. The churches commit themselves 'to act together at all levels of church life wherever conditions permit and there are not reasons of faith or overriding expediency mitigating against this; to defend the rights of minorities and to help reduce misunderstandings and prejudices between majority and minority churches in our countries' (Charta, 2001, II.4).

5. *Common (social) responsibility in Europe*: 'Christianity constitutes an empowering source of inspiration and enrichment for Europe'. The parties undertake to work towards 'a humane, socially conscious Europe, in which human rights and the basic values of peace, justice, freedom, tolerance, participation and solidarity prevail'; and 'reverence for life, the value of marriage and the family, the preferential option for the poor, the readiness to forgive, and in all things compassion'.

6. *Reconciling peoples and cultures*: Diversity of regional, national, cultural and religious traditions is enriching; the churches are called upon to serve together the cause of reconciliation among peoples and cultures. The churches 'value the person and dignity of every individual as made in the image of God' and 'defend the absolutely equal values of all human beings'; they join forces in *the process of democratisation in Europe*; and in the non-violent resolution of conflicts (Charta, 2001, III.8).

Several other churches also have an individual presence in Brussels. The Brussels Bureau of the EKD has a small full-time staff to act as a channel of communication with the EU institutions (including making formal and informal representations). Britain's Yearly Meeting of the Religious Society of Friends maintains a small office, namely the Quaker Council for European Affairs. There is also a European Network of Health Care Chaplaincy which has issued Standards for Health Care Chaplaincy in Europe (2002). Its areas of activity include: to proclaim and defend the infinite value and dignity of every person; to be a reminder of the existential and spiritual dimension of suffering, illness and death; to endeavour to see that the spiritual needs of people from different religious or cultural backgrounds are met, respecting everyone's beliefs; to provide research and advocacy; and to assess and evaluate the effectiveness of provision for spiritual care.

In May 2008 the Church of England installed a cleric at the Anglican chaplaincy at Holy Trinity, Brussels, as the archbishop of Canterbury's representative to the European institutions in Brussels. The focus for the appointee, in the first instance, will be issues of climate change but it is to be hoped that a broader remit and a more animated mode of intervention will be carved out.

The Visibility of the Church of England

In the light of the religiosity which permeates the EU and contributes substantially to the concept of identity, why does the Church of England seem to lack visibility in Europe? A number of possible reasons may be ventured:

1. It does not have the *resources* to maintain a diplomatic mission at the institutions of the EU,[18] nor does it have the skills constructively to feed into its legislative agenda: far more personnel would be needed in Brussels if the archbishop's representative is to make a meaningful contribution.

2. It is a *state church*, or more accurately the established church in one part of the geographical territory of the state. The Diocese in Europe, being a creature of statute (the Diocese in Europe Measure, 1980), is a jurisprudential anomaly.[19] The Church of England's interests are mainly national and not supra- or trans-national.[20]

3. It is a *numerically small church*. The number of Anglicans whose names are on the rolls of the various chaplaincy councils scattered throughout the Diocese in Europe (the territorial jurisdiction of which extends beyond EU member states) are statistically few in number. Even factoring in the Old Catholics, the Spanish Reformed Episcopal Church, the Lusitanian Church, and members of congregations of the Episcopal Church of the United States of America, their numbers remain modest. Most Anglicans within the EU reside in the UK.

4. European legislation, in practice, is centrally declared but nationally applied. Unlike regulations, automatically binding on EU member states, directives need to be brought into force by domestic legislation in each such state. Julian Rivers highlights specific techniques of accommodation and ways by which EU lawmaking is localised (Rivers, 2007a).[21] The *religious element is felt at a local level* and, arguably, it is here that the effective lobbying on the part of religious organisations should be happening. If finance is limited, it is best spent where it can be most effective. However, the logic of combining with faith communities Europe-wide to influence the content of directives would greatly ease the pressure on all churches at national level to cajole their own governments. A number of Church of England bishops of differing churchmanships, when addressing the manner in which religious organisations respond to the gay marriage legislation in EU states, commented that what is needed is an 'early warning' system giving notice of flashpoints where the churches are likely to have a legitimate interest, which would allow them to be pro-active rather than re-active.[22]

5. There seems to be a tacit assumption that all religious organisations would want the same concessions from both EU and national legislators. Their interests are not necessarily coterminous, nor may they be in agreement as to the strategy and profile to be adopted in any negotiation, but as the UK transgender experience indicates, they all have an interest in the promotion of religious liberty and tolerance, and this can produce some unexpected, almost unholy, alliances.

Equal Treatment Directive

A further example, derived from the Employment Equality (Sexual Orientation) Regulations 2003 (SI, 2003), provides a real-life illustration of the working out of these issues. In *R v Secretary of State for Trade and Industry ex parte Amicus and others* (2004) Mr Justice Richards was asked to consider challenges brought by seven public sector unions in relation to several of the Regulations. The challenges were targeted against regulations that allowed exceptions to the general prohibition against discrimination on the grounds of sexual orientation where employment or vocational training is for the purposes of an organised religion (Sandberg and Doe, 2007).

The judge was being asked to rule on the correct balance to be struck between these two competing rights: the right of non-discrimination on the grounds of sexual orientation and the right to manifest one's religion or beliefs. At the core of the case were submissions put before the court by the Christian Action Research Education, the Evangelical Alliance and the Christian Schools Trust who were permitted to intervene in the litigation. They submitted that their ability to hold their religious beliefs and to carry on their teaching and practices would be undermined if they were forced to employ persons whose sexual practices and beliefs about those sexual practices were at odds with their own beliefs, teachings and practices. It was argued that employees working for Christian organisations were expected to behave in accordance with a Christian ethos and belief. Employing those who did not share this ethos would fatally undermine such an organisation's ability to achieve its objectives.

The public service unions maintained that the exclusions contained within the Regulations permitting religious organisations to discriminate against potential or existing employees or trainees on the grounds of sexual orientation were too wide and, therefore, were incompatible with the obligations imposed on the UK by an EU Directive and with Articles 8 and 14 of the European Convention on Human Rights.

The judge held that the exception was intended to be a very narrow one and, on its proper construction, was very narrow, affording an exception only in very limited circumstances. He said that the tests set out were objective not subjective and were going to be far from easy to satisfy in practice. He held it unlikely that this exception would apply to the various situations put forward on behalf of the Applicant unions to illustrate their concerns, namely a church unwilling to employ a homosexual man as a cleaner; a Catholic school for girls dismissing a science teacher on learning that she had been in a lesbian relationship; a shop selling scriptural books and tracts unwilling to employ a lesbian as a sales assistant; or an Islamic institute unwilling to employ as a librarian a man appearing to be homosexual.[23]

There is now a second wave of EU legislation concerning sexual orientation discrimination in the provision of goods and services.[24] Religious organisations mounted much-publicised protests outside the Palace of Westminster, supported in the columns of the *Times* newspaper by a former lord chancellor (Lord MacKay, 2007). In this instance the protest was in vain, and the legislation was confirmed (see Sandberg, 2008), but it emphasises, however, the real need for greater dialogue and earlier intervention on the part of religious organisations.

Conclusion

Religion presents a problem for national governments and for the institutions of the European Union. While content to afford respect to the tradition of faith bodies informing the structure of society and governance as a matter of historic fact, contemporary pluralism places a severe strain on the dynamic tension between church and state particularly where establishment gives rise to benefits and burdens for a particular denomination. The difficulty lies in protecting a voice for religion, albeit plurally, and in resisting the hegemony of secularism. These voices need to be heard in the heart of the EU just as much as in the Westminster Parliament, and the Church of England must become more adroit so as to operate to best effect both at home and abroad.

Acknowledgment

I am grateful to Frank Cranmer, fellow of St Chad's College, Durham, and honorary research associate at the Centre for Law and Religion, Cardiff University, for the generous provision of additional material for this paper and for his insightful comments on previous drafts. I must also thank Professor Norman Doe, director of the Centre, and Russell Sandberg, an associate, for their assistance in its preparation.

Notes

1 For analysis and commentary, see Cranmer (2001) and McClean (2004).

2 For an overview of the present position, see McClean (2005).

3 He continued: 'There is no Act of Parliament that purports to establish it as the Church of England: *Sir Lewis Dibdin, Establishment in England: Essays on Church and State* (1932), p 111. What establishment in law means is that the state has incorporated its law into the law of the realm as a branch of its general law. In *Marshall v Graham* [1907] 2 KB 112, 126 Philimore J said: "A Church which is established is not thereby made a department of state. The process of establishment means that the state has accepted the Church as the religious body in its opinion truly teaching the Christian faith, and given to it a certain legal position, and to its decrees, if rendered under certain legal conditions, certain civil sanctions." The Church of England is identified with the state in other ways, the monarch being the head of each.'

4 It is arguable that the Church of England Assembly (Powers) Act 1919, as amended by the General Synod Measure 1969, represents the delegation to General Synod of Parliament's legislative function. Measures are primary legislation passed by the General Synod, albeit subject to parliamentary approval.

5 For a full discussion, see Hill, M. (2007, para. 1.19).

6 *Aston Cantlow and Wilmcote with Billesley Parochial Church Council v Wallbank* [2002] Ch 51 CA, Sir Andrew Morritt V-C, Robert Walker and Sedley LJJ. Both the conclusion and reasoning of the Court of Appeal were subsequently overruled by the House of Lords in 2003.

7 See Oliver (2002), Leigh (2002), Dawson and Dunn (2002), Whale (2002) and Hill, M. (2001, 2004). Note, however, the partial dissent of Lord Scott of Foscote in the House of Lords decision in *Aston Cantlow* at paras 130–32. A full discussion of the House of Lords judgment may be found in Hill, M. (2007), at paras 1.01 and 1.19.

8 The Green Paper itself asserts: 'The Church of England is by law established as the Church in England and the Monarch is its Supreme Governor. The Government remains committed to this position' (Governance, 2007, para. 57). Curiously this appears in the Green Paper in a chapter entitled 'Limiting the powers of the executive' (ch. 1).

9 See the motion (of which this quotation forms part) passed by 297 votes to 1 in a debate by the General Synod on 9 July 2007 on the Pilling Report, *Talent and Calling: Report of the Senior Church Appointments Review Group* (London, Church House Publishing, GS 1650, 2007).

10 See House (2000), which recommended that the representation of the Church of England remain though cut from 26 bishops to 16 representatives, chosen however the church itself decides and not necessarily bishops. Alongside these would be five church representatives from other parts of the UK, five from other Christian churches within England and five from other faiths. This was superseded, *inter alia*, by a White Paper (Reform, 2007), published shortly before the House of Commons expressed a preference for an entirely elected second chamber (on 7 March 2007) and the House of Lords for one that was wholly appointed (on 14 March 2007).

11 The Rt Hon. Jack Straw MP confirmed, however, that the government would prefer a second chamber that was fully elected or substantially so, and intended to put that option to the electorate in the next Labour manifesto (Hansard, 2006–07). This would leave little (if any) room for the bishops or for other religious leaders.

12 It was set up in 1941 to coordinate negotiations with the government over compensation for war damage. It is now an ecumenical body that acts as a channel of communication between

the churches and government – in the widest sense – on issues of secular law as they affect religion.

13 Note however the Equality Act (Sexual Orientation) Regulations 2007 which now seek to outlaw discrimination on the ground, among others, of gender reassignment.

14 See generally Ahdar and Leigh, 2005, particularly ch. 5, 'Is Establishment Consistent with Religious Freedom?' (pp. 127–54) which concludes, entirely correctly, that 'non-coercive state endorsement of religion is consistent with freedom of religion'.

15 In August 2006 the UK government set up a Commission on Integration and Cohesion to consider how local areas could make the most of diversity while responding to the tensions it might cause. The Commission's final report, *Our Shared Future* (Future, 2007), included lots of references to faith communities, and boldly asserted that 'Faith communities should be encouraged to work with Government, the LGA, and other relevant agencies to develop a programme to help increase "religious literacy" on the part of public agencies and the ability of these agencies to establish effective patterns of engagement with religion and belief groups as part of wider public engagement; to strengthen their engagement with the process of policy development and implementation, and enable local areas to make targeted use of their resources.' As recently as 14 November 2007 the prime minister himself made proposals for a new forum of headteachers to advise on protecting young people from extremism and encourage social cohesion, a government-sponsored national framework for teaching religious education in schools, including a multifaith syllabus, and an advisory group to work with local communities to support the citizenship education classes run by mosque schools. The government also intends to publish a Green Paper to encourage interfaith groups to come together in every constituency (Hansard, 2007–08).

16 I am grateful to my colleague Frank Cranmer for this material and its analysis which I draw from his unpublished paper *The Europeanisation of Church Law and the Common Law of Religion in the EU* (Cranmer, 2007) delivered in Stockholm in November 2007.

17 'As a matter of historical fact, it is Christianity and the Christian message that have built the "inheritance of Europe" from which have developed the universal values of the inviolable and inalienable rights of the human person, democracy, equality and the rule of law. The Preamble does state that these values have derived from the religious inheritance. The *Constitutional Treaty* draws its inspiration from specific traditions that have shaped Europe, thus implicitly referring to the centre of this tradition, which is Christianity' (COMECE, 2005, p. 14).

18 It remains to be seen whether the new representative of the archbishop of Canterbury to the EU institutions in Brussels will be significant in raising the profile of the Church of England and increasing its influence.

19 Its governing instrument is a constitution, para. 2 of which declares that the diocese 'shall be deemed to be within the Province of Canterbury'. Para. 22(a) makes provision for the canons and ecclesiastical law of the Church of England to apply in the diocese 'so far as the local law of any state or country shall permit' and 'with such modifications or exceptions as … are deemed appropriate by the Archbishop of Canterbury acting with the concurrence of the vicar general of the Province …'.

20 However if one speaks in terms of the Anglican Communion (autonomous churches throughout the globe each of which is formally in communion with the See of Canterbury) then there is a universality of issues to be considered and Europe-wide matters legitimately be addressed. The Anglican Communion maintains a permanent observer and modest mission at the United Nations in New York.

21 For a summary of the conference at which this paper was presented, see Rivers (2007b).

22 An invited symposium 'Same-Sex Unions and the Churches: Problems and Responses in an European Perspective' was organised by the Ecclesiastical Law Society in London on 31 March 2006. For a full summary, see Hill, C. (2007).

23 For an analysis of the judgment, see Samuels (2005). A high profile decision, albeit only at employment tribunal level, has been the judgment in the case of *Reaney v Bishop of Hereford* (2007) which considered that the ambit of the exemption is a fact-specific case.

24 The Northern Ireland High Court recently gave consideration to the particular legislation brought into force in the Province, namely the Equality Act (Sexual Orientation) Regulations (Northern Ireland) 2006 (Statutory Rule 2006, No. 439). The decision of Mr Justice Weatherup is lengthy and finely nuanced: *R (on the application of the Christian Institute and others) v The Office of the First Minister and Deputy First Minister* (unreported) Weatherup J. For the position in England and Wales, see the Equality Act (Sexual Orientation) Regulations 2007, and the treatment given to this legislation in Sandberg and Doe (2007).

References

(a) Books, Articles and Papers

Ahdar, R. and Leigh, I. (2005) *Religious Freedom in the Liberal State* (Oxford, Oxford University Press).

CEC (1992) Constitution of the Conference of European Churches, www.cec-kek.org/content/preamble.shtml (last accessed 6 November 2008).

Charta (2001) CEC/COMECE, *Charta Oecumenica*, April, http://cofe.anglican.org/info/ccu/europe/ecumbackground/charta.rtf (last accessed 6 November 2008).

COMECE (2005) COMECE, The Treaty Establishing a Constitution for Europe: Elements for an Evaluation (11 March) (Brussels), http://www.comece.org/upload/pdf/pub_const_treaty_050311_EN.pdf (last accessed 6 November 2008).

Cranmer, F. (2001) 'Church–state relations in the United Kingdom: a Westminster view', *Ecclesiastical Law Journal*, 6, pp. 111–21.

Cranmer, F. (2007) *The Europeanisation of Church Law and the Common Law of Religion in the EU*, paper presented at a conference in Stockholm, November, unpublished.

Cranmer, F. (2008) 'Parliamentary report', *Ecclesiastical Law Journal*, 10, pp. 97–102.

Dawson, I. and Dunn, A. (2002) 'Seeking the principle: chancels, choices and human rights', *Journal of Legal Studies*, 22, pp. 238–58.

Evans Pritchard, A. (2004) '1m Christians sign EU religion plea', *Daily Telegraph* (London), 25 November.

Future (2007) *Commission on Integration and Cohesion: Our Shared Future*, http://www.integrationandcohesion.org.uk/Our_final_report.aspx (last accessed 6 November 2008).

Governance (2007) Government Green Paper: The Governance of Britain, The Stationery Office, London, Cm 7170, July, http://www.official-documents.gov.uk/document/cm71/7170/7170.pdf (last accessed 15 November 2008).

Hansard (2006–07) HC Deb (2006–07) c 449, http://www.publications.parliament.uk/pa/pahansard.htm

Hansard (2007) HC Deb (2006–07) 3 July 2007 c 817, http://www.publications.parliament.uk/pa/pahansard.htm

Hansard (2007–08) HC Deb (2007–08) 14 November c 667 ff. http://www.publications.parliament.uk/pa/pahansard.htm

Hill, C. (2007) 'Same-sex unions and the churches: problems and responses in a European perspective', *Ecclesiastical Law Journal*, 9, pp. 120–25.

Hill, M. (2001) 'Case note', *Ecclesiastical Law Journal*, 6, pp. 173–74.

Hill, M. (2004) 'Editorial', *Ecclesiastical Law Journal*, 7, pp. 246–49.

Hill, M. (2007) *Ecclesiastical Law* (3rd edn) (Oxford, Oxford University Press).

House (2000) *A House for the Future* (the Report of the Royal Commission on Reform of the House of Lords) (London, The Stationery Office, Cm 4534, January), http://www.archive.official-documents.co.uk/document/cm45/4534/4534.htm (last accessed 15 November 2008).

John Paul II (2003) *Ecclesia in Europa* (Apostolic Exhortation, 28 June), http://www.vatican.va/holy_father/john_paul_ii/apost_exhortations/documents/hf_jp-ii_exh_20030628_ecclesia-in-europa_en.html (last accessed 6 November 2008).

Leigh. I. (2002) 'Freedom of religion: public/private, rights/wrongs', in M. Hill (ed.), *Religious Liberty and Human Rights* (Cardiff, University of Wales Press), pp. 128–58.

Lord MacKay of Clashfern (2007) *The Times*, 9 January.

McClean, D. (2002) 'Letter from Brussels', *Ecclesiastical Law Journal*, 6, pp. 375–80.

McClean, D. (2004) 'The changing legal framework of establishment', *Ecclesiastical Law Journal*, 7, pp. 292–303.

McClean, D. (2005) 'State and church in the United Kingdom', in G. Robbers (ed.), *State and Church in the European Union* (2nd edn) (Baden-Baden, Nomos).

Oliver, D. (2002) 'Chancel repairs and the human rights', *Public Law*, pp. 651–53.

Reform (2007)*The House of Lords: Reform* (London, The Stationery Office, Cm 7027, February), http://www.official-documents.gov.uk/document/cm70/7027/7027.pdf (last accessed 15 November 2008).

Rivers, J. (2004) 'In pursuit of pluralism: the ecclesiastical policy of the European Union', *Ecclesiastical Law Journal*, 7, pp. 267–91.

Rivers, J. (2007a) *The EU, Religion and Techniques of Accommodation*, paper presented at the conference 'The European Union and the Religious Dimensions of Law: Issues and Challenges' at the Centre for the Study of Law and Religion, University of Bristol, School of Law, 12–13 January.

Rivers, J. (2007b) 'The European Union and the religious dimensions of law', *Ecclesiastical Law Journal*, 9, pp. 221–22.

Samuels, L. (2005) 'Sexual orientation discrimination and the church: balancing competing human rights', *Ecclesiastical Law Journal*, 8, pp. 74–79.

Sandberg, R. (2008) 'Gods and services: religious groups and sexual orientation discrimination, *Ecclesiastical Law Journal*, 10, pp. 205–09.

Sandberg, R. and Doe, N. (2007) 'Religious exemptions in discrimination law', *Cambridge Law Journal*, 66, 2, pp. 302–12.

SI (2003) SI (Statutory Instrument) 2003/1661, giving effect to Council Directive 2000/78/EC, http://www.statutelaw.gov.uk

Soul for Europe (2000) *'A Soul for Europe': Ethics and Spirituality: Annual Report 2000* (Brussels, European Commission Secretariat General Budget Heading A–3021).

Whale, S. (2002) 'Pawnbokers and parishes: the protection of property under the Human Rights Act', *European Human Rights Law Review*, 67, pp. 78–79.

(b) Court Cases

In the following citations the following abbreviations are used:
AC: *Appeal Cases*
Ecc LJ: *Ecclesiastical Law Journal*
IRLR: *Industrial Relations Law Reports*
NIQB: *Northern Ireland Queen's Bench*

References are given in the form '1 AC 546', which means that the case was published in volume 1 of AC starting at page 546.

Aston Cantlow and Wilmcote with Billesley Parochial Church Council v Wallbank [2004] 1 AC 546.

R (on the application of the Christian Institute and others) v The Office of the First Minister and Deputy First Minister [2007] NIQB 66.

R v Secretary of State for Trade and Industry ex parte *Amicus and others* [2004] IRLR 430.

Reaney v Bishop of Hereford (2007), judgment 17 July 2007, noted at (2008) 10 Ecc LJ 131.

Religious Lobbies in the European Union: from Dominant Church to Faith-Based Organisation?

MARTIN STEVEN

Introduction

A changing policy environment is altering the political behaviour of national, state or dominant churches in Western Europe in two ways.

First, while the Amsterdam Treaty protects the right of the individual citizen to freedom of religious expression, the European Union (EU) is an inherently secular body with no mention of Christianity in any of its other treaties or directives. Within this context, the harmonisation of fundamental citizen rights in policy areas such as education and employment has led to a situation in which churches that have traditionally enjoyed an automatic form of domestic political influence are beginning to resemble one interest group amongst many others. For example, the EU Equal Treatment Directive has been used in order directly to challenge the Church of Scotland's 'special' political status, as well as the Scottish Catholic Church's independent state school system.

Second, the transfer of power from national level to Brussels has meant that the territorial political influence of national churches is no longer clear: the wider impact of European integration is proving to be as significant as specific directives. Thus 2006 witnessed a controversy over a British Airways flight attendant not being permitted to wear a cross, following a debate in 2004 over the place of religious symbols or clothing in French classrooms – both issues that transcend the boundaries of the traditional nation state. These trends also reflect the wider debate about the role of religion in an enlarged and secular EU: does integration inevitably mean a less certain – if not necessarily less influential – political role for individual Christian churches?

Churches and European Integration

EU member states are increasingly integrated, with supranational legislation now taking precedence over national laws. Brussels offers a specific policy focus where a wide variety of different types of interest groups can lobby: supranational political institutions like the European Commission and the European Parliament have become more central to decision-making, working in conjunction with the intergovernmental Council of Ministers. The development of different tiers of multilevel governance – supranational, national, and subnational – has created a constantly evolving legal and political framework with which interest groups and political organisations must engage. Against the backdrop of 'ever closer union' (Dinan, 2005), centuries-old traditions of national or state churches being given special political rights or status in the domestic societies of their respective member states are inevitably affected.

Fourteen EU member states continue to maintain a formal link between church and state (Madeley and Enyedi, 2003, p. 13), and as a result sustain official channels between religion and politics. As Mirjam Künkler and Michael Meyer-Resende explain, 'the relationship of the state to religious institutions in established democracies takes such a variety of forms that it is impossible to speak of one general pattern' (2007, p. 2). Yves Meny and Andrew Knapp highlight the European tradition of a 'dominant' church or religion 'marking' the political systems of both Italy in Southern Europe and the UK in Northern Europe (1998, p. 26). All the Nordic nation states – so often perceived to be socially liberal – have a tradition of sustaining the work of their respective Lutheran Churches via taxation, although this practice is now much reduced in practical significance. In Denmark, for example, the Lutheran Church is still supported by the state under the Danish Constitution, and there is a minister for ecclesiastical affairs, that is, a cabinet member who handles the political side of church affairs. Meanwhile in France there exists a strict separation of church and state, but one church – the Catholic Church – continues to 'dominate' what is still a relatively homogeneous society with 82 per cent of the population continuing to claim adherence in 2000 (Bale, 2005, p. 25; Barrett *et al.*, 2001).

One of the consequences of the dynamics of European integration is a challenge to justify the 'established' place traditionally held by various types of national, state or dominant church in Western Europe – and in two key ways. First, the development of supranational legislation in policy areas where emphasis is placed upon the shared and uniform fundamental rights of citizens across the EU has had a significant impact on the nature of this role. Churches are finding it increasingly difficult to justify their automatic right to unique political privileges such as state funding or legal exemptions – particularly in policy areas relating to education and employment where EU legislation seeks to ensure equal opportunities. Second, the wider 'hollowing out' of the conventional parameters of the nation-state has led to Europe-wide political issues in the twenty-first century rendering the conventional model of church and state relations more peripheral.

Religious Interest-Group Behaviour

The role of religion in EU politics – both at a national and at a supranational level – is multidimensional. I have mentioned the question of church–state relations. There is also a continuing clear correlation between religious denomination and voting behaviour, but as Russell Dalton argues (2002, p. 134), the emergence of a 'new politics' has meant that postmaterialist issues such as environmental protection and women's liberation have replaced the old 'cleavages' of religion and class as factors which condition this behaviour (see Lipset and Rokkan, 1967). While significant links between religion and voting remain across Western Europe, the decline in church attendance has led to a weakening of this correlation, and the pattern is now less uniform. Nevertheless, it remains more prevalent in Europe than in the USA (Miller and Niemi, 2002, p. 171). Meanwhile the fundamental question of whether the accession of Turkey to the EU remains problematic for further integration impinges upon any discussion of politics and religion in Europe (see Klausen, 2005).

In addition to the dimensions of church–state relations, voting behaviour and European values, there is another less researched dimension to the ways in which politics and religion interact, namely when churches act as political interest groups, lobbying decision-makers on aspects of social policymaking which concern them. Literature on the various lobbying activities of churches – both domestically and in Brussels – is limited. Carolyn Warner's analysis of the political behaviour of the Catholic Church in Europe is one of the few self-contained studies that analyses a mainstream church as if it were a 'conventional' interest group.

> The Church has lobbied democratic governments, via political parties and other means, to retain its monopoly over education and to have the costs of it paid for by governments; it has lobbied them to impose its morals on society through legislation; it has lobbied governments to gain or retain preferential tax status; and it has lobbied to keep some of its employees from being conscripted .... To put it bluntly, the Catholic Church is, in addition to being a religion, an interest group (Warner, 2000, pp. 6–7).

The study of interest groups is dominated by American literature. While significant research has been conducted on lobbying in the EU (Mazey and Richardson, 1993; Greenwood and Aspinwall, 1998; Richardson, 2001), it remains small-scale in contrast with a number of very large-scale studies of lobbying behaviour in the USA (Heinz *et al.*, 1993; Baumgartner and Leech, 1998). This is a direct consequence of the traditional difference between the pluralist US political system, where different interest groups compete to exert influence over government, and the more corporatist European political systems, where only the most prominent 'peak associations' have any meaningful contact with those in power.

In the pluralist system of US politics, religious lobbies have long-established influential voices, despite the fact that no one church is formally linked to the state. President George W. Bush provided an increase in public funds for churches and religious organisations involved with social care, establishing the Office of Faith-Based and Community Initiatives, as well as faith-based centres in five cabinet-level federal agencies to assist with its work (Wilson, 2003, p. 30). Ever since the early 1980s religious interests, particularly on the political right, have become 'perennial participants in U.S. electoral politics' (Guth *et al.*, 2002, p. 162); the two most important religious right organisations of that period, 'Christian Voice' and 'Moral Majority', were both founded in 1978, but as Clyde Wilcox states, it was actually the 1976 Carter presidential campaign which 'mobilized the evangelicals as no candidate had done before' (1992, p. 11). President Carter made his 'born again' Southern Baptist faith central to his campaign, and won many votes for the Democrat cause as a consequence. Alongside evangelical Christian lobbies, the pro-Israel lobby, the American Israeli Public Affairs Committee, is generally considered to be one of the most influential interest groups in American politics.

Religious lobbies in the EU are neither on a scale, nor in a form, such that any meaningful comparison can be drawn between them and US faith-based lobbies. For one thing, 'religious right' activities in Washington are essentially issue-based, for example, lobbying against abortion, or stem cell research, as opposed to representing one particular church or religious denomination. However, I am not arguing that churches are any less politically influential as a result of EU integration, and for three reasons. First, the question of evaluating interest-group effectiveness is methodologically difficult, if not impossible. Writers in the field have tried to address the difficulties involved, although as Paul Whiteley and Stephen Winyard argue, 'the question of interest group effectiveness is probably one of the least adequately researched aspects of the study of pressure groups' (1987, p. 111). As Grant correctly states, it is often easier to assess the ineffectiveness of a pressure group, or a change in its levels of effectiveness, than its effectiveness *per se* (2000, p. 211). Second, the central and important place of religion in American politics demonstrates that churches need not necessarily be formally tied to the state in order to exert influence. Third, my focus is on the fact that churches in the EU are now being challenged to justify their political role in a more open and transparent way, within a modern policy environment of equal opportunities and civil liberties (see Norris and Inglehart, 2004).

'Fundamental Rights' in the European Union

The contemporary debate concerning the nature of Europe's 'common values' is not merely theoretical. On a practical level, 'ever closer union' has involved the harmonisation of human rights and civil liberties across the EU. For example, British people are no longer simply 'subjects' of the queen – they are EU citizens, with their freedoms protected by pan-European legislation, enshrined in the EU Charter of Fundamental Rights, and safeguarded by both the European Court of Justice and the European ombudsman. In policy areas such as education and employment, 'equal opportunities' are an important component of European law. As integration has advanced, European directives on laws in the work-place and schools have tightened up practices across different member states.

The issue of harmonising 'common values' goes to the very heart of the European integration project as it focuses on the sensitive political issue of 'foreign' values being 'imposed' upon traditionally independent territorial areas. For example, the British Conservative Party's enthusiasm for the type of free market economics represented by the EU is substantially tempered by its dislike of what it perceives to be the centralising and overly bureaucratic aspect of the Single Market. Eurosceptics argue that there exists a quantifiable difference between conceding aspects of sovereignty for tangible economic benefits and an undemocratic body imposing unfamiliar laws (Holmes, 2001). Supranational EU laws are at their most contentious when they are perceived to be alien to the values of an individual member state – for whatever reason. Defining the limits of human rights – and the nature of civil liberties – is a difficult and a delicate task, where compromise and harmonisation are not always easily achieved.

This problem was highlighted in 2004 when the Italian Christian Democrat politician Rocco Buttiglione was nominated to become the new EU commissioner for justice, freedom and security. His nomination was blocked by a group of Socialist,

Green and Liberal/Democratic MEPs (members of the European Parliament) who expressed 'reservations' that his devout Catholicism was incompatible with the role of promoting and protecting equal opportunities across Europe, with its distinctive 'union of values' (Charlemagne, 2004). This was despite Buttiglione's assurance that he drew a clear distinction between the theological concept of a 'sin' and 'crimes' recognised by European law, and that he would feel entirely comfortable implementing the EU Charter of Fundamental Rights. In this context, we should note that the European Parliament maintains an all-party Working Group on the Separation of Religion and Politics (WGSRP) whose aim is to

> 1. Identify issues pertaining to the intersection of religion and politics in which the political values and principles of the European Union are at stake;
> 2. Identify ways MEPs and civil society can work together to raise awareness of these issues;
> 3. Promote knowledge, understanding and acceptance of freedom of religion and non-religion, and the impartiality of the EU regarding organizations of faith and conviction;
> 4. Take action, where appropriate, to counter any attempts to undermine democracy, human rights and in particular women's rights and minority rights, sexual and reproductive health and rights, pluralism and the rule of law. (European Parliament, 2008)

The language used in the WGSRP's mission statement epitomises the wider debate over the role of religion within the EU: the Group is ostensibly concerned with maintaining a healthy balance between religion and politics, but also makes pejorative references to democratic values potentially being 'at stake' or 'undermined' by religious organisations.

In contrast, European leaders seem to ask for official recognition of the place of religion – and particularly Christianity – in the political development of the EU. German Chancellor Angela Merkel has backed Pope Benedict's call for the EU Reform Treaty to make reference to the importance of Europe's Christian values and heritage (Traynor, 2007). In November 2007 Donald Tusk, the new Polish prime minister, announced that his government would refuse to sign the EU Charter of Fundamental Rights, as a result of concerns that some of the provisions relating to 'moral' or 'family' policy areas, namely same-sex marriages, would contradict domestic law in Poland (BBC, 2007b).

Can there ever be compromise between such polar viewpoints, or is this type of conflict an everlasting process within the EU? Is it possible for a 'third way' to be developed between those who believe in moral relativism and those who stand for objective truth? Secular values are not necessarily being promoted as a consequence of antireligious sentiment – more as a consequence of the practical need for uniformity and consistency. The Buttiglione case was really more of a political dispute between the integrationist values of those serving on the European Commission and MEPs arguing for the safeguarding of individual freedoms, rather than between liberal, secular northern Europeans and conservatively religious Mediterraneans.

Philosophical debates on the relationship between the state and the secular also have practical consequences for policymaking – and this applies to the wider debate on the role of religion in the new Europe. Churches are directly affected by new legislation and directives particularly when these challenge their right to hold a special status as the 'national' church. In addition, churches are influenced by a change in 'political culture' (Almond and Verba, 1963) initiated by the EU: the prevalence of equal opportunities, and a change of political status which means that the role of the nation-state is no longer central and links between church and state are also less important.

European Legislation and the Political Behaviour of State Churches: the Case of Scotland

The direct impact of European legislation on churches can be seen particularly in the devolved Scottish political system. The EU recognises Scotland as an official 'region' of Europe, and Scottish government has a permanent, distinctive and prominent presence on Rond Point Schuman, the hub of lobbying activities in Brussels. Edinburgh is one of only three cities which are not member state capitals to have a permanent European Parliamentary Office as a consequence of its cultural/national status (Barcelona and Munich are the others). This particular position reflects Scotland's historic political independence from England. Various 'political' institutions which survived intact after the Act of Union with England in 1707, namely, the legal system, the education system and the Presbyterian Church of Scotland, have now been joined by the new Scottish Parliament (and devolved government) created in 1999. The Church of Scotland is one of the defining features of Scottish national identity and simultaneously part of the establishment (as the 'national' church). Prior to the reintroduction of devolved government in Scotland in 1999 the annual General Assembly of the Church of Scotland was even described as the closest body to a Scottish legislature. The Church of Scotland is however free from any political interference. This is a different situation from that of the Church of England, which has the queen as its head, seats in the House of Lords, and its senior clergy appointed by the prime minister. The Catholic Church in Scotland has prominent status because of its significant population centring on Scotland's largest city, Glasgow, and its own unique school system, educating large numbers of Scottish school children, and making it a 'quasi-governmental body' (Kellas, 1989, p. 179).

The special status enjoyed by the two churches has been challenged as a consequence of the EU's Equal Treatment Directive (ETD), which came into effect in November 2000, and established a general framework for equal treatment in employment and occupation. The ETD prohibits discrimination against individuals in the workplace on the grounds of disability, sexual orientation, age or religion: 'Employment and occupation are key elements in guaranteeing equal opportunities for all and contribute strongly to the full participation of citizens in economic, cultural and social life . . .' (European Union, 2000).

In December 2005, referring to the ETD, the House of Lords ruled that the Revd Helen Percy, a minister in the Church of Scotland, could take the church to an employment tribunal after she was suspended from her post in 1997. The ETD covered working conditions, pay and dismissals as well as recruitment. Church lawyers had argued that because of the content of the 1921 Act, which stipulated that the church alone can fully adjudicate in all matters of doctrine, worship, government and discipline in the church, and that it is therefore 'subject to no civil authority', ministers were not protected by employment law in the same way as employees in other areas of work; that is, they did not have the same rights of procedure and appeal. The House of Lords interpretation of European law did not accept the legitimacy of that argument.

The Scottish legal system is distinctive from its English equivalent, which means that British-wide bills often have to be amended or revised before they can become law in Scotland. One of the consequences of this is that the Church of Scotland has full autonomy over the running of its affairs, including legal exemption from certain acts of parliament concerning employment rights. Traditionally, the church's principal clerk (who, as well as being an ordained minister, is legally trained) acts as the church's 'chief executive', setting up *ad hoc* courts to deal with cases such as the one of Revd Percy. However, while the Percy case was eventually settled out of court in October 2006, a new legal precedent was set, with the church's automatic exemptions from standard elements of employment law being challenged. The concept of national churches being able to conduct their affairs without any interference from the state was judged to conflict with the spirit of the ETD.

A second example of EU employment legislation impacting upon a Scottish church comes from the area of education, the 'third pillar' of the Scottish political system. Although the Church of Scotland is the official state church of Scotland, a formal link exists between the Catholic Church and the Scottish political system, in the shape of denominational primary and secondary schools. As a consequence of the 1918 Education Act the Catholic Church possesses more *de facto* importance in Scottish society than at national level. The main teachers' union in Scotland, the Educational Institute of Scotland (EIS), has regularly shown signs of frustration that Catholic teachers have an inherent advantage over their nondenominational colleagues when applying for promoted jobs in Catholic schools. Appointments of teachers are made in accordance with the wishes of the representatives of the Catholic Church on the local authority education committee. Non-Catholic teachers can be hired to work in Catholic schools; however, they cannot be promoted as they are not allowed to teach Religious Education or to handle related pastoral issues. In May 2007 the EIS publicly cited the European Convention on Human Rights as the basis for arguing that no teacher should be denied a job on 'religious or moral grounds' (Denholm, 2007). The issues involved are also relevant to the ETD, which specifically refers to equal opportunities in relation to promotion, as well as recruitment and dismissals. The EIS stance dates back to 1979, when a motion was passed at its annual conference calling for religious integration in schools. However, employment rights lawyers have continued to show an interest in the case, and since 1999 the EIS has resolved to 'formulate a policy on campaigning for denominational schools' abolition – subject to the consent of churches and parents' (Devine, 2000, p. 163). There have been various tribunals involving teachers who have been blocked from promotion in denominational Scottish schools as a consequence.

These examples suggest that European integration is weakening the established link between church and state. These legal changes have a deeper 'ripple effect', with main churches readjusting to the new political landscape. For example, both churches have appointed their own parliamentary officers to lobby the Scottish Parliament on their behalf over policy issues of concern. In 2003 the Catholic Church even decided to set up the Scottish Catholic Education Service in order to promote the existence of its denominational schools against the backdrop of calls for increased integration in the 'new' Scotland. In the context of EU politics, both churches' special status is being challenged by individuals or groups who believe they should be brought 'into line' with other employers – and they are responding accordingly to protect their interests.

EU 'fundamental rights' are having a practical impact upon everyday life – and the advancement of equal opportunities and civil liberties do not always sit particularly comfortably with traditional religious values. Constitutional anomalies are inevitably going to be ironed out as member states grow ever closer. New political institutions promulgate new laws and the place of older values is re-evaluated in the process.

European Institutions and the Political Behaviour of State Churches: the Cases of the UK and France

As well as examining the impact of European integration upon church behaviour, we must also examine the changing role of the nation-state. This has also resulted in the political climate for national churches becoming more challenging, fuelling changes in their behaviour. In particular, there have been significant effects in the areas of employment and rights in the workplace and schools in the UK and France.

In November 2006 the decision of British Airways to stop one of its flight attendants from wearing a cross prominently around her neck prompted senior figures in the Church of England, including the archbishops of Canterbury and York and the bishop of London, to speak out strongly in her defence. The debate was particularly intense because it involved Britain's 'national carrier', with many of the subsequent criticisms focusing on the country's Christian heritage and traditions. Dr John Sentamu, the archbishop of York, stated that 'British Airways needs to look again at this decision and … at the history of the country it represents, whose culture, laws, heritage and tradition owes so much to the very same symbol it would ban' (BBC, 2006). Ultimately the church won the argument and in January 2007 the airline dropped the ban. The British Airways case represented a challenge to the traditionally prominent political role of the Church of England similar to the challenge in the Scottish case to the political status and behaviour of the Scottish churches.

The Church of England exerts considerable power – the queen is its head, its bishops are part of the parliament and formulate British law. However, in the context of the British Airways row, the established church became an interest group. Its most senior clergy were compelled to speak out on behalf of Anglican communicants in the modern workplace to defend the right of people to wear the most recognisable symbol of Christianity while working for *British* Airways. In contrast to the Percy and EIS cases in Scotland, European law was not directly involved. The airline did not seek to justify its ban on the grounds that it was adhering to EU legislation. Willie Walsh, the chief executive of British Airways, stated that 'unintentionally, we have found ourselves at the centre of one of the hottest social issues in current public debate' (BBC, 2007a). Nevertheless, a very similar pattern can be identified here in that a traditionally dominant church in a EU member state was compelled to take radical political action in order to 'defend' its place in its own domestic society, with the harmonised and secular political values of the EU again playing a prominent role.

The fact that British Airways took a decision of this nature is itself a statement about the role of religion and/or Christianity in modern Europe. The decision reflects a wider trend across Western Europe: churches are no longer automatically powerful. It suggests that the values of churches are not as important as the secular equal opportunities or civil liberties expounded by the EU. With European law superseding British law, and sub-state institutions like the Scottish Parliament bypassing established central government decision-making, the overall importance of Church of England bishops having a vote in the House of Lords is in decline. Part of New Labour's attempts to modernise British government has been to include representatives of different faith groups, so while the 'lords spiritual' still constitute a component part of the chamber, their unique special political status is much reduced. In 2002 the British government appointed the member of parliament John Battle to act as an 'envoy to the faith communities' – a direct channel of communication between all faith groups and the prime minister (BBC, 2002).

The political power of the church has been substantially altered. The 'non-decision-making' model of Peter Bachrach and Morton Baratz (1970, p. 9) sees controversial items being deliberately kept off the political agenda by political elites. Steven Lukes (1974, p. 23) goes further than Bachrach and Baratz, arguing that power can also be exercised by 'shaping or determining' the entire political climate, so that individuals are not even aware they are being influenced. As the political climate of European integration develops, churches in the EU are increasingly forced to be much more proactive in order to protect their interests. In Denmark, for example, the Lutheran Church is considering setting up an office in Brussels to lobby on behalf of 'liberal Protestants' in Europe, linking in with representatives from Swedish, Finnish and German churches (Danish Lutheran Church, April 2007). The Conference of European Churches already maintains an EU office in Brussels to liaise with the decision-makers.

France provides another example of the secular culture of the EU challenging religious values. The French Catholic Church was a powerful institution at the start of the twentieth century but in 1905 a law was passed in order to curtail its political influence. French society remains relatively homogeneous, with only eight per cent of its current population made up of ethnic minorities (Bale, 2005, p. 25; Barrett *et al.*, 2001), and the *de facto* influence of the Catholic Church has remained across France, in terms of its values and culture. France's revolutionary tradition, however, provides an interesting contrast with the tradition which has evolved in some 'Protestant' nations of empowering the church's involvement in politics by linking it to the state.

In 2004 the comprehensive separation of church and state in France was brought up to date as the Chirac government resolved to apply the secular principle to the case of 'conspicuous' ('*ostensible*') religious symbols in the classroom. The French parliament subsequently banned pupils from wearing Muslim headscarves (the most high-profile and contentious aspect of the new law), Sikh turbans, Jewish skullcaps or 'prominent' Christian crosses in state schools, arguing that these practices contradicted the principle of *laïcité* embodied in the 1905 law that formally separated church and state.

The impact of European integration can be perceived here. The twenty-first-century French application of church–state separation is in keeping with the harmonised neutral values of a secular EU. Parallels can also be drawn with the British Airways controversy, in that both have international and supranational implications, rather than simply being restricted to domestic politics. The question of how modern, multicultural political systems define the boundary between religion and politics is not only a French debate but a European issue.

From a behavioural perspective, the French secular law of 1905 designed to moderate the power of one church is effectively being used to maintain a parity of equal religious interests. Political motivations are the same, namely to keep the spiritual separate from the temporal, but the effects are different. The public perception is not one of a powerful institution like the Catholic Church being restricted but of the French state acting like an referee, trying to be scrupulously fair to all religions (and none) in French society, and the political status of the dominant church in France is substantially altered as a consequence.

Conclusion

The cases of churches in Scotland, the Church of England and the Catholic Church in France raise interesting issues in the context of the wider debate on the role of religion in Europe. While the European institutions have not always been directly involved in these cases, they are responsible for helping to create a secular political climate that is questioning the role of religion in European society. They have wider implications for church–state relations, employment rights and interest-group politics. Churches can no longer expect automatically to enjoy a pre-eminent position in their domestic societies, and the traditionally close formal relationship between politics and religion in most European nation states has been fundamentally altered. A pattern is developing within the EU, which one could cautiously compare with the situation in the USA, eclipsing the older European model of a group of homogeneous nation-states where one official religion or church is dominant in each autonomous territory. Brussels is increasingly providing a focus for churches to lobby decision-makers for their own ends, becoming one interest group among many, albeit one with potentially substantial influence.

References

Almond, G. and Verba, S. (1963) *The Civic Culture* (Princeton, Princeton University Press).

Bachrach, P. and Baratz, M. (1970) *Power and Poverty: Theory and Practice* (New York, Oxford University Press).

Bale, T. (2005) *European Politics: a Comparative Introduction* (Basingstoke, Palgrave Macmillan).

Barrett, D. B., Kurian, G. T. and Johnson, T. M. (2001) *World Christian Encyclopedia* (Oxford, Oxford University Press).

Baumgartner, F. R. and Leech, B. L. (1998) *Basic Instincts* (Princeton, Princeton University Press).

BBC (2002) BBC News, 17 January, http://news.bbc.co.uk (last accessed 20 April 2008).

BBC (2006) BBC News, 21 November, http://news.bbc.co.uk (last accessed 20 April 2008).

BBC (2007a) BBC News, 19 January, http://news.bbc.co.uk (last accessed 20 April 2008).

BBC (2007b) BBC News, 23 November, http://news.bbc.co.uk (last accessed 20 April 2008).

Charlemagne (2004) 'Real politics, at last?', *The Economist*, 30 October, p. 52.

Dalton, R. (2002) *Citizen Politics in Western Democracies* (New York, Chatham House).

Danish Lutheran Church (2007) Council on International Relations of the Evangelical Lutheran Church in Denmark, *Church News from Denmark*, 2/6 (April), www.interchurch.dk/cn/archive.php (last accessed 11 October 2008).

Denholm, A. (2007) 'End church veto over jobs, say teachers', *The Herald*, 16 May, p. 1.

Devine, T. M. (ed.) (2000) *Scotland's Shame?* (Edinburgh, Mainstream).

Dinan, D. (2005) *Ever Closer Union: an Introduction to European Integration* (Basingstoke, Palgrave Macmillan).

European Parliament (2008) All Party Working Group on the Separation of Religion and Politics, http://politicsreligion.com/group.html (last accessed 11 October 2008).

European Union (2000) Council Directive ... Establishing a General Framework for Equal Treatment in Employment and Occupation, http://europa.eu/scadplus/leg/en/cha/c10823.htm (last accessed 20 April 2008).

Grant, W. (2000) *Pressure Groups and British Politics* (Basingstoke, Macmillan).

Greenwood, J. and Aspinwall, M. (eds) (1998) *Collective Action in the European Union: Interests and the New Politics of Associability* (London, Routledge).

Guth, J. L., Kellstedt, L. A., Green, J. C. and Smidt, C. E. (2002) 'A distant thunder? Religious mobilization in the 2000 elections', in A. J. Cigler and B. A. Loomis (eds), *Interest Group Politics* (Washington DC, CQ Press), pp. 161–84.

Heinz, J. P., Laumann, E. O., Nelson, R. L. and Salisbury, R. H. (1993) *The Hollow Core* (Cambridge, MA, Harvard University Press).

Holmes, M. (2001) *The Eurosceptical Reader 2* (Basingstoke, Palgrave).

Kellas, J. G. (1989) *The Scottish Political System* (Cambridge, Cambridge University Press).

Klausen, J. (2005) *The Islamic Challenge: Politics and Religion in Western Europe* (New York, Oxford University Press).

Künkler, M. and Meyer-Resende, M. (2007) *A Missing Link: Why Europe Should Talk about Religion when Promoting Democracy Abroad* (Berlin, Democracy Reporting International).

Lipset, S. M. and Rokkan, S. (eds) (1967) *Party Systems and Voter Alignments: Cross-National Perspectives* (New York, Free Press).

Lukes, S. (1974) *Power: a Radical View* (Basingstoke, Macmillan).

Madeley, J. T. S. and Enyedi, Z. (eds) (2003) *Church and State in Contemporary Europe: the Chimera of Neutrality* (London, Frank Cass).

Mazey, S. and Richardson, J. (eds) (1993) *Lobbying in the European Community* (Oxford, Oxford University Press).

Meny, Y. and Knapp, A. (1998) *Government and Politics in Western Europe* (Oxford, Oxford University Press).

Miller, W. L. and Niemi, R. G. (2002) 'Voting, choice, conditioning and constraint', in L. LeDuc, R. Niemi and P. Norris (eds), *Comparing Democracies 2: New Challenges in the Study of Elections and Voting* (London, Sage), pp. 169–88.

Norris, P. and Inglehart, R. (2004) *Sacred and Secular* (Cambridge, Cambridge University Press).

Richardson, J. (ed.) (2001) *European Union: Power and Policy-Making* (London, Routledge).

Traynor, I. (2007) 'As the EU turns 50, pope says it's on path to oblivion', *The Guardian*, 26 March, p. 23.

Warner, C. (2000) *Confessions of an Interest Group: the Catholic Church and Political Parties in Europe* (Princeton, Princeton University Press).

Whiteley, P. F. and Winyard, S. J. (1987) *Pressure for the Poor* (London, Methuen).

Wilcox, C. (1992) *God's Warriors: the Christian Right in the Twentieth Century* (Baltimore, Johns Hopkins University Press).

Wilson, P. A. (2003) 'Faith-based organizations, charitable choice, and government', *Administration and Society*, 35, 1 (March), pp. 29–51.

The European Union and the New Religious Movements

SABRINA PASTORELLI

Introduction

The relationship between religion and space presents interesting and important issues at a European level. According to Daniel Dory, thinking, organising and controlling are the three fundamental elements characterising this connection. Religion allows 'thinking the space' (cognitive appropriation), can influence the 'organisation of the space' (for example, designating sacred and profane places) and can act in 'controlling' the management of particular spaces (Dory, 1995, pp. 367–75).[1] This raises questions in the wider context of European construction about the role of religions and the ways in which European space structures and manages religious phenomena.

In general, the legislative measures of the European Union (EU) make little reference to religious phenomena. European religious law is residual and religious matters are regulated at the national level (Ferrari, 1999, p. 359). In Marco Ventura's opinion, religious factors represent 'the cultural pattern of European identity as well as factors of socio-cultural cohesion' and, as a consequence, 'religious factors and European integration interact at several levels' (Ventura, 2001, pp. 121–22). European decision-making has a direct impact on religious matters through directives, regulations[2] and the jurisprudence of the European Court of Justice, while it is indirectly implemented through political acts, such as parliamentary recommendations and resolutions, informal dialogue with European institutions and discourses (Ventura, 2001, pp. 126–33).

Between 1994 and 1997 the suicides–homicides of the Order of the Solar Temple, Aum Shinri-kyo and Heaven's Gate attracted the attention of the public and stimulated the interest of the political authorities regarding the diffusion of new religions. Several European member states set up parliamentary committees in order to study this phenomenon and develop appropriate national policies. European institutions have become involved in the debate on new religious movements (NRMs) through political actions and court decisions. A comparison between national and transnational levels of religious management is of particular interest, as it reveals the ways in which European institutions have come to influence public policy on religious matters in the EU member states.

The European Parliament

The European Parliament has intervened in the debate on new religions through resolutions and recommendations, although at the European level there are no legal definitions of NRMs. In its 1984 Resolution on a Common Approach by the Member States of the European Community towards Various Infringements of the Law by the New Organizations Operating under the Protection Afforded to Religious Bodies, the European Parliament recognised that the development of NRMs represented a 'world phenomenon', generating delicate juridical problems. It asked member states for the creation of common criteria 'for the examination, the registration and the evaluation of the activities' of these organisations (Resolution, 1984). The Cottrell Report, which prepared the way for the 1984 resolution, used the term 'new religious movement' to classify the bodies identified in the resolution as 'new organizations acting under religious freedom'. This terminology was adopted in order to avoid possible discrimination as Community institutions 'have no right to judge the value of either religious beliefs in general or individual religious practices' but 'rather the lawfulness of the practices used to recruit new members and the treatment they receive' (Resolution, 1984; Sarra, 2003, p. 203).[3]

In 1996 the European Parliament pointed out that 'groups of cults or cult-type associations are a phenomenon that is rapidly proliferating, and taking diverse forms, throughout the world'. In this situation, it recognised that while many 'religions and other sects' were perfectly legitimate, some 'cults' were engaging in activities of an illicit or criminal nature and in violations of human rights. As a consequence, the European Parliament called on 'the governments of the Member States not to make the granting of religious status automatic and to step up the exchange of information between them' (Resolution, 1996).

The Parliament instructed its Committee on Civil Liberties and Internal Affairs to propose to the corresponding committees of the national parliaments that their next joint meeting should be devoted to the subject of 'sects'. Information on the organisation, working methods and conduct of sects in each member state were to be exchanged and conclusions drawn on the best means of restraining undesirable activities and of raising public awareness.[4] Since 1996 no other resolutions focusing exclusively on cults have been adopted, although several Annual Resolutions on the Situation of Fundamental Rights in the EU and their respective reports have referred to 'illegal or criminal activities sometimes carried out by "cults" or "sects" or "cult-like movements"'.[5]

The European Court of Justice

The jurisdiction of the European Court of Justice applies to the interpretation of existing Community law and EU treaties, where there is no mention of churches or religious communities. However, two decisions (in 1974 and 2000) concerning the Church of Scientology, a movement often designated as a 'cult' in several reports of national parliaments, have indicated that the Court neutralised the religious character of the case issued to its attention. In doing so, the Court has made its judgments on the basis of conformity to 'community free market principles', for example, the free movement of capital and workers (Macrì, 2004b, p. 116).

The 1974 van Duyn case showed that the refusal of entry into the United Kingdom to a Dutch Scientologist, for reasons of public order, was considered a limitation of the principle of free movement of persons. The Court ruled the application of the public order clause *sufficient* for derogating from the fundamental principle of Community law of the freedom of movement of workers and recognised the British right to refuse the right of entry to a foreign national, for reason of public order. The ban remained in force for 12 years (*Yvonne van Duyn v Home Office*, 1974; Barker, 1997, p. 114).

In 2000 the Court issued a judgment concerning France and the Church of Scientology. The latter requested the Court to cancel a system of prior authorisations for direct foreign investment to NRMs which were considered by French law 'a threat to public policy or public security' (*Eglise de scientologie and Scientology International v Prime Minister*, 2000). Under the system of prior authorisations, the French government refused to authorise the Church of Scientology to import foreign funds in order to pay taxes levied by the French government. The *Conseil d'Etat* referred to the European Court of Justice the question of whether the system of prior authorisations was compatible with the Community law principle of free movement of capital under the Treaty. The Court stated that a system that restricts movement of capital can be justified only by public policy or public security concerns; such concerns must be in any case strictly interpreted and subject to review by European institutions. Applying this standard, the Court declared that foreign investors were given 'no indication whatever as to the specific circumstances in which prior authorisation is required'. Thus the Court held that the regulation was 'contrary to the principle of legal certainty' because it did not apprise individuals of the extent of their rights and obligations under the Treaty (*Eglise de scientologie and Scientology International v Prime Minister*, 2000).

In those two decisions, because of its incompetence *ratione materiae*, the Court evaluated religious elements only *indirectly*, as they can fall under other Community competences or subjects (Macrì, 2004b, pp. 114–26).

The Dialogue with the Bureau of European Policy Advisers

In the early 1990s the European Commission started to develop an informal dialogue with religions, churches and communities of conviction. The Bureau of European Policy Advisers (BEPA) has been placed in charge of this issue. It dealt with preparing the participation of the European Commission's president in dialogue meetings; regularly informing churches and religious communities of European policies, projects and objectives; exchanging ideas on particular topics; encouraging interreligious and ecumenical dialogue; and counselling general directorates on relations with churches and religious communities (Jansen, 2002, pp. 81–85). The dialogue has had no juridical-institutional formalisation, except in Article I-52 of the draft Treaty establishing a Constitution for Europe, which stated that 'the Union shall maintain an open, transparent and regular dialogue with churches and non-confessional organisations'.[6] With this lack of a legal basis, it cannot be said that there is a formal or political recognition of religions and it is the president of the Commission who personally conducts the dialogue.

In this situation, the transparency of religious denominations present in Brussels is of particular interest: the type of religious communities, namely minority religions or NRMs; the technocrats in charge of taking part in dialogue with religious communities; and the main requirements for access to dialogue meetings.

For majority churches, as well as for humanist associations, participation in the construction of the EU is a prime issue allowing contribution to European construction as well as protection at the EU level of national prerogatives. For minority religions, informal dialogue with the Commission means that they are legitimate, and have social recognition and respectability. Among the minority religions, sometimes indifferently designated as 'cult' or 'sect' in the parliamentary reports of several member states, the Church of Scientology, Soka Gakkai and *Invitation à la Vie* are all recognised as dialogue partners by the BEPA (Dialogue, n.d.).

In Pauline Côté's opinion, religion can legitimate political authority which, in return, provides a sort of 'religious authentication' (Côté , 2001, pp. 236–37). The question is therefore not only the legitimation of public and social authorities by religions, but the legitimation of religious beliefs by public authorities (Leca, 2005; Adams *et al.*, 2005). Political authorities have become involved in 'a new policy of religious prestige', accrediting orthodox-conventional religions and handling a process of 'religious authentication' (Côté, 2001, pp. 235–52). For new religions, therefore, presence at the European level implies legitimation, the main indicators of which are reputation, confidence and social capital (Leca, 2005, pp. 392–95; Gambetta, 2005; Forse, 2003). In addition, new religions often engage in litigation, both at European and national levels, which can support the legitimation process (Côté and Richardson, 2001, pp. 11–25).

The BEPA does not make distinctions between religion, 'sect' or 'cult', and in the early 2000s, no religious movement has been refused as a dialogue partner. It operates as an 'open door to a part of civil society' where movements can 'enrol' as nobody has the authority to exclude them from participating as dialogue partners. At present, almost 60 movements are included in the list of dialogue partners, as compared to 14 in 1999 (Jansen, 1999);[7] however, only approximately 30 representatives, mostly Catholics and Jews, usually take part in these meetings.

The number of dialogue partners has been continuously growing since 2001–02. According to Bérengère Massignon, there is an 'accelerated pluralisation' in the relations between the European Commission and religions and a sort of 'deinstitutionalisation of the dialogue' since the arrival of Michael Weninger[8] (Massignon, 2005, pp. 333–36; Massignon, 2007). There are no particular criteria for qualifying as dialogue partners, only self-designation to represent a church, a religion or a community of conviction, as the dialogue is conceived as *informal*. In the future, after the ratification of the Lisbon Treaty, it will be of particular interest to observe if a more formal procedure will be introduced concerning the criteria to become dialogue partners.

Among the events organised by the BEPA, there are some debriefing meetings after the European summits (at least four in a year), dialogue meetings on subjects of common concern (twice a year), and information meetings providing the opportunity for an exchange of views with all dialogue partners on a regular basis. However, there are also meetings of limited participation, for example, when President Barroso met only the high representatives of the three principal monotheistic religions on 15 May 2007 (Barroso, 2007).

Soka Gakkai

An example of dialogue between religions and the BEPA is offered by Soka Gakkai, a Buddhist movement of the Mahayana tradition. Its presence in Brussels is relatively recent; in 1999 Thomas Jansen mentioned only the participation of the European Buddhist Union (EBU) in informal dialogue with the EU Commission (Jansen, 2002, pp. 3–12). Soka Gakkai started its dialogue with BEPA in 2006 as the '*Institut Européen Soka Gakkai International*' (IESGI).

Soka Gakkai claims to have 70,000 adherents in Europe (http://www.sgi-europe.org). The name Soka Gakkai means literally 'value-creating society'. Members follow the teachings of Nichiren Daishonin, a Buddhist monk who lived in thirteenth-century Japan. Nichiren considered the *Lotus Sutra* to contain the essence of the Buddha's enlightenment and affirmed that all people inherently possess Buddha's qualities. Therefore everyone can attain enlightenment and enjoy happiness. The chant of *Nam-Myoho-Renge-Kyo* enables people to manifest the Buddhahood inherent in their lives and gain the strength to challenge and overcome any adverse circumstances. Soka Gakkai members chant *Nam-Myoho-Renge-Kyo* to a *gohonzon* – the object of devotion in Nichiren Buddhism – kept in their own homes. The *gohonzon*, together with a practitioner's faith and chanting, acts as a stimulus to activate the condition of Buddhahood innate in one's life (Wilson and Dobbelaere, 1994; Macioti, 1996; Dobbelaere, 2001). Soka Gakkai conducts activities in the field of culture, education and the promotion of peace. The movement has often been described as a 'sect' or 'cult' by parliamentary reports in France and Belgium as well as by reports of specialised state agencies of 'cult' control.[9]

The European Institute Soka Gakkai was created in 1973, as an association under the 1905 French law (Law, 1905). It is a European umbrella organisation of Soka Gakkai for 28 European countries. Soka Gakkai's president, Daisaku Ikeda, conducted a European tour in 1960, aiming to create a 'chapter', which is a territorial grouping, covering a country or a region, typical of the space administrative organisation of Soka Gakkai. However, he did not have a real European project; his aim was simply to help various countries to support and encourage, usually by visits and lectures, the practice of Soka Gakkai in each country. The European Institute is therefore largely the result of country-level initiatives. The Institute, with its headquarters in Trets, in the South of France, was initially set up with the participation of 13 European countries. In an internal publication, the Institute is conceived as having the following aims:

1. Developing international relations of friendship on a Buddhist basis;
2. Speeding up the development of Nichiren Shoshu[10] in Europe;
3. Organising ceremonies and prayers for global peace;

4. Helping Nichiren Shoshu organisations to develop and overcome difficulties;
5. Studying other religions and philosophies concerning Nichiren Buddhism and helping in the translation of religious documents and other publications (Une soirée, 1973, p. V).

The fourth point is particularly interesting as, in the opinion of the movement's leaders, Soka Gakkai's activity in dialogue with the BEPA would help relations between the movement and EU member states, especially in countries where the movement is still considered as a 'cult', as well as in Eastern European countries.

In Brussels, after some preliminary meetings with Michael Weninger, the organisation regularly participates in BEPA activities. The organisation has not opened an office in Brussels and both the president and the vice-president live and work in Germany. As with the other minority dialogue partners, Soka Gakkai does not receive the agenda of meetings beforehand and its representatives have no special knowledge on European matters; in many cases they are not prepared to intervene in the discussions. However, Soka Gakkai Buddhists are confident about dialogue and its results. They claim that there is a real participation, and that they can support the process of European integration and give advice on decisions and on European politics. They are convinced that being recognised as a dialogue partner by the European Commission gives them the possibility of influencing national state attitudes towards their religious movement.

Soka Gakkai's approach is more enthusiastic than that of other religious minorities, for example, the Vaishnava Communication Institute, representing Hindu communities in Europe. Organised as a trust, whose executive members are mainly from the UK and Belgium, the Institute wanted to contribute to the dialogue initiated by the Soul for Europe programme established by Commission president Jacques Delors. Vaishnava's representatives have worked on the European Convention and the Constitution and intervened in the dispute on the language used in the text and Preamble. They have actively worked with other organisations for this purpose and made suggestions on the formulation of Article I-52. In particular, they proposed 'a more egalitarian language', recommending that the text refer not to 'church' but to 'religions'. Their representatives participated in the meetings of the Commission of the Bishops' Conferences of the European Community (COMECE) and the Conference of European Churches (CEC) but expressed doubts about the utility of the BEPA meetings, especially for any movement which has no office in Brussels. Expressing some doubts about the utility of the BEPA meetings, they considered it more useful for the EU to deal directly with minorities, to observe and see people working in the field, instead of waiting for the movements to act as lobbies.

The two main Buddhist organisations at the BEPA, the EBU and Soka Gakkai, are not in contact and do not interact with each other. The EBU is the umbrella organisation representing Buddhist communities and organisations in Europe. Up to the time of writing (2008) it has not been very active at the European level and at present it participates only rarely in the BEPA's meetings. In the future, the EBU wishes to modify its organisation and to act more efficiently at the European level. It is interesting to note that Soka Gakkai is affiliated with some Buddhist national unions which are members of the EBU.[11] At the European level, therefore, Soka Gakkai operates both directly as a dialogue partner and, in addition, could act indirectly through the EBU.

Considering the case study of Soka Gakkai and the relation between religion and space, it is interesting to point out how this movement thinks, organises and attempts to control European space. I observed that the movement perceives European space as one for diffusion of the Soka's principles. The European Institute, and more particularly the European centre in Trets, are the places for European as well as transnational meetings, but each country is thought of as having its opportunities and problems. Participation in EU dialogue is significant for the movement, not only for the diffusion of Buddhist principles of peace and welfare, but as part of a larger process of legitimation in the different EU member states.

The Council of Europe

Another European institution which has adopted recommendations on NRMs is the Council of Europe, through its Parliamentary Assembly. In 1992, Recommendation 1178 with a reference to Article 9 of the European Convention on Human Rights considered specific legislation on NRMs inappropriate (Recommendation, 1992). The Council recommended that the Committee of Ministers call on member states to include in their educational curriculum objective and factual information concerning established religions and their major variants and supplementary information on the nature and activities of sects and NRMs, and to set up independent bodies to collect and circulate this information.

Since then, the Council of Europe's approach towards NRMs has become more vigilant. The conclusions of Adrian Nastase's report on the 'illegal activities of sects' stated that 'the attitude of the state authorities ought to be tolerance on the one hand and vigilance on the other' (Report, 1999). The report was issued six years after the first recommendation of the Council of Europe in response to the estimated rise in the number of people joining sects in Central and Eastern European countries. It took into account the national parliamentary reports from France, Belgium, Germany and Switzerland. The project proposed the setting up of a European Observatory, the interdiction of some groups and penal proceedings against the indoctrination programmes conducted by these groups (Torfs, 1999, pp. 41–42).

Following the Nastase report the Parliamentary Assembly passed Recommendation 1412, which recognised that religious pluralism was a natural consequence of freedom of religion. It called upon state authorities to refrain from taking measures based on value judgments concerning religious beliefs and concluded that it was unnecessary to define what constituted a sect or to decide whether particular cases represented a religion or not. On the other hand the Assembly called on member states 'to use the normal procedures of criminal and civil law against illegal practices carried out in the name of groups of religious, esoteric or spiritual nature' but 'to take firm steps against any action which is discriminatory or which marginalises religious or spiritual minority groups' (Recommendation, 1999).[12]

The European Court of Human Rights

Despite the absence of specific provisions on minority rights in the European Convention on Human Rights and its Protocols the European Court of Human Rights (ECHR) has reviewed several cases concerning minority issues and freedom of religion (Richardson, 2006, pp. 284–89; Richardson, 2004, pp. 223–34; Richardson, 1995, pp. 39–59). The jurisprudence on freedom of religion is mostly concerned with the non-admissibility of cases or the indirect protection of religious freedom through other rights (Rolland, 1998, pp. 275–77), for example freedom of expression, freedom of assembly and association, and the prohibition of discrimination. The Court operates more on the basis of those principles which are better defined and more specific than the freedom of religion, which has been difficult to define (Macrì, Parisi and Tozzi, 2006, pp. 162–63). As a matter of fact, Article 9 has been cautiously interpreted and the Court has shown reluctance to define the word 'religion' (Cumper, 1999, p. 173; Rolland, 1998, p. 273; Evans, 2001, p. 204).

In the *Manoussakis* case of 1996, the Court recognised that 'states are entitled to verify whether a movement or association carries on, ostensibly in pursuit of religious aims, activities which are harmful to the population'. 'Nevertheless, it recalled that Jehovah's Witnesses come within the definition of "known religion" as provided for under Greek law' (*Manoussakis and Others v Greece*). In other decisions, the Court has referred to the 'margin of appreciation' in which member states must consider the extent of necessary interference with protected manifestations of religious belief. For example, in the *Kokkinakis* case the Court introduced a distinction between proper and improper proselytism. The latter should be prohibited or restricted when it takes 'the form of activities offering material or social advantages with a view to gaining new members for a Church or exerting improper pressure on people in distress or in need', sometimes even entailing 'the use of violence or brainwashing'.[13] According to Silvio Ferrari, with this judgment the Court wanted to point out the way to face the activity of NRMs, prefiguring the possibility of creating a juridical notion of 'unauthorised proselytism' (Ferrari, 1997, p. 20).

In the *Paturel* case, the Court reached a particular decision concerning France and a French citizen, Christian Paturel, a Jehovah's Witness. The case related to the publication of *Sectes, religions et libertés publiques* in which Paturel – the author – denounced the activity of anti-cult movements, particularly the *Union Nationale des associations de défense des familles et de l'individu victimes de sectes* (UNADFI). This organisation carried a complaint for slander against the author and the editor, and after three French levels of judgment both the author and the editor were found guilty. The author therefore made a complaint of breach of Articles 9 and 10 of the European Convention on Human Rights at the ECHR. French courts recognised Paturel guilty of slander, judging that there was absence of serious investigation and the proper limits of debate had been exceeded (*Paturel*, 25 March 1997, 15 October 1997, 5 October 1999). The first court made direct reference to the personal animosity of Paturel as a Jehovah's Witness against UNADFI, after having asked directly if he was or was not a Jehovah's Witness. Regarding Article 9, the ECHR held that there was no violation of religious freedom and only the Court of First Instance referred to the particular animosity of Paturel as a Jehovah's Witness. Regarding Article 10, the ECHR considered that there was interference by the public authorities in Paturel's freedom of expression. Following the wording of Article 10, the ECHR had to consider if the limitation of freedom of expression was prescribed by law with a legitimate aim and if it was necessary in a democratic society. The ECHR argued that the limitation of Paturel's freedom of expression was prescribed by law (Law, 1881, Articles 29 and 32) with a legitimate aim (the protection of the reputation of others). It considered the need to limit freedom of expression in a democratic society in order to protect a social need and the proportionality of the interference by the member state. A margin of appreciation was recognised to states but the ECHR considered that the French jurisdiction had exceeded this margin and disproportionately interfered in Paturel's freedom of expression. The ECHR therefore concluded that there was a violation of Article 10 and France was condemned to pay pecuniary sanctions.

According to Patrice Rolland, the French conception of slander differed from that of the ECHR, as shown not only in the Paturel case but also in other cases, such as

Giniewsky v France. According to the French interpretation, slander was conceived as a potential offence made by the media. In this regard, a journalist had to conduct any investigation in an impartial and serious manner. The ECHR's conception paid much more attention to the notion of 'public debate' and considered the debate on NRMs as being 'general, of public interest and particularly necessary because of the non-definition of "sect" in law' (Rolland, 2006, pp. 131–40).

Conclusion

New religions consider it an important issue to be represented at the EU level. They adopt legitimacy strategies at both national and international levels. They conduct judicial activities both at the ECHR and at the European Court of Justice and they lobby European institutions. The litigation conducted by NRMs, both at the European and at the national level, is part of a more general 'legitimation process' (Lewis, 2003). The 'vigilant litigation', as defined by Pauline Côté and James Richardson (2001, pp. 11–25), undertaken by Jehovah's Witnesses is conceived as a 'model for defensive moves taken by controversial religious minorities' but is also part of the minority religions' strategy in seeking legitimacy. In this situation the question remains: can a sort of *European legitimation* have an effect at the national level and influence national attitudes towards a particular minority religious group?

The White Paper on European Governance (Commission, 2001) suggests that relations between the EU and religious communities should be based on the notion of governance[14] and that religions can have a significant contribution to make. Governance allows new forms of confrontation and social involvement where space is given to cohesion in a system of equal opportunities for all religions instead of the public management of religious phenomena. The EU's management of religious matters could therefore constitute a model for its member states in the context of increasing religious pluralism (Macrì, 2004a, p. 198).

Acknowledgment

This paper is the result of several interviews conducted in 2007. I am grateful to the representatives of Soka Gakkai France, Soka Gakkai Italy and the IESGI for sharing with us their experiences regarding the dialogue with BEPA and European issues; to the representatives of the EBU and the Vaishnava Communication Institute; and to the representatives of the BEPA office in Brussels. I am also grateful to James T. Richardson for his comments on an earlier draft of this paper.

Notes

1 For an application of Dory's model, see Wydmusch (2001).
2 For example, the Directive (2000) for the fight against racism, discrimination and xenophobia.
3 The Cottrell Report was adopted by the European Parliament in 1984 and was withdrawn on 13 July 1998.
4 The Committee on Civil Liberties and Internal Affairs released an amended resolution, Resolution on Cults in the European Union, rejected by the European Parliament in January 1998.
5 Expressions used in 2000, 2001, 2002, 2003 resolutions and their reports. See: Resolution (2000); Report (2000); Resolution (2001); Report (2001); Resolution (2002); Report (2003).

6 Now Article 17 of the Treaty on the Functioning of the European Union, as it results from the amendments introduced by the Treaty of Lisbon, signed on 13 December 2007 in Lisbon. The Treaty of Lisbon is still in the process of being ratified by the member states, in accordance with their respective constitutional requirements. Article 6 states that the Treaty will enter into force on 1 January 2009, provided that all the instruments of ratification have been deposited, or, failing that, on the first day of the month following the deposit of the last instrument of ratification (Consolidated, 2008).

7 The list of dialogue partners which was published on the BEPA website is no longer there. A written question to the European Parliament in October 2008 asked for clarifications about the classification of the organisations listed and as a consequence participating in dialogue meetings. See De Keyser (2007).

8 Michael Weninger was the European Commission political adviser responsible for dialogue with faith-based communities at the BEPA under the EC presidency of Manuel Barroso. The current adviser is Jorge César das Neves.

9 For example: MILS (*Mission interministérielle de lutte contre les sectes* (Interministerial Mission in the Fight Against Cults)); MIVILUDES (*Mission interministérielle de vigilance et de lutte contre les dérives sectaires* (Interministerial Mission for Monitoring and Combatting Cultic Deviances)), www.miviludes.gouv.fr

10 Nichiren Shoshu Buddhism follows the teaching of the Buddhist monk Nichiren Daishonin. Several movements refer to Daishonin's teachings; the best known is Nichiren Shoshu based in Japan, which looks after the original *mandala* prepared by Daishonin, the Dai-Gohonzon. Soka Gakkai was created as a lay organisation with the aim of spreading Nichiren Shoshu Buddhism and as a consequence it depends on the Nichiren Shoshu monastic organisation in Japan. In 1990, as a consequence of a long crisis, there was a split between the laypeople of Soka Gakkai and the monks of the Nichiren Shoshu organisation, who excommunicated Soka Gakkai.

11 Soka Gakkai is a member of the Buddhist national unions in United Kingdom and Austria: see http://www.e-b-u.org/members_list.html (last accessed 10 April 2007).

12 In 2002 the Council of Europe intervened once again in the NRMs issue. The resolution on Freedom of Religion and Religious Minorities in France referred to the French law 'on the reinforcement of the prevention and suppression of sects which infringe on human rights and fundamental freedoms'. While considering 'unnecessary to define what constitutes a sect or to decide whether it is a religion or not' the Assembly invited the governments of member states 'to use the normal procedures of criminal and civil law against illegal practices carried out in the name of groups of a religious, esoteric or spiritual nature'. It further argued that it was not competent to decide whether or not the French law was compatible with the European Convention on Human Rights.

13 The case concerned Greece. Following a complaint, two members of the Jehovah's Witnesses were convicted of proselytism. The case was referred to the ECHR which, following the Commission's report, considered that this conviction violated Article 9 of the European Convention on Human Rights because the prohibition on proselytism in this specific case was not a necessary measure in a democratic society, within the meaning of Article 9 para. 2 of the Convention. However, the Court accepted that improper proselytism should sometimes be prohibited or restricted (*Kokkinakis v Greece*). The terms 'brainwashing' and 'mental manipulation' are used several times in the report of this judgment, but, as various scholars have remarked, the report is not clear on how groups carrying on this kind of activity are to be identified. The above-mentioned report of the Council of Europe on 'illegal activities of sects' makes reference to the term 'brainwashing' concerning the protection of 'those most vulnerable, and particularly the children of members of religious, esoteric or spiritual groups, in case of ill-treatment, rape, neglect, indoctrination by brainwashing' (Report, 1999). On this issue see Richardson and Introvigne (2001, pp. 161–62).

14 Governance has become the prevailing mode of political regulation in Europe; it leads to less formal modes of decision-making. The concept is well known in political science, even if the

notion is sometimes not very clear, as scholars often use diverging concepts and aspects to define it. According to A. Benz, the concept was introduced in political science in view of the fact that the traditional mode of the nation-state was no longer adequate to guide reform policies. The shift from government to governance involves a plurality of decision centres with non-formal hierarchies and consisting of networks. In governance, elected politicians play a secondary role compared to experts and public and collective actors, and the result is more intense interaction between the public and the private sectors (Benz and Papadopoulos, 2006). At the European level, the concept of governance was established by the EU Commission in the White Paper of 2001 (Commission, 2001). The main aim was to seek out new forms of governance in order to consolidate EU democracy and enhance the legitimacy of EU institutions. In this sense, governance should lead to EU institutions connecting more and more with civil society, including churches and religious communities, in the formulation of policies (Commission, 2001). For more on the notion of governance, see Benz and Papadopoulos (2006), Moreau Defarges (2003) and Commission (2001).

References

(a) Books, Articles and Papers

Adams, J. L. and Mikelson, T. (2005) 'Legitimation', in L. Jones (ed.), *Encyclopedia of Religion* (2nd edn) (New York, Macmillan), pp. 5396–404.

Barker, E. (1997) 'New religious movements in Britain', in H. Meldgaard and J. Aagaard (eds), *New Religious Movements in Europe* (Aarhus, Aarhus University Press), pp. 99–123.

Barroso, President J.-M. (2007) *Building Europe on the Rock of Human Dignity*, speech, 15 May, http://ec.europa.eu/dgs/policy_advisers/activities/dialogues_religions/events_en.htm (last accessed 26 October 2008).

Benz, A. and Papadopoulos, Y. (eds), (2006) *Governance and Democracy: Comparing National, European and International Experiences* (London, Routledge/ECPR Studies in European Political Sciences).

Commission (2001) Commission of the European Communities, European Governance: a White Paper, COM (2001) 428 Final, Brussels, 25 July, http://ec.europa.eu/governance/index_en.htm (last accessed 5 November 2008).

Consolidated (2008) Consolidated Versions of the Treaty on European Union and the Treaty on the Functioning of the European Union, *Official Journal of the European Union*, 9 May, http://eur-lex.europa.eu/JOHtml.do?uri=OJ:C:2008:115:SOM:en:HTML (last accesssed 17 November 2008).

Côté, P. (2001) 'Echange généralisé et politique de prestige religieux dans l'espace public-monde', in P. Côté (ed.), *Chercheurs de dieux dans l'espace public/Frontier Religions in the Public Space* (Ottawa, Presses de l'Université d'Ottawa), pp. 235–52.

Côté, P. and Richardson, J. T. (2001) 'Disciplined litigation, vigilant litigation, and deformation: dramatic organization change in Jehovah's Witnesses', *Journal for the Scientific Study of Religion*, 40, 1, pp. 11–25.

Cumper, P. (1999) 'The rights of religious minorities: the legal regulation of new religious movements', in P. Cumper and S. Wheatley (eds), *Minority Rights in the 'New' Europe* (The Hague, Martinus Nijhoff), pp. 165–83.

Dialogue (n.d.) BEPA, *Dialogue with Religions, Churches and Communities of Conviction*, http://ec.europa.eu/dgs/policy_advisers/activities/dialogues_religions/index_en.htm (last accessed 26 October 2008).

De Keyser, V. (2007) Written Question P-5288/07, Véronique De Keyser (PSE), BEPA Meetings and Working Methods to the Commission, 24 October, *Official Journal of the European Union*, 29 July 2008, C191/1, http://eur-lex.europa.eu (last accessed November 2008).

Directive (2000) Council Directive 2000/43/EC of 29 June 2000 Implementing the Principle of Equal Treatment between Persons Irrespective of Racial or Ethnic Origin, http://eur-lex.europa.eu (last accessed 5 November 2008).
Dobbelaere, K. (2001) *Soka Gakkai: from Lay Movement to Religion* (Salt Lake City, Signature Books).
Dory, D. (1995) 'Religions et territoires: éléments de théorie et propositions de recherché', in J.-F. Vincent, D. Dory and R. Verdier (eds), *La construction religieuse du territoire* (Paris, L'Harmattan), pp. 367–75.
Evans, C. (2001) *Freedom of Religion under the European Convention on Human Rights* (Oxford, Oxford University Press).
Ferrari, S. (1999) 'Le droit européen en matière religieuse et ses conséquences pour les sectes', in F. Champion and M. Cohen (eds), *Sectes et démocratie* (Paris, Seuil), pp. 359–72.
Ferrari, S. and Ibán, C. I. (1997) *Diritto e religione in Europa occidentale* (Bologna, Il Mulino).
Forse, M. (2003) 'Capital social', *Dictionnaire de sociologie* (Paris, Larousse), p. 202.
Gambetta, D. (2005) 'Confiance', in B. Vakade, M. Cherkaoui, M. Borlandi and R. Boudon (eds), *Dictionnaire de la pensée sociologique* (Paris, PUF), pp. 118–20.
Jansen, T. (1999) 'Dialogue entre la Commission Européenne, les églises et les communautés religieuses', in J. Adoración Castro (ed.), *Iglesias, confesiones y comunidades religiosas en la Unión Europea* (Zarautz, Universidad del País Vasco), pp. 77–85.
Jansen, T. (2002) 'La Commission Européenne en dialogue avec les églises et les communautés religieuses: l'action de la cellule de perspective', in A. Chizzoniti (ed.), *Chiese, associazioni, comunità religiose e organizzazioni non confessionali nell'Unione Europea* (Milan, Vita e Pensiero), pp. 3–12.
Law (1881) Loi du 29 juillet 1881 sur la liberté de la presse, www.legifrance.fr
Law (1905) Loi du 9 décembre 1905 concernant la séparation des Eglises et de l'Etat, *Journal Officiel de la République Française: Lois et Décrets*, 11 December.
Leca, J. (2005) 'Légitimation', in B. Vakade, M. Cherkaoui, M. Borlandi and R. Boudon (eds), *Dictionnaire de la pensée sociologique* (Paris, PUF), pp. 392–95.
Lewis, J. R. (2003) *Legitimating New Religions* (New Brunswick, Rutgers University Press).
Macioti, M. I. (1996) *Il Buddha che è in noi: germogli del sutra del loto* (Rome, Seam).
Macrì, G. (2004a) 'Europa, *governance* e gruppi religiosi', *Diritto pubblico comparato ed europeo*, 1, pp. 191–201.
Macrì, G. (2004b) *Europa, lobbying e fenomeno religioso* (Turin, Giappichelli).
Macrì, G., Parisi, M. and Tozzi, V. (2006) *Diritto ecclesiastico europeo* (Bari, Laterza).
Massignon, B. (2005) *La construction européenne: 'un laboratoire' pour la gestion de la pluralité religieuse: clivages nationaux et confessionnels et dynamiques d'européanisation*, PhD thesis, Ecole Pratique des Hautes Etudes, Paris.
Massignon, B. (2007) *Des Dieux et des fonctionnaires: religions et laïcités face au défi de la construction européenne* (Rennes, Presses Universitaires de Rennes).
Moreau Defarges, P. (2003) *La gouvernance* (Paris, PUF, QSJ).
Pour (1975) 'Pour la première fois en Europe', *Troisième Civilisation* (Sceaux), 1 October 1975.
Recommendation (1992) Parliamentary Assembly of the Council of Europe, Recommendation 1178, Sects and New Religious Movements, adopted 5 February (23rd Sitting), http://assembly.coe.int (last accessed October 2008).
Recommendation (1999) Parliamentary Assembly of the Council of Europe, Recommendation 1412, Illegal Activities of Sects, adopted 22 June, http://assembly.coe.int (last accessed October 2008).
Report (1999) Council of Europe, *Illegal Activities of Sects*, Doc. 8373, 13 April, Committee on Legal Affairs and Human Rights, Rapporteur: Mr Adrian Nastase, Romania, Socialist Group, http://assembly.coe.int (last accessed October 2008).
Report (2000) European Parliament, Committee on Citizens' Freedom and Rights, Justice and Home Affairs, *Respect for Human Rights in the European Union (1998–1999)*, A5-0050/2000, 29 February, Rapporteur: Bertel Haarder, http://www.europarl.europa.eu (last accessed October 2008).

Report (2001) European Parliament, Committee on Citizens' Freedom and Rights, Justice and Home Affairs, *The Situation as Regards Fundamental Rights in the European Union*, 21 June, Doc. 2000/2231 (INI), Rapporteur: Thierry Cornillet, http://www.europarl.europa.eu (last accessed October 2008).

Report (2002) Council of Europe, Committee on Legal Affairs and Human Rights, *Freedom of Religion and Religious Minorities in France*, Doc. 961231, October, Rapporteur: Mr Cevdet Akçali, Turkey, European Democratic Group, http://assembly.coe.int (last accessed October 2008).

Report (2003) European Parliament, Committee on Citizens' Freedom and Rights, Justice and Home Affairs, *The Situation as Regards Fundamental Rights in the European Union*, 21 August, A5-0281/2003, Doc. 2002/2013 (INI), Rapporteur: Fodé Sylla http://www.europarl.europa.eu (last accessed October 2008).

Réputation (2004) 'Réputation', *Le Nouveau Petit Robert* (Paris, Le Robert).

Resolution (1984) European Parliament, Resolution on a Common Approach by the Member States of the European Community towards Various Infringements of the Law by the New Organizations Operating under the Protection Afforded to Religious Bodies, *Official Journal*, C 172 (2 July), p. 41.

Resolution (1996) European Parliament, Resolution on Cults in Europe, Minutes, Sittings of Thursday 29 February 1996, http://www.europarl.europa.eu (last accessed October 2008).

Resolution (2000) European Parliament, Resolution on Respect for Human Rights in the European Union (1998–1999), A5-0050/2000, http://eur-lex.europa.eu (last accessed October 2008).

Resolution (2001) European Parliament, Resolution on the Situation Concerning Basic Rights in the European Union 2001, Doc. 2001/2014 (INI), http://eur-lex.europa.eu/ (last accessed October 2008).

Resolution (2002) Parliamentary Assembly of the Council of Europe, Resolution 1309, Freedom of Religion and Religious Minorities in France, adopted by the Standing Committee acting on behalf of the Assembly, 18 November, http://assembly.coe.int (last accessed October 2008).

Richardson, J. T. (1995) 'Minority religions, religious freedom and the new pan-European political and judicial institutions', *Journal of Church and State*, 37, pp. 39–59.

Richardson, J. T. (2006) 'The sociology of religious freedom: a structural and socio-legal analysis', *Sociology of Religion*, 67, 3, pp. 271–94.

Richardson, J. T. and Garay, A. (2004) 'The European Court of Human Rights and former communist countries', in D. Jerolimov, S. Zrinšcak and I. Borowik, *Religion and Patterns of Social Transformation* (Zagreb, Institute for Social Research), pp. 223–34.

Richardson, J. T. and Introvigne, M. (2001) '"Brainwashing" theories in European parliamentary and administrative reports on "cults" and "sects"', *Journal for the Scientific Study of Religion*, 4, 2, June, pp. 143–68.

Rolland, P. (1998) 'Le fait religieux devant la Cour Européenne des Droits de l'Homme', in R. Goy (ed.), *Du droit interne au droit international* (Rouen, Publications de l'Université de Rouen), pp. 275–77.

Rolland, P. (2006) 'Sectes, libertés de religion et liberté d'expression (arrêt Paturel du 22 décembre 2005)', *Cahiers du CREDHO*, 12, pp. 131–40.

Sarra, R. (2003) 'Nuovi movimenti religiosi tra diritto comune e legislazione speciale: prospettive europee e legge francese sui "mouvements sectaires"', *Archivio Giuridico*, 223, 2, pp. 195–255.

Torfs, R. (1999) 'Les nouveaux mouvements religieux et le droit dans l'Union Européenne', in European Consortium for Church–State Research/Consortium Européen pour l'étude des relations églises-état, *New Religious Movements and the Law in the European Union/Les nouveaux mouvements religieux et le droit dans l'Union Européenne* (Milan, Giuffré), pp. 37–66.

Tozzi, V. (2005) *Persone, chiese e stati nell'evoluzione del fenomeno europeo*, http://www.olir.it/autori (last accessed 27 October 2008).

Une soirée (1973) 'Une soirée européenne', *Troisième Civilisation* (Sceaux), 1 June.

Ventura, M. (2001) *La laicità nell'Unione Europea: diritti, mercati e religione* (Turin, Giappichelli).

Wilson, B. R. and Dobbelaere, K. (1994) *A Time to Chant* (Oxford, Clarendon Press).
Wydmusch, S. (2001) 'Intégration européenne et réseaux transnationaux: le lobbying européen des églises', in J. B. Bastian, F. Champion and K. Rousselet (eds), *La globalisation du religieux* (Paris, L'Harmattan), pp. 249–62.

(b) Court Cases

European Court of Human Rights (http://www.echr.coe.int/echr/)

Kokkinakis v Greece, 25 May 1993.
Manoussakis and Others v Greece, 26 September 1996.
Paturel v France, 22 December 2005.
Giniewski v France, Judgment 31 January 2006.

European Court of Justice (http://curia.europa.eu/)

Yvonne van Duyn v Home Office, Judgment of the Court of 4 December 1974, C-41/74.
Eglise de scientologie and Scientology International v Prime Minister, Judgment of the Court of 14 March 2000, C-54/99.

French Courts

Paturel, Tribunal Correctionnel de Paris, 25 March 1997.
Paturel, Cour d'Appel Paris, chambre XI, 15 October 1997.
Paturel, Cour de Cassation, chambre criminelle, 5 October 1999, no. 97-85.828.

The Logic of Structured Dialogue between Religious Associations and the Institutions of the European Union

KENNETH HOUSTON

Introduction

Incorporated into the Consolidated version of the Treaty on European Union (TEU) and the Treaty on the Functioning of the European Union, as amended by the Lisbon Treaty of 2007, is a provision for structured dialogue between the institutions of the European Union (EU) and communities of faith and conviction.[1] While demands for the inclusion of a reference to God and Europe's Christian heritage in the Preamble of the defunct Draft Constitution were unsuccessful, the controversy they generated overshadowed more muted opposition to this proposed provision.

The informal links that preceded this dialogic provision and the provision itself developed largely at the behest of churches (COMECE, 2002; CEC, 2002; Jansen, 2000). The function of religious representation in Brussels was to remain informed of initiatives and changes in European policies that might impact on their interests and to utilise links with European institutions to influence policy formulation at the highest possible level (Jansen, 2000, p. 104). The formalisation of this interaction was opposed by several NGOs: among them Catholics for a Free Choice (CFFC) and the European Humanist Federation (EHF). CFFC drew attention to the potential misuse of the provision to further conservative social agendas by the churches and by the Vatican in particular (CFFC, 2003a, 2003b). The EHF concentrated on the totality of Article 52 and pointed to the manifest imbalance in relations between the churches and European institutions (EHF, 2003). This imbalance, the EHF contended, emerged through the effective granting of immunity against interference in the status of churches under Section 1 of Article 52, while Section 3 granted churches access to the highest echelons of EU decision-making.

Notwithstanding the perspectives of these nongovernmental organisations (NGOs), the provision for dialogue is closely connected with two interrelated questions: What salient issues at the supra-national level of European governance would conceivably fall within the remit of such a provision? And can structured dialogue contribute tangibly and meaningfully to the life of the EU?

The BEPA Perspective

An explicit reference to the provision's function is alluded to on the website of the Bureau of European Policy Advisers (BEPA):[2] 'The benefits lie in better knowledge of the significance of European integration on the part of the religions and other communities of faith and conviction and in the light that they for their part are able to shed on contemporary political trends' (BEPA, 2007). This statement indicates a clear transactional relationship.[3] One aspect concerns the EU, primarily the European Commission, and the desire to ensure that religious organisations are favourably disposed to the concept of integration. As the engine of integration, the Commission perceives that elements of civil society have the potential to influence positively public perceptions of integration to some degree. If churches are inclined to oppose integration this might erode popular acceptance. Churches with strong societal influence, particularly the Roman Catholic Church, have been supportive of the broader European project (Nelson *et al.*, 2001). However, the extent to which public opinion beyond that of committed adherents can be influenced by church leaders is not easily determined.

The second transactional aspect outlined by BEPA is somewhat nebulous and arguably more controversial, in that it opens the possibility alluded to by CFFC of churches' pursuit of conservative social agendas. Whereas human rights, environmental or professional bodies and associations might be accorded contributory status in relation to certain policy issues on the basis of their objective expertise, BEPA lays considerable emphasis on religious associations and churches as 'transcendental institutions' and alludes to the specificity of their 'religious component' (BEPA, 2007).[4] The transcendent element of religion, and more specifically of the Abrahamic faiths, is viewed as a distinguishing and defining characteristic of religious institutions, one that sets them apart from wider civil society and justifies the incorporation of *specific* structured dialogue in an intergovernmental treaty text.

The existence of many religions and the sects within each tradition is testament to the various interpretations of the nature of transcendence and the extent of its perceived influence in human affairs. There is no reason to assume any profound homogeneity among religions in their interpretation of the transcendent beyond a generic acknowledgment of its existence. This aspect of religious adherence is specifically experiential, and is therefore a basis of knowledge and action that is not universally accessible. Particular clerical perspectives on tangible socio-political issues, which are grounded in the acceptance of and belief in an omnipotent being or power, limit the scope of wider understanding and exclude those who hold a different view of transcendence, or those who hold none. Religious actors – whether individuals or collective bodies – are required to contribute to socio-political issues by appealing to the acceptability criterion of reasonable argument rather than faith in transcendence. Doubtless their normative perspectives on socio-political issues are animated by the place of transcendence and specific doctrinal tenets in their respective worldviews, but that is not a sufficient basis on which to interact at an *elevated* level with the wider public space and its political representatives. It should be questioned whether useful and meaningful dialogue can be conducted when premises such as God and the idea of morally purposive transcendence are not identically conceived among the interlocutors.

BEPA also assumes that 'religious values play a very important role for the European citizens and consequently the European Union enjoys a spiritual dimension' (BEPA, 2007).[5] The importance placed on religious values is open to empirical refutation. The most recent Eurobarometer survey at the time of writing (Eurobarometer, 2006, pp. 34–35) questioned a cross-section of citizens throughout the member states on the values to which they attached greatest personal importance. Peace ranked in first place (52 per cent), respect for human life second (43 per cent), followed by human rights (41 per cent). Religion was placed last out of 11, with seven per cent ranking it greatest in personal importance. Crucially, when asked what values represented the EU only three per cent indicated religion. This is despite other indicators that show just over half (52 per cent) declared a belief in God (Eurobarometer, 2005). The weak place of religion in the body politic parallels a desire not to externalise and incorporate it into the objective values of the EU. The most comprehensive indicator of societal attitudes available, the European Values Study (EVS, 2004), supports this position. In presenting evidence indicating that citizens across the countries surveyed are less inclined to attach their religious belief to traditional religious authority the survey draws a stark conclusion: 'People leave the churches not only because they no longer accept the rules and dogmas proclaimed by church leaders, but also, and perhaps mainly, because people's religious convictions and beliefs are on the decline' (EVS, 2004, p. 311). The underlying premise of strong religious convictions among EU member state citizens lacks any evidential basis. Closer cooperation between religious authorities and the EU's political leaders is not necessarily supported by significant portions of the EU population. Furthermore, the transactional basis of structured dialogue is not sufficiently grounded in a tangible advantage over existing mechanisms of interaction, or alternative articulations of civil society engagement such as that established through inclusion of Article 11.2 of the Lisbon Treaty. It should be questioned whether the principle of transcendence adds anything significant to the value of dialogue or whether emphasis on it has inadvertently excluded relevant nontranscendent ideational perspectives. The ability of civil society bodies, including the religious, to 'Europeanise' their memberships and the wider citizenry is open to challenge (Warleigh, 2001).

Intercultural Understanding

The coexistence within the same socio-political space of alternative religious and philosophical world views has problematic potential (Ruthven, 2004). Since the events of 11 September 2001 this debate has tended to centre on the issue of Islam and Europe's Muslim adherents, and the issues of pluralism and multiculturalism, immigration and enlargement have become salient. As EU competencies have increased and the integration has deepened, member states have been prompted to expand their focus from economic cooperation and interstate politics to wider issues. Christianity and Islam prescribe within their doctrines the unique validity of their particular tradition and the necessity of adherence to these for moral and spiritual fulfilment. The putative dynamic of desecularisation and the creation of a multireligious space may not inevitably lead to a more peaceful European polity. Managing these competing and potentially incompatible perspectives so as to ensure the integration of diverse perspectives and tolerance within a liberal democratic framework, and the avoidance of interconfessional (and intraconfessional) cleavages, is not without its challenges.

There is little doubt that any meeting of different perspectives in a civilised forum grounded on mutual respect for the participants is a desirable end in itself. The question becomes whether the existence of such a space at the supranational level can add significantly to the quest for greater tolerance beyond the forum confines as currently configured. There are a number of interrelated issues.

First, there is the ability of religious leaders to 'represent' their adherents. It is perhaps more accurate to describe their role as representatives of their religious ideology and tradition, rather than of multitudes of adherents who range from apathetic to nominal to traditionalist, and who ultimately have little influence on their faith's institutional form. The question of congruence looms large here, and the White Paper on Governance (2001) made clear that greater congruence among civil society organisations and their constituencies was required if EU engagement was to become effective. However, the follow-up report indicated profound opposition to such a condition from civil society actors, including churches (Commission, 2001, 2003).

Second, there is the question of the coherence of religious perspectives even in their organised or corporate form. There is no doubt that an institution such as the Roman Catholic Church can readily present coherence in any dialogical forum, but this is not an institutional feature of other religious traditions. Even within Protestant Christianity the ecumenical impetus that underpins international organisations, such as CEC, is not one that is universally endorsed within Protestantism.

Third, there is the practical extent of church capacity to influence EU policy formulation in areas of interest to them that have a realistic chance of being implemented at national, regional and municipal level. The concept of subsidiarity, invoked by religious authorities in the context of consolidating their status at national level, renders the provision for dialogue an inert instrument in relation to pan-European policy proposals of relevance to churches. Beyond the airing of their perspectives on intercultural understanding at supranational level a certain paralysis might well limit the ability of policy initiatives to impact directly on other governance levels.

Despite a potentially quasi-apocalyptic scenario of a divided confessional European political space, no such widespread or pronounced confessional division exists. Europe is, with respect to religious conflict, a 'quiet continent' (Crouch, 2000). There is not an absence of tension, still less the presence of unqualified tolerance, but it remains a curious feature of Europe that religious diversity has not developed into much sharper religious cleavages. The predominant view among Europeans concerning religion's place in society – that is, its *private* status – has perhaps rendered elite-led initiatives at multireligious dialogue obsolete. The dilution of faith provides a useful explanation. The dilution of faith can be defined as the conscious rejection by nominal adherents to formal religious authority of tenets, teachings and practices through a process of evaluation and filtration in light of socio-culturally available alternatives. People inevitably choose to ignore certain aspects of their inherited faith while retaining nominal affiliation. A relevant element of this phenomenon is the extent to which the *universal* claims of prominent religious traditions, implicitly upheld by the clerical strata who administer their institutionalised forms, are endorsed by ordinary adherents. It is important to consider the extent to which Europeans nominally affiliated to particular religious traditions agree with the idea that their faith is *uniquely* valid. Given the evident popular support for human rights cited above, it is reasonable to assume that most Europeans overwhelmingly endorse the view of religious association articulated within the Universal Declaration of Human Rights, the European Convention and the more recent European Charter. The fact that these documents endorse the freedom of choice in religion, in worship, teaching, practice and observance, and the right to change one's faith, indicates that the idea that a particular religion embodies the *universal truth* is not necessarily endorsed by most adherents, still less the wider citizenry.

The question of diluted faith is not sufficiently acknowledged and its importance to the subject is undervalued. The idea of 'believing without belonging' (Davie, 2000) has gained wide scholarly currency, but has obscured the concept of 'belonging without believing', referring to those who neither belong nor believe but still affiliate themselves to their inherited tradition (Voas and Crockett, 2005). The levels of secularisation in Europe across its distinct dimensions – in its social, institutional and individual forms – vary across national contexts (Halman and Draulans, 2006). What is clear is that higher levels of religiosity tend to correlate with lower levels of economic development and less religiously plural societal contexts (Halman and Draulans, 2006). What is less often emphasised is that those who do declare affiliation to a faith may not necessarily believe in everything that this tradition advocates; the widespread rejection by Roman Catholics of Vatican teachings on the use of contraception and on divorce is an obvious case in point. When advocating and conducting dialogue with representatives of organised religion, there is insufficient empirical evidence permitting EU decision-makers to infer the preferences of either adherents or the wider population from the preferences of religious representatives when formulating policy.

Religion is a complex phenomenon and cannot be reduced to assumptions based on quantitatively discerned affiliations to major traditions. Strong adherence is the minority position in Europe when measured as regular attendance at services (Gallup, 2004). The reasons for strong adherence, where it is more than mere apathetic affiliation inherited from birth, might also be complex. They can range from personal/existential to political and identitarian. Yet they may not be all of these, and they can even shift from one to the other within a lifetime. Simplistic views of Europe's 'diversity', concentrating on broad inferences from percentages of the population affiliated to this or that religion, obscure as much as they illuminate.

This foray into considerations of micro-level religious adherence bears ultimately on the matter of intercultural understanding because throughout the late twentieth century member state policies toward integration of migrants have been rooted in the 'UNESCO tradition', which substituted the discredited notion of biological racism with diversity of culture (Lentin, 2004; Malik, 1996; UNESCO, 1968). Though the 'celebration of diversity' has become a catchword among political authorities across the continent, not all its consequences have been positive. A recent case in Germany serves to illustrate a tendency toward exceptionalism and antiuniversalism born of this 'cultural' emphasis. A recent court ruling in Germany rejected the application by a Moroccan woman to speed divorce proceedings on the basis that, as a Muslim, she was subject to Quranic teaching (German, 2007).

How interreligious questions are framed by religious leaders gives the impression that greater mutual understanding is something urgent and necessarily spearheaded by these leaders, when in fact the evidence indicates considerable apathy in relation to religion and confessional difference. We must consider whether such apathy is necessarily a bad thing. An illustration of the divergence between elite clerical and lay opinion emerged recently in Ireland, where a concelebration of religious service between Catholic and Protestant clergy in one parish became a source of serious controversy, not for the people of the parish, who were largely enthusiastic about the event, but for the hierarchies of both traditions (Cooney, 2006; Controversy, 2006). Indeed, if anything, growing suspicion of religion (and not just of any one faith tradition) across Europe has coincided with an increase in organised religion's involvement at the public and political level (Berger, 1999; Westerlund, 1996; Kepel, 1994; Juergensmeyer, 1993). Reconciling these apparently contradictory trends means grasping the dynamics of desecularisation. Caution should prevail in assuming the veracity of the 'desecularisation' of the public space (Norris and Inglehart, 2006; Mazlish, 2006; Bruce, 2002). A more plausible interpretation is that the reassertion of strong faith is a reaction to the increasing apathy and indifference of most Europeans. In addition, other countertrends are emerging. Educationalists and parents in the UK, for example, are becoming more concerned about the rising number of 'faith schools' as advocated by the then prime minister Tony Blair (Blair, 2006; Wyatt, 2007). The fear has been expressed that segregating children on the basis of religious adherence will only exacerbate interfaith misunderstandings rather than solve them (Frean, 2007; Casciani, 2006). Similarly, the establishment of the Council of Ex-Muslims in Germany by Mina Ahadi among others (and latterly in the UK) and groups such as Women Living under Muslim Laws, as well as the recent conference of secular Muslims in Florida, are indicative of the diversity of opinion about one religion's role in the political sphere (Not possible, 2007; Ghitis, 2007).

The objective suitability of the provision for structured dialogue in providing a forum for greater intercultural understanding may well be an academic question. BEPA has made it clear that 'The dialogue ... is a communication tool between the European Commission and the religions, churches and communities of conviction. It should not be confused with inter-religious dialogue (between religions), which concerns only the churches themselves' (BEPA, 2007). The capacity of this provision to enhance intercultural understanding is therefore limited by the bounded scope of the provision's remit.[6] In effect, this specific limit on the provision's broader terms of reference (as yet ill-defined) means that the religious bodies are not compelled by the political institutions to examine their own perspectives on interfaith understanding and the role of religion in society. Therefore it is unclear just how any meaningful intercultural or interreligious exchange can take place.

Identities and Values

The contribution of civil society to contemporary issues is a necessary feature of any political space, whether national or supranational. With the increase in competencies, the importance of new technologies and greater interconnectedness and interdependence, the identity and values dimension of the European project – and what Europe stands for – has become more salient (Laffan, 1996).

An important consideration is whether common values are necessarily underpinned by the idea of a single European identity. BEPA, in its declaration on dialogue with religions, explicitly assumes the existence of this identity, albeit one composed of marked diversity (BEPA, 2007).[7] As far back as 1973 the nine member states of the European Economic Community issued a declaration on the need to clarify a European identity (European Communities, 1973). However, this declaration is viewed in the context of its time, and its focus on establishing a common perspective on relationships with non-member states in the midst of deepening economic instability. It is, therefore, distinctly outward-looking in orientation. The founding documents of the EU were not explicit about the concept of a supranational identity, and focused invariably on the need to 'merge their essential interests' and 'give direction to a destiny henceforward shared' (Treaty of Paris), and later 'strengthen the safeguards of peace' (Treaty of Rome). It was only with the finalisation of the Maastricht Treaty that the idea of a European identity became enshrined in a European treaty document. Even here it was linked explicitly to the framing of the Common Foreign and Security Policy.

In the Preamble of the EU Draft Constitution there was a bold assertion that a '*re-united* Europe' (my italics) allows its peoples to transcend ancient divisions (European Communities, 2004). Eurosceptics argue that such an idea is another example of Euronationalism, something to be challenged as a threat to national identities. The idea of a pan-Europa has always been embedded in ultimately unsuccessful attempts to extend a particular version of Europeanness over the wider European space (Delanty, 1995). There has always been tension between pan-Europeanism and fragmentary particularism (Snyder, 1984). As David Mitrany asks, 'Could a European union, in the long run, benefit its own peoples if it tends in the least to split the world afresh into competing regional sovereignties? Is not breaking through that dour barrier of sovereignty the ultimate test?' (Mitrany, 1965, p. 145).

It remains questionable whether the term 'identity', when used to denote an essentialist historical–cultural underpinning as the basis of the modern EU, is viable. This is especially true of one that emphasises a particular confessional perspective. Drawing on the insight of Schmuel Eisenstadt (2001), one might say that modern Europe and the impetus toward integration in modern Europe have more to do with *modernity* than cultural essentialism. Identity is, as Rogers Brubaker and Frederick Cooper (2000) contend, a much used term, which adds little to academic analysis and serves only to reify subject matter unnecessarily. The real deficiency undermining effective collective EU action is not the absence of a pan-European identity among its peoples, but rather the absence of *solidarity* among its governments, particularly when confronted with external issues. The distinction between identity and solidarity is a very real one (Hollinger, 2006). The absence of solidarity among EU member states on emergent issues properly describes the teleological crisis confronting the EU. Shorn of the organising imperatives of postwar reconstruction and the looming communist threat, and more recently the focus on eastward enlargement, the Union has struggled to display the unity of its diversity. Whether it is exogenous crises, such as the break-up of Yugoslavia, or positions on the Iraq war, rendition flights and US missile defence systems, the EU member states have been more often divided than not. Recourse to invoking a deity and referring explicitly to Europe's Christian heritage in treaty documents is not likely to supply the glue to bind Europe's diverse population, providing little remedial benefit for the imperatives either of solidarity or of legitimacy.

In 1992 Jacques Delors, the Commission president, emphasised the need to give a 'soul to Europe, to give it spirituality and meaning', as a prelude to further integration. The idea of a European 'soul' seems somewhat vague. Chancellor Merkel argued that the EU does not require the creation of values so much as their discovery, which she believes to be underpinned by liberty (European Council, 2007), while the current Commission president, Manuel Barroso, similarly suggests that Europe's values lie in freedom of expression, of religion and of conviction, and the institutions of democratic government (Commission, 2006, 2007).

The values indicated as being central to ordinary citizens throughout Europe correlate with documents such as the European Convention and the Charter of Fundamental Rights: peace, respect for human life, human rights, equality and democracy. The lack of a coherent identity has not prevented the emergence of salient core values among Europeans (Kantner, 2006). It might even be argued that it is precisely the absence of a single European identity that is causative of the core values that underpin the interaction of diverse groupings. As a value, tolerance would doubtless have much less emphasis if everyone thought the same way and led a similar kind of life, or followed the same religion. Religion's contributory role to value formation is therefore ambiguous to an extent. Research on the correlation of levels of religiosity with societal dysfunction indicates that high levels of religiosity correlate to greater societal dysfunction, while the normative potential of higher religiosity levels contributing to societal improvement is not proven (Paul, 2005).

There is doubt about the ability or viability of religious bodies making significant contributions to the question of identity and values within the European Union. The attempt to articulate or promote a *European* identity is not based on widespread support, and the proposed incorporation of an explicit confessional element into official treaty documents has already proven divisive. However, a latent identification of member states' citizens with Europe is already gaining ground (Lutz *et al.*, 2006). This indicates that younger European citizens tend to see no contradiction in being both a national *and* a European. This lends credence to the emergence of a European identity that may well occur *despite* elite designs, rather than because of them (Kostakopoulou, 2001). Notwithstanding marked differences both across national boundaries and along generational lines toward issues such as family and sexual and reproductive rights, most Europeans share similar outlooks on many issues. The absence of consensus on moral norms located around sexual/reproductive issues should not lead into viewing Europe as 'morally bankrupt'. Religious emphasis on the 'deviancy' of sexual liberalism has too often allowed debate on values to become narrow and unproductive, and has tended to deflect attention from the real improvement in overall life quality among Europe's populations.

It is difficult to see how a greater role for religion can contribute definitively to the issues of values and identity. Indeed, societal issues have impinged directly and divisively on the religious institutions, as the recent controversy and threatened schism within the Anglican Church over homosexual clergy has shown (Bates, 2007). The EU has made explicit its support for the inclusion of barrier contraception methods in the fight against HIV/AIDS in its development aid programmes, which is in line with the goals articulated by the International Conference on Population Development (European Council, 2005). In this instance the EU diverged not only from the prevailing policy in the USA but also from that of a number of prominent religious associations.

Religious Freedom

One explicitly relevant area where religious institutions could conceivably be accorded a voice is in the area of religious freedom. Nevertheless, the ability to practise religion is largely upheld across the EU, though there have been local controversies surrounding the location of mosques in some urban centres (Triandafyllidou, 2002).

The question of what constitutes 'freedom' is a significant and underexamined aspect of the issue of religious freedom. There is a clear distinction between the freedom of individuals to practise their faith and the freedom of religious institutions to administer it in the context of a democratic society (Westerlund, 1996). Religious freedom assumes a much more nuanced character. The right of individuals to practise their faith is guaranteed under national and European laws, and it is generally respected (Boyle and Sheen, 1997). The issue of religious freedom becomes somewhat more fraught when the objectives pursued by religious organisations come into conflict with the obligations of the governing authority to uphold the equal rights of citizens.

Two examples illustrate the nature of this conflict. The first relates to the recent controversy in the UK over new adoption legislation, whereby no adoption agency would be legally permitted to discriminate on the basis of gender or sexual orientation (Woodward and Bates, 2007; Hurst, 2007). Religious groups, led by the Roman Catholic Church, sought an exemption, claiming that it could not in conscience allow gay/lesbian couples to adopt children from its agencies, as this ran contrary to Catholic/Christian teachings. The government rejected the exemption clause and the law was enacted. The second case was the recent opinion of the EU Network of Independent Experts on Fundamental Rights in relation to the right to conscientious objection and the conclusion of concordats between the Vatican and EU member states (Commission, 2005). Specifically, this controversy concerned the Slovakian/Holy See agreement on the right to conscientious objection, which would have permitted doctors to opt out of performing abortion services. The expert group concluded that this situation conflicted with obligations to citizens and the state's obligations under international treaty conventions.

Both cases exemplify a critical dilemma for political authority. The freedom of religion, particularly the accordance of freedoms to religion in its *corporate* form, can potentially conflict with the wider freedoms that a government is obligated to uphold for all citizens. This is particularly true when the agencies (adoption agencies and hospitals respectively) administered by the religious institutions concerned are being funded by tax revenue. Unlike instances where religious institutions or agencies merely voice objection to proposed laws, such as the objection by many Christian and Muslim clergy to the enactment of civil unions for gay/lesbian couples in the UK, the demand for exemptions that may ultimately permit such tax-funded/state supported bodies to discriminate against citizens is inherently problematic.

The initial praxis of the provision for structured dialogue with the EU has symbolically concentrated on 'world' faiths, namely, Judaism, Christianity, Islam and Buddhism. Aside from the substantial numbers (18 per cent) who declare no belief in a God, it is not insignificant that a considerable number of Europeans (27 per cent) described their belief in the transcendent as being: 'I believe there is some sort of spirit or life force' (Eurobarometer, 2005, p. 9). A significant number of Europeans do not subscribe to an *authoritative* interpretation of transcendence, as exemplified by the monotheistic and dharmic religions, and instead embrace various spiritualities and personal creeds. Defining religion therefore becomes central for reasons of equality and equity of participation in dialogue. National governments rarely embody complete neutrality (Madeley and Enyedi, 2003) and while constitutions uphold the right of religious freedom, there remain implicit and established restrictions on minority and alternative religious and philosophical movements. The 1997 world report on religious freedom noted that

> With the establishment of constitutional guarantees of protection, at least for majority religions, throughout Europe, the debate about religious liberty

> has largely shifted away from how governments practise tolerance to how religious communities show tolerance and afford freedom of conscience and belief to their own members and to their neighbours of other faiths and ideologies. (Boyle and Sheen, 1997, pp. 259–60)

While there is room for improvements in state neutrality with regard to religious freedom, the report makes clear that restrictions on religious freedom no longer emanate solely from state organs. The various majority religions concerned have been implicated in the restriction of religious freedom and freedom of conscience, whether between majority and minority faiths or within religious traditions. One particular instance of this is in relation to the use of 'brainwashing' rhetoric in cases involving 'cults'. Several European states have refused to recognise the right of individuals to practise a religion when that religion has been deemed eccentric by states with particular majority faiths (Richardson and Introvigne, 2001).

Social Justice and Equality

The most significant role of religions in the public sphere is in their contributions to questions of social equality and justice. Major religious organisations, in particular the Vatican (primarily through COMECE) and the Conference of European Churches (CEC), have made submissions and contributions to a range of issues. These contributions had been envisaged by the European Commission in its 2001 White Paper, which emphasised the role of churches in highlighting injustice and giving voice to weaker members of European society (Commission, 2001, p. 14). This leads to questions about the validity of the provision envisaged within Article 17.3 of the Lisbon Treaty as the appropriate forum. The Lisbon Treaty provides for elements of civil society to interact with the institutions of the Union through participatory democracy under the auspices of its Article 11.2 (formerly Article I.47.2 of the Draft Constitution), which states that 'the institutions shall maintain an open, transparent and regular dialogue with representative associations and civil society'.

Commission representative Jacques Barrot, in his address to the European Parliament following the first occasion of formalised dialogue in 2005, emphasised that

> The Commission believes that such dialogue comes under its normal relations with all members of civil society in the member states ... the Commission intends to pursue an *established practice*, which will be developed in parallel with efforts to develop its entire links with civil society. (European Parliament, 2005; emphasis added)

Dismissing the questions raised by several MEPs concerning the absence of transparency and the exclusion of humanist groups from the discussions, Barrot maintained that the Commission was free 'to develop certain discussion with particular speakers to as great an extent as is necessary' (European Parliament, 2005). This indicates that, for the Commission, the function of the provision established under Article 17.3 somehow differs and improves upon that established under Article 11.2, where the Union's institutions have committed to maintain regular dialogue with *all* of civil society. However, the tautological inclusion of two provisions with the same function has no obvious benefit beyond differentiating religious actors from wider civil society, and the stress on monotheistic world faiths has served only to exclude – rather than include – a greater multiplicity of ideational voices.

A further issue concerns the extent to which religious institutions contribute *uniquely* to various areas of policy formulation, to warrant a differentiated dialogue provision. Churches can and do make relevant contributions to emergent issues, particularly in areas such as refugees and asylum, development aid and bio-medical ethics. However, these contributions become markedly less salient when viewed within the wider totality of EU interest representation. Within the EU's lobbying apparatus a veritable plethora of groups and sectional interests make regular and frequent parallel representations to its bodies on issues that concern churches. Within the area of social issues, religious contributions to specific areas have the potential to diverge from the broader liberal consensus. Areas include equality in gender and sexual orientation, education, reproductive rights and, as demonstrated by controversy in the UK, Spain and Italy, civil unions.

Conclusion

The desecularisation and resurgence of religion premises cannot be considered a foregone conclusion, as the available data most certainly do not indicate a decisive shift toward higher levels of religiosity among Europeans. Justification for the inclusion of a differentiated provision for church–EU dialogue, such as that embodied in Article 17.3, on this basis is at best premature – and at worst flawed. In addition, a number of key premises underlying the BEPA perspective on the dialogue do not stand up to scrutiny. The potential of religious groups to become torchbearers of integration, and their potential to 'Europeanise' broader public opinion, is dubious. The second aspect of the transactional relationship appears to view religious transcendence as a specific justification for the establishment of an exclusive, *religiously* focused forum. However, the absence of shared conceptual premises, and a need for churches to debate within the paradigms of socio-political discourse, renders this aspect ambiguous. The third assumption, the importance of religion in the life of the citizenry, is not supported by empirical evidence.

The role of structured dialogue in fostering greater intercultural, and in this case greater interfaith, understanding is hampered by the explicit rejection of this function by the Union. The absence of congruence between a clerical elite and the myriad shades of 'adherent' renders this justification difficult to sustain. There has been a failure to appreciate the distinction between representing an idea, or set of ideas, and speaking on behalf of people. The dilution of religious faith appears not to have been sufficiently factored into the EU's calculations.

The attempt to establish greater political legitimacy for the EU through promotion of a common European identity linked to common values appears a distant possibility. There is little to indicate that it is viable beyond a superficial acknowledgment of weak affiliation augmented by a much stronger national affiliation. What is more problematic is the assumption that strong identity is a prerequisite for the more instrumental goal of strengthening core values. The viability of a contrived European consciousness based on a perceived Judaeo-Christian essentialism among the citizens of member states has found little support. As regards values, it remains debatable whether the assumption that strong religiosity connotes a strong sense of values holds true and whether apathy toward religion is necessarily a negative attribute of European society.

Regarding religious freedom, the conflation of individual religious freedom with corporate privileges and exemptions is misleading. Individual religious freedom has been largely upheld by EU member states. Exemptions and privileges extended by member states to majority religious institutions have had the effect of curbing the freedom of those who affiliate or adhere to minority faiths and more loosely defined personal creeds, and of nonbelievers.

Where churches have a valid contribution to make – and where they have done so – has been in the area of social justice and equality. What remains problematic is whether this function needs a specific arena such as that established by Article 17.3. Existing channels, coupled with the provision to engage in dialogue with all of civil society under Article 11.2, appear more than adequate for this purpose.

Despite the failure of ratification of the Draft Constitution, the representatives of the Union's institutions have had formal meetings with representatives of the monotheistic faiths on several occasions: July 2005, May 2006, May 2007 and May 2008.[8] It seems that the provision for dialogue is very much a solution in search of a problem. The rhetorical justification for the inclusion of this provision, on such grounds as intercultural understanding, managing tolerance of diversity, contributing to the values/identity dimension and shoring up support for deeper integration, has been ill thought out. The vigour with which religious institutions pursued the inclusion of this provision indicates an unexplored dynamic behind its establishment. It is not clear, from the consideration above, why churches should feel that these issues would benefit from a specific forum for religious representatives. Furthermore, the initial exclusion of other bodies, such as that of the humanists and other minority faiths, and the narrow interpretation of the term 'religion', hinders meaningful consensus-orientated exchanges. As a consensus-building forum capable of contributing substantially to the life of the EU, the provision for structured dialogue fails to meet the requirements of full inclusiveness, clear and realisable goals, appropriately defined scope and equality of participation. For administrative ease, EU actors might see the merit in dealing with major faiths with strong, or at least coherent, organisational structures. However, if the objective of engaging with civil society is to bring the EU closer to Europe's wavering citizenry, this instance of elite-driven interaction does little to dampen scepticism.

Notes

1 The full text of Article 17 reads as follows:
'(1) The Union respects and does not prejudice the status under national law of churches and religious associations or communities in the Member States.
(2) The Union equally respects the status of philosophical and non-confessional organisations.
(3) Recognising their identity and their specific constitution, the Union shall maintain an open, transparent and regular dialogue with these churches and organisations.' (Consolidated, 2008)

2 The Bureau of European Policy Advisers is attached to the Commission and advises the president and members of the Commission on policy formulation and strategic issues. Extracts from the BEPA webpage referred to here were available at the time of writing (2007). In mid-2008 this webpage was significantly updated and the original text is no longer accessible there. In the newer version, BEPA presents the background to the dialogue provision, outlines its legal basis and elaborates briefly on its operationalisation. There is a further link to a list of events conducted under the auspices of the dialogue provision articulated in Article 17.3 of the Lisbon Treaty (see note 8 below).

3 The transactional benefits are also alluded to in the newer text. However, in this case the explicit benefits mentioned refer only to the churches. The benefits of the dialogue process for the EU are not outlined.

4 This aspect is not retained in the new text.

5 Once again, this rationale is not retained in the new text.
6 It should be pointed out that this explicit limitation on the remit of the dialogue provision is not alluded to in the new text.
7 The updated text similarly alludes (in para.2) to the necessity of a European identity and a 'sense of belonging'.
8 See http://ec.europa.eu/dgs/policy_advisers/activities/dialogues_religions/events_en.htm for a full list of events.

References

Bates, S. (2007) 'Archbishop battles to ward off final Anglican split on homosexuality', *Guardian*, 12 February.

BEPA (2007) *Dialogue with Religions, Churches and Communities of Conviction*, http://ec.europa.eu/dgs/policy_advisers/activities/dialogues_religions/index_en.htm (last accessed 30 May 2007).

Berger, P. L. (1999) *The Desecularization of the World: Resurgent Religion in World Politics* (Washington, Ethics and Public Policy Center and Eerdmans).

Blair, A. (2006) 'Teachers demand end to state cash for faith schools', *The Times* (London), 12 April.

Boyle, K. and Sheen, J. (eds) (1997) *Freedom of Religion and Belief: a World Report* (London, Routledge).

Brubaker, R. and Cooper, F. (2000) 'Beyond "identity"', *Theory and Society*, 29, pp. 1–47.

Bruce, S. (2002) *God is Dead: Secularization in the West* (Oxford, Blackwell Publishing).

Casciani, D. (2006) 'So who's right over segregation?', *BBC Magazine*, 4 September, http://news.bbc.co.uk/1/low/magazine/5304276.stm (last accessed 23 September 2008).

CEC (2002) Conference of European Churches, *Churches Ask for Structured Relations between Civil Society and European Institutions*, press release, 8 October, http://www.cec-kek.org/News/cq0238e print.htm (last accessed 30 May 2007).

CFFC (2003a) *Catholics Join Coalition of 165 European NGOs in Appeal to Convention not to give Religion Unfair Influence in Constitutional Treaty*, press release, 22 May, http://www.catholicsforchoice.org/news/pr/2003/20030522eurongocoalition.asp (last accessed 30 May 2007).

CFFC (2003b) *Catholics Join Broad Coalition of Civil Society in Protest against Special Status of Vatican Granted through Article 51 in European Draft Constitution*, press release, http://www.catholicsforchoice.org/news/pr/2003/20031105vaticaneruoconstitution.asp (last accessed 30 May 2007).

COMECE (2002) Commission of the Bishops' Conferences of the European Community, *The Future of Europe: Political Commitment, Values, and Religion: Contribution of the COMECE Secretariat to the Debate on the Future of the European Union in the European Convention*, 22 May, http://www.comece.org/upload/pdf/secr_conv1_020521_en.pdf (last accessed 30 May 2007).

Commission (2001) Commission of the European Communities, European Governance: a White Paper, COM (2001) 428 Final, Brussels, http://europa.eu.int/eur-lex/en/com/cnc/2001/com2001_0428en01.pdf (last accessed 30 May 2007).

Commission (2003) *Report from the Commission on European Governance*, http://ec.europa.eu/governance/docs/comm_rapport_en.pdf (last accessed 30 May 2007).

Commission (2005) EU Network of Independent Experts on Fundamental Rights, Opinion No. 4–2005: The Right to Conscientious Objection and the Conclusion by EU Member States of Concordats with the Holy See, http://www.reproductiverights.org/pdf/CFR-CDFopinion4-2005.pdf (last accessed 31 May 2007).

Commission (2006) *A Soul for Europe*, speech by Commission president Barroso at the conference 'A Soul for Europe', Berlin, 17 November, http://europa.eu/rapid/pressReleasesAction.do?reference=SPEECH/06/706&format=HTML&aged=0&language=EN&guiLanguage=fr (last accessed 31 May 2007).

Commission (2007) *On the Occasion of the Inaugural Speech of the President of the European Parliament*, speech by Commission president Barroso in a plenary session of the European Parliament, 13 February, http://europa.eu/rapid/pressReleasesAction.do?reference=SPEECH/07/77&format=HTML&aged=1&language=EN&guiLanguage=en (last accessed 30 May 2007).

Consolidated (2008) Consolidated Version of the Treaty on European Union (as amended by the Lisbon Treaty), http://register.consilium.europa.eu/pdf/en/08/st06/st06655.en08.pdf (last accessed 19 April 2008).

Controversy (2006) 'Controversy over joint mass continues', *RTE News*, 19 April, www.rte.ie/news/2006/0419/religion.html?rss (last accessed 31 May 2007).

Cooney, J. (2006) 'Monks apologise for sharing mass with Anglican priest', *Irish Independent*, 16 May.

Crouch, C. (2000) 'The quiet continent: religion and politics in Europe', *The Political Quarterly*, 71 (s1), pp. 90–103.

Davie, G. (2000) *Religion and Modern Europe: a Memory Mutates* (Oxford, Oxford University Press).

Delanty, G. (1995) *Inventing Europe: Idea, Identity, Reality* (Basingstoke, Macmillan Press).

EHF (2003) European Humanist Federation, *Coalition for the Withdrawal of Article 51*, press release, http://www.humanism.be/in/doc/pdfs/const08-en-parl%20press%20bis.pdf (last accessed 30 May 2007).

Eisenstadt, S. (2001) 'The civilisational dimension of modernity: modernity as a distinct civilisation', *International Sociology*, 14, 3, pp. 320–40.

Eurobarometer (2005) *Special Eurobarometer 225: Social Values, Science and Technology*, http://ec.europa.eu/public_opinion/archives/ebs/ebs_225_report_en.pdf (last accessed 30 May 2007).

Eurobarometer (2006) *Standard Eurobarometer 66: Public Opinion in the European Union*, http://ec.europa.eu/public_opinion/archives/eb/eb66/eb66_highlights_en.pdf (last accessed 30 May 2007).

European Communities (1973) 'Declaration on European identity', *Bulletin of the European Communities*, Supplement 12, pp. 118–22, www.ena.lu/mce.swf?doc=6180&lang=2 (last accessed 12 October 2006).

European Communities (2004) Treaty Establishing a Constitution for Europe 310/11, http://europa.eu/constitution/en/lstoc1_en.htm (last accessed 21 November 2006).

European Council (2005) *EU Statement on HIV Prevention for an AIDS Free Generation*, 24 November, http://www.dfid.gov.uk/eupresidency2005/EU-statement-dec2005.pdf (last accessed 31 May 2007).

European Council (2007) *Speech by Angela Merkel, Chancellor of the Federal Republic of Germany, to the European Parliament in Strasbourg on Wednesday, 17 January 2007*, http://www.eu2007.de/en/News/Speeches_Interviews/January/Rede_Bundeskanzlerin2.html (last accessed 31 May 2007).

European Parliament (2005) *Dialogue with Churches and Non-Denominational Organisations*, debate on Monday 5 September 2005, Strasbourg, http://www.europarl.europa.eu/sides/getDoc.do?pubRef=-//EP//TEXT+CRE+20050905+ITEM-020+DOC+XML+V0//EN&language=EN (last accessed 31 May 2007).

EVS (2004) Arts, W., Hagnaars, J. and Halman, L. (eds), *European Values at the Turn of the Millennium: Findings, Explanations and Reflections from the European Values Study* (Leiden, Brill).

Frean, A. (2007) 'British schools "face US-style segregation"', *The Times* (London), 26 April.

Gallup (2004) 'Religion in Europe: trust not filling the pews', 21 September, http://www.gallup.com/poll/13117/Religion-Europe-Trust-Filling-Pews.aspx (last accessed 23 September 2008).

German (2007) 'German justice failures: paving the way for a parallel Muslim society', *Spiegel Online*, 29 March, www.spiegel.de/international/germany/0,1518,474629,00.html (last accessed 31 May 2007).

Ghitis, F. (2007) 'Secular Muslims speak out: are we listening?', *World Politics Watch*, 21 March, http://worldpoliticswatch.com/article.aspx?id=646 (last accessed 31 May 2007).

Halman, L. and Draulans, V. (2006) 'How secular is Europe?', *The British Journal of Sociology*, 57, 2, pp. 263–88.

Hollinger, D. A. (2006) 'From identity to solidarity', *Daedalus* (fall), pp. 23–31.

Hurst, G. (2007) 'Catholics refuse to accept gay adoption law', *The Times* (London), 23 January.

Jansen, T. (2000) 'Europe and religions: the dialogue between the European Commission and churches or religious communities', *Social Compass*, 47, 1, pp. 103–12.

Juergensmeyer, M. (1993) *The New Cold War? Religious Nationalism Confronts the Secular State* (Berkeley, University of California Press).

Kantner, C. (2006) 'Collective identity as shared ethical self-understanding: the case of the emerging European identity', *European Journal of Social Theory*, 9, 4, pp. 501–23.

Kepel, G. (1994) *The Revenge of God: the Resurgence of Islam, Christianity and Judaism in the Modern World* (University Park, Pennsylvania State University Press).

Kostakopolou, T. (2001) *Citizenship, Identity and Immigration in the European Union: Between Past and Future* (Manchester, Manchester University Press).

Laffan, B. (1996) 'The politics of identity and the New Europe', *Journal of Common Market Studies*, 34, 1, pp. 81–102.

Lentin, A. (2004) *Racism and Anti-Racism in Europe* (London, Pluto Press).

Lutz, W., Kritzinger, S. and Skirbekk, V. (2006) 'The demography of growing European identity', *Science*, 314, 5798, p. 425, http://www.sciencemag.org/cgi/reprint/314/5798/425.pdf?maxtoshow=&HITS=10&hits=10&RESULTFORMAT=&fulltext=european+identity&searchid=1&FIRSTINDEX=0&resourcetype=HWCIT (last accessed 23 September 2008).

Madeley, J. T. S. and Enyedi, Zs. (eds) (2003) *Church and State in Contemporary Europe: the Chimera of Neutrality* (London, Frank Cass).

Malik, K. (1996) *The Meaning of Race: Race, History and Culture in Western Society* (Basingstoke, Macmillan Press).

Mazlish, B. (2006) 'Globalization and God – part II: religious revivalism may win a few battles, but secularism will ultimately win the war', *YaleGlobal Online*, 28 November, http://yaleglobal.yale.edu/display.article?id=8466 (last accessed 31 May 2007).

Mitrany, D. (1965) 'The prospects for integration: federal or functional', *Journal of Common Market Studies*, 4, pp. 119–49.

Nelson, B. F., Guth, J. L. and Frazer, C. R. (2001) 'Does religion matter? Christianity and public support for the European Union', *European Union Politics*, 2, 2, pp. 191–217.

Norris, P. and Inglehart, R. (2006) 'Sellers or buyers in religious markets: the supply and demand of religion', *Hedgehog Review*, 8, 1–2 (Spring/Summer), pp. 69–92.

Not possible (2007) 'Not possible to modernize Islam: interview with founder of Council of Ex-Muslims', *Spiegel Online*, www.spiegel.de/international/spiegel/0,1518,468828,00.html (last accessed 31 May 2007).

Paul, G. S. (2005) 'Cross-national correlations of quantifiable societal health with popular religiosity and secularism in the prosperous democracies: a first look', *Journal of Religion and Society*, 7, http://moses.creighton.edu/JRS/pdf/2005-11.pdf (last accessed 23 September 2008).

Richardson, J. T. and Introvigne, M. (2001) '"Brainwashing" theories in European parliamentary and administrative reports on "cults" and "sects"', *Journal for the Scientific Study of Religion*, 40, 2, pp. 143–68.

Ruthven, M. (2004) *Fundamentalism: the Search for Meaning* (Oxford, Oxford University Press).

Snyder, L. L. (1984) *Macro-Nationalisms: a History of the Pan-Movements* (Westport, CT, Greenwood Press).

Triandafyllidou, A. (2002) 'Religious diversity and multiculturalism in southern Europe: the Italian mosque debate', *Sociological Research Online*, 7, 1, www.socresonline.org.uk/7/1/triandafyllidou.html (last accessed 31 May 2007).

UNESCO (1968) 'UNESCO statement on race and racial prejudice', *Current Anthropology*, 9, 4, pp. 271–72.

Voas, D. and Crockett, A. (2005) 'Religion in Britain: neither believing nor belonging', *Sociology*, 39, 1, pp. 11–28.

Warleigh, A. (2001) '"Europeanizing" civil society: NGOs as agents of political socialization', *Journal of Common Market Studies*, 39, 4, pp. 619–39.

Westerland, D. (ed.) (1996) *Questioning the Secular State: the Worldwide Resurgence of Religion in Politics* (London, Hurst & Co.).

Woodward, W. and Bates, S. (2007) 'Anglicans back Catholics in gay adoption row', *Guardian*, 24 January.

Wyatt, N. (2007) 'UK schools dividing along race lines', *Observer*, 27 May.

Index